MURDER
IN
ATLANTA!

Skyline of Modern Atlanta

The towering skyscrapers of Atlanta in the 1980s reach upward from the remnants of a city that has been

MURDER
IN
ATLANTA!

SENSATIONAL CRIMES
THAT ROCKED THE NATION

By
James S. Jenkins

ATLANTA
CHEROKEE PUBLISHING COMPANY
1981

Library of Congress Catalog Card No.: 81–68541
International Standard Book No.: 0–87797–056–4

Portions of this book appeared originally in a paperback book entitled
Murders and Social Change (1974) under LC Catalog Card No. 73–
91479.

Copies of *Murder in Atlanta!* may be obtained through leading booksellers
everywhere or by ordering directly from Cherokee Publishing Company's
sales office: P.O. Box 1081, Covington, Ga. 30209. Send $8.95 plus 86¢ post-
age. Georgia residents include 3% state sales tax and, where applicable, 1%
MARTA or local option tax.

PRINTED IN THE UNITED STATES OF AMERICA

To
the Memory
of
the Victims

Table of Contents

Illustrations

(For credits, see p. 201)

Introduction

The facts in the case were extremely sketchy. There was little for the investigators to go on. A young man found murdered. No weapon was located at the scene of the crime, but it was believed to be a large rock or boulder—the victim having died from a blow to the head. No eyewitnesses to the homicide came forward. Persons in the vicinity, when questioned, related a story of family rivalry and jealousy. A neighbor told investigators that he was present a few days before during an argument between the victim and his older brother. The older brother accused the victim of conspiring against him with their father to cheat him out of his inheritance. Afterwards, others came forward and related in detail the malice and jealousy of the older brother, who had made threats against his brother. It appeared to the investigators to be an open and shut case. The victim, Abel, had been slain by his older brother, Cain. Motive—jealousy. The accused was condemned, sentenced, and banished away into the land called Nod.

Crimes of violence are the oldest known to mankind. The crime of homicide, the killing of one person by another, is a type of behavior that all cultures tend to condemn regardless of differences in social organization and values. Not only is homicide condemned by most societies but an attempt is made to control such crimes, and the usual method of control is a penalty commensurate with the crime. What should be the punishment for a person who commits the crime of homicide? In the above-mentioned murder the authority passing on the case decided that banishment was the proper punishment. In time, harsher penalties were instituted. Society decided that a person who takes another person's life should be made to pay with his own life. Consequently, society began committing murder as punishment for persons who committed this type of crime. The results of such punishment seemed not to have lessened the crime of homicide, and, if anything, by the

xii MURDER IN ATLANTA!

violent nature of such a policy, actually contributed to the increase of such crimes. As a result, the punishment of murder in most Western nations has been modified. Now murderers, when tried and convicted, are banished from society. They suffer essentially the same punishment meted out by the Almighty in the case of Cain.

The murder of Abel by Cain has had a profound effect not only on the punishment of people who commit this crime, but an effect upon how investigators of subsequent homicides go about solving them. It was duly noted that Abel was slain because of a family disagreement, or rather a rivalry within the family, which ultimately was resolved by a crime of violence. Investigators still assume that practically all homicides basically follow the Cain-Abel pattern. Abel was murdered by someone known to him, in this case a relative, in most cases by either a relative or a close friend. To find out who committed such a crime the proper procedure for the investigator to follow is to take a close and searching look at relatives and persons known to the victim. There you will usually find the murderer. With all the technological changes and variations in life-styles, this principle in nearly all cases holds true. Today, in practically all instances, a person who becomes a homicide statistic was done in by a relative or close friend.

But not always. The unpredictable. cases which do not follow the Cain-Abel pattern is often what makes detective work harrowing. Some murder cases have become famous due largely to what we might call the investigators falling prey to the Cain-Abel syndrome. In detective work this means that you cannot always follow the Cain-Abel pattern in attempting to solve all murders. Insofar as most homicide victims are murdered by a relative or close acquaintance, and since the police are confronted with this type of crime and see it repeated day in and day out, detectives must be on guard not to assume that a friend or relative is the murderer in a particular homicide case in which there appears to be no quick solution.

The crime of homicide through the years continues to follow the Cain-Abel pattern. Bitter squabbles among members of a family, or close friends, is resolved by a killing. How much or actually how little of this activity goes on is a pretty good index of how civilized a society has become. Throughout history as a society becomes more technologically advanced, offenses against property (burglary and theft) have risen in the United States and in other urbanized countries. On the other hand, crimes of violence (murder, rape, aggravated assault) have decreased. Even in the decade of the sixties when crimes in all categories moved upward, the crime of homicide did not rise at the same rate as crimes against property. This would seem to indicate that people still usually don't sit down and plan the death of another. In spite of all the increase in many areas of crime, the murder of the Cain-Abel pattern seems, if not to be lessening, at least to be undergoing certain changes.

That is not to say that we do not have an increase in the homicide rate at the present time. We do. What appears significant, and admittedly is more of an impression than anything else, is that the pattern is changing. The emphasis of homicides appears to be shifting away from premeditation and, as the lawyers say, malice aforethought, to an act more akin to exasperation, unkept promises, and boredom.

The typical homicide today follows the Cain-Abel pattern to the extent that it is usually committed by a relative or close friend. The change occurs very subtly as you look over hundreds of cases. The homicide begins as a matter of assault triggered by a spur-of-the-moment fit of anger. A cheap .22 caliber pistol is readily at hand. A domestic squabble ensues. To end the argument the wife or husband ends up snatching the gun and shooting the other. One or more shots are fired and the victim, even if hit more than once, often recovers. But fired at close range, a gun costing less than ten dollars can readily kill with one bullet. If so, the perpetrator then usually calls the police and states matter of factly that a homicide has occurred.

Let's suppose that in the above example the crime was committed by the wife. For this crime the wife receives a ten-year probated sentence. This is not only a possible sentence but one which is quite probable. Her only inconvenience is that of going to court and then living up to the terms of her probation. Hard-liners would insist that if the wife knew she would get the electric chair she would not have shot at her husband and would have vented her anger in some less lethal fashion, such as throwing a plate or coming at him with her rolling pin like Grandma used to do.

But in our present-day world the rolling pin has been replaced by the handgun, with a resulting rise in the number of homicides. This increase in the number of murders is of great concern to the police, the press, and all persons involved in the fields of crime prevention and social welfare.

This book is a study of several legendary murders which occurred in the Atlanta area. They have been selected for study because of the enormous impact which they had upon the times in which they occurred. These homicides were an essential part of the social fabric of the Atlanta scene and as a result made people more aware of the nature and numbers of homicides then occurring, an awareness which led in some instances to an overall decrease in the homicide rate in the community.

These cases have also been selected for study because they not only illustrate the nature of police practices of the times, but show how in periods of sociological and technological change police methods in attempting to solve murder cases became modified.

MURDER
IN
ATLANTA!

1

A Miscellany of Early Twentieth Century Murders

Crimes of violence tend to increase in periods of social upheaval. In the past homicides have increased in times of economic depression and after wars. The period following World War I was a time notable for social change. In Atlanta, there was an increase in business activity stimulated by the pent-up demand of the war years. New suburbs to the north and east of downtown Atlanta reflected the need for new housing in a growing city. Industry was on the move. The automobile brought about easier transportation and enabled people previously restricted by the confines of quaint, but slow, public transportation to move about the city in their business affairs and to live farther out from town in the mushrooming suburbs. The better means of communication made possible by telephones and modern newspapers brought about a flurry of activity in a city which has always been uninhibited and "on the make." As a rail center in this era of the railroads, trains brought people from everywhere into Atlanta. This brought about an increase in crime.

In the past, criminal activity was hampered by lack of communication and transportation. Lawbreaking among the citizenry was confined to a few kingpins who pretty well governed activity in their neighborhoods. There would be disagreements and fights—and homicides. But these were usually family or gang feuds that were confined to particular areas and had little effect upon life in other sections of the city.

But the boom following World War I, and the enormous advances in technology that followed, changed the crime pattern. The police became more aware and the press began to speak openly about the existence of crime in the city being better organized. Like the city which surrounded it, crime also was being affected by the tremendous shift in living patterns and a rapidly changing society. What came to be called organized crime, which had no doubt been evolving for some time, began to be recognized and identified for what it was.

This doesn't mean that one so-called crime lord came to have sway over all criminal activity, not in Atlanta anyway. What it did mean was that certain persons who carried on illegal activity expanded their operations and became involved in larger and more diversified kinds of crime. It is always the new crime problem that is the most difficult for the police and the public to deal with. Maybe there aren't any new kinds of crime, but there always appear to be people, often very brilliant people, who can constantly come up with endless variations of well-worn schemes that at least give the appearance of a new kind of crime. What they do is refine older forms of criminal activity to meet new and changing conditions. Business, in order to survive in a changing and violatile society, must constantly do this. Somehow the criminal element seems to be ahead not only of the press and the police in this regard, but also the business community. Those persons who originate a new scheme attract countless, less subtle imitators. This leads to conflict between groups, which in turn often leads to homicides. The more usual result, however, is conflict within a certain criminal group that leads to murder. Thus for all the technological advances and what have you, the homicide still follows the Cain-Abel pattern. The players remain the same and only the times and scenery are different.

Some colorful criminal characters flourished in Atlanta in those pivotal years of 1918, 1919, and 1920. People like Walter Clyde Smith, Mark Tillery, Jay "Old Dad" McBride, Abe Powers, Floyd Woodward, and Military Brown were busily engaged in many schemes and rackets outside the law. They talked with their lieutenants over the telephone. They drove fast cars that whipped about the city in defiance of all traffic and safety regulations. In their own gangland world they were the law unto themselves.

Floyd Woodward was the reputed head of the bunco ring in Atlanta during the get-rich-quick days following the end of World War I. The word bunco was a term used to define any of several forms of illegal swindling games or schemes. The bunco business flourished in this period of upheaval and change. Floyd Woodward reportedly devised a scheme that raised the level of the bunco business to a near art form. He understood not only how to take advantage of people but how to bend technological advances to his own criminal ends. His operation was not only organized but took advantage of a new trend in living patterns. During the winters of 1918, 1919, and 1920, Atlanta was crowded with affluent and well-to-do Northerners stopping-over on their way to winter vacations on the Florida coast. This was the beginning of the first Florida land boom and during this time people were flocking southward with legitimate get-rich-quick plans of their own dancing in their heads. As a rail center Atlanta was a connecting point and lay-over stop for these tourists. Many became victims of the bunco ring.

Although the bunco racket as allegedly operated by Woodward and his cohorts had many angles and variations, the best known was the fixed horse race, in which the victim was led to believe he could share in a take on a race that could not possibly go wrong. An elaborate set of props (there was, of course, no actual race) was used in this build-up, and the idea was to let the unsuspecting tourist win a small amount the first time. Greed being what it is among mortals, the would-be tourist decided not to go on to Florida that night on the train, but to stay in town for a few days and play the game again. If the victim bet a small amount the second time, he was allowed to win once more. But ultimately, if he was a real sucker, he would bet that roll of bills intended for a down payment on some choice seacoast acreage on a sure thing, and of course he would lose. His contact would vanish and the sadder but wiser tourist would end up at the police station with a sad tale and empty pockets. Such a racket on a large scale would have a hard time making it in our sophisticated world of today, but in that era the bunco ring was a booming business.

Public, newspaper, and law enforcement scrutiny was cast upon the bunco ring on April 2, 1919. At 8:30 that night, Edward P. Mills, member of an old and respected Atlanta family, was found shot to death on the ninth floor of the Ansley Hotel. Whatever the prominence of his family in Atlanta, Ed Mills was somewhat of a loose branch on the family tree. He was quite a man-about-town, an alleged gambler, and probable associate of Woodward in the capacity of a "steerer" in the bunco ring operation. It was alleged that Mills, a man of debonair appearance and respectable connections, was one of Woodward's men who first made contact with the unsuspecting tourist and steered him toward Woodward and his bevy of con artists. Woodward was no doubt thinking of public relations. He knew his own goons could not approach high-class, honest people successfully; so, he employed someone better suited for this aspect of the job. It would appear from his selection of Mills that Woodward understood not only public relations but also job counseling and the importance of fitting the right man in the right job where he could most effectively serve the organization.

The police, however, were not without some leads in the Mills case. For one thing—all those moaning, sad-eyed, empty-pocketed, winter tourists had given them a clue that something new in the way of swindles had hit the crime market in Atlanta. Officers confided to the press that they were searching for Floyd Woodward for questioning in the case. They had been told that he was a close friend of Mills and that he was in the hotel lobby with Mills a short time before the shooting occurred. Several checks on the body of Mills were examined, one of them for $1,000, a far heftier sum in those days than now. It appeared to Detective Chief A. Lamar Poole that "cards, gambling, and liquor" were responsible for the killing of Mills. A hotel guest who had the room next to Mills was arrested but he vigorously denied that he had any connection with the case. He said that he was from Memphis, had only been in town two weeks, and knew Mills only as someone to drink and play cards with. He certainly didn't kill him. Another hotel guest, a woman from Rome, Georgia, was one of the first people to reach Mills after the shooting and she heard him say before he died: "I have the right kind of nerve to die. I know who shot me, but I won't tell. I'm going to die like a man . . . " A house detective at the hotel told police that Mills was a "known" gambler and had been forbidden to enter the hotel because of his reputation, and he (the house detective) had in fact been on his way up to the ninth floor to evict Mills from the building when four shots rang out. Now there is a conscientious hotel employee for you! Don't let the hotel get a bad name. If someone is murdered on the premises say that you were just planning to throw the bum out. No doubt if Mills had not been shot to death and had continued to pay the bill, he would have remained in residence. Homicide is like the plague; people believe it is infectious.

The police had a lot of information and, as in all such cases, had many reports that turned out to be nothing but gossip. There were no people in town (Had you been fleeced by the bunco ring wouldn't you move on to a friendlier city?) at the time who could identify Mills to the extent of even tying him in with Woodward. Besides, the bunco business was one thing, homicide quite another, and just because the two might have been in business doesn't mean that Woodward shot Mills. Police asked themselves, What was the motive? It was certainly not robbery. Then it must have stemmed from some disagreement. No likely suspects appeared on the scene. The police were making little progress in the case when something very dramatic occurred.

Seventeen hours after the shooting, accompanied by his attorney, Floyd Woodward walked into police headquarters and gave himself up. Twenty-four hours later a coroner's jury was convened to hear the evidence in the case. Woodward testified that he shot Mills in self defense. He stated that Mills had threatened him several times and when the two of them walked into the hotel room Woodward started to leave and Mills followed him out of the room. Mills drew his gun and Woodward shot him first.

Ten minutes after Woodward's testimony the jury returned a verdict: "We, the jurors, find that Edward P. Mills died of wounds inflicted at the hand of Floyd Woodward, the same being a case of justifiable homicide." The coroner was outraged at the hasty verdict.

As a result of the jury's findings, Woodward was set free. On the surface the case might appear to be closed, but the jury's somewhat swift deliverance, and the fact that more questions were unanswered than answered at the inquest, led to widespread public outrage.

A murder within a crime organization very often is the one thing that will lead to public demand that something be done about the crime organization itself. In the eyes of the public Mills was forgotten. Maybe it did happen as Woodward stated. The rumors and talk created as a result of the homicide proved far more interesting to the public than the murder itself. What was all this business about a bunco ring? It was all anybody talked about. An aroused public was demanding to know the facts. The police rushed about in response to public outcry.

In November of 1919, six months after the death of Edward Mills, Solicitor General John A. Boykin and his deputies, in response to public pressure, swung into action. They pulled a surprise raid on a gambling house operated by Woodward on Central Avenue. The raiders were disappointed because they did not snare Woodward in the raid. While the solicitor and his aides placed numerous crap table and poker game players and those in charge of the place under arrest, they failed to find Woodward at the scene. Word had reached him that the raid was in progress and he never showed up at the establishment that night. In fact, Floyd Woodward vanished from the Atlanta scene.

The Central Avenue raid by Solicitor Boykin and his men was but the beginning of a crack-down that eventually put an end to the bunco enterprise in Atlanta. Woodward, who could not be found, was indicted nevertheless on over a dozen counts of larceny after trust, gaming, larceny from the person, and related state charges, in addition to numerous federal charges against him.

The state charged in the murder of Mills that Woodward employed Mills in his bunco operations, and that he had sent Mills to Philadelphia to lure a wealthy merchant to Atlanta to be buncoed. Instead of doing this, the state alleged that Mills went on a spree and Woodward had to send in another steerer to bring the merchant to Atlanta, where he was relieved of between $25,000 and $50,000 in various games and schemes conducted by the Woodward organization. Mills claimed a share of this loot, warning that if he did not receive it he would expose the bunco racket to the authorities. That is why Floyd Woodward killed Edward Mills on the night of April 2, 1919.

Not until twenty years later was Floyd Woodward located by federal authorities at Monrovia, California, where he was living with his second wife and adopted daughter. He was brought back to Atlanta on a federal warrant charging mail fraud, for which he served two years and eight months in the Atlanta Federal Penitentary.

On April 17, 1943, the old murder indictment was returned and Woodward was placed on trial for the killing of Edward P. Mills 24 years before. The one-time bunco king was given life imprisonment. He was placed on parole by the State Pardons and Paroles Board on June 12, 1947. Returning to California, he died there in 1952 at age 60, known to his neighbors as a kind and gentle man.

THRILL KILLING

On the night of October 20, 1928, Willard H. Smith, a clerk in a drugstore at Boulevard and Tenth streets in Atlanta was shot and killed as he resisted an attempt to rob the store. A few nights later E. L. Meek, clerk in a grocery store at Tenth Street and Hemphill Avenue, was killed in an exchange of gunfire between the store manager and two would-be holdup men. Several days later an unidentified caller to Atlanta Police Headquarters told Chief of Detectives A. Lamar Poole that a student who had attended Oglethorpe College, George Harsh, had been receiving private treatment for a leg wound. The store manager was certain that he had wounded one of the holdup men in the leg during the attempted robbery of the grocery store. George Harsh, the son of wealthy Milwaukee, Wisconsin, parents, was taken into custody by police while on his way to a Georgia Tech football game.

The police rushed Harsh to headquarters, where he was relentlessly questioned for several hours. Ultimately he broke down and confessed to the murder of Willard H. Smith, the drugstore clerk. But he insisted that, although he participated in the gun battle at the grocery store, Meek was actually killed by a bullet from the store manager's pistol. Also in his confession Harsh named his accomplice, Richard G. Gallogly, member of a prominent and well-to-do Atlanta family. Gallogly was arrested and questioned for four hours. He vehemently insisted that he did not participate in the robberies, and only went to the front doors of the two stores in an attempt to prevent Harsh from carrying out his announced intention of robbing them. In his trial Harsh did not deny his guilt, but stated that he committed the crimes under the influence of alcohol. He told the court that he didn't want to commit these crimes, but the alcohol made him do it. He never intended to kill anyone and the whole episode had begun somewhat as a lark. Obviously he did not need the money. His wealthy parents paid for the best legal assistance obtainable to defend him.

Gallogly, who was tried later, was defended in a sensational trial by a battery of prominent Atlanta lawyers. He maintained his innocence throughout the trial, and Harsh, although he had been sentenced to die in the electric chair in his own trial, refused to testify against his former comrade in crime. As a result, the Gallogly trial ended, when the jury was unable to agree, in a mistrial. Gallogly was tried again but this ended in a mistrial. By the time the third trial came around the prosecution had persuaded Harsh to testify against Gallogly, whereupon Gallogly immediately plead guilty and accepted a life sentence. Harsh was then granted a new trial and given a life sentence. Gallogly insisted that he only plead guilty to save Harsh from the electric chair, but few people believed him. In 1939 both Harsh and Gallogly were pardoned by then-Governor Ed Rivers.

At the outset of World War II Harsh joined the Royal Canadian Air Force; he was shot down on a mission over Germany in 1942. As a prisoner-of-war he participated in the heroic but unsuccessful "tunnel escape" from Stalag III German prison camp, which later served as the basis for the movie *The Great Escape*. Afterwards, he wrote a book entitled *A Lonesome Road*, in which he described life on a chain gang and his efforts to redeem himself. In the book he revealed that the downward course of his life began when he became one of five university students who drew straws to pull robberies. He had pulled the short straw when he killed the drugstore clerk. George Harsh died in Toronto, Canada, in 1980 at the age of 72.

This case closely parallels the famous Leopold and Loeb thrill murder in Chicago in 1924. The newspapers at the time referred to Harsh and Gallogly as thrill killers and naturally made the comparison with Leopold and Loeb. The unanswered question remains: Did reading about Leopold and Loeb give Harsh and Gallogly the idea to commit a thrill murder themselves, or rather was it just the trend of the times that brought about these two murders so similar in nature, but occurring in widely different sections of the country? We cannot really know. Gallogly never said, but Harsh stated that he was aware of the Leopold and Loeb case. Both Harsh and Gallogly must have heard over the radio and read in the newspapers about the Leopold and Loeb case. The question is: Would they have committed these thrill murders in Atlanta, four years later, had they never heard or read about the thrill murder in Chicago?

Changes in the level and pattern of criminal activity reflect changes in American life. Just as the unsettled conditions following World War I had an effect on crime, as did the development of technology in the fields of transportation and communication, so did the effects of the Depression.

Hard times and an increase in crime accompany one another. Perhaps spurred on by the example of the kidnapping of wealthy Atlanta banker John K. Ottley, who was held for ransom by two very amateur bandits but escaped unharmed (the case occurring just one year after the much-publicized Lindbergh kidnapping), throughout the early thirties there was an epidemic of ride-rob crimes in Atlanta. Driving at night, or even during daylight hours, often became a hazardous adventure as people without jobs or hope very often turned to banditry. A person would stop at a traffic light in his automobile, and before he realized what was happening a pistol-carrying or knife-wielding bandit was sitting beside him. The bandit would order him to keep quiet and to keep driving. On some lonely road on the outskirts of town, the victims would be robbed, often assaulted, relieved of their cars, and, if lucky enough, spared any further harm. Some were not so lucky.

VICTIM RESISTED

In the early evening of Saturday, September 22, 1934, Max Sjoblom, aged 35, a traveling salesman from Davenport, Iowa, met sudden death at the hands of a ride-rob pair who forced their way into his automobile when he halted for a red light at the intersection of Marietta and Spring streets.

At around midnight that same evening, Detective Lieutenant J. Hiram Davis and his partner answered a call to a downtown hotel where they interviewed Mrs. Max Sjoblom. She was only 23 years old and had been married but a short time. The journey south with her husband on a business trip was also a delayed honeymoon; otherwise she would not have accompanied him on this routine trip. Mrs. Sjoblom was hysterical as she told police of how she and her husband had lunch at the hotel around 1 p.m., and that then her husband had gone out alone to call on some customers. When he did not return for dinner, Mrs. Sjoblom tried to reach her husband at the business address where he had an appointment earlier in the afternoon. She was told by the party there that, yes, Mr. Sjoblom had been at their office earlier in the day, but had departed. No; he did not mention where he was going when he left, but he had been gone for some time and certainly he should have arrived at the hotel by now. Mrs. Sjoblom tried to reach her husband at some other business locations where she thought he might have gone, but failed to do so. She became very worried as evening faded into darkness and notified the police.

Detective Davis and his partner decided, in talking with Mrs. Sjoblom, that Mr. Sjoblom was a devoted husband and not the sort of person who would just stay out all night drinking or playing cards when he had a beautiful wife waiting for him at the hotel. Detective Davis did not realize it just then, but this case would consume his time and energy for the next 35 hours.

The police learned from Mrs. Sjoblom that her husband was a traveling representative of an automobile repair equipment firm and that he traveled in his own car, a business coupe. The officers were then able to determine that the last person to see Sjoblom was the engineer of a local automotive plant about 7:00 that evening. He was alone and had driven off in the direction of his hotel. At this point Detective Davis began to believe that his missing man was the victim of foul play. It followed this new pattern of crime that the police had been plagued with lately—the ride-rob bandits. There was mounting public pressure to put an end to this kind of crime. Just two days earlier a prominent local citizen had been the victim of a pair of ride-rob bandits and had turned up at police headquarters with a black eye and broken nose, the results of having been beaten mercilessly by his two abductors. He wanted something done. He wanted his car returned. He went in to talk with the Chief. Detective Davis knew the pressure was there, and if this case turned out to be what he thought it was, he knew that he had better have all the answers—and quick. Detective Davis started checking the route he presumed Sjoblom took to his hotel, figuring that if he had been abducted it would have been along this route.

The early morning hours of Sunday passed quickly without any break in the case. Lieutenant Davis needed time; he needed a lead before the papers broke the story on Monday.

Then at nightfall a startling development took place. On East Main Street in College Park, an automobile identified as Sjoblom's car was found with blood on the front seat. An identification bureau officer examined the vehicle and found a .38 caliber lead slug embedded in the automobile upholstery. Lt. Davis was fairly certain then that he had not simply another ride-rob case on his hands, but a homicide. This intensified the pressure. Developments came fast.

Police in Fulton and Clayton counties began working with Atlanta police and an intensive search was begun of the area where other ride-rob victims had been put out and assaulted. A man was located who recalled seeing two young men in the College Park area about 10:45 p.m. Saturday. One of the men had his hand bandaged and both men had blood on their trousers. A College Park druggist recalled that two men came into his store about 11 p.m. to use the telephone. One had a bandaged right hand and both had blood on their trousers. They remained in the store until a taxicab came by.

The taxicab driver was found. He told police that he had made a pickup at the drugstore Saturday night but that only one of two young men had entered the taxi—the one with the bandaged right hand. He reported that he drove the man to Kirkwood.

At 7:00 Sunday night Detective Davis received an anonymous tip that a man with a bandaged right hand could be found at an Eleanor Street address in Kirkwood. This was in the vicinity where the taxi driver had let his fare out the night before. Detective Davis went to the address and arrested Robert Riley, white male, aged 20. The taxicab driver immediately identified him as the fare from College Park the night before. His right hand was still bandaged. In a search of the Riley home police found a pair of white flannel trousers spotted with blood stains. At the police station Riley said nothing. In spite of intense police questioning, he stuck doggedly to his story that he had cut his hand in a fight. He had never heard of Max Sjoblom. Detective Davis knew he would have to release Riley unless he found witnesses who had seen him in company with Sjoblom. Even had Riley confessed to Sjoblom's abduction, it would be of little use since Georgia law requires production of the body before a conviction can be obtained in a homicide trial. No body; no homicide. It was as simple as that.

In his interrogation, Riley did give an account of his activities of Saturday night and Sunday. He told police that he and Robert H. Summers had been downtown on Saturday night and met another young man with some girls in their rounds. They had gone for a ride out through College Park. A quarrel occurred and a fight ensued. A door glass was broken and he (Riley) cut his hand. Riley stated that he and Summers were put out of the car and made their way to a drugstore in College Park. When Summers was taken into custody and brought to the police station, he told essentially the same story as Riley. Lt. Davis was convinced that it was a cover that both men had worked out and agreed on beforehand. But he had no proof. The only thing Summers could not explain was why he did not return in the taxicab with Riley to Atlanta, instead of taking the streetcar as he claimed.

There was still no definite connection of the two suspects with Sjoblom's disappearance. Meanwhile a number of Saturday night ride-rob reports had reached the police department, as Lt. Davis had expected. A postal clerk had been waylaid at about 7:30 p.m. by two youthful looking men who leaped onto the running board of his automobile as he was parking at Carnegie Way and Spring Street. They pointed a gun at him; and, when he refused to open one of the car doors, one of the gunmen smashed the window with his fist and fired at him—the bullet grazing his head. Then both bandits fled.

The postal clerk identified Robert Riley in a lineup at headquarters as the man who had broken his car door glass and shot him. Another ride-rob victim, a visitor from Arizona, identified Riley as one of two bandits who had held him up on June 24, taking $50 cash and a .38-caliber revolver. Ballistics tests later showed the bullet found in Sjoblom's car was fired from a .38-caliber weapon.

A drugstore employee identified both Riley and Summers as having entered his business about 8:30 p.m. Saturday. He said Riley's hand was cut, and there was no blood on the clothing of either man. Riley's hand was bandaged in the drugstore.

An anonymous tip to Lt. Davis stated that a relative of Robert Riley had turned a pistol over to a lawyer, and this led to the recovery of the gun. A test bullet fired from the weapon, a .38-caliber revolver which proved to be the one taken from the Arizonian in the robbery weeks previously, compared perfectly with the one found embedded in Sjoblom's abandoned car.

When confronted by Lt. Davis with these findings, Riley

confessed that he shot the salesman when the latter resisted. He also implicated Summers in the Sjoblom case and in numerous other ride-rob jobs during the previous weeks. When asked by Lt. Davis why he had become involved in this ride-rob spree and why he killed Sjoblom he blamed it all on drinking. He said he was under the influence of liquor when he shot Sjoblom. He said that if it had not been for liquor he would never have become involved in all of this. He said that he was glad, in a way, that it was all over.

At 5:45 Monday morning, Riley led detectives to the spot where the Iowan's body had been dumped. The entire investigation had taken from midnight Saturday until early Monday morning. For Detective Davis it was 35 hours of grueling work.

Robert Riley was found guilty and given the death sentence on a murder conviction on September 10, 1934. He was granted several stays of execution, and the death sentence was commuted to life on October 31, 1934 by Governor Eugene Talmadge. He was placed on parole on September 15, 1949, but the parole was revoked on January 19, 1951, and he was confined to prison once again. He was later released.

Robert H. Summers was given a life sentence on a murder conviction in the Sjoblom case. He was paroled on February 17, 1947 and moved to Ohio.

It took a homicide to bring to an end the rash of ride-rob crimes that plagued the city in this time of economic depression. For his swift solution of the Sjoblom case, Lt. Davis received much favorable attention from the press and had a long and respected career with the Atlanta Police Department. He always stoutly maintained that the swift solution and attendant publicity generated in the Sjoblom case deterred other would-be ride-rob bandits and prevented any other innocent persons from suffering a fate similar to that of Max Sjoblom.

THE APPARATUS

Not only the Depression, but the passage of the 18th Amendment to the Constitution, had an effect upon the nature of violent crimes in America in the early thirties. While we usually think of culprits like Al Capone and Dutch Schultz and cops like Elliot Ness, many less well-known individuals were caught up in the crime patterns of the times and became gangster products to a lesser degree than the more famous lawbreakers whom they often imitated. These small-time hoodlums operated in many areas of the country, and Atlanta, unfortunately, had its share of them. Again due to its location as a rail center and stop-over point between North and South, many of these criminals drifted into the city from somewhere else.

Organized crime, like organized business, tends to branch out in order to grow and flourish. To lieutenants of Al Capone's gang in Chicago or Dutch Schultz's Brooklyn waterfront gang passing through Atlanta on their way to the warm sunny beaches of Florida, Atlanta in the thirties often appeared not only a convenient stop-over point but a virgin field where small-time mobsters felt they could become bosses on their own and heads of giant crime syndicates. Although many came, few succeeded in realizing their dreams, and those who did, didn't for long.

Jimmie Rosenfield drifted from New York to Atlanta in the early thirties, allegedly because he had to get out of New York in a hurry and lie low until things there cooled off. Rosenfield was an underling in the Dutch Schultz gang; and it was said at that time that he had shot someone in a holdup in New York, and the police were hot on his trail. In Atlanta he had visions of becoming a big-time gangster in new territory. Ultimately it was discovered that he was involved in gambling activities and he and several associates were responsible for over two dozen burglaries and robberies in the Atlanta area in the years 1934 and 1935.

Rosenfield was clever enough to keep the police from tying him to any of these robberies and burglaries and was well on his way to an increasing life of crime when fate intervened.

Exactly as in the Sjoblom murder, it was a homicide which he committed that ultimately did Rosenfield in. It would appear that society in general was more aroused by murders in those times than today. Perhaps because the murder rate was not as high then, a homicide made a greater impression upon the police and public when one was committed. Certainly a study of crime reports of this time indicates that the criminal was severely weakened and the individual criminal brought to justice and his criminal enterprises smashed most often when, unplanned and for no predictable reason, the criminal committed an act of murder. This really got the press, the public, and the police in high gear.

They strongly believed that the homicide rate more than anything else reflected the true crime index of the community. When a homicide was committed, the reaction was that crime was on the increase. Whether or not the homicide rate is the surest barometer of criminal activity within a community, it is certainly the most dramatic indicator; and then, as now, it received the most attention from the police, press, and public. Whatever, the individual criminal in this era could carry on his criminal activity much better if he refrained from killing. But being gangsters and often lacking subtlety of mind, most never mastered this basic fact. A small-time operator like Jimmie Rosenfield never comprehended it at all.

On Confederate Memorial Day, April 26, 1935, Jimmie Rosenfield, aged 35, and late of Brooklyn, New York, shot and killed Lester V. Stone, Jr., aged 35, of Atlanta, whose mother on that day was presiding at Confederate Memorial Day services. Lester Stone's wife and young son had also gone to the Confederate Memorial Day services. At the last moment Stone changed his mind and decided not to accompany his family. Had he not done so, it would have saved his life. The homicide of Lester V. Stone turned out to be one of the most bizarre crimes of this period.

Lester Stone and his family lived in an apartment building at 572 Parkway Drive, N.E., Atlanta. He had been a star football player in his youth and later became a boxer, but he gave up the career at his mother's insistence. At the time of his death he worked in the radio department of a downtown Atlanta furniture store. A long-time friend and old football mate of Stone's, R. B. Bullock, and his wife, Frances, a beautiful brunette who was the mother of two children by a former marriage, lived in the apartment across the hall from Stone and his family. On the evening of April 26, 1935, Bullock had called Stone to come over to his apartment. When Stone got there, he found his old friend very upset. Bullock told him that his wife had been gone all afternoon, and he did not know where. He told Stone that he was afraid his wife was seeing another man, and he just didn't know what to do.

Soon Mrs. Bullock returned to the apartment, and an argument developed between her and Bullock. Stone got up to leave the apartment, but Bullock urged him to stay. The telephone rang. Mrs. Bullock answered. It was Jimmie Rosenfield wanting to know if she had gotten home all right. She and

Rosenfield had been to a movie earlier, and he was checking to see if she had gotten home safely. Before the conversation was over, Bullock grabbed the phone away from his wife, uttered a remark into the receiver, and then slammed it down. There were more heated words between Bullock and his wife. He accused her of having an affair with another man. The doorbell rang. Bullock went to answer, but Stone restrained him and told him to sit down. Then Stone went to the door, opened it, and stepped out into the hallway and closed the door behind him, without either of the Bullocks seeing who was at the door. Seconds later a shot rang out and Bullock rushed to the door; he found Stone sprawled in the hallway, dead from a bullet in his heart.

Bullock didn't want his wife to leave him. After the murder occurred, she was scared and contrite and promised her husband she would always love him and would never go with another man. They both knew that the murderer was Rosenfield, and they were afraid that if they talked they would get the same treatment that Stone received. Mrs. Bullock told her husband that Rosenfield was tied in with mobsters and recounted frightening stories that Rosenfield had told her of his exploits on the Brooklyn waterfront. Bullock was convinced. If he needed further proof concerning what Rosenfield might do, the body was lying in the hallway in front of the door.

When the police arrived, the Bullocks had their story worked out. They told police they heard an argument in the adjoining apartment and then a shot fired in the hallway. They went out and found Stone. They said they did not see anyone else. They told the police that Stone must have come home and surprised a burglar, who shot him. They could not give any other information.

There was no progress in the case. No one came forward, and of the people the police talked with, none of them linked Rosenfield with Mrs. Bullock. Not until a burglary suspect being routinely questioned supplied them with information did the police get a break in the murder case. The burglar told police that if they would give him a break he would give them some good information.

The burglar related that an associate of his forced him at gun point to drive him to Marietta, Georgia, leaving him with the warning: "I think I have a shot a man . . . don't you put me on the spot . . . " The man's name was Jimmie Rosenfield.

On June 25, 1935, Rosenfield was traced to New York City. Lt. Cal Cates and two other officers went to New York to find him. With the assistance of New York City detectives, and after searching for their suspect for three weeks, Rosenfield was arrested by Lt. Cates as he strolled down Broadway. Lt. Cates testified: "I asked him if he had ever been in Atlanta and he said yes. I asked him if he was the person who had shot and killed Lester Stone, and Rosenfield looked shocked. He told me all the time that he thought he had killed Bullock." It was a mistaken-identity slaying.

Rosenfield was returned to Atlanta to face charges of murder. It was a dramatic trial. Defense attorneys attempted to imply that Mrs. Bullock fired the fatal shot, then passed the gun to Rosenfield. Possibly because of this, the jury, when it found Rosenfield guilty, recommended mercy. Both Mr. and Mrs. Bullock were arrested, and Mrs. Bullock was charged with being an accessory after the fact; but nothing was done about this charge. The gun which killed Stone had been pawned in Chattanooga during Rosenfield's drive north from Atlanta. The pistol was recovered from a prominent physician in Trion, Georgia, who had bought it at the pawn shop. The weapon, a .38-caliber automatic, was taken to Atlanta, where ballistics tests showed it fired the bullet that killed Lester V. Stone, Jr.

On September 9, 1935, Jimmie Rosenfield was sentenced to life imprisonment. On the eve of his retirement from office, Governor Ed Rivers granted Rosenfield a full pardon: January 14, 1941. At this time Rosenfield left the South and returned to New York City, never to be heard from again.

His departure from Atlanta closed the book on the saga of a small-time gangster whose involvement in a mistaken-identity killing spelled the end of his dreams of bigger things.

2

Banker Henry Heinz

In the past crimes of violence have taken on an aura of mystery and intrigue when prominent people have been involved. Homicides of wealthy people then proved more interesting to the general public than homicides of poor people. The more interesting and noteworthy the life, the more absorbing the details if this life ends abruptly in sudden and violent death. Factors enter into such a homicide investigation that are not present in the ordinary case. The victim is not merely known to his family and associates, but well known throughout the larger community. People are interested in the homicide because they are acquainted with the victim or have heard of him. The case receives broad coverage from the news media. The police are under great pressure to apprehend the culprit who committed the murder. People discuss the case and theorize about various motives and angles. Everyone is an amateur sleuth and develops his own ideas about the case from what he has read and heard. The case becomes more than a homicide; it becomes a part of the folklore, as much a part of a town as the waterworks. Such homicides, because of their complexity, are seldom solved to the satisfaction of everybody.

Coca-Cola is an Atlanta institution. The founder of the Coca-Cola Company was an Atlanta druggist, Asa Griggs Candler, a very prominent Atlanta citzen in the early decades of the present century. He was president of the Coca-Cola Company and later chairman of the board. He served as mayor of Atlanta in the period prior to World War I and was active in all aspects of life in the city. In 1908 he had been the moving force behind the development of the Druid Hills neighborhood.

Asa Griggs Candler was the father of four sons and a daughter. In 1943, his only daughter, the former Lucy Candler, lived at 1610 Ponce de Leon Avenue. At this time she was married to Henry C. Heinz, an Atlanta banker. Their beautiful home in Druid Hills was a notable estate in this section of fine homes. Mr. and Mrs. Heinz were charming hosts and entertained often. The Heinz home was one of the showplaces of the city; in the dogwood season the estate was opened to the public, and thousands visited its grounds and gardens. On the night of September 29, 1943, there took place at the Heinz estate not an elegant party, or a tour of the grounds and gardens, but a murder. At approximately 9:50 p.m., Henry Heinz was shot to death in the library of his home.

Officers I. A. Thomas and Ralph Hulsey were patrolling in squad car No. 19 on the north side of the city when they received a call over the police radio to 1610 Ponce de Leon Avenue, signal 4 (burglar in the house.) Though they were the officers who initially received the call to the Heinz home that fateful night, they were not the first officers to reach the scene. But since the call was given to car No. 19 originally, it was the responsibility of the officers in this car to file at police headquarters that night the initial report of the events which transpired at the Heinz home on the night of September 28, 1943. The first report in the Heinz case as submitted by Officers Hulsey and Thomas reads as follows:

We backed car No. 19 up to 1610 Ponce de Leon Avenue on a signal 4 (burglar in the house.) We entered the house and found Mrs. Henry Heinz in a very hysterical condition. She stated to us [that] earlier in the evening she heard a dog barking on the property outside and Mr. Heinz started to go out and investigate. She called him back and told him not to go out. Mrs. Heinz went out to use the telephone, and she could either not reach her party or decided not to call. Mr. Heinz had gone back in the library and she heard him cry out. She went into the library and saw Mr. Heinz scuffling with a Negro man. She went into her bedroom to get a gun, while there she heard two shots. She went back into the library and the Negro man was gone. She described the man as being a large Negro man wearing a blue shirt, brown pants, skull cap and with a handkerchief tied over his face. She said that his back was to her and she could give no other description.

Upon examination the victim, found lying on the divan in the library, had eight bullet holes in his body, and this included both entrances and exits. One bullet entered six inches below the arm pit, another entered at the fifth rib, one entered in the center of the chest, and one entered in the right arm three inches above the elbow. Mr. Heinz was pronounced dead by Dr. J. L. Campbell, a private physician, and the body was removed to Patterson's funeral home. The fingerprint man arrived on the scene and in going over the room, he immediately located three bullet holes in the room. As far as could be determined at the time, there was no property loss at the scene of the crime.

THE ESTATE

The Heinz estate is located on several acres of land at the corner of Ponce de Leon Avenue and Lullwater Road. The house faces Ponce de Leon and sits on a gently rising hill some distance from the street. Although the grounds adjacent to the house are wooded, the front lawn is landscaped, and the house is plainly visible to traffic along Ponce de Leon Avenue. The entrance to the estate is up a driveway that enters the grounds at both the left and the right of the house itself. It is a circular drive which on the left side (facing the house) comes up next to the house, where there is a covered drive-through entryway, screened porch, and side door into the house. A person coming up the drive in an automobile would stop under the entryway, get out of his car, and walk through the porch and side door directly into the library of the house, which is a large corner front room. The driveway does not stop at the entryway, but continues beyond the house and forks; the drive to the left continues in a circular fashion to a three-car garage and storage house located directly behind the main house. Because of tall trees and hollies the garage is practically hidden from the main house. The drive toward the garage is through wooded grounds, and here the land of the estate reaches the crest of the hill and just beyond the drive begins sloping downward to the end of the Heinz property. On the drive, just before one reaches the garage and to the left, there is a children's playhouse built in the style of the estate. Also to the left, and farther down the hill, are a tennis court and a swimming pool. Beyond the garage are greenhouses. The property is planted in azaleas, camellias, hollies, magnolias, and dogwood. The entire Heinz estate, except for the front lawn and the immediate side yards and gardens, is heavily wooded.

A visitor coming up the drive from the street on the left side of the estate would, as stated, drive under the entryway, stop, and enter the house from the side door or else walk around to the front of the house and enter through the front door. Leaving the estate, one would not have to back down the drive, but could continue driving around the house (but would not take the fork to the left to the garage) and would continue driving on the driveway to the right. This drive swings around behind the main house all the way, and bears right and then goes directly toward the street to Ponce de Leon Avenue. The driveway on the right side of the house (facing the house from the street) does not contain an entryway or door, and a person entering the estate up this driveway must go into the house through the front entrance. Therefore to gain access, one must go up the circular drive, entering from the street at either the left or right of the main house. It is an unusual circular driveway in that it circles around behind the house rather than in front of it, in the more ordinary manner. The driveway was constructed in this way to accommodate and be in harmony with the style of architecture of the house.

The house is white stucco with a dark-orange roof and is a replica of a Mediterranean-Spanish villa of the period; and although this type of architecture flourished in Florida and Southern California, in this era it was unique in Druid Hills, where most of the homes tend to be either red brick traditional or English estate limestone. The great charm of the Heinz mansion was certainly due, in part, to its setting on Ponce de Leon and the uniqueness of its architecture in this location.

Flanking each entrance to the driveways are twin white stucco pillars, and suspended above and supported by the pillars there is an ornamental Spanish-design grillwork. In the center of the iron decoration there is an elaborately designed letter "H".

Although the two entrances to the estate are flanked by these pillars, they were placed there for effect and ornamentation, rather than protection, for there was no barrier to entering the grounds of the mansion, either by automobile or on foot. There was no wall or fence enclosing the grounds, or any type of structure to mar the natural beauty and flow of the landscape. Although it was an imposing residence, to the casual visitor it was a home which appeared warm and inviting. The house, even from the outside, reflected the friendliness and old-style Southern charm of the inhabitants. The openness of the Heinz estate is a clue to the character of the people who lived there. It was also an important factor contributing to the tragedy which occurred there one harvest night long ago.

SHOTS IN THE DARK

Officers Marion Blackwell and Bill Miller were not surprised when they heard over the police radio in their squad car the signal 4 to 1610 Ponce de Leon Avenue. It was an address they knew well and a place they had been many times before, for the Heinz estate had been plagued by prowlers in the past several months. At the time the call went out over the radio, the two officers were patrolling in their squad car in the Little Five Points section. Officer Blackwell was at the wheel, and although he was driving along Moreland Avenue from the Druid Hills section when the call came over the radio, Blackwell turned the car around in the middle of the street, driving up over the curb and onto the sidewalk in order to do so. Pressing the accelerator to the floor, Blackwell and Miller roared off as fast as the car would go in the direction of the Heinz mansion, oblivious to all traffic rules.

Blackwell and Miller encountered few cars as they thundered down Moreland Avenue and turned right on Ponce de Leon, the tires squealing as Blackwell negotiated the turn without slowing down. Back then, during World War II, people parked their cars at nightfall, because of gasoline rationing and did not drive around on nonessential errands—hoarding their precious gas coupons for work and other important trips. In this era the police, unhampered by traffic congestion, could wheel about the city in their sleek 1941 black-and-white Fords at breakneck speed.

Within minutes after the first call, Blackwell and Miller were roaring up the drive on the left side of the house at 1610 Ponce de Leon Avenue. Blackwell noted that the light was on in the outside entryway, but that otherwise the house appeared dark. As he approached the entryway, Miller leaped out of the patrol car and ran toward the front door. Just as Miller reached the front entrance, he heard a woman's scream from inside the house. It was dark outside in front of the house and there was no moonlight. There were no outside lights with the exception of the lighted porch and entryway around on the left side of the house. Miller tried to enter the front door and found it locked. He tried to enter the tall front windows which reached to the floor, but found that they too were locked. Then there was another scream and Miller managed to squeeze through a small window of the library on the front of the house. The room was dimly lit and as Miller came through the window, he collided headlong with Mrs. Heinz, who had been doing the screaming and now screamed again; but then recognizing Miller as a policeman said: "Thank heaven you have come—I think he is still in the house!!" Miller saw Mr. Heinz lying on the divan in the library. From his experience as a police officer, he immediately knew that the man was dead.

After Miller had leaped out of the car and raced toward the house, Blackwell drove through the entryway and around to the back, whipped the car around, and faced it toward the house, leaving the lights on. His object was to snare the burglar if he was still on the premises or attempted to come out of the house somewhere in the rear. Then Blackwell ran back toward the house, through the lighted entryway and entered through the side door that opened into the library. Blackwell took one look at Heinz and, like Miller, knew at once that the banker was dead. He ran back to the patrol car and placed a lookout for the murder suspect. The only description he could give was that of a large Negro man. He then called for an ambulance and detectives to come to the murder scene. As he returned the police receiver to its place on the dashboard of the car and walked toward the house, a shot rang out, and Blackwell felt the sting of a sliver of concrete graze his cheek as a bullet ricocheted off the stucco abutment of the driveway and sent small pieces of concrete flying. Blackwell thought that the burglar was shooting at him. He wheeled around just as another shot rang out, and from the inky darkness in the shrubbery about half-way down on the side of the drive away from the house, he saw the unmistakable orange glow of pistol fire aimed directly at him. He leaped out of the drive and away from the lighted entryway and took cover behind a tree; grabbing his service revolver and blindly returning the fire toward the orange glow in the darkness. Blackwell called for Miller:

"Here!! He is out here!!! He is shooting at me!!" Inside the house, Miller heard the gunfire and his partner calling out that the slayer was in the yard shooting. Miller ran out through the door of the library and into the porch and lighted entryway. He was in full police uniform and standing there in plain view. Blackwell screamed for him to get down just as the assailant fired toward Miller from his place in the bushes. Blackwell heard the gunfire again and then saw Miller fall off the porch into the dark as though he had been shot. Blackwell thought the murderer had shot and possibly killed his partner. He could not see Miller because of the darkness; his partner had fired once but did not fire again, and he was closer to the slayer than Blackwell. Enraged, Blackwell advanced on his assailant with his service revolver blazing. The gunfire was returned, but even though he drew closer, none of the bullets hit Blackwell. As he advanced, his assailant began moving backward down through the shrubbery toward Ponce de Leon Avenue. At this point, Miller, who had not been shot but had broken his ankle as he leaped off the porch of the entryway to escape the line of fire, managed to make his way painfully down the driveway. This put the assailant almost in a cross fire between the two officers, and, as he turned to fire at Miller, Blackwell ran toward the assailant and fired the last bullet in his gun. Because of the darkness and dense shrubbery, Blackwell was right in front of his assailant before he could actually see him. Miller got within two feet of the person and fired his gun directly at the person's head. The bullet failed to fire properly. With his pistol empty, Blackwell managed to use it to knock the gun out of the assailant's hand. Then, Blackwell grabbed the assailant, leaping upon the back of the man, and began beating him on the head with the butt of his gun. Miller also got into the scuffle. At this point officers Hulsey and Thomas (*remember them*) and Officer Cody arrived on the scene and they joined the fray. Even with five policemen struggling with him, the supposed slayer managed to stay on his feet; and the fight continued furiously until the man was forced to the ground, one of the officers sitting on his chest, another on his stomach. At this point the man shouted:

"I am not the burglar! I am not the burglar!! I have been shot! I am Doctor Vann, Mrs. Heinz's son-in-law." The police backed away in stunned amazement from the darkened form sprawled before them. Officer Blackwell remembers thinking it was all a nightmare: the blazing gun battle, the murder, everything. There in the confusion and darkness it just did not seem real.

SCENE OF CHAOS

While the gun battle was taking place on the grounds, Mrs. Heinz was in the house alone. She thought, too, that the police had cornered the killer before he made a get-away. In the turmoil she had forgotten all about her call to Dr. Vann. When the police came up to the house with Dr. Vann, and Mrs. Heinz learned that the shooting had been not at the slayer, but at her son-in-law, she collapsed.

At this point the situation at the Heinz home was complete chaos. No one was sure exactly what had happened. No more than ten minutes could have elapsed since the original call went out over the police radio; yet at this point one of Atlanta's most prominent citizens was dead and for the moment being ignored, the police were rushing about trying to comfort Mrs. Heinz, and Dr. Vann was thinking he was going to die before anyone came to his aid. Officer Blackwell remembers the oppressive, overwhelming sense of darkness, of trying to get Dr. Vann into the house, of trying to get Miller, who could not walk, into the house, of everybody stumbling over one another and bumping into each other, and of nobody being able to see more than two feet in front of him in the darkness; also, of trying to see by lighting matches, of getting everybody into the house and trying to find the light switches and towels and giving first aid, and all the time the overwhelming sense of frustration bred in the darkness. He also remembers Mrs. Heinz coming around after fainting and rushing about trying to tell them what happened.

Officers Hulsey and Thomas calmed Mrs. Heinz and then examined the body. They sent out several help calls over their police radio. Office Blackwell, as the full impact of what had happened dawned on him, turned his attention to Dr. Vann. To have one of the town's most prominent citizens murdered on your beat was bad enough, but to shoot and possibly kill an in-law at the scene of the crime in a mistaken gun battle had implications almost too frightening to imagine. Blackwell immediately went to Dr. Vann's aid. He determined that Vann had been shot in the right wrist and chest, either from the same bullet or a second bullet. Although understandably in a state of shock, Dr. Vann was coherent. He managed to relate what had happened that night and to explain his presence on the Heinz property.

He stated that his first wife, then deceased, was the daughter of Mrs. Heinz by a previous marriage. Vann lived at 761 Lullwater Road, around the corner from the Heinz home. The backyard of his home backed up to the rear of the Heinz estate. There was a well-worn pathway which both families used to walk back and forth to each other's homes. The path started at the end of Dr. Vann's property and continued uphill by the tennis court and pool and came into the Heinz home at the back entrance. This pathway, easily traveled in daylight hours, was pitch black at night. Dr. Vann stated to Blackwell that he was in his home getting ready for bed when the phone rang. He was tired and disinclined to answer, but the phone kept ringing and he felt that it might be something urgent, possibly a patient (Dr. Vann was a dentist), and that he had better answer. When he answered, Mrs. Heinz began screaming something about a burglar and told him to get a gun and come over to her home at once. Dr. Vann stated that he grabbed his army .45 and loaded it with a full magazine. He started out of the house through the back path but realized that it was so dark that he could not find his way; so he changed his mind and ran out the front of his house, up to the intersection at Ponce de Leon, and entered the Heinz estate from the front.

As he rushed toward the house, he saw Officer Blackwell and thought he was the burglar, about to get away in the car, so he opened fire. When Blackwell returned the fire, his first or second shot hit Vann in the right wrist, thus crippling his firing arm and ruining his aim, for in order to fire the gun after that, Vann had to support his right hand with his left. The wound was very painful, he could not keep his hand steady, and the bullets missed their mark.

At this juncture the ambulance which had been called for Mr. Heinz arrived, and Dr. Vann was quickly placed upon it by the police and attendants. Blackwell noted as Dr. Vann was placed on the stretcher that he was wearing a pajama shirt and a pair of plain khaki trousers of the army uniform type. He wore bedroom shoes and no socks. His mode of dress seemed to match his story.

People were rushing to the estate from everywhere. Senior police officials arrived, summoned by continued calls for assistance and confusion at the Heinz home. As they arrived the police officials encountered Vann being carried out on a stretcher. They realized that the man had been shot, but he did not appear to be in bad shape; certainly he was not a corpse. No doubt the report of a homicide was not accurate. They soon learned otherwise.

Neighbors and curiosity seekers, attracted by the commotion and gunfire, began to invade the estate. A streetcar had been passing in front of the house when the shots were fired, and when the motorman stopped it and ran to investigate, all of his passengers piled out of the car after him to see what had happened. Relatives learned of the tragedy and went from their own homes in Druid Hills to the scene. It would be long after midnight before family and friends, police and press, and the plain curious departed.

After the body was removed from the house, Officer Miller was sent to a hospital. At this point what seemed like a full battalion of Atlanta police officers and investigators was on the scene. Men from the fingerprint and identification sections were going over everything in the house. Four detectives and the chief of the detective bureau were on the scene beginning to unravel the strange goings-on of the evening.

The major portion of the city of Atlanta lies within the boundaries and political and police jurisdiction of Fulton County; however, a portion of the northeast section of the city lies within DeKalb County. 1610 Ponce de Leon Avenue lies within the city of Atlanta but in the county of DeKalb. This jurisdictional anomaly would further confuse and hamper the investigation of the Heinz case.

The sheriff of DeKalb County went to the scene and called for the bloodhounds. The chief of the DeKalb County police was next on the scene. When the dogs were brought there, the officials discussed the possibility of the bloodhounds being able to search for the killer; but it was the unanimous opinion of all the police there that due to the confusion and delay, at that juncture any attempt to use the dogs would be futile.

The police therefore gave their attention to the house and the only person present at the time of the murder—Mrs. Henry C. Heinz. Mrs. Heinz had been taken upstairs and given a sedative by her doctor. Although very distraught and confused, she faced a battery of questions from the police and the press.

She told essentially the same story that is related in the report of officers Hulsey and Thomas. She and Mr. Heinz were alone in the house. They were both sitting in the library awaiting a news broadcast. Mr. Heinz was sitting in a large chair, next to a floor lamp, reading the editorial page of the evening edition of *The Atlanta Journal*, as was his custom before retiring. Earlier they had heard a commotion outside and a dog barking on the left side of the estate, the side on which the library is situated. Mr. Heinz started to investigate, but Mrs. Heinz restrained him. Then Mrs. Heinz stated that she went into another downstairs room to make a phone call, and, before the call was completed, she heard Mr. Heinz cry out. She rushed back to the library and found Mr. Heinz struggling with a Negro man. She stated that it seemed like the struggle went on a long time, and there was gunfire. She could not say exactly what happened after the struggle, but she said she had the impression that the slayer was still in the house when she ran back to the telephone and called Dr. Vann and then the police.

She went back into the library and found her husband lying on the divan. She tried to talk to him, to get him to answer her; but he said nothing, and she stated that she felt sure that he was dead. Mrs. Heinz stated that she had the feeling the slayer was still in the house when the police arrived, but she could not actually say that she saw anyone.

In the library the police inspected an overturned floor lamp and disarranged furniture—the only evidence of a scuffle there. As investigators went over every detail in the library a few meager clues were unearthed. The battered inner workings of a man's wrist watch were found on the library floor. Several relatives and friends stated to police that Mr. Heinz did not wear a wrist watch. An ordinary shirt button was also found on the floor. Three badly smashed bullets were dug out of the library walls. Then the fingerprint man went over the room and lifted prints from furniture, door facings, window sills, and venetian blinds. At this point it was all the available evidence the police had to go on.

Next an attempt was made to determine the route the burglar used in both entering and leaving the house. As you enter the Heinz home through the front door, you step directly into a large reception hall which is a massive room that is two stories high. Standing at the front door, facing the room, there is an enormous fireplace to the left, and to the right a stairway leading to the second floor. Beyond the fireplace, on the left side of the house, is the library—the room in which the murder was committed. To the right, and beyond the stairway, is the dining room. This is the layout of the rooms in the entire front part of the house. There are, of course, other rooms to the rear and bedrooms on the second floor. The only lights burning in the front part of the house that night were in the library and the outside light in the entryway beyond the library. The dining room and reception room were dark. The French windows in the reception room and the front door were locked. Officer Miller had tried to enter the house through all of these entrances and had been unable to do so. There was a small library window on the front of the house which Miller had found opened and through it he entered the house. At this hour, however, Miller was at the hospital, and his partner, Blackwell, was at the police station, making his report concerning the shooting of Dr. Vann. A detective on the scene immediately concluded that this window was too small for a man to enter (he was a very large detective) and that the burglar must have entered the house some other way. A window on the far right corner of the side of the dining room was found raised, and it was thought that the burglar must have entered the house through it. If this were the case, it would mean the killer had to traverse the immense reception hall, both before and after the shooting, which was completely dark. This might account for Mrs. Heinz's impression that the killer was still in the house after the murder, and in the darkness he could have had as much difficulty making his way back to the dining room window as the police had in the darkness outside.

It was also theorized by the police that the floor lamp in the library, when knocked over in the struggle between the intruder and Mr. Heinz, went out. It was not touched by the police until the fingerprint man had been over everything in the room, and it was not burning when the police arrived. Other lights in the room were turned on for light when Dr. Vann and Officer Miller were brought in. The fallen lamp explains why the police found the house in total darkness.

Members of the press, the police, and the curious continued to mill about the house far into the night. Mrs. Heinz left with relatives to escape the confusion and relentless questions. It would be a long while before she returned to the house at 1610 Ponce de Leon.

BACKGROUND

At Atlanta police headquarters investigators began sorting through the meager details they had of the case. The best sources of information were officers Blackwell and Miller. Inasmuch as Miller was at the hospital that night with a broken ankle, it was up to Blackwell to give an account to his superiors and the press concerning the events that evening at the Heinz home.

How was it that he and Miller managed to get to the Heinz home when the original call was given to officers Hulsey and Thomas? It was at this point that some of the background of the case began to emerge.

During the past two or three years burglars had frequented the Heinz home, and Blackwell and Miller had handled those calls. On one occasion, a burglar had entered the Heinz home and stolen a small amount of money, awakening Mr. Heinz in the process. Mr. Heinz had gotten a brief glimpse of the burglar as he fled the house, and when Officers Blackwell and Miller arrived, the banker described him as being a large Negro man. In this same period other homes in the Druid Hills section had been burglarized, and the thief always took only money. Another victim had gotten a glimpse of the burglar and described him as a large Negro man. The press had become aware of the situation in Druid Hills and had written several articles about the robberies. The pattern was always the same. At night, when the victims were either away from home or asleep, someone quietly entered the house and stole money—and sometimes during the daylight hours. Nothing in the houses was ever disturbed or taken, and the burglar or burglars were very careful to enter an unlocked door or window. A fleeting glimpse of a large Negro man was the only clue to the burglaries, and the alleged thief had been dubbed the cat burglar by the press.

After he was robbed the second time, Mr. Heinz decided that enough was enough. He bought a .38-caliber pistol and began target practice in the rear of his estate. He stated to the police that if the burglar came to his house again, he would shoot him.

The police were very concerned about the cat burglar situation in Druid Hills. The most influential people of the community lived there. It was a situation they did not wish to see continue. In attempting to catch the so-called cat burglar, Blackwell and Miller began making nightly checks on several of the estates in Druid Hills that had been visited by the burglar. They made it a practice to drive through the Heinz estate every night between ten and twelve o'clock. They would vary the time of their patrol in order not to establish a pattern for a would-be burglar, thereby allowing him to rob the Heinz home as soon as they departed. If they were not entertaining or up for some special occasion, Mr. and Mrs. Heinz would be in bed by 10 p.m., and all the lights would be out. Blackwell and Miller would ride through the grounds and cruise behind the house, shining the car lights and their police spotlight about the house and grounds. When Mr. Heinz bought that gun, the officers were concerned he might shoot them, thinking they were the cat burglar. Mr. Heinz, a fearless man himself, laughed at this notion and said there was no danger of that. He said he always knew if it was the police, because they shined that spotlight; however, he did caution them never to come onto the grounds without shining the light.

Officer Blackwell was concerned about two things on the Heinz estate: the gun and the total lack of security. He had several conversations with Mr. Heinz about the gun. He pointed out to him that burglars seldom carried guns (we are talking about 40 years ago) and they wished to appear peaceful; and if caught or surprised while on a job, if they had a gun, they might use it. It would be better to face a burglary charge than a murder charge. Mr. Heinz scoffed at this suggestion and continued with his target practice. Blackwell also urged him to take some precautions on the estate. The Heinz place was not enclosed by a wall or fence, and Mr. and Mrs. Heinz owned no dogs. They lived on the estate alone, and the people who worked for them in the daytime left at nightfall. Blackwell stated that when he and Miller drove through the estate on patrol, the grounds were as dark and spooky as a cemetery. They were ready to make their visit to 1610 Ponce de Leon Avenue that night when the call came over the police radio. This explains how Blackwell managed to put a lookout over the police radio for a Negro man in the vicinity, even before talking with Mrs. Heinz.

A second question Blackwell had to answer was the Vann shooting. Members of the press wanted to know, Why did he and Miller shoot Dr. Vann? Blackwell stated that it was all a horrible mistake. They thought Vann was the cat burglar, and he thought they were. But why couldn't Vann see the police car, or see that Miller was in police uniform when he came outside on the lighted entryway? Blackwell stated they would have to ask Dr. Vann that question. When interviewed, Dr. Vann stated that the police fired at him as he entered the grounds and he returned their fire thinking they were the burglars. Upon examination, it was determined that Dr. Vann fired nine times, Blackwell six, and Miller once. Vann stated that when he answered the telephone call from Mrs. Heinz that night, she stated to him in a very frantic voice: "By! By! Come over here this instant! *They* are killing Mr. Heinz!"

"I started to go down the path through the gardens," Dr. Vann continued. "But then I decided that whoever was over there might be outside or have accomplices, so I went down Lullwater Road to Ponce de Leon and up Ponce de Leon to the entrance of the Heinz home."

Blackwell maintained that he could not have fired at Dr. Vann first because he did not know that he was there. Blackwell insisted that he could not see Vann until he was within two feet of him, even after the shooting started. Dr. Vann was not in the drive, but, by his own account, hidden in the bushes; so, how could Blackwell, or Miller, for that matter, know he was there until he opened fire? Blackwell was sure Vann opened fire on him thinking he was the burglar, and he thought this a rather normal reaction considering the hysteria of the moment and the pitch darkness of the setting. In the black night all Vann saw was the form of a man beside the entryway and another darkened silhouette leap from the house. All things considered, it was impossible to tell they were police officers. A man preparing for bed had been thrust into a crazy series of events. Upon reflection, his behavior seems quite normal.

Most Atlantans learned about the Heinz murder the following morning over the radio or by reading the morning edition of *The Atlanta Constitution*. The entire city was shocked and horrified that such a thing could happen in Atlanta. The first news accounts of the events that had transpired at the home the night before painted a rather strange and confusing picture. Needlss to say, on the morning after the shootings the police performance did not come off very well.

Henry C. Heinz was not only a well known but a highly

regarded citizen of the city. Although born in New Haven, Connecticut, on August, 18, 1879, Henry Heinz's father and grandfather had been native Atlantans. Heinz as a young man began a long career in the banking business. He began with the Central Bank and Trust Company, which had been founded by Asa Griggs Candler; and in 1922, when this bank merged with Citizens and Southern, Henry Heinz became a director and vice president of the Citizens and Southern Bank—a position he held at the time of his death. Like other men of wealth of the period, he was very active in civic affairs and devoted much of his time and energy to helping the less fortunate. In 1938 he was a founder of the Atlanta Boy's Club and served this organization as president from then until the time of his death. He took great interest in the work of the Boy's Club, and his desk was cluttered with ashtrays and other artifacts made by members of the club in their projects.

Mr. Heinz was involved in countless civic affairs. He was city chairman of the banking division of the Third War Loan Drive; and he had heard over the radio, just moments before his death, that the drive had reached its goal. Indeed, it was to hear whether the drive had been a success that Mr. Heinz had remained up beyond the time at which he usually retired for the night. Beside Mrs. Heinz, he was survived by a brother, two sisters, and a son and a stepson.

By mid-day all Atlanta knew of the murder, and the police assigned to the Heinz residence had a time of it shooing sightseers and photographers away. People flocked to the scene of the crime hoping to get a glimpse of Mrs. Heinz. And she was forced to stay away from the home she had built back in 1922. For several days Atlanta was agog over the murder, and even the war in Europe and the Pacific had to take second place to the Heinz case.

The Atlanta Journal headline of Wednesday, September 29, 1943, stated:

GREATEST ATLANTA MANHUNT
LAUNCHED FOR HEINZ KILLER

When Officer Blackwell put out that alert for a large Negro man shortly after the shooting, it had some results. No large Negro man anywhere in the northeast section of the city was safe from either search or seizure. Three suspects had been picked up that night; but by the following morning they had been released, the police satisfied that they were guilty only of being large Negro men.

Following a night of panic, a quiet calm hung over the Druid Hills neighborhood. That night, as news of the murder spread, residents of Druid Hills began to flood the Atlanta police station and DeKalb police station with calls of prowlers on the property and burglars in the house. The police not at the Heinz murder scene were scurrying around all over Druid Hills answering these frantic calls. The residents were gripped by fear. There had never been a murder in the neighborhood before. It was not that kind of neighborhood, and it was in a frenzied atmosphere that the police, in searching the grounds of various homes for reported prowlers, collided with one another—with pistols drawn—in the darkness. It was a replay of the scene at the Heinz home earlier. The miracle of the night of September 28, 1943, is that only one person was murdered.

ENVY SPAWNS RUMORS

As the shock of the murder wore off and the initial reaction of fear ebbed, tongues began to wag. All at once, the city was flooded with a host of wild and unfounded rumors. The case, in that pre-television time, became something to talk about, and as people talked and speculated, fiction very often supplanted fact. Some of the rumors were the result of the dual police investigation of the crime. Some were spread by newspaper writers and radio commentators speculating about the murder, but many of the rumors originated simply from wild imaginations.

Due to the twin police jurisdiction of the case, investigations by two separate police agencies were going on at the same time. The major investigation was being conducted by the Atlanta Police Department, but insofar as the murder occurred in DeKalb County, the police agency there was involved. The chief of the DeKalb County Police stated to the press that he had had several conversations with Mr. Heinz about the burglaries at the Heinz home and had instructed a patrol car from his department to check on the house at various times. The chief's statement strengthened the case against a burglar as the likely murderer.

There were other police detectives assigned to the case who did not agree. Some of them felt the case was more involved;

one detective leaned toward a Cain-Abel theory, and felt that
Mr. Heinz had been killed by someone close to him, that probably his death was the result of some kind of conspiracy. Although he did not actually name the conspirators, Mrs. Heinz
and Dr. Vann were the implied villains in the case. The impression grew and persisted and flowered into full-blown
speculation that Mr. Heinz was killed by Mrs. Heinz and Dr.
Vann because the two of them wished to marry and had to get
rid of Mr. Heinz in order to do so! This rather absurd notion
was given some credence when the press printed what were
supposedly the last words of Heinz:

"Don't shoot me . . . you will get more if you don't shoot me."

This really set the rumor mills to churning for it was inter-
preted to mean that if Vann didn't kill Heinz, Heinz would
give him whatever he wished. The idea persisted that Heinz
was killed because Mrs. Heinz and Vann wished to marry and
wished to "get their hands on the money." Meaning that Mrs.
Heinz would get Vann and all the money too. Many people
believed this was the true motive in regard to the Heinz murder, and that the "facts" never came out because Mrs. Heinz
was a rich woman and the police and press hushed everything
up. For several years afterwards, the press always referred to
the conflicting opinions of various police officials when mentioning the Heinz case.

It was exceedingly difficult for investigators to get a complete picture of events because of numerous rumors and false
reports concerning the case. Both Mrs. Heinz and Dr. Vann
were under seige from the police and the press who wished to
question them endlessly concerning what happened. They
grew weary of the ordeal and quit talking to anyone; and
when it appeared in print that Mrs. Heinz was at an undis-
closed location and that Dr. Vann's attorney had told him not
to talk to the press anymore, the "I told you so's" had a field
day.

The Atlanta Police Department issued a directive for all
officers working on the Heinz case not to discuss it with anyone not involved. This order was issued in good faith in an
attempt to cut down on false reports and rumors concerning
the case; however, it was widely regarded as a cover-up.

The first reaction to the Heinz murder had been one of
shock and fear. This could not happen in the city, certainly not
in Druid Hills. People were truly saddened by the violent

death of a fine citizen. But as rumors continued to spread, they began to grow uglier. The viciousness of the attacks on Mrs. Heinz were directed at her because she was a person of wealth.

Soon, strange and threatening letters began to arrive at police headquarters and at editorial offices of the newspapers. Sometimes letters written by near-illiterates, but just as often by people who could write legibly and spell correctly. What they had to say was very clear: Because Mrs. Heinz was a rich woman, a member of the most famous Atlanta family of the era, she could get away with anything, even murder. That is the way it was with rich people: If you had enough money, you could buy your way out of anything; only the poor were ever convicted.

The facts in the Heinz case were swept aside, the police being accused of having been bought out by big money and paid to cover things up. It was a conspiracy which the letter writers felt powerless to do anything about; but the message came across on paper, loud and clear—this terrible hatred and predjudice against the rich. In our present day we are aware of this kind of prejudice existing against certain minority groups within our society, but hatred has not always been so directed. Different times and different conditions create different hates. The era of the Heinz murder was a time when people still lived under the pall and anguish of the Depression. That era of hunger and economic failure had generated a prejudice against the wealthy that even in 1943 had not abated. Strangely enough, it was a homicide that caused this hatred to surface into full view.

PANIC AND FALSE LEADS

The acrimony generated by the Heinz killing severely restricted the murder investigation. The police had become rather sensitive on the subject. They were working very hard for a solution of the case, but they had been accused repeatedly of a sell-out, of treating rich people better than poor people, and any attempt to look for the killer was regarded by many as a mere diversionary tactic to take the heat off Dr. Vann and Mrs. Heinz. But some investigators believed in this Heinz-Vann conspiracy theory and proceeded to try and prove it. This they were unable to accomplish. In fact, about the strongest case against any kind of conspiracy was Dr. Vann's presence on the estate the night of the murder in his pajama top shooting at anything that moved. It would be absurd to believe that people engaged in a conspiracy would behave like that.

A report persisted that because the killer was masked he must have feared recognition and was therefore known to Heinz. An elaboration of this theory held that the man was actually a former employee of Heinz, who was not a Negro man at all, but a white man disguised as a Negro to throw the police off the trail. Very extensive and thorough police investigation could turn up no one who was an enemy of Mr. Heinz. He was the type of man who was beloved by the people who worked for him, and the type of person who would give anyone he knew anything they asked of him. He was constantly coming to the rescue of people who worked for him when they needed money or came upon hard times. If any of these people had any grudge against Henry Heinz, it was not discernable. But Heinz was a man of strong character who did not cotton to being robbed, and it was, with him, as much a matter of principle as of money.

Another theory was that if burglary was the motive the intruder would hardly have gone from the darkness of the dining room into the well-lighted library, especially if he was at the dining room window at the time Mr. and Mrs. Heinz heard the commotion outdoors. Officers Blackwell and Miller felt that the theory that the murderer entered the house through the dining room window did not hold water, and they were convinced that the burglar went in the same front window of the library and entered the house directly into the library as did Officer Miller himself a few minutes later. Others insisted no burglar would enter a well-lighted room with people awake in the house. It was ridiculous! Burglars did not operate in that manner. Never! Only the murderer himself could say what happened that night. Although the search for the so-called cat burglar continued, the quest proved fruitless.

The Druid Hills section of Atlanta was never quite the same after the Heinz murder. Few places are following a homicide. Mrs. Heinz never lived in the house afterwards, and it was closed up and stood empty and forlorn.

Burglaries in Druid Hills did continue, however. Officers received hundreds of calls, but most of them proved to be false. Whereas before the Heinz murder Officers Blackwell and Miller had been handling several prowler calls a week in the Druid Hills neighborhood, after the murder, they were answering dozens of calls a night.

The police thought they had a good break in the Heinz case when they arrested George Arnold, a black male, who fit the description given by Mrs. Heinz. He had been arrested for larceny and burglary in 1936, and for burglary in the northeast section of Atlanta in 1942. The newspapers, too quickly, headlined that a solution to the Heinz murder was imminent. For something more priceless than his own peace of mind, indeed his life, Georgia Arnold had an alibi. He was at work the night of the murder. His white boss stoutly maintained that Arnold was at work loading trucks from 6 p.m. until after midnight on September 28, 1943. Whew! for George Arnold. For the police and the press the speculators had no mercy. A storm of protest from the public followed the Arnold fiasco, and the police and the press became very leery of anything touching upon the Heinz case. Both investigation and reporting of the case came to a near-standstill. It seemed that whatever was done or written about the case created a backlash from the public. The gossips who were saying the case was "too hot to handle" knew more than they thought. Due to the notoriety surrounding the case, nobody wanted any part of it.

Two months after the Heinz murder the police answered a burglary call at a house only two blocks away from the Heinz home. When officers Blackwell and Miller reached the house all the lights were out and a very hysterical lady met them at the front door and in a whisper stated:

"I had turned out the lights in the house and gone to bed and I heard somebody breaking in the back door so I crept downstairs and called the police and waited here by the front door until you got here. He is still in the house."

Blackwell went through the front of the house back to the kitchen where he encountered a large Negro man, who immediately started out the back door and ran right into Miller. The officers had their man. They immediately placed him in the patrol car and began to question him. Upon interrogation, while riding through the Druid Hills area, the suspect confessed and pointed out some 17 homes that he had either prowled around or burglarized. He denied ever burglarizing the Heinz home or being anywhere near it. The suspect was booked at the police station on suspicion of burglary, and the

officers were certain that, if not the Heinz killer, they had at
least arrested the culprit who was causing them so much
havoc in the Druid Hills neighborhood. When the suspect's
fingerprints were identified by the FBI in Washington, it developed that the man was from Chattanooga, Tennessee; and
upon further questioning and investigation, he revealed that
he had arrived in Atlanta for the first time in his life the
afternoon before on a Greyhound bus. When asked why he so
readily admitted to being a burglar and fabricated such an
elaborate but false scenario of his activities in that field, he
replied that he was terrified by the obvious eagerness of the
officers to implicate him in the Heinz slaying, and felt that if
he confessed to something of a lesser nature they would be
satisfied with that and not try and pin a murder rap on him.
The man had an arrest record of traffic violations and petty
theft in Chattanooga and was very frightened by the mess in
which he now found himself. When asked why he had come to
Atlanta, he stated that he had heard about the Heinz murder
and other burglaries in Druid Hills and thought he would
come down to Atlanta and do himself some good. When he
reached the bus station in Atlanta, he asked for directions to
Druid Hills and rode on the streetcar out there. He walked
around awhile until it was dark and then entered the first
house he could manage to break into, whereupon he found
himself quickly in the hands of the police. Blackwell stated
that this incident, early in his police career, taught him something about investigative work he never forgot: never put
pressure on people to tell you things.

Several days afterwards, Blackwell spent an afternoon
talking with Mrs. Heinz. It was three months after the murder, but this was the first time Blackwell had seen Mrs. Heinz
since that fateful night. He had some difficulty in locating her,
for she still found it necessary to keep where she was staying
a secret, to keep from being badgered by the various police
from two departments, the press, and the plain curious. Mrs.
Heinz had heard the rumors then circulating the city, and
they much distressed her. They talked about the case and
Mrs. Heinz recounted the facts of the evening once more. They
discussed the events in detail, but only one important new
fact that Blackwell was previously unaware of emerged from
his conversation with Mrs. Heinz. She stated that while she
and Mr. Heinz were in the library listening to the news over

the radio, and while he had been reading the newspaper, she had been sewing for the Red Cross, and that she carried her sewing in a bright red knit bag. It did not appear significant to Blackwell then, but it was something he had not heard before; and Mrs. Heinz said that in the excitement of that evening she had not recalled it.

The next day Blackwell talked with Dr. and Mrs. Vann for the first time since the murder. Dr. Vann was out of the hospital and recovering from his wounds, but he still appeared dazed by the events of the past few months. The hysterical phone call from Mrs. Heinz that night, the gun battle at the Heinz home, his injuries; and then, the gossip about himself and Mrs. Heinz. It was all a terrible nightmare. He shook his head and wondered out loud about how such things could happen to people. Blackwell wondered how any responsible person could talk with Dr. Vann and then conclude that the man could possibly be involved in the Heinz murder.

CLOSING IN

On Sunday night, January 14, 1945, a year and four months after the Heinz murder, Fulton County police officers, on patrol in the area of north Fulton County, noticed a car driving somewhat erratically with the headlights out. They halted the car, and Officer Thompson got out to investigate. They found a Negro man in the car alone, and they asked him what he was doing in that neighborhood at that time of night, driving around with the lights off.

"I just a railroad nigger trying to get home," the man answered respectfully. "My lights went bad." The officers didn't find this unusual in the third year of World War II when people were finding it difficult to keep cars in good shape or to secure parts for much-needed repairs. The man appeared to be perfectly sober, and nothing else aroused Officer Thompson's suspicions. He told the man to drive on—and get those lights fixed. The Negro man thanked him profusely and drove off. Almost as an afterthought Thompson jotted down the license number of the man's car.

At approximately 8:30 that same night, the wife of prominent Atlanta attorney Hughes Spalding went into the well-lighted bedroom of the Spalding home on Peachtree Road and found a Negro man, gun in hand, his face hidden with a handkerchief, calmly moving about the room. She called to him and demanded to know what he was doing there, but he paid no attention to her, walked over to a closet, removed a pocketbook from the shelf, and then left. When Fulton County police arrived, Mrs. Spalding described the intruder as a large Negro man who walked a short distance from the house and got into a blue car. The police found a bandanna-type handkerchief that the intruder dropped as he left the Spalding home.

When the lookout was placed over the police radio, Officer Thompson felt sure the man involved was the one he had stopped earlier less than a mile from the Spalding home. He immediately called over the police radio and gave the license number of the wanted car.

At 9:40 the same evening, Atlanta police, having been alerted for the wanted man, spotted the car with the license number driving west on Simpson Road. They stopped the car, placed the man under arrest, and took him to the city jail. He offered no resistance. From there he was picked up and taken to the Fulton Tower jail by Fulton County police. He was questioned that night but did not admit entering the Spalding home. Officer Thompson interviewed the suspect and positively identified him as the man driving a blue car with the lights off.

Fulton County police went to the suspect's home and interviewed his wife. She identified the handkerchief found at the Spalding home as the property of her husband. One of their children had given him a set of four for Christmas. When confronted with this, the suspect confessed and took officers to the spot where he had thrown Mrs. Spalding's pocketbook. He admitted also breaking into 14 other houses in the North Atlanta area. In the interrogation the suspect stated that he "didn't have to wait until people went to bed before breaking in." The suspect was booked and held for indictment by the Fulton County grand jury.

The arrest report gave the man's name as Horace Blalock, a black male, of 1986 Simpson Road, Atlanta. He was born in Cobb County, Georgia, on June 26, 1909 and attended school there until he dropped out in the eighth grade. He was a man of large build and was 6'3" tall and weighed 230 pounds. His complexion was described in the report as medium brown. He had a large burn scar on the left arm, inside and above the elbow, and two smaller scars: one on the left side of the forehead and another on the inside right thumb. He was married and the father of three children and had two brothers living in Cobb County. He gave his occupation as porter.

Upon checking, Fulton County police discovered that Blalock had received three citations for traffic violations by Atlanta police over the past three years but had no record of burglary. When he was arrested for burglary of the Spalding home, Horace Blalock was fingerprinted for the first time.

Since the Heinz murder, the fingerprints of all persons arrested for burglary had been compared with the prints found in the Heinz home the night of the murder. When the prints were compared, Fulton County police were amazed at the similarity of the prints taken from the Heinz home and those of Blalock. However, they proceeded with great caution. There had been so much publicity on the Heinz case, so many false leads that in fact led nowhere, that the Fulton County police moved forward warily. But they became the third police agency involved in the case. Blalock was told nothing about the check on fingerprints.

Identification experts of the Georgia Bureau of Investigation, the fourth law enforcement agency to be involved in the case, were called in to examine the prints. Captain Ben Seabrook of the Atlanta I.D. Bureau also studied the prints carefully. It was the unanimous opinion of all these people that the index and small-finger prints taken from the venetian blind in the library of the Heinz home the night of the murder matched those of Horace Blalock. This appeared to make the identification positive. But speculation in the Heinz murder had come in waves in the past year since the homicide, and when the police came upon each speculation they tried feverishly to trace down every possible clue. No case in Atlanta history had ever caused so much unrestrained theorizing. This time officers had to be sure, for if the prints did not match conclusively, then the results would be just more waves of speculation and another dead-end.

Both Blalock's prints and the prints lifted at the Heinz home were sent to Washington for comparison. The FBI, the fifth law enforcement group in the case, was the most respected authority in the country on the subject of prints. The investigators wanted the FBI's evaluation before proceeding any further with their latest lead.

It was an anxious 24 hours for the police connected with the

case as they awaited word from Washington. Then, a terse
one-line telegram arrived from the FBI:

> Latent print identical with print of suspect Blalock.
>
> [signed] Hoover.

Now the police knew that Blalock was at the Heinz home at
one time or another, and it would be up to the suspect to provide an explanation of his whereabouts the night of September 28, 1943.

Blalock was being held in Fulton Tower jail for trial on the
burglary charge. He had been told nothing about his fingerprints matching with those from the Heinz home. He had not
asked to see an attorney.

On Thursday, January 18, 1945, four days after he had been
picked up on the burglary charge, Blalock admitted he had
burglarized the Heinz home several weeks before the slaying
and accompanied officers to the crime scene, showing them
how he entered the house (through the library window) and
the route he took to Mrs. Heinz's bedroom, where he said he
took $80 from a purse on a dressing table. The same after-
noon, Mrs. Henry Heinz picked Blalock out of a lineup as
the man she saw grappling with her husband the night of the
murder.

Blalock was taken into the detective office and questioned
extensively by Fulton County police, the chief of the DeKalb
County police, and Captain Seabrook of the Atlanta police.
Questioned constantly for some 15 hours, Horace Blalock confessed that he murdered Henry Heinz. One of the participants
of that session described it later as follows:

> Everybody was seated about the office very casual like. We
> would talk among ourselves about the case. Officers would
> come in and out on other business, there would be discussion of
> other cases, of routine police business and then we would begin
> talking about the Heinz case again. We would ask Blalock
> questions, mainly about his activities the night of the murder.
> Blalock was seated at a desk—an ordinary desk there in the
> office. There were no bright lights or the suspect being sub-
> jected to any discomfort, except the questions. Blalock was
> friendly and agreeable and showed no anger toward any of us.
> His replys [sic] were always well thought out and intelligent.
> He was a very likeable person and in the questioning there was
> none of the seething hostility that often develops in this type

of situation. Food and soft drinks were brought in from time to time, and we would not talk about Heinz during these breaks.

Blalock gave the appearance of being very fond of his family. I don't know how to say it exactly except that he was not care-free. In many ways he was different from your ordinary sus-pect; his manner, his very conservative way of behaving, his politeness, and his intelligence. All this made him different. Talking about his family and children seemed to get to him. We went over again and again all we knew about the case—which was a good deal—and tried to get Blalock to fill in the answers. Bit by bit he began to tell us things we hadn't known before. When he realized this, and this was quickly, he sat quietly for a long time and would not talk to us. We were on the verge of sending him back to his cell and giving it up for the night when he suddenly asked for a paper and pencil. It was handed to him and he began writing vigorously. While he was writing no one in the room said anything, and no one came in to interrupt while he was writing. He took a long time. It was kind of eerie . . . the long silence.

CONFESSION

For the time and the person and the place, Horace Blalock laboriously wrote out in long hand that night a rather re-markable statement. Then, he was writing down a confession to the murder of Henry Heinz; today, it reads more like a com-mentary, or social document of a by-gone era.

The following statement was written by Horace Blalock on January 19, 1945. Ryburn G. Clay, referred to in the state-ment, had once employed Blalock for a short time.

On the day of Sept. 14, 1943 I had to go to the hospital for a serious operation on the brest left side and I stay in the hospi-tal until Sept. 18th cause I had a cold. They operated on me on the 18th day of Sept. 1943. I left the hospital on the 23 to go home. I was very weak until the 15 day of Oct. 1943. I began to gain my strain, I need some money. I was get $7.00 a week out of my policy that was not anof and I try to figer out some way to get some more money. I was at home that nite. My wife and myself. So some body came by my house going to Dallas, Ga. to see my sister-in-law. They ask my wife and myself to go with them so I say I am to weak to ride up there so I demand my wife to go ahead so she did but she say will you be allwright. I say sure I will be so when she left I come out of my house and got in my car and left. I went down on out in Druid Hill and look around. I stop and Mr. Heinzy home on ponde de leon Ave. I went up there and I look around it was about 7:30 at night so I spoted them sitting in the side room. They were reading so I waited until Mrs. Heinzy went into the bedroom then I went to the winder and walk slower to the side room I thought both of them was goind to the bed room and I thought I spotted a red pocketbook on the sofa but it was a sewing bag and I hat a gun in my pocket when I got there there he was I was sorprised I turned to run and fell over the tables and he grab me and we tussle for a few minute he was so strong I could hardly hold him so he got my gun before I did and point it at me and shoot my thum half in two, and I got the best of him but I did never get the gun he had the gun but I twisted the gun point at him and it was fire every once in awhile. I don't know how many times it fire I got it in a little while in my hand and I ran out. Then I saw my finger was bleeding so and I all ready weak I could hard make it. I went strait home got me some little stick and did it up. I went to bed it bled all night. I went to the doctor the next morning and he fix it up. But I have not rested a nite since it have been worried me so much I could not sleep I say awake all night if it had not been for my wife and children I would have done give up. I go to church I could feel right it was sometime on my mind all the time I am sorrow I don't no what to do. I bought the gun from a boy on the west side of town. I dont no who he was. I throw the gun in the river at Marietta Bridge I was brought up in the church and made to do wright. My mother and father are dead they made me do wright but when I got up I staid away from her and his raised. They was very nice to me I have worked for some very good white people in Atlanta I work for Mr. Clay for a year or more. I do wont Mr. Clay to speak for me at my trial gentlemen I need mercy of you all for my family I have a wife and 3 little children. One 3-8-9 for the sake of my little children I ask mercy of Mrs. Heinzy please mirm just in order so see my children grow up and not let the make the same mistake I have made in life I am ask that you gentlemen please sir, I am so sorrow have mercy on me for wife and my children. Crime dont pay everbody that is doing wrong quit it now dont pay. The trial will come off in Decatur, Ga. High Cort some time in March. I hope you gentlemen will consider my case by that time please sir and please mirm I am sorrow I turned out to be what I did I married a fine girl for a wife she is a chrisen woman and not a better one she beleave in wright and wright a long I hope she will be happier again someday. She is a mitre sweet girl I will have to give her critic for my little children that so much of me and there mother it is hard for me to part from them but the lord says the best of friend must part from one another I wont you all to pray for me and I will pray for me. My time is all mose up but I hope not cose I am so sorrow I dont know what to do please pray for me and my family and children I hope no more of my people dont no crime. So sorrow.

[signed] Horace Blalock

Blalock's statement was printed in the papers and received wide readership. When the trial came up in March, it was very unlikely that anyone on the jury would not have read and been aware of the confession. And the remarkable thing is that is just what Blalock intended, for the confession is not really a confession at all, but a shrewdly worded defense of a man, knowing then that he was fighting for his life. For the person who could reason well and think things through and write it down coherently even to remembering dates without checking, and then slip back into the Negro idiom of the era, indicates that Blalock, from a lifetime of experience, knew well the softer spots in the Southern armor of black-white relationships of the period. Blalock was trying to get the point across that even though he was guilty of stealing money and had unwittingly killed a respected and wealthy white man, and in spite of all these terrible crimes, a person could read the statement and if saying nothing else for the defendant, could conclude that he certainly wasn't uppity. That would be a far worse crime for Blalock to be guilty of than either burglary or homicide. Making himself lowly and being properly humble, Blalock hoped to appeal to the sympathy and prejudice of the incoming jury. That he knew so well how to say not only everything that he knew the white man wanted to hear, and phrase it in a way that he knew the white man wanted it to sound, Blalock probably did himself more good than either of the two attorneys who would ultimately plead his case in court.

When the fifteen-hour session was concluded, Blalock's statement was distributed to the press, which had gotten wind of what was going on and was camped en masse outside the detective office.

The press and photographers were allowed inside to take pictures and interview Blalock, who was totally unperturbed by the mayhem in the rather crowded office and faced the press with quiet composure and unruffled answers to their sometimes-barbed questions and requests for pictures. Blalock had not talked to a lawyer or asked to see a lawyer. It was normal police practice in such cases to get the confession and the case wrapped up before even considering a lawyer for the accused. It was the way all police departments operated then. Had someone suggested that Blalock's rights had been violated, the police would have been incredulous. The police in the case had treated Blalock very fairly, they thought. It had all been very friendly, and Blalock and the police seemed relieved when it was over.

Blalock stated that he earned approximately $200 a month on his railroad job, a good salary for a man at that time. It was certainly deemed sufficient to support his family adequately. Then why did he feel compelled to steal? Blalock told the press that soon after he moved to Atlanta and got a job with the railroad, he began playing the "bug." In no time, he was spending at least $15 a day playing the bug, and most days he would lose; but when he did win, he would put all his winnings on the bug; and as a result he never seemed to get ahead. He stated he wanted to quit playing the bug but that he could not, for it had become a part of him, a part of his everyday life. Blalock stated also to the press in his interview that he took $45 and a billfold from Heinz after killing him.

HEARING

The grand jury of DeKalb County was in session at that time, and, insofar as the Heinz home was located in that county, all facts and data pertinent to the case were turned over to DeKalb County authorities for prosecution. Immediately the grand jury took up the case and called witnesses. The main witness was Mrs. Heinz. She had identified Blalock in a lineup as the man whom she saw grappling with her husband. She had congratulated the officers for finding the slayer and stated to the press how relieved she was that it was all over and that the strain of the past year had at times been more than she could bear. In her sworn statement to the grand jury Mrs. Heinz said in part:

I was sewing something for the Red Cross. Henry was reading. We were in the library. A few moments before ten p.m. I grew sleepy and decided to go to bed. I laid my sewing bag on a sofa in the library, and went and took a shower. I had just stepped out of the shower when I heard Henry calling:

"Momma, Momma, that devil is in here. Get the gun quick!" I knew who he meant because he said, more than once to me: 'If that devil who has been stealing from us comes back I will kill him with my own hands.' I put a robe on and went rushing around. I do not remember what he said but I heard Henry cry out again and I heard two shots. I went into the library and saw a Negro man struggling with Henry. I went into another room to get a gun, but ran back to the library instead and found Henry on the sofa and the Negro man was gone. I went to the telephone and called Grady Hospital, the police, and Dr. Vann."

The jury heard from the police who had worked on the case and then it indicted Horace Blalock for the murder of Henry Heinz. The case was set for trial in March 1945.

A roar of speculation, gossip, and pure vindictiveness swept the city. Previously friends and relatives had offered a $2500 reward for the solution to the murder of Henry Heinz. There were charges that the police were railroading a Negro man into prison to earn the reward. Some police on the case again speculated about the guilt or innocence of Blalock and the press picked up these rumors. The press often described Heinz as a "rich capitalist" and Mrs. Heinz as the "widow of the rich capitalist"—somewhat inflammatory terms for the era.

The gossip against Mrs. Heinz reached a fever pitch. The rumor-mongers said that of course she was relieved that the case was closed because then the heat would be off to find the real killer, who was someone in league with Mrs. Heinz. At this point Dr. Vann had faded from the picture, for his statements and appearances made it difficult for even the most determined to believe him a villain. Now, it was said, persons unknown who were responsible for the murder were being paid off by the rich to protect Mrs. Heinz. Mrs. Heinz was also criticized for looking too cheerful at the hearing and for not wearing the proper clothes for a truly grieving widow.

THE TRIAL

In March Horace Blalock went on trial in DeKalb County with Judge James C. Davis of the Stone Mountain circuit presiding. Blalock was represented by two lawyers who immediately disavowed the alleged confession and asked the court not to allow it to be placed in evidence. They also asked that the fingerprint evidence not be allowed because it could not be proven beyond a shadow of a doubt that they were Blalock's prints. After hearing from all sides and lengthy deliberation, Judge Davis ruled that both the alleged confession and finger-print evidence was admissible. For the first time in Georgia court history, a projection machine and screen were set up in the courtroom to explain the fingerprint technique to the twelve-man, all-white jury.

Once again, Mrs. Heinz was the principal witness. Visibly shaken by the long ordeal and the attacks made against her, she left a sick bed to testify. In deference to public opinion, she wore a black suit and hat with veil for this appearance in court. Her testimony was essentially the same as that at the inquest. However, following intense cross-examination on the witness stand, she stated that Blalock "looked a lot like" the man in the Heinz home the night of the murder.

The prosecution witnesses were the various police investigators who worked on the case and a jeweler, Harold Jacobson, who testified that he had sold Blalock a watch similar to the one found at the scene of the crime. He could not identify the inner workings of the watch found at the scene as definitely being the watch he sold Blalock because it was an inexpensive watch and did not have a serial number on it. However, two weeks after the murder, Jacobson testified that Blalock had come to him and told him he had lost the inner workings out of his watch and wanted it replaced. The jeweler replaced the inner workings of the watch for him.

Blalock's lawyers alleged that during the fifteen-hour interrogation that the police had put some kind of "truth serum" (that was the new thing then) in Blalock's Coca-Cola, and that as a result Blalock was under the influence of drugs when he signed the so-called confession. It appears the lawyers might have erred in their strategy here. The best defense Blalock had was his confession.

THE VERDICT

The case went to the jury after a three-day trial. After six hours there was no decision, and Judge Davis had the jury locked up for the night. They deliberated all the next day and were locked up a second night, spending the night on cots hastily set-up in the court house. After some 50 hours of deliberation the jury found Blalock guilty—with a recommendation for mercy. Under Georgia law it was automatic that Judge Davis sentence Blalock to life imprisonment. It was reliably reported that the jury was split 9 to 3 in favor of giving Blalock the electric chair. In spite of intense pressure, three jurors held out to the end for life instead, and rather than have a mistrial the other nine jurors agreed on life imprisonment for Blalock. It would be interesting to know if the three jurors who held out were influenced by humanitarian considerations, Blalock's confession, or a belief that Blalock was taking the rap for a murder he did not commit. Maybe it was a combination of these factors, but it is likely the last consideration was the most overriding.

It was the opinion of many that Blalock took the blame for higher-ups. No manner of evidence or reasoning could convince some people otherwise. The police were severely stung by the rumors and accusations in the Heinz case. They felt that a super-human effort had been made to solve it. However, many of the rumors developing around the case could be traced directly to certain police investigators who were influenced by and believed in the conspiracy theory—and became captives of it, themselves prisoners of the prejudice against people of wealth. Certainly the possibility of a conspiracy was thoroughly gone into, for the investigators wanted to find a basis for their beliefs. But no evidence of a conspiracy was ever uncovered. The officers closest to the case and best informed from all the police departments involved felt then, and later, that any implication linking Mrs. Heinz with the murder of her husband was absurd.

Those who attempted the most to make a conspiracy out of the Heinz case and felt that Blalock had been abused of his rights by the police and the rich were often those who thought nothing of insisting that Negroes should go to the back of the streetcar and take seats behind the white folks, and if any Negroes were seated and whites got on the streetcar and needed a seat, then the Negroes should stand, as was the custom. Clearly the prejudice voiced in the case was against wealth.

Following the events of the night of the murder, Mrs. Heinz's role in the case was endlessly speculated upon. In a way, she was also a victim of the case. Some years later when she remarried, all the innuendoes concerning her role in the murder were revived once more, and they still linger to this day. Many people insist that there was "something funny" about the Heinz murder.

Officer Blackwell managed to interview Blalock prior to the trial. Blalock stated he left the house through the door opening off the library to the entryway. But he also said that he started out of the house through the reception room but changed his mind and doubled back and went out of the house through the side entryway. Blackwell thought that Blalock was probably somewhat disoriented following his fierce struggle with Heinz. It also explains Mrs. Heinz's statement that she felt the slayer was still in the house moments after the struggle. After leaving the house, Blalock stated he went down the path and through the gardens, the same route that Dr. Vann almost took seconds later. Blalock also said his car was parked across the street from Dr. Vann's house on Lullwater Road and that he got into his car, started it up, and as he was approaching the intersection of Lullwater and Ponce de Leon he realized there was a car coming east on Ponce de Leon at breakneck speed. In order to avoid being hit by the speeding car, he came to a complete stop, and the other car roared through the intersection and quickly turned left into the driveway at the Heinz estate. It was Blackwell and Miller in their patrol car.

On May 18, 1955, Horace Blalock, having served ten years of a life sentence for the murder of Henry C. Heinz, was paroled by the Georgia Pardons and Paroles Board. On June 28, 1956, Blalock's wife swore out a warrant in Fulton Superior Court charging him with abandonment. For this he received a twelve-month probationary sentence which was terminated July 1, 1957. Blalock then moved to Vidalia, Georgia, where he worked as a porter for an automobile agency. This was the last the police heard of him. Some years later Mrs. Heinz married Enrico Leide, conductor of the first Atlanta Symphony Orchestra. They were prominent in social and musical circles in Atlanta until Mrs. Leide's death in September 1962.

The Heinz home became the property of a somewhat eccentric lady who lived in the downstairs section of the main house with a bevy of dogs and converted the second story and garage and out-buildings into apartments. People who rented the apartments stated that the place was spooked and that strange things went on there which attracted the attention of occult groups. It was said that on particularly dark nights a person could be heard walking about the grounds, but no one could be seen. It was also said that pistol shots could be heard late at night, like someone target-practicing on the rear of the estate, but no one could be found. People living on the estate began to believe that the ghost of Henry Heinz returned to the scene of the crime periodically. Others moved away, for the darkness, the overgrown estate, and the memories of murder became too much to contend with. The estate was never kept up properly after the murder, and the grounds rapidly deteriorated. Today the house stands vandalized and forlorn. A walk upon the grounds in the dead of night has nothing to recommend it.

Now Ponce de Leon Avenue is a busy thoroughfare for commuters driving into the city from surrounding suburbs. Most of the old estates of another time have been converted into churches or clubs or cleared away to make room for apartments or town houses. The time when this section was regarded as being way out from town has long since passed. Time and the city have caught up with Druid Hills and overgrown it. Busy people driving along gaze at the Heinz home and wonder about its past. Sitting there, on a cloudy misty day, waiting for the developers and earthmovers, its shadow-white stucco makes the house appear like a ghost, and it looks, even to the casual passer-by, like a house with a past.

Just prior to the Civil War a German immigrant came to Atlanta and opened a gun shop. During the war he rendered valiant service to the Confederacy in the manufacture and repair of rifles and small arms. After the war, his son joined him in the business and the firm grew and prospered in the manufacture, repair, and sale of handguns. The firm was a prominent business establishment on Alabama Street in Atlanta. The father died in 1906, but the son continued the business until his own death in 1928, when the business was ended. Obviously the grandson of the founder and the son of the man who operated the business until it closed had no interest in the manufacture or sale of guns, for he took no part in the business. He was a peaceful man, well-liked and highly regarded by everyone who knew him. That man was Henry Heinz.

3

Socialite Peggy Refoule

Paul and Peggy Refoule (*Reh´-fo-lā*) moved most of their furnishings into their new home on April 30, 1947. The unusual house on fashionable Howell Mill Road was converted from an old woolen mill dating from the Civil War period, when the area had been a battleground in the Atlanta campaign. The house was located in the sparsely-settled neighborhood of northwest Fulton County, beyond the city limits of Atlanta. The property had a thousand-foot frontage on Howell Mill Road and ran back about 300 feet from the road to the middle of Peachtree Creek, a winding stream in a very wooded tract. There were no close neighbors, and the house sat near the street—all the expanse of property being the wooded area behind the house down to the creek. The old mill part of the house was to be used by Paul, an artist, as a studio. It was a gigantic room 20 by 50 feet with two-feet thick granite walls. It had a beamed ceiling and concrete floors. Several tapestries adorned the walls, and Refoule paintings rested on easels about the room. The studio had an enormous fireplace, with a huge mantel. In the new section of the house which the Refoules had just added to the old mill structure there was a kitchen and small bedroom downstairs, and two bedrooms and two baths upstairs. In the master bedroom upstairs there was a large fireplace. A dry creek bed ran directly behind the home and resembled a moat, and the house from that vantage point looked like a medieval castle, which is exactly the way that Paul Refoule, who was a Frenchman, wanted it to look; for it reminded him of the houses in his hometown of Orleans, France.

On May 5, 1947, the Refoules moved into their new house. The first social gathering which took place there was on the afternoon of Sunday, May 11, 1947, during which time the Refoules were visited by their friends, many of whom brought their children. Among those friends were Dr. and Mrs. Jack Varner, Major and Mrs. William V. Durkin, Mr. and Mrs. Howard Smith, and others. Major and Mrs. Durkin stayed on for dinner that night, and the two couples decided to have dinner together the following night, Monday, at Emile's French restaurant in downtown Atlanta, which they did.

While on his way to Oglethorpe University to teach his art class that afternoon, May 12, 1947, Paul Refoule stopped at the Fulton Hardware Company on Peachtree Road, at the request of Mrs. Refoule, and purchased a cotton clothesline. He asked the clerk in the hardware store for a clothes wire, specifying that his wife wanted one which would not rust, but at the time the store did not have clothes wire in stock; so, the clerk suggested the cotton clothesline instead. In giving Refoule change, the clerk made a mistake of one dollar against Refoule, which the latter called to his attention. Later that same evening, after coming home from Oglethorpe, Paul Refoule attached the clothesline to three small trees on the back of his property near the remains of an old brick retaining wall which runs parallel to Howell Mill Road.

On Tuesday morning, May 13, 1947, Mrs. Refoule drove the family automobile to Buckhead, taking with her soiled clothing of the family which was put through a washing machine at the laundromat in Buckhead. When she returned from the laundromat, Mrs. Refoule hung the clothes on the new clothesline. She told her husband he would have to find a better place for the clothesline, as the pathway leading to and from the line had too steep an incline.

On the morning of May 14, 1947, Mrs. Refoule drove the family automobile, a 1936 Ford Coupe, to Buckhead where she did some shopping. She went to a store which stocked venetian blinds, draperies, shades, etc. and asked one of the owners to send someone to her home that afternoon to make some measurements for draperies. (The man was too busy to go to the Refoule house that afternoon, however.)

Paul Refoule did not notice when his wife left to go to Buckhead or note the time of her return because he was busy doing some cement work about the premises. She must have returned home by 11 or 11:30 a.m., however, for she fixed lunch, which she ate with her husband. Before they had finished eating, two ladies stopped by for a visit and to look at the house. One of these ladies was a lifelong friend of Mrs. Refoule, Mrs.

Cook, and a friend of hers, Mrs. Cason, who met the Refoules for the first time on this occasion. When these two ladies came to the front door, they saw Mr. and Mrs. Refoule at the table finishing lunch. They decided they would go on and not disturb them. Mr. and Mrs. Refoule saw them through the glass front doors, and both came to the front door and insisted that the two ladies come inside. The ladies had coffee with them, and the Refoules showed their guests around the house. While the ladies were there, Refoule made several telephone calls, one of them to a building supply house, and ordered some materials for the house. Refoule said during the course of the conversation that he wanted to go into Buckhead and buy some paint to paint the floor, but Mrs. Cook told him that all the stores in Buckhead closed on Wednesday afternoon. These ladies arrived at approximately 12:30 p.m. and left the Refoule home at 1:45 p.m., at which time Paul Refoule was ready to leave to go to his classes at Oglethorpe University; but he remained until after the departure of the guests. Mrs. Refoule asked him to go by the home of her mother, Mrs. William Ott Alston, Sr., on his way to Oglethorpe, and pick up some of her things which were stored in her mother's basement.

Paul Refoule left his home immediately after the departure of the two guests. He arrived at the home of his mother-in-law a few minutes later, the time of arrival being sometime between 1:50 and 1:55 p.m. He drove into the backyard, parked the car, went to the basement, and began loading into the car some books and other articles which he was to take home after he completed his afternoon's work at Oglethorpe.

At approximately 1:50 p.m. Refoule's mother-in-law returned to her home. She had been out all morning. Just as she came into the house the telephone rang and she had a telephone conversation with her daughter Peggy Refoule.

Mrs. Alston: Hello?

Peggy: Hello, Mother, what are you doing?

Mrs. Alston: Nothing right now. I've just come in. I've been gone all morning and haven't even taken off my hat yet, and it is (looking at the clock) ten minutes until two.

Peggy: Mother! Where have you been?

Mrs. Alston: Oh, I went to my club, then to the stores to try and find some rice for Son (W. O. Alston, Jr., Peggy's brother, who was ill); then to the hospital to see Miss DeGraffenreid.

Peggy: Well . . . why don't you come over to see me? When are you going to help me to do some more sewing?

Mrs. Alston: I'm just not going to sew on that sofa cover in that upstairs room until you can get your window shades in. Have you seen about them yet?

Peggy: Yes. I went to that place in Buckhead this morning, and the man there says he can make the drop curtain the way Paul and I wanted it at first. So he is going to get the measurements for the window this afternoon and make it right away. Don't you think that kind will be all right?

Mrs. Alston: Well . . . it isn't the kind I would want, but I suppose it will be all right if you like it. It is at least the cheapest way to make it.

Peggy: It really will be all right, I think, Mother.

Mrs. Alston: Well, if you are satisfied . . . go ahead and order everything and charge it to me.

Peggy: Thank you, Mother. Oh Mother, is Paul still there?

Mrs. Alston: I think he is downstairs packing.

Peggy: Well; please send me the box of Kotex I left there.

Mrs. Alston: All right. Wait and let me call him before he leaves. (At this point Mrs. Alston went to the stairs and called her son-in-law.)

Paul: Mother?

Mrs. Alston: Paul, come upstairs before you leave. I want to send something to Peggy.

Mrs. Alston: (into the phone) Hello, I got him Peggy.

Peggy: Well now, you be sure to come over. I have a lot of new things to show you. Mrs. Cook and Mrs. Cason came to see us. Mrs. Cason is going to give us a chandelier.

Mrs. Alston: Will it suit the place where you need one?

Peggy: Oh yes, I'm sure it will!

Mrs. Alston: Well, that's fine! People certainly have been nice to you.

Peggy: You haven't seen the new stone steps that Paul just made, have you?

Mrs. Alston: No, I haven't.

Peggy: Well, you have to see them. They are just beautiful. All my new house is beautiful.

Mrs. Alston: Well, I am in a hurry now, Peggy. I must go. Carrie (an old family servant) is here waiting to wash my hair. Maybe I will come over later and bring Carrie. But I must go now and prepare lunch.

When Mrs. Alston said goodby to her daughter she did not hear Mrs. Refoule say goodby or remember hearing any click of the receiver. Mrs. Alston was in a hurry to prepare lunch for her son, who, under doctor's orders, was required to have meals at stated times which were made up of special foods. A few minutes after Mrs. Alston hung up the phone, Paul Refoule came upstairs. She gave him the box of Kotex and talked for a few minutes before he left to return to packing his car.

At 2:10 p.m. Paul Refoule started the motor of his car to drive from his mother-in-law's house to Oglethorpe University. The car had been parked almost immediately underneath a window of the bedroom of William Ott Alston, Jr., which was upstairs. Mr. Alston had been dozing but was awakened by the sound of the car starting, glanced at the clock, and saw that it was 2:10 p.m. He noted the time because he was making a mental calculation as to whether or not Paul would have time to meet his classes at Oglethorpe on schedule.

Art classes at Oglethorpe University were taught by Paul Refoule on Mondays and Wednesdays of each week, commencing at 2:40 p.m. Upon this occasion, as was his custom, Refoule arrived fifteen minutes or more ahead of time, in order to see that everything was in readiness for his art class. He set up a still life of a green vase with honeysuckles in it for the students to draw. At 2:45 p.m. he explained to the students in the class what he wanted them to do. After giving these instructions, he was occupied for the remainder of the afternoon working with individual students as each worked on his painting of the still life.

Upon leaving Oglethorpe University at 5 p.m. or a few minutes thereafter, Paul Refoule drove to a home on Lenox Road to keep an engagement he had previously made to talk with two ladies about the painting of a portrait. Refoule arrived at this home at approximately 5:20 p.m., and he left at approximately 5:55 p.m. The time was noted particularly by one of the women because she was disturbed by the fact that the preparation of dinner was being delayed.

The Refoules' young son, Jon Paul, aged 9, had been taken to school that morning by his father. When he got out of school at 3 p.m., he caught the bus and went over to the Fritz Orr Camp. At 5 p.m. the station wagon of the camp left with young Refoule aboard, and the driver let him out at the Refoule home at approximately 5:30. The driver was later to recall the time because he had been delayed in getting started that day by the time taken up in giving out some awards to the children at the camp for horsemanship. When the driver let young Refoule out of the station wagon, he did not see anyone at the house. It was his practice, when letting children out, to wait and see that they got indoors or if someone met them; but on this day he was already behind schedule and the traffic on Howell Mill Road was brisk, so he drove away quickly.

When Jon Paul got home he tried to go in the front door of the house but found that it was locked. Rather than wait for his mother to come and open the door to let him in, he decided to go around to the back door in order to surprise her. At the back door, he saw muddy footprints on the small back porch, which had a concrete floor, and wondered about them because his mother had always required him and his father to clean their shoes carefully before entering. He did not see any muddy footprints in the kitchen or inside the house. He called for his mother but she did not answer. He looked all over the house but could not find her. The radio was on full. He then went upstairs to his room and read a comic book.

Paul Refoule arrived at his home at approximately 6:10 p.m. He went in the front door, using his key to do so, as the door was locked. He called for Peggy, but she did not answer. He called for his son, and the boy answered him. He asked his son where his mother was, and the boy said that he did not know. He asked him how long he had been there, and young Refoule told him about an hour and that he had come in through the back door, which was unlocked. Refoule unloaded his car and brought the things into the house that he had previously gotten at Mrs. Alston's earlier in the afternoon.

Refoule waited awhile to see if his wife was coming. He called her grandmother and mother, asking if Peggy was at either one of their homes, or if they knew if she was over at Frances', Peggy's sister. They both said that Peggy was not at their house, that they did not know where she was. Refoule thought his wife might be at a neighbor or friend's house and did not worry. He went outside and worked on a ditch by the new retaining wall he was building. He then went inside and made some more calls but received no information concerning his wife's whereabouts. By 7 p.m. Refoule began to worry. Since he had arrived home, he had not left the immediate vicinity of the house because he thought his wife might telephone, and he did not want to leave his son in the house alone. By now very agitated, he once again called his mother-in-law, who was very upset when she realized for the first time that her daughter had not been at home when her grandson arrived from camp. She was convinced that had her daughter gone out, she would have arranged to return to the house before her son came home, or either arranged for someone else to be there. Mrs. Alston called her brother, Mr. Douglas Wright, apprised him of the situation, and asked him to go to the Refoule home at once.

FAMILY ARRIVES

It was still daylight, about 7:30 p.m., when Douglas Wright, Peggy's uncle, arrived at the Refoule home. It was just about dusk when Mrs. Alston arrived at the Refoule home. Shortly, several other members of the family arrived. Mrs. Alston and the others searched the house for Peggy or some trace of her. Mr. Wright and Paul searched outside the house and went as far on the back of the property as the creek but saw no sign of Peggy. Now it was nearly dark.

Mrs. Alston and the others in the house were upset; and when her brother and son-in-law returned to the house and reported no sign of Peggy anywhere, they became frantic. Mrs. Alston kept repeating that if something was not wrong her daughter would have been at home when her grandson arrived from camp. She insisted that the police be called at once. A call was placed to the Fulton County Police Department by Mr. Wright at 8:10 p.m.

By 8:20 p.m. there were no less than four police cars at the Refoule home. Other relatives and friends came to the house. The large studio in the Refoule home began to fill with people; soon everyone was standing around, not knowing what to do. Mrs. Alston requested that the police send for dogs. The police thought that because of the length of time any trail would be lost; however, Mrs. Alston begged them to call for the dogs.

When the keeper of the hounds and his helper, an experienced trusty, arrived at the Howell Mill Road home, one hound was released at a point near the new stone retaining wall, which is at the side and rear of the home. The hound first ran a trail down a slope in the direction of the dry creek bed. One of the policemen told the keeper to call the dog back, as it was the trail of the policeman the dog was following. To call the hound back the keeper fired two shots—which totally shattered the nerves of everyone in the Refoule house, until someone told them that the shots were just for calling the dogs. The police told Refoule and everyone else to remain in the house. By now it was dark.

Upon being called back, the dog picked up another trail which led from the house down into a ravine, to the left side of the Refoule property. The hound was closely followed by the helper this time, and the keeper proceeded along an old dirt road which ran parallel with Peachtree Creek in the rear of the home. When the dog had proceeded for a considerable distance along the ravine, he turned westward into the road at a point approximately 100 feet north of the dead end of the road. He then proceeded southward, to a point just past the dead end of the road, then turned toward the creek. While following the trail he had barked several times. He disappeared into the darkness and was silent.

SHOCKING DISCOVERY

The keeper followed the dog to the edge of the water and looked toward the creek. Standing along the bank of the creek, he allowed his flashlight to play over the shallow, rippling water, then focused on a single spot. There he saw the body of Peggy Alston Refoule.

Lieutenant Cal Cates was one of the first officers at the Refoule home and the first superior officer to view the body. He and two patrolmen started searching the rear of the house as they had been told that Mrs. Refoule was in the habit of picking wild flowers in the woods. When the dog found a track down the creek bank about 200 yards to the rear of the house, Lt. Cates and his men were right behind. There they found a white plastic hairpin, and upon looking further, they found the body lying face up in the creek. Her head was on a rock— her left arm was twisted to her back. She was still limber and not as cold as the water in the creek. Her body was about 300 feet from where they found signs of a scuffle and her pin clasp. The woman's feet had been tied together with her shoe laces and her throat had a mark around it as if it had been corded with a rope or some object used to choke her. One finger had signs of a ring being removed.

Lt. Cates immediately began an examination of the ground in a search for footprints. It was his intention to have the dog undertake to follow the trail away from the point at which the body had been discovered in an effort to find the direction taken by the slayer when he left the scene. Soon after the discovery of the body and before the keeper of the hounds could help Lt. Cates and his men complete an examination of the ground for footprints or resume his work with the dog, a number of persons came to the point at which the body was found. Lt. Cates had observed several footprints in the sandy soil which appeared to him to have been made by someone wearing tennis shoes, the bottoms of which had been worn smooth so that the tracks bore no imprint of grooves or serrated surfaces. The tracks did not contain definite heel prints, but the arrival of the curious in large numbers so confused any trail which the slayer may have left that the keeper of the hounds and Lt. Cates deemed it useless to try and follow the trail, as the dog would have been by that time confronted with a maze of trails. Any footprints that might have proved useful were soon obliterated by the large number of people rushing to the scene.

Paul Refoule from his house saw a car driving up the dirt road that entered his property about 300 yards below the house. He kept inquiring and someone told him that they had found his wife. At this time he went to the front of the house to meet the car when it was coming. He heard one of the policeman say that they needed blankets. He heard a relative say something about blankets and another relative say something about calling Dr. Davison, the family physician; and he gathered from this that Peggy was sick or injured, but alive. He ran out the driveway and on the way saw Peggy's uncle, Douglas Wright, walking slowly up the driveway shaking his head. Refoule asked him what happened to his wife, and her uncle told him that she was dead. Refoule was in a state of shock, and several other relatives came forward and helped him and his son into a car and drove them away from the scene to his mother-in-law's house.

Policemen at the front and rear doors of the Refoule home were attempting to keep the public away from the house and off the property. Some friends of the family arrived, and policemen guarding the front door would not admit them; however, they called to Mr. Wright, and he told the policeman to admit them and anyone else who wished to enter. In a matter of hours, the press and the public were swarming all over the house like bees after honey. Before the night was over, approximately 2,000 people visited the house and property!

After the body was removed from the scene, Assistant Police Chief E. G. Fitzgerald and Detective Captain Fred Bradford attempted to learn from friends and relatives as much as possible about what had happened. They gave up on going over the grounds that night, as it was completely dark by this hour. Missing after the murder were two diamond rings in unusual settings, a plain gold wedding band, a lady's wrist watch, and an inexpensive camera. The two diamond rings cost approximately $1000 apiece at pre-war prices in France. The wrist watch was an ordinary lady's wrist watch and had been purchased in France. Mrs. Refoule's wedding band was missing. She wore the wedding band at all times, except that she sometimes removed it when working around the house. The finger upon which she customarily wore it bore its imprint when the body was discovered, but the ring had been removed. She wore only the other two rings, both heirlooms handed down in the Refoule family, upon special occasions. Before moving to the new home, and while she and Paul were living with her mother, she had been in the habit of keeping the two diamond rings in a small sewing cabinet. When they moved to the new home, this little cabinet, which had several drawers or trays, was placed upon a shelf in one of the closets in the large master bedroom. The cabinet was located by police and relatives, and upon examination the rings were found to be missing. Upon the bed in this same room was Mrs. Refoule's handbag, which was open and contained a few small coins. As she had been in the habit of paying for most of her purchases by check, she would have taken very little money with her to Buckhead that morning.

Since Lt. Cates had been the first officer on the scene, he informed Fitzgerald and Bradford of everything that had happened that evening. Since Cates was a long-time resident of the neighborhood, he had some other interesting comments. Cates told his superiors that there was no evidence or signs that Mrs. Refoule had been dragged through the heavily wooded area that separated the house from the creek. Her body bore no scratches or bruises, and Cates said if she had been carried through the woods it would have been necessary for a man to have carried her on his shoulders. To cross a dry creek bed immediately back of the house and then cross the wooded area with a heavy burden would have been an almost superhuman task. Furthermore, the rear exit, overlooking the woods and creek, was visible from Howell Mill Road, and if Mrs. Refoule had been slain inside the house, the killer would have had difficulty carrying her body outside without being seen by passers-by. Cates said that the dead end road leading to the secluded creek bank was used frequently, and he described it as a perfect lovers rendezvous. He also pointed out that the dirt road was there and being used long before the Refoules started renovating the old mill, and prior to the time they moved into the mill house the lovers' lane road had complete privacy and was secluded day or night. He felt that it might be significant that the Refoules moving into the mill affected the purposes, whatever they might be, of the dirt road. He recalled also many years ago he helped drag the body of a woman from Peachtree Creek near the exact spot where Mrs. Refoule was found. He said the mystery of the woman's death by drowning in the then-higher creek waters was never solved.

Captain Bradford and other detectives searched the Refoule house thoroughly. They did not find any signs of there having been any scuffle or struggle with anyone, and the house had not been ransacked. In the upstairs bedroom, an iron and ironing board were out, and a stack of neatly folded laundry was found nearby. Bradford noted that the position of the ironing board was such that if Mrs. Refoule had been at work there she would have been facing the only door to the second-story room. It would have therefore been difficult for an intruder to come upon her by surprise while she was at work ironing.

Assistant Chief Fitzgerald concluded that Peggy Refoule had surprised a burglar in her home and had been murdered. He thought it followed the pattern of the Heinz case. Fitzgerald had worked on the Heinz case and was instrumental in gathering the evidence against Blalock, who, incidentally, at this juncture was still in prison (although his guilt was still questioned by the public).

At 10 p.m. the feverish activity inside the Refoule home continued. Remnants of the curious wandered about. Relatives talked with the police detail on the scene. The atmosphere at the Alston home was quite different. Everyone sat around in stunned silence or else talked perfunctorily. Paul Refoule sat alone in a room by himself. No one bothered him. Around 1 a.m. the police arrived at the Alston home and asked Paul Refoule if he and Jon Paul would come downtown to headquarters and make a statement.

At 11 p.m. Captain Bradford had left the Refoule home in order to be present at the funeral home when the county coroner arrived there. Preliminary tests of the body by Dr. Jernigan, county coroner, indicated that Peggy Refoule had not been sexually assaulted. A complete autopsy on the body would be performed the following day.

Paul Refoule and his son and a cousin of his wife's arrived at Fulton County Police headquarters at about the same time that Bradford arrived from the funeral home. Assistant Chief Fitzgerald and Captain Bradford questioned Refoule and his son about their activities of the previous afternoon. They both gave written statements to the police and were then returned to the Alston home around 3 a.m. At this point the investigation of the Refoule case rested until later in the day.

Captain Bradford and other detectives went on duty at 8 o'clock on the morning of May 15, 1947. They went directly to the banks of Peachtree Creek below the Refoule house on Howell Mill Road, the scene where Mrs. Refoule was found murdered, to search for any evidence which they might find. It was a beautiful spring morning and on Peachtree Creek the sun shone on the rippling water and birds sang in branches of nearby trees. It did not seem possible that murder could occur in such a setting.

A police detail had closed off the dirt road that ran parallel along the creek, and another police detail was keeping sightseers off the property and out of the area. However, the bridge spanning Peachtree Creek was just below the Refoule property, and people on their way to work downtown the morning afterwards, intrigued by Mrs. Refoule's murder, slowed down and craned their necks as they viewed the police all about the vicinity.

A search of the Peachtree Creek murder scene revealed no new clues, and Bradford, leaving other officers to continue searching, left and drove to Buckhead. There he talked to a man who stated to him that he had seen a torn piece of garment on a branch of a tree about 400 feet from Northside

Drive on the north bank of Peachtree Creek. He added that the torn cloth was not there on Tuesday, May 13, 1947. The man had a distinct recollection of seeing the cloth, and stated that it was his custom to take his dogs down to walk along the creek banks every evening. He said the torn cloth looked like an army jacket or shirt.

While in Buckhead, Bradford talked with a lady who stated that she had passed the Refoule home just a few minutes before and saw there a black coupe automobile with a large rear light flashing on and off. It was parked across the street from the Refoule home. She further stated there was more than one person in the car—a black-haired young man and two women. She did not see the people well enough to be able to identify them later. She thought they looked very suspicious and ought to be investigated by the police. She lectured Captain Bradford for several minutes about how poor the police protection in this area of the county was. She had always said they did not have enough police and now the Refoule murder proved her correct. If the police did not find the murderer, and quick, something would have to be done about the situation. Bradford suggested that the people in the car the lady saw were sightseers. He pointed out that cars would be driving by as people tried to get a look at the murder scene. He said also that sightseers had hampered the investigation of the case. After some more conversation, the irate citizen appeared somewhat mollified and relieved that the police were trying to solve the case.

Bradford then returned to the Refoule home where he conferred with two of his investigators who told him that they had learned that two young men had been down on Peachtree Creek all day May 14, hunting turtles. Bradford and his investigators then went and talked to these two men, and they stated they went to the creek about 10 a.m., where the branch runs into the creek about 300 yards from where the body was found, and went down the creek barefooted toward Moores Mill Road, away from the murder scene. The two men, both of whom worked as gas station attendants, were taken to their homes and agreed to allow investigators to search for the missing Refoule rings, none of which could be found. Reliable witnesses told police the two young men were away from the creek area and at work by 2 o'clock that afternoon. One witness stated that he thought the whole thing was some kind of prank—that some friends of the two men knew they were down by the creek the day of the murder and called the police and told them about it, in a playful effort to upset the men. This appeared to make sense. The two young men were certainly terrified when they realized the police considered them murder suspects. If they had been involved in the murder, it appears unlikely they would have told dozens of people they were going to be in the vicinity of Peachtree Creek.

Bradford then stopped at Marvin Cleaners on Howell Mill Road, and the owner told him that he had seen a car parked about a block and a half away from the Refoule home on Howell Mill Road the day of the murder. The car, a 1941 Ford Club Coupe, was parked under the shade of a tree on the first curve, south of the Refoule home, about 4:45 p.m. with a man and a woman in the car. The man looked to be in his late thirties. Bradford wondered if these people could be considered as suspects or just people out in the springtime afternoon. The Howell Mill-Peachtree Creek area was well known as a place for lovers to go driving. It was spring. The setting was conducive to romance. Many people would be out driving in the afternoon. Bradford had the feeling this could greatly complicate the case.

That afternoon, Captain Bradford talked with Mrs. George Craft at her home. She said that she was a personal friend of Peggy Refoule and that she had started to town and decided to stop by and see Mrs. Refoule. She sent her son, George, Jr., age 5, to the front door of the Refoule home to see if anyone was at home. The front door was locked and she blew the horn on her automobile but there was no response. After waiting a few minutes, she drove away. She stated this was around 4 p.m. on May 14, 1947. She stated that she saw a white man about 50 or 55 years old walking north on Howell Mill Road, wearing a plaid shirt and felt hat. He passed by the house and continued walking south on Howell Mill Road.

Bradford returned to the Refoule home late in the afternoon. The investigators who searched the creek reported that they had found no new evidence or clues in the creek areas. The police detail at the house said they had a difficult time trying to keep the curious off the property and out of the house. The police said some people acted like the Refoule home and grounds had become public property. It was a repeat of what had happened at the Heinz estate three years before.

NO RESPECT FOR GRIEF

Paul Refoule had returned to his home on Howell Mill Road that afternoon. He went into the studio and played the piano softly. He paced about the house smoking. He appeared very remote to friends and relatives who dropped in to offer their condolences. He talked about the murder and paced about, chain-smoking all the time. He asked everyone who came to the house that day, "Who do you think could have committed such a terrible crime?"

Refoule became very upset later in the afternoon when members of the press and the curious tried to enter the house and people stopping in front of the house tried to get a glimpse of those inside. To a friend he muttered:

"In France, they would leave you alone. There people have respect for grief."

Refoule became so upset by all the people about that relatives said it would be impossible for him to have any peace in the house. The police reluctantly agreed. It was therefore decided that Refoule and his son should continue living with his mother-in-law for the time being.

That night, in the studio of the Refoule home, Bradford and his investigators went over everything they had learned about the case thus far. As the two guests who had coffee with the Refoules had not departed until approximately 1:30 or 1:45 p.m. and as Mrs. Refoule talked first with her grandmother, and later with her mother, after the departure of her guests and did not conclude these telephone conversations until approximately 2:05 p.m., and as it was known that no ironing had been done before the arrival of the two guests, it was plain that all of the clothes which were found to have been ironed had been done after the telephone conversation with Mrs. Alston had been concluded. Bradford and the investigators examined the bedroom once more. They examined the number of freshly ironed clothes and estimated that it would have taken approximately 45 minutes for her to have done this ironing. Expiration of 45 minutes after the conclusion of the telephone conversation with her mother would seem to establish that she must have been alive as late as 3 p.m., and thus the fact that Mrs. Alston could not recall her daughter saying goodby or hearing a click of the receiver appeared to have no significance.

Bradford noted that the Refoule home was so constructed that in the absence of curtains a person walking around the house and looking into the windows could see practically all over it. At a right-angle corner formed by a meeting of two brick walls of the house was a water spigot, which was frequently used by a black man, apparently a convict trusty, in carrying drinking water to the convicts who had been engaged in building a sewer line across Howell Mill Road from the Refoule home. Situated near this corner was a narrow but very tall window, which extended from a point about 30 inches above the ground to ceiling height. From this window it was possible to see the upstairs hallway as well as the stairway. It would not have been possible for anyone to have passed from one of the upstairs bedrooms to the other, or to have passed down this stairway, without being in plain view of anyone standing near the water hydrant. This was a temporary hydrant and, instead of having a spout, water had to pass out of the upright pipe, which resulted in some spilling and kept the ground muddy at that point. Bradford thought this might be significant in view of the statement by Refoule's son that he saw muddy footprints upon the back concrete stoop.

Friday, May 17, 1947, two days after the Refoule murder. The first thing that Captain Bradford encountered that morning when he reached police headquarters was the newspaper headline from the morning edition of *The Atlanta Constitution*:

SEX SLAYER INDICATED IN MATRON DEATH

The news account stated that the police thought that burglary was the motive. However, the paper stated also that according to Dr. Herman Jones of the Fulton County Crime Laboratory, Mrs. Refoule had been criminally assaulted. Bradford read this with a start. He had been present on Wednesday night when the coroner first examined the body and told him that the victim had not been assaulted. And yesterday at the inquest Dr. Jernigan, in sworn statement, testified: "After having carefully examined the deceased's body and finding only evidence of an external bruise, located about her neck, having performed an autopsy and having found nothing abnormal, I feel confident that the deceased met her death due to strangulation. There are no signs of drowning. There are no signs that she was raped."

From his own police experience, Bradford surmised that

Mrs. Refoule had not been sexually assaulted. He had seen the bodies of women who had been criminally assaulted and then killed, and it was not an easy memory to forget. He had seen the body of Peggy Refoule, and it did not appear to be a case of sexual assault because, except for the bruise around her neck, where she was choked to death, there was not a mark upon her body. Women who are sexually molested and then killed by a sex slayer do not appear afterward as Mrs. Refoule's body appeared, for there is a struggle until the woman is subdued, and the woman's body always has marks which are a result of the struggle, and there are usually not only severe bruises but broken bones.

Bradford began to have doubts about the case. Things did not appear to add up. Dr. Jernigan stated also at the inquest that it appeared that the victim was strangled with a rope or cord that was a garrot looped around her throat and apparently twisted from the front. He said he thought that from an examination of the body it could be concluded that Mrs. Refoule was killed at the scene rather than carried there later, and that certainly she was not dragged from the house through the wooded area to the creek. He stated that the victim's feet had been tied together by the laces of her shoes.

Next, Bradford got a report from the detectives who had been checking the pawn shops in search of the rings stolen from the Refoule home. One was a plain gold wedding band. One was an heirloom ring with two round diamonds and a square diamond in the center. The third was a platinum ring with a large center saphire and small diamonds on each side. The two diamond rings had been handed down in the Refoule family. The detectives had covered the shops and investigated several tips but had come up with no trace of any of the missing rings.

At 9 a.m. the funeral of Peggy Refoule was held at the Cathedral of Christ the King. Although from an Episcopalian family, Peggy had become a Catholic when she married Paul Refoule. The funeral was held at an early hour in an attempt to keep away curiosity seekers, and with police assistance the funeral was not disturbed.

Peggy Alston Refoule was survived by her son and husband, her mother, and a brother and sister. Her death brought to an end the life of a courageous young woman who had overcome religious barriers, war, starvation, and Nazi occupation to first marry, and then to be with, her French artist husband. All her life a willful fate had doggedly followed Peggy Refoule.

EARLY YEARS

It all began when 19-year-old blonde, blue-eyed Peggy took the grand tour with her mother in the fall of 1935. They traveled to Italy, Switzerland, Belgium, Holland, and France. In the winter of 1936 Peggy became a student at the Sorbonne in Paris. There she met Paul Refoule, an artist. They began dating and soon were very much in love. Paul wanted to marry Peggy at once, but Peggy's family thought she was too young. They considered Paul, although the son of Robert Refoule, Judge Advocate of Orleans, France, where the Refoule family had been prominent for generations, as an artist, a Frenchman and a Catholic, as not the most suitable prospective husband for their daughter. The family prevailed upon Peggy to return to Atlanta in the spring, but the romance continued and in six months time Paul followed Peggy to America, reaching Atlanta by Christmas. Paul and Peggy decided to get married, and the Alston family gave their consent. The couple were married in Atlanta on January 19, 1937, in the chapel where now is located the Cathedral of Christ the King. Atlantans who recall the event say that there was never a more beautiful and radiant bride nor a handsomer groom, for Paul Refoule possessed the dark good looks and magnetic charm which caused people to compare him with actor Charles Boyer.

After their marriage the Refoules lived in Paris, where Paul had a studio at 26 Rue des Plantes. There their son, Jon Paul, was born. While the Refoules were visiting Peggy's seriously ill father in Atlanta, Hitler's invasion of Poland brought war to Europe. Paul returned immediately to France and enlisted in the French Army. Despite pleas from family and friends that she remain in Atlanta, where it was safer, Peggy returned to France with her young son. The Nazis swept into France, and Paul was taken prisoner at Dunkirk. He was held first in Germany, then in Poland. Peggy lived with her son and her husband's family at Orleans, protected from the worst of things by the means of the elder Refoules. Peggy's letters to her mother told of chopping up furniture for kindling and of giving her share of the dwindling food supply

to her son. Gradually money became worthless and hunger
stalked everyone. There were long silences when there was no
news from Peggy at all.

Conditions were so bad in France following the German
surrender that the Refoules came to Atlanta to live and to
rest after their ordeal. Paul got jobs teaching art at Oglethorpe University and at the High Museum of Art. He also
had a private studio in downtown Atlanta. He did the murals
of Emile's French Restaurant, the Cox-Carlton Hotel bar, and
the then-well-known Mammy's Shanty. At first the Refoules
lived with Peggy's mother, who was now widowed. Then they
bought the old mill and converted it into a home. It was the
only home that the war-weary couple had ever owned. Peggy
Refoule would live there only nine days. For her family and
old friends, it was impossible to comprehend. That Peggy
could have survived the war and suffered its privations—to at
last come home—and be murdered, murdered in the wealthy
residential neighborhood of northwest Atlanta. It should have
been the safest place in the world, and it was not. The family,
friends, and neighbors wanted to know: Why?

Captain Bradford spent the morning of Mrs. Refoule's funeral going over the telephone messages that had come into
the police department. The pressure on the police was enormous. People were upset about the murder. Housewives in the
Refoule neighborhood were greatly alarmed over the slaying
and were barricading their doors and putting guns in handy
places, lest they had to face an intruder. The newspaper headlines stating that the killer was a "sex-slayer" further terrified the inhabitants of the Buckhead area, and because of the
excitement generated by the case and the information that
was coming into the police department, the full force of the
Fulton County Police Department was thrown into the investigation of the slaying. (In 1947, the areas of Fulton County—
including Buckhead—and beyond the old Atlanta city limits
were policed by an independent police department.) It was
proving to be a difficult job for the department to conduct an
orderly investigation of the murder, for the department had
few specialists, and it was the practice for officers to work all
types of cases—murder, robbery, and larceny. The investigators had no special training for these cases and often had to
learn on the job. Up until this point the investigation had
been headed by Assistant Chief Fitzgerald and Captain Brad-

ford. The head of the Fulton County Police Department, Chief G. Neal Ellis, was out of town when the murder occurred but would return the following day. Bradford had a lot of loose ends to clear up before then.

Bradford went to the county work camp and talked with the man in charge of the camp. He learned that a black male, Francis Goodman, had been released at noon Monday, May 12, 1947, from the camp, and this man had been working with Loy Reeves, who was in charge of the sewer construction work that the county had been doing in the Howell Mill Road section during the month of April 1947. Bradford was told also that Francis Goodman had been the water boy on this gang. Bradford and another officer then went to Mr. Reeves' home and picked him up and he went with them to the Howell Mill Road section showing them the different roads and the different water plugs that Goodman had been carrying the water from. Reeves stated that Goodman was bad about wandering off and not getting water always from the plugs that he was told. Reeves said that he did not know, but it certainly was possible that Goodman carried water from the Refoule house part of the time the work was being done. Mr. Reeves also told Bradford that in April, when the sewer construction work was being done, that one day a terrific rainstorm came up, and Paul Refoule allowed the workmen to seek refuge from the storm in his then-unfinished house. Refoule, who was there working on his house, also provided hot coffee for the workmen.

Next, the police went to the home of Francis Goodman and questioned him. He stated that he had gone to work at the Atlantic Steel Plant on Wednesday morning, May 14, 1947; he went to work at 7 a.m. and got off from work at 3 p.m. The police found $24 and some change on Goodman, which he told them represented wages that he had coming to him from the steel plant. The police thought it unusual that a man just off the chain gang would have this money coming to him; so, they went to the steel plant and talked with Goodman's supervisor, who told them Goodman was correct, that he did come to work at the steel plant on Wednesday and that he had $25.84 which was back pay that he received that day. Bradford removed Goodman's name from the list of possible suspects in the case.

Bradford and another investigator then interviewed the foreman on the job in building the addition to the Refoule home on Howell Mill Road. They wanted to know if the foreman could account for the whereabouts the day of the murder of the men who worked on the house. The foreman told them that all but two of the workers were with them that day on another job, on the opposite side of town. Upon checking, the police learned that of the two unaccounted-for workers, one was in the city stockade on a drunk charge and the other was home sick the day of the murder. When interviewed, the sick man was deemed by officers to be too old and enfeebled to bother anyone. Bradford struck these two men from the list of possible suspects.

On Friday, Bradford and two other officers returned to the Peachtree Creek murder scene and searched the area but could find no new clues. They went through the house again and searched it. Bradford carefully examined the sashcord that they had first seen the night of the murder. They had found this cord on the tool chest under the kitchen range. Paul Refoule told them it was the excess rope that he had left over from the clothesline. Could this be the rope that strangled Peggy Refoule? The clothesline was still intact. Bradford went upstairs and examined the cord of the electric iron. It was the retractable-type cord. Did the killer strangle Mrs. Refoule with the ironing cord? It did not seem likely, for the cord appeared like new and was not shredded at any point. Neither the sashcord nor the ironing cord appeared to be the murder weapon. Then, was Mrs. Refoule surprised while ironing and strangled in the house and then carried to the creek? The case was a puzzle, and none of the pieces appeared to be fitting together logically.

Saturday, May 17, 1947. The police received a report on a stolen car with a Georgia tag which had been recovered in Austin, Texas. Captain Bradford called the police there and had them question the two occupants of the car concerning their activities the day of the murder. Later in the morning, the police called back from Austin and said that after extensive questioning and a search of the two suspects and of their car and belongings, there appeared to be no link between these two car thieves and the Refoule murder. None of the items stolen from the Refoule home were in their possession. A similar communication was had with the Chattanooga, Tennessee, Police Department concerning another suspect, but it also proved to be fruitless.

G. Neal Ellis, Chief of the Fulton County Police Department, had returned to the city and was conferring with Fitzgerald and Bradford concerning what progress had been made on the case. In the past two days Bradford had checked on a dozen workmen who had labored on the remodeled mill house, hunted an unidentified white man who had been seen loitering May 14 on the Peachtree Creek bridge (found him and cleared him in the case), had checked out the men who had been doing sewer work in the vicinity in the month of April, and had checked out the workers on the Refoule house. A young yard boy had been taken into custody and released.

In spite of all this investigation, Bradford did not have a suspect, and it seemed to Chief Ellis that the department was no nearer solving the case than it was the day of the murder. Some investigators insisted to Chief Ellis that Bradford had done nothing—absolutely nothing—during his four days of investigation!

Ellis, a traffic specialist, had no extensive training as an investigator. Three months before, he had been made chief of the department. Pressure was on him from all sides. He had to rely on what the men in the department reported to him. But he was more aware of certain aspects of the case than others in the department who were working on it.

RUMORS

Ellis asked Fitzgerald and Bradford if they were aware of rumors that Paul and Peggy Refoule were about to divorce? No, they were not. He wanted to know what truth there was to the rumor that Paul Refoule was conducting love affairs with two women and that he planned a flight to Egypt with one of them? The detectives could not say.

The chief made it clear that the information was all just rumors but that he had received several telephone calls. He pointed out also that the information coming to him was from prominent people, *not* crack-pots, and consequently *had* to be treated seriously. The chief implied that his sources were very close to the Alston family.

Bradford insisted that Refoule had an air-tight alibi. Fitzgerald proposed that there could be some kind of conspiracy— that Refoule might have had someone murder his wife. Ellis pointed out sternly that this was merely a theory: How could they prove it? Ellis again made it plain that he was not accusing anyone, but he wanted all the people working on the case not to limit themselves in any way in their investigation and to consider everyone a suspect until proved otherwise. Bradford wanted to know if this included Mrs. Alston, Peggy's mother. Rumors persisted that there was some kind of conspiracy between Refoule and his mother-in-law, and many people felt that her statement concerning the phone call with Peggy the day of the murder was a cover for Refoule. Chief Ellis discounted this entirely, but again, no one was to be ruled out. There were to be no "higher-ups" in this case. Again and again the officers would be cautioned not to spare the higher-ups. The comparison with the Heinz case was already being drawn by the public, and the newspapers were hinting at it. Many people at the time believed the police had protected Mrs. Heinz in that murder and were very vocal in insisting that the Fulton County police not fall into *that* trap in their investigation of the Refoule case. Chief Ellis was determined not to fall into that trap, and probably he and his men were more sensitive to this charge than they, or anyone else at the time, realized. Much of their future action would indicate that this was a factor.

The pressure was building in the Refoule murder. Both Atlanta newspapers had carried the story in its page-one headlines for four consecutive days, something of a record; even more coverage than the Heinz case. The pressure was on to find and punish the guilty party. There was a victim; there had to be a culprit. The police had to locate him—and quick. All other leads in the case had proved futile. Why not look for a Cain-Abel motive in the Refoule case?

Both Bradford and Fitzgerald had little alternative in the matter. Their search for the culprit had proved ineffectual. And there were many details, even discounting all the gossip they had heard, which did not add up.

Two of Bradford's investigators reported on their activity Saturday morning. They had been investigating two former boy friends of the victim. From members of the Alston family, the police had learned that before Peggy married Refoule, she had dated a young man who wanted very much to marry her, but she spurned him. Even so, after her marriage the young man had written her several peculiar letters. The police checked with this man's family and discovered that he was confined to the Shephard-Pratt Hospital in Maryland. He could not be involved in the murder. They had interviewed the other man, now a prominent businessman in the city, and he told them that he had not seen Peggy since before the war. The police were satisfied with this statement and said this individual could not be considered a suspect. One investigator told Bradford that he had heard rumors of marital discord between the Refoules, but no one had had anything derogatory to say about Peggy Refoule.

Chief Ellis and his men went to the Howell Mill Road home Saturday afternoon. Ellis suggested that Peggy Refoule was murdered in her home and then carried by automobile along the dirt road to the point where her body was dumped in the creek. This would explain, he stated, why there were no marks or scratches on the body. But Chief Ellis had not been on the scene when the murder occurred. He was, in a sense, second-guessing the case.

How could the slayer surprise Mrs. Refoule at her ironing since she would have been facing the door to the upstairs bedroom? Well, Chief Ellis told his men, if the slayer was known to Peggy she would not have been surprised, would she? Ellis was pretty well convinced that the slayer was someone known to her, someone who would know where the rings were kept. An ordinary burglar would not know what in the house was valuable and would have to search, and as a result make a mess of things in the process. But the Refoule home was not ransacked. Little by little, as the investigators talked among themselves, the idea of a Cain-Abel killing seemed more real, and they were becoming willing captives of the proposed theory, participants of the syndrome.

Sunday's papers carried a statement of Chief Ellis saying that the police were investigating all leads in the case, but that no one had been accused or arrested for the murder. When the reporters wanted to know if the investigation included the background of both Mr. and Mrs. Refoule, Ellis made a strong statement saying that absolutely nothing had come to the attention of anyone in the police department concerning anything bad about Peggy Refoule and that he was convinced she was a person of the highest character and was the victim of a brutal murder; and that his department would find the killer. Ellis refrained from commenting on Paul Refoule.

Chief Ellis stated also to the press his theory that Peggy

Refoule was murdered in her home and that then her body was carried in an automobile to Peachtree Creek. When asked by reporters what evidence he had to substantiate this theory, he stated that he thought it was obvious! He stated to the press that the method of tying the feet together as Peggy Refoule's were was taught to servicemen during the war and taught also to first-aid workers, but that he was inclined to believe this crime was committed by a young man and that the slayer was an ex-serviceman. Ellis made public instructions he had issued to the men of his department not to talk about the case to persons with no official interest in its solution. This was an effort to clamp a lid on the wild rumors and false reports circulating that were hampering the efforts of officers dealing with the case. Unknowingly or not, the chief was doing just what he was urging his men not to do by his public statements of unproven theories concerning the case. Gradually Chief Ellis and his department would become total captives of the Cain-Abel theory.

THE CURIOUS

Sunday afternoon was a beautiful spring day with temperatures in the high eighties. Hundreds of people took advantage of the holiday to drive by the scene of the slaying. Others brought picnic lunches and spread their sandwiches and Coca-Cola in the wooded area across the road from the Refoule house. With binoculars they tried to see as much as possible of the house and grounds. The police detail at the Refoule home spent a busy afternoon shooing people away and keeping the traffic moving along Howell Mill Road.

SLAYER OF MRS. REFOULE WAS KNOWN TO VICTIM, SAYS NEW POLICE THEORY

This was the page-one headline of *The Atlanta Constitution* on Monday, May 19, 1947.

It had been a busy Sunday for the Fulton County police. Chief Ellis had assigned four more investigators to work on the case. The fact that two of these men were beat patrolmen was not considered. This made a total of nine investigators then working on the Refoule case. The renewed activity had brought forth results.

A nineteen-year-old art student had been located and, under questioning, had admitted to having an affair with Paul

Refoule. At 8 o'clock that night, Captain Bradford and other investigators brought the girl and Paul Refoule to the Refoule home on Howell Mill Road. Refoule was now living with his mother-in-law but was brought to his home for the purposes of interrogation. Both the girl and Refoule agreed to come, and neither asked that a lawyer be present. They both stated to police that they wished to cooperate. The questioning was conducted in the room that was to have been the studio, the old mill part of the house. Most of the furniture had been removed. The granite walls gave the room a dungeon-like appearance. The intensive questioning of the girl and Refoule began around 10 p.m. and continued until 3 a.m. on May 20— some six hours.

Captain Bradford was both astonished and pleased with what the grilling of the two suspects produced. He felt that the case had taken such a turn that Chief Ellis should be present; he felt also that the police had gotten their first big break. He telephoned Chief Ellis to come to the Refoule home, and, while they were waiting for the chief to arrive, one of the investigators went out for food, and everyone had a bite to eat. When Ellis arrived, he was briefed privately by Bradford, and then he (Ellis) questioned Elaine, the young art student, and Refoule separately.

At 7 a.m. the former gave a sworn statement to the police.

ELAINE'S STATEMENT

I won a scholarship from Girls High School for three years at the High Museum of Art School, located on Peachtree Street, near Fifteenth Street. I started going to the High Museum of Art in September of 1945, this is my second year. Mr. Paul Refoule was my composition teacher. During that entire year, that is, the first year, he talked to me just as he did any of the other students. It was known to all the students that Paul Refoule was interested in one of the other students, whose name was Pat Sue, who is now married.

I did not know Mr. Refoule except what she told me about their affair. Pat Sue told me that Mr. Refoule told her that he loved her and that he wanted to marry her and that he had made love to her. She told me in class once that Mr. Refoule made love to her beautifully, and that he had kissed every part of her body. We discussed it later in the second year, after I had been with Mr. Refoule.

About two days before school was out in 1946, in May a year

ago, Mr. Paul Refoule asked me if I would like to come to his studio at Wesley Memorial Church Building and paint from a model who posed for him. I told him that I would like to. I had painted with him about 2 or 3 times but never quite finished because I started to work in the advertising department at Rich's, Inc. I became pretty interested in my advertising work but I still wanted to do some painting because I wanted to keep up my interest in fine art. He called me at Rich's. At the time, there was some talk between the two of us about doing some work together, murals, or paintings. I discussed it with the people in the office at Rich's, not very much, but they answered the phone. I told the people in my office that we were planning to do some painting together. About this time, I had my first sexual intercourse with Paul Refoule in his studio at Wesley Memorial Church Building.

This was during my lunch hour when I met him, maybe three times a week. From then on, about three times a week, we would have sexual intercourse. This lasted for about two months. Mr. Paul Refoule told me his life story, about his family in France, his family at home, about how he was not happy at home. He told me that he loved me. I told him not to say it because the word just gave me the cold chills. It was trite. I didn't believe it. I think he could convince himself that he was in love with anyone, any woman, that he was with. The reason I was so sure of this was because of what the other students thought of his relationship with Pat Sue. When he did mention marriage to me, it was because I was airing my views on marriage. I said that I didn't plan to get married. I never had. I wanted a career. After that, he didn't go into very much detail about his trouble with his wife except that it was the same situation, and that I couldn't imagine how miserable he was. At the time I thought it was self-pity. And I wasn't sympathetic enough to encourage him, to talk about it very much. He did tell me that he didn't feel very affectionate towards his wife, and that he didn't love her, and that he never did love her. He married her, he told me, because he thought she was attractive, cute, and felt like getting married. He told me about the way he met her. He further told me that he did not know her at all, but that they weren't together enough because of the war for him to realize this fully until he came back to this country. He told me that he had been planning to divorce her ever since he came back here. I knew this before through Pat Sue. On almost every occasion that we were together he would tell me that he loved me and he thought that I could love him someday, but I always told him that I did not love him, and when he

mentioned marriage, it wasn't a definite plan because I had
never told him I would marry him, even if he got a divorce.

That was through the summer of 1946 and when school
started again, I went on a free lance basis at the store and did
my work at home at night. As I got busier with it, I became
more interested in my advertising work, so that I lost all interest in Paul Refoule. I told him not to call me either at home or
at the office that it was embarrassing to me and I didn't want
to see him again. He didn't try to call me after that or see me
for six months. I didn't talk to him or see him even on the street
because I got busy with my work at Rich's.

It was necessary to stay out of art school a few days to catch
up with my work. I had to go to night school at the High Museum, that is, the High Museum School of Art, to make up this
time. Paul teaches in the night school and he talked to me
there. I told him at first that I didn't want him to give me a
ride home because the whole thing might get started again,
but then, because I didn't have another ride, I let him carry me
home from night school, but we always went straight from the
museum to my home. The longest period of time that I was ever
out with him after night school was about thirty minutes, sitting in front of my house talking. At night school, I was talking
with Bill Gray, a boy who had helped Refoule in the house and
had posed for him, for a portrait. I suggested to Paul that he
get Bill Gray to come out and pose and that I would come paint
him too. This wasn't to get together with Paul, but because I
thought Gray was an interesting model and I can't afford to
hire my own models. This is how our sketching trip became a
plan.

On Sunday, May 4, 1947, Paul came by my house with his
little boy and told me that we were coming out here, to his
home on Howell Mill Road, to sketch. We came in the house,
and he asked me if I would like to see the house. I said yes and
he showed me through the house. He asked me if I like it and
I told him that I did, but that I thought everything followed his
taste exactly and that it wasn't the accepted sort of house in
Atlanta. He said that it was a little silly to build the house
because he would never live in it, that he would probably sell
it. Then he played the piano.

We got our things together, went down by the creek in back
of the house. I sketched in one place and he sketched in another
place further down this dirt road. Then his little boy came out
and told us that lunch was ready and so we came and that is
when I met Mrs. Refoule. After lunch, I went back out. He
came out and I told him that I thought Mrs. Refoule was very

charming and nice, and we talked a few minutes and he went
back to the place where he was painting. When we finished our
sketches, we came in and he played the piano again. Mrs. Refoule complimented my painting and then they had guests.
After the guests left I told them that I had to go home and Paul
offered to take me home. Mrs. Refoule was there at the time
and she agreed that he should take me home. On the way
home, we planned to sketch again on the following Tuesday,
May 6, 1947.

I went down to the studio at Wesley Memorial Church about
10 a.m. Then we left immediately and went down to Decatur
Street to sketch a store down there. The store was Harry's Loan
Office. We went to lunch at the cafe about a half a block from
the church. Here we were talking and he talked about how
hard he had worked in the house and how everything was
going to be all right. The only thing he was unhappy. I told him
that I thought he was very lucky to have the studio he had.

We went back to the studio at Wesley Memorial Church to
finish our ink and wash drawings and after an hour or so, we
had sexual intercourse. This was last Tuesday, a week ago. On
the way home I told him that I would never go back to the
studio again or any place where any sexual relationship could
take place. He agreed to this because it depressed me. I did not
go to night school that night or the next Thursday, so the next
time I saw him was a week later on Tuesday night, May 13,
1947, the Tuesday night before Mrs. Refoule was killed on
Wednesday. The reason I saw him was that I went to night
school. It wasn't planned at all. We talked about my work. He
mentioned that he loved me and asked me if I even liked him.
He made no mention of his wife that night. We went straight
home. I talked to him about five or ten minutes, then went into
the house. All I know after that was what I heard over the
radio and read in the newspapers. According to the newspaper
accounts, there was no suspicion cast upon him, so I began
wondering how it had affected him. I thought that underneath
he had loved his wife very much and that the brutality of it all
had probably shocked him out of his mind. I wanted to express
my sympathy, so I called him at his mother-in-law's house and
told him that I was very sorry and asked him if there was anything I could do to help. He said that there was nothing anyone
could do that it was very, very hard to take. Then he said that
he was awfully confused and that he didn't know what he was
going to do. He said he wasn't going to live in the new house.
He said that he was going to live with his mother-in-law and
after that he didn't know what he was going to do. It wasn't a

definite plan because I had never told Paul Refoule that I wanted to marry him, but he suggested that if I ever married him, ever changed my mind, that we would probably go back to France, or he went alone after he divorced his wife. He said he could go to Egypt because he had very good friends there. When I returned from lunch at school yesterday, there was a note for me at the High Museum of Art, from Captain Bradford, telling me to meet him at a place down the street from the school. He asked me about my relationship with Paul Refoule and I told him the same thing that I am telling you now.

Paul Refoule has told me that he has slept with one or both of our models. I don't remember their names, but they were the two models we had at the High Museum last year. He told me about one relationship, that is a sexual relationship, he had with a girl who has since gone north. That was during the six months when I did not see him. I would like to say that although he was interested in me, during this time, Refoule had told Pat Sue the same things he told me about his home life. Also, other people around the school. All the students around the school knew about his affair with Pat Sue and anybody who talked to him any length of time, would hear about his work, his family, and his plans. I heard no plans of any murder. All I know about it is what I read in the paper and heard over the radio. I know absolutely nothing else about it.

Chief Ellis remained at the Refoule home until Elaine completed her statement, and it had been typed, and she had signed it. He then left the Refoule home and returned Elaine to her own home. The time was between 6 and 7 a.m., May 20, 1947.

Captain Bradford then had Paul Refoule make a written statement.

PAUL REFOULE'S STATEMENT

I met my wife in Paris, I think it was in 1936, probably the winter of 1935–1936. We had dates and I thought to myself that someday I would like to marry her. I knew she was in love with me. I went with her a few months, and saw her once or twice a week. We would attend movies and other functions together.

In 1936, I arrived in New York in December and came to Atlanta, Georgia immediately. I had some money which I had brought from France with me and had enough to live on. We decided to get married. After we got married, we had a honeymoon trip to Florida to Daytona Beach and southward. Then we came back to Atlanta. We stayed in Atlanta a very short time and then left and went to Washington, New York, and we sailed from New York on the Hansa, a German boat, and went back to France, and landed at LeHarve probably in February or March, 1937. After I went back to France, I was painting and teaching in Paris.

In 1938, we came back to the states, and to Atlanta, Georgia. We stayed probably about two months and left the states from either Mobile or New Orleans and landed at Cherbourg, France. I went back to painting at the same place. In 1939, my wife came back to the states, and stayed awhile and visited her father who was ill, and then came back to France.

When the war started, I went into the army. I was a liaison officer in the French army, attached to the English army. I was in the army about nine months and was captured in the north of France near Tournei, Belgium. I was sent to Meinz, Germany, where I was held prisoner by the Germans for about four years. I tried to escape many times. I was sent to Poland, where a French doctor gave me an X-ray for someone else and was released as being sick. I went to the south of France, Monein, to be exact. I stayed there until the end of the German occupation. I then came back to Orleans, which is my hometown, and met my wife there, we had met together in the south of France previous to this. I went back to painting and decided to move to this country. During the four years I was a prisoner, I did not see a girl, that is, I did not touch a girl, I saw them from a distance only.

After awhile I came back from the war and had been with my wife, my feeling for her was not the same. I thought that after we came back to this country, everything would straighten out. Instead, it didn't straighten out and my feeling was still not the same I had for her when I first knew her and married her. I had a very deep affection and respect for her, because of the child and because of her.

When we got back to the states, we went to my wife's mother's house. While staying with my mother-in-law, we were not too happy. I tried to have sexual feeling for my wife, but she was unhappy and did not like it.

We bought a place on Howell Mill Road. It was the old mill house. I started building and got a loan from the bank and another from my wife's grandmother. All together, I have a total investment in the place of $28,000, including the lot, remodeling, the addition, everything. The studio was built here and was remodeled from the old mill. During the time I was teaching at the High Museum of Art and also at Oglethorpe University. I had a class of students at both places.

I met a girl named Pat Sue who was a student in the class at the High Museum, and she posed for me privately for portraits and paintings. I went with her and was in love with her for a short while, a very short while. I also had a personal studio located in the Wesley Memorial Church Building in downtown Atlanta. During the time I had this place, Pat Sue came down to the studio to do some posing for me. I thought she was pretty and I tried to make love with her, but she never let me. I tried to sleep with her, and I never did. One day I got to kissing her and she consented and I put my tongue inside her and she did not like it. She wanted to stay a virgin so I did not try to have intercourse with her. This was during the month I worked on the Taj Mahal Bar in the Cox Carlton Hotel. She went to Florida, her home, for Christmas. I went down to see her, and see her mother. I had given her a black leather bag, which I bought down on Peachtree somewhere. It was an inexpensive bag. I wanted to give her a nice present because she had helped me work on the Taj Mahal Bar for no pay. During this time, I had difficult days of temper and humor with my wife and I asked Pat Sue to marry me and she told me no. When I went down to her house I told my wife I was going down to the seashore to draw some sketches and she never knew the difference. I stayed at a hotel, near the seashore. Last year, 1946, I had a student, a very fine art student, named Elaine who was in my class at the High Museum of Art. I never saw her out of class or the school before the end of the school year. She was my best pupil, very talented, and I thought she was very nice. I was interested in her paintings. We got to be better friends. She got a job down at Rich's. I called her several times and I saw her off and on and had lunch together and sometimes we would go back by my studio at Wesley Church, sometimes during the summer. On a lot of occasions we would have sexual intercourse in my studio at Wesley Memorial Church. I probably had sexual intercourse with her on her lunch hour at one time or another. Sometimes she would drop in after school and during paintings and I would have sexual intercourse with her.

I told Elaine my whole life history. After December, 1946, I saw her less and less. I was very fond of Elaine. I told her I loved her. I was very much impressed with her. I told her about my family relations. I asked her to marry me. I told her if she would marry me, I would take her to Paris and that if she didn't want to I would go alone to Egypt where I had friends. She always said no to the idea of getting married. Last Tuesday, two weeks ago, Elaine and I were at the Royal Cafe on Auburn Avenue. I told Elaine that me and my wife were very depressed at home and that we were having trouble again. I asked her what she thought about getting married now. She said no, that she was interested in a career.

From time to time, I gave Elaine presents of a book, a water color painting, some second hand odd books. On her birthday, I went to a florist and sent her flowers. Last Tuesday night, the night before my wife was murdered, I carried Elaine home from school from the High Museum of Art. We left there about 10 p.m. and had a flat tire. I got the tire fixed and carried Elaine on home and probably kissed her goodnight. I told her I loved her and that I cared a lot about her. I was home by 10:30 p.m. During the time I went with Elaine, I told her about my relations with Pat Sue and told her that I had put my tongue in her. I also told her about having an intercourse with one of the nude models, whose last name I never did know, but her first name was Caroline. I had intercourse with Caroline, just as I told her.

Last Sunday, two weeks ago, I called Elaine and asked if she wanted to come out and make some sketches at my home. She came, and I went to pick her up and my son was with me. She got here about 9:30 a.m. We went through the ditch in back of the house and I completed a sketch I had already started and she started a sketch down the dirt road. Elaine met my wife before lunch time. My wife did not like for me to bring Elaine or the other girls in the class, and she did not like it at all. During the week, I had one of my boy students, Bill Gray, over here to do some portraits and other painting. I asked him over here to help me paint the bathroom walls and to make some sketches on the outside. My wife treated him very well. When the girl came she did not like it, that is, my wife did not like for the girl to come here. I showed Elaine through the house when I first got here. She said it was beautiful and very nice, and that it was the home of an artist. I told her maybe I would never live much in it that I could always sell it. I have told other students at the High Museum that I was not happy with my wife.

By the time Refoule had completed making his statement and it had been typed and he had gone over the document and signed each page, it was noon on Tuesday, May 20, 1947. The session had lasted some fifteen hours. Everyone had lunch and Refoule went upstairs to take a nap. By this time the press had learned something was going on at the Refoule house, and reporters and photographers descended upon the house and surrounded it. When Chief Ellis learned of this he was greatly concerned that something in the statements would be leaked to the press, and he was not ready for that at this point. He called the editors of both papers and asked them to call off their boys. He assured the press that nothing was being kept from them and that the police were merely going over the details in the case once again. The press retreated from the house but continued to keep the house under surveillance from their automobiles. In this way they could see who came out.

For the fifth time, the police on the case walked over the wooded area and examined the house and grounds carefully. Since the night following the murder, the police had patrolled the grounds and kept the public away.

THE POLICE CLOSE IN

In the eyes of the police, the statements of Paul Refoule and Elaine now made Refoule a suspect in the murder of his wife. It was a turn of events that the police should have found hard to believe, but this was not the case. They had not liked Refoule much from the beginning. They wanted to believe he was guilty of the murder. Since all other avenues of solving the case appeared to lead nowhere, it was a valid excuse for blaming Refoule for the murder. At least it seemed so to the investigators at the time.

Refoule's own words cast the most suspicion upon him, the investigators thought. The police now felt that it was their job to either prove Refoule guilty of the crime of which many of the investigators in their own minds had already found him guilty or else clear him of any suspicion whatsoever.

The man Refoule had to be thoroughly investigated. With relish, the police moved in to find out everything they possibly could about this Frenchman, this artist, this man who would seduce a young blond girl and then take her to lunch on Auburn Avenue—of all places. It was ghastly. Horrendous! Good white folks did not behave that way.

For one last attempt, one other suspect in the case was not overlooked. Robert Griffin, a black male, aged 30, was arrested for burglary in the area of the Refoule home. He was questioned briefly about his activities on the day of May 14; but he had an alibi and was then released. This suspect may have had nothing to do with the murder. He may have. The point is that this suspect was not thoroughly checked as were suspects in the beginning. The police were beginning to zero in on Refoule, and other suspects did not interest them much.

There was other pressure. The newspapers noted that some investigators thought that Griffin might play the same role in the Refoule case that Blalock played in the Heinz case. This caused a rash of telephone calls to come into the police station castigating the police completely for attempting to follow this line. It was just another sell-out. Go after the French artist husband, the callers urged—and his mother-in-law. They both looked pretty suspicious to the general public. Like villains. Such feeling on the part of the public was not lost upon the police. They did not like Refoule. The public was beginning not to like Refoule and the entire family. What the police felt about Refoule, they began to realize, many other people felt the same. It would be a popular thing to prove Refoule guilty. The public would be grateful. Public pressure was pushing at the police dangerously.

On Wednesday, May 20, 1947, the police took into custody a white male, aged 22, who was questioned concerning the slaying. The young man's family hired a lawyer and threatened legal action if the police did not quit questioning this man, who had nothing to do with the case and the police had no evidence whatsoever that he had any connection with the case. This supposed suspect came to the attention of the police because he had been hitchhiking on Howell Mill Road the day of the murder and had been given a ride by a prominent citizen, who, upon reading and reflecting about the murder, decided that his hitchhiking passenger of that day appeared highly nervous. The man was nervous because his car had run out of gas and he was late for work.

Many tips to the police proved to be just this far off base. Hundreds of other tips from persons interested in helping the police solve the case poured into headquarters. Many were the wild notions of people whose neuroses had been turned on by the publicity in the Refoule case. People in the area were jittery and insisted that what was needed were more police to patrol the Peachtree Creek area and that it was not safe for people to be on the streets. Women wrote in to tell the methods they used for protecting themselves while walking in the vicinity. Some of the reports, those which helped the police retrace the activities of the Refoule household the day before and of the murder, were helpful.

Letters and phone calls continued to come into police headquarters stating in essence that Refoule was somehow implicated in the murder of his wife. Even these calls, when coupled with Refoule's own statement of May 19–20, which made the police more suspicious than they were before, were not sufficient evidence to indict Refoule for murder.

In the mail addressed to police headquarters which arrived on May 22, 1947, there was a letter that altered the complexion of the case even further. Written in ink on a plain white sheet of bonded typing paper and placed in a plain envelope with no return address, the letter stated that the police were on the wrong track in the Refoule case. It claimed that Peggy was murdered by her husband Paul. The unsigned letter accused Paul Refoule of being a sexual pervert and said that he gave wild parties at his studio home. The anonymous note alleged that the last wild party was held on Monday, May 12, 1947, two nights before Peggy Refoule was murdered. The letter further stated that Refoule wanted to divorce his wife and go back to France, but he was Catholic, and in the event of a divorce Peggy would never give up Jon Paul. Refoule's parents had written letters urging him not to divorce Peggy and leave America because of the boy. The mystery informant concluded by stating that these letters were in the Refoule studio at the Wesley Memorial Church Building.

Whether it was a combination of factors—the fact that all other leads in the case came to nothing, there were unusual facts of the actual murder scene that did not add up, that there was continuing information coming to the police that the Refoules were on the verge of divorce, that Refoule was French, Catholic, an artist, and now, by accusation, a sexual pervert; or whether it was the continuous demand from the public to "get the higher-ups" the "untouchables"—whatever, from this point onward the police would concentrate all their efforts on proving that Refoule was responsible for the death of his wife. All other considerations in the case were out the window. Attempts to trace the items stolen from the Refoule home were abandoned in the rush to prove Refoule guilty. Other possibilities in the case were forgotten. The police, even if they were not totally convinced of Refoule's guilt, were now hell-bent on proving it.

Friday, May 23, 1947. Captain Bradford and his investigators visited the Refoule studio in downtown Atlanta and searched the room thoroughly. In a trash can they found letters that had been torn up and thrown away. The letters were painstakingly pasted together again like a jig-saw puzzle, and the police discovered that several were from a girl in New York named Mary, who was a former student of Refoule. They were, for all intents and purposes, harmless love letters. The police found the letters from Refoule's parents. They were also pasted back together again and, because they were in French, sent out to be translated. When the letters were returned to the police from the translator, the letters said exactly what the anonymous note to the police said they contained: that Refoule wanted to leave Peggy, leave America, but that his parents urged him to stick it out. The anonymous note proved its authenticity to the extent that the police realized it was not from a crackpot—the anonymous note writer knew what he, or she, was talking about. It was obviously written by someone who knew Refoule quite well, had been to the studio, and learned the content of the letters either by reading them or being told what they contained by Paul Refoule. The anonymous note was sent to a handwriting expert to try and determine something about the mysterious author. It became vital for the police to discover who wrote the note and why. Was it truth or vengeance? Some personal grudge or a legitimate lead in the case?

NEW EVIDENCE

On Saturday, May 24, 1947, ten days after the Refoule slaying, county convicts, under police supervision, were dragging and sifting the rocky bottom of Peachtree Creek, once again going over the area of the slaying in search of clues in the case. By chance, they came up with a startling discovery.

Eight feet above the spot where Peggy Refoule's barrette was found swung a noose over the limb of an oak tree. The six-foot length of rope had spots of blood upon it. It was a sashcord identical with that found on the Refoule tool chest under the kitchen range. It was knotted exactly as the shoelaces binding Mrs. Refoule's legs had been knotted, with an extra turn or loop. After observing the grooves in the tree bark made by the sashcord, police determined the cord had supported considerable weight.

Chief Ellis was called to the scene. He concluded that "the killer strung up Mrs. Refoule. The welt was high on her jaw because of the upward pull. That is why her feet were tied, to control the action of her legs." This appeared to be an accurate analysis. But then the chief went on: "Maybe the murderer left Mrs. Refoule there two or three hours before he put her in the water." Perhaps the slayer left her there, went to the house and burglarized it, returned to the creek, and, now certain that the victim was dead, placed the body in the creek. But this is not what Chief Ellis had in mind. He did not say so publicly but privately he felt the finding of the rope implicated Refoule more than ever.

Why had not the police discovered the rope before now? The creek area had been gone over many times. All one had to do is look up. In time, there would be talk that the police placed the rope in the tree to implicate Refoule. This possibility appears remote. If the police wished to implicate Refoule, they could have found a better means. The discovery of the rope confused the case more than ever. It certainly was not ironclad evidence of Refoule's guilt.

Was there some connection between the rope and the anonymous note? Was the same person responsible for both? If Peggy Refoule was hung from a tree, would an ordinary burglar go to such lengths? Not usually. But obviously this was no ordinary case.

Chief Ellis felt it all did not add up. He theorized to the press that Peggy Refoule was strangled in her home, then hung in the tree, and finally placed in the creek much later. Again, by inference, he was strongly pointing at the husband as the murderer. He told the press that the police had eliminated robbery as a motive in the slaying and that an intruder in all probability would have fled the house, leaving the body where it lay—regardless of the fact that previous police investigation had clearly established that the house was burglarized the day of the murder. Ellis said also that the rope in the tree was tied in a distinct navy knot, further implicating Refoule.

The day was full of surprises for the police. They learned also that the will of Peggy Alston Refoule had been filed for probate. The will left her entire estate, estimated at ten thousand dollars or more, to her nine-year-old son and named her uncle, Mr. Douglas Wright, as executor.

On the night of May 24, 1947, Captain Bradford went to the Alston home and talked with Paul Refoule. He asked him to come downtown for further questioning. Refoule agreed to do so. Mrs. Alston and her son, William Ott Alston, Jr., strongly urged that a lawyer be present during the questioning. Refoule did not want an attorney and said that he could speak for himself, that he had nothing to hide. Refoule wanted to go over the details with the police. He appeared eager to do so. Perhaps he felt that to do otherwise would make him appear guilty in their eyes. The Alstons felt that Refoule, being French, had little appreciation for American police procedure and custom and that in these interrogations with the police he was in need of legal assistance. On the other hand, Refoule looked upon the American police in the same way as he did his German captors during the war—both held the trump cards, and Refoule wished to escape. In this instance, Refoule felt that he had the best chance of not being accused of his wife's murder if he cooperated with the police in every way; so, Refoule voluntarily went with Bradford to the Hurt Building in downtown Atlanta. When they had gone, Mrs. Alston and her son discussed the situation, and Mrs. Alston decided to call an attorney, Hal Lindsay. She told him what was happening and asked him to represent Refoule whether he wanted a lawyer or not. Mr. Lindsay immediately accepted the defense of Paul Refoule and drove in his automobile to the Hurt Building.

Around midnight Chief Ellis arrived at the Hurt Building, and by this time Assistant Chief Fitzgerald and other detectives who were working on the case were present too. Lindsay and Ellis went into a private office to discuss the situation. Lindsay stated that he had been hired as counsel for Paul Refoule and he wished to be present at the questioning of his client, that this was his practice and custom. But Chief Ellis abruptlydeclined Lindsay's request. Assistant Chief Fitzgerald then joined them. He told Lindsay that he had just spoken to Refoule and that Refoule stated to him that he had not employed Mr. Lindsay, that he did not have a lawyer, and that he did not need a lawyer. Lindsay asked to speak with Refoule. Ellis denied this request. Fitzgerald told Lindsay that if Refoule requested his presence during the questioning, he would be summoned. Mr. Lindsay agreed reluctantly. He said that he would be at his home if his presence was requested by Refoule. While at the Hurt Building, neither Chief Ellis nor Mr. Lindsay actually saw or spoke to Refoule directly, his wishes being communicated to them through Fitzgerald.

At 1 a.m. Refoule was taken to the Fulton County Courthouse. There he remained from 1:30 a.m., May 25, 1947, until 4:30 a.m., May 26, 1947—a period of some 27 hours! At no time during this questioning in the courthouse did Refoule ask for an attorney or indicate in any way that he desired an attorney, according to all those present at the questioning.

First, the police questioned Refoule about the sashcord that had been found in Peachtree Creek Saturday afternoon. They asked him about the sashcord on the toolbox under the kitchen range. Refoule explained that when they moved to their new house, he strung the cord between two trees for the clothesline. It was much too long. He sawed off a piece and threw it on the toolchest and forgot about it. The police wanted to know if the cord found in the tree was cut from the left-over cord on the tool chest. Refoule said he did not know. He could not remember exactly how much cord was remaining. It could have been from the same cord.

Next, the police put Refoule through extensive and arduous knot-tying tests. Each time, Refoule tied his knots with the extra loop—as the shoelaces and the noose found in the tree had been knotted. The police were jolted. Refoule could tie this intricate knot with ease. They thought this was highly significant. Refoule insisted that it was a simple knot which an ordinary person could, and would, tie—that it required no special talent. The police thought differently. One detective suggested that the knot with the extra loop was a distinctively "foreign" knot. But this was only his thought; he could not prove it.

The questioning turned next to the subject of Refoule's sex life. The police wanted to know if he was a sexual pervert. They wanted to know, too, if he had a sex party at his home on the night of May 12, 1947. Refoule denied both assertions. As for Monday night, he and his wife went out to dinner with another couple. They were out late and were seen by many people. But the questioning on these points continued for several hours. Then, Refoule was questioned again about everything concerning the case. He gave essentially the same answers as he had given to the police on May 19–20 when he and Elaine were questioned at his home.

While the investigators went over Refoule's statement carefully, the artist took a nap on a couch in a judge's chambers in the courthouse. While Refoule was asleep, the detectives went to the home of Bill Gray and brought the art student to the courthouse for questioning. All the police knew about Gray was that he was a student and model of Refoule and had helped Refoule do some work on the mill house. After extensive questioning Gray made the following statement:

I was discharged from the U.S. Navy at Charleston, S.C., in December, 1945 and returned to Atlanta and got a job at Conley Depot. I worked there six months to the day. I then went to work for the National Traffic Guard and worked there one month and a half. About three or four months ago through the G.I. Bill of Rights handled by the Veterans Administration, I started attending the High Museum of Art. I attended school two nights a week, Tuesday and Thursday. When I first started attending the school Mr. Paul Refoule was my teacher. I attended his class approximately one month, then went into the classes of Mr. Rogers and Mr. Shute in the portrait class and saw Mr. Refoule every night that I attended, and started having conversations with him. He told me about his house that he was building and his plans of completing it. He told me about the studio and his plans of holding a school out there but he said there was no bus service that far out. He said that he had never run a school like he was planning and he did not know if it would pay or not. About this time he told me that both he and his wife were unhappy. He stated that his wife was not interested in his work anymore. He said that it made him very unhappy because she was that way. This conversation took place in his car as we were riding to school. I had been helping him paint his bathroom upstairs and we talked about building a bridge over a big ditch in the back of the house so other students could get to the creek to sketch.

I had supper with the Refoules before we left for school. I was out there one other time. I helped him do some painting in one of the rooms on the right of the bathroom. I went out there about 10:30 a.m. and stayed there until around 6 p.m. that evening. While we were eating supper Peggy Refoule said that she would like to get someone to rent a room there so she would have someone to stay with her at night for protection. On the way to school that night Paul told me again that Peggy was not happy and neither was he. These were the only two times I was ever at the Refoule home. I know absolutely nothing else about the case.

Two other male students were brought to the courthouse and gave statements that day, but their testimony added nothing further to the case. Late that afternoon Refoule returned to the Alston home.

GHOULISH CURIOSITY

On Sunday, for the first time since the case broke on May 14, sightseers had the run of the Refoule premises on Howell Mill Road. The police had gone over everything numerous times and no longer kept a guard on the property. The press estimated that some 10,000 persons went through the Refoule home and grounds! The sightseers parked their automobiles and proceeded to conduct their own investigations, retracing the route through tangled underbrush where many thought the slayer had taken his victim. They tramped down the foliage, peered into windows, opened closet doors, and remarked on paintings in the Refoule studio. Various groups got into conversations with others and exchanged theories and gossip about the murder. They voiced their opinion on art and crime. When the police rushed to the scene to clear everyone out of the house, many people were very indignant, and a near-riot ensued between the people and the police. The people felt that they had a perfect right to be there. They considered the Refoule home and crime scene now to be public property, and, if the public wanted to know and see everything concerning the Refoule case, then the police should not deny them. The murder was now public entertainment. If you are prominent and get murdered then you lose certain rights of privacy—like a politician running for office. This was how people felt at the time. For many, the Refoule murder was one of the big events of their lives.

The week of May 26 through May 31 the Fulton County police spent gathering all the evidence possible against Refoule. They went to Oglethorpe University and had all the students in Refoule's art class make notarized statements. The statements were practically all the same.

> I am a student at Oglethorpe University and study art under Paul Refoule. On Wednesday, May 14, I came to class at 2:45 p.m. by the school clock. The class starts at 2:40 p.m. and I was five minutes late. When I got into class at 2:45 p.m., Mr. Refoule was present. He had already set up a still life which we

were supposed to draw. He had already explained what he wanted the class to do. When I came in five minutes late, he explained to me again what the instructions were. My wrist watch is usually ten minutes faster than the school clock. I set up my board and started working on the drawing about 2:50 p.m. About 3:15 p.m. Mr. Refoule checked the roll. I cannot say definitely just when Mr. Refoule left our classroom. Evidently, Mr. Refoule left the classroom between 3:15 and 3:30 p.m. and went into the other classroom, because when I went into the other art classroom to get a bottle of water, I saw Mr. Refoule in the other room. I sat down by him and talked with him for about 15 minutes. I left the classroom about 5 p.m. and Mr. Refoule was still there. The class is rather informal since the students have to go in and out for water and supplies. This is all I know about the case.

All the statements of his students taken together verified that while Refoule was in and out of his own classroom, he did not leave the building at anytime. The statements of the Oglethorpe students tended to firm up Refoule's alibi. It should have been obvious to anyone that Refoule could not have murdered his wife. But the police continued to confine their investigation only to the husband.

Next the police department took on the High Museum of Art. It was not possible that two institutions of the period could have had less in common. Neither understood the other. The police interviewed practically the entire school, faculty and students, and took lengthy statements. Needless to say, the police were operating in a rather unusual environment for them, and what they learned about life among artists in art school was a terrific shock. They thought it deplorable that models posed in the nude. They had never heard of such a thing! They listened wide-eyed to stories about wild sex parties and loose morals. Most of this was just gossip and student pranks to play games with the police, and the murder investigation went rather far afield at this point. A spokesman for the High Museum of Art stated: "High-handed, Gestapo-like, and intimidative methods in questioning art students and models were being used by the Fulton County Police Department." The director of the museum was indignant. But the High Museum depended upon both tax money and civic contributions to stay in operation, and its officials were appalled at what the investigation was doing to the school's reputation.

They wished the police would go away. But the more the police learned about art school, the more they were fascinated and the more active they were in questioning the art students. They requested that the young art student who had written love letters to Refoule from New York and was now back in Atlanta on vacation come and make a statement, and she eagerly did so.

I started going to the High Museum of Art in 1946. I had a class and the instructor was Paul Refoule. I attended his class from February 1946 until May, 1946. All the girls in the class thought Mr. Refoule was very handsome and a good teacher. Mr. Refoule would tell me as an instructor any criticism that he might have of my drawing. I never saw Paul until I started back to the High Museum of Art in October of 1946 and he was my instructor once again. I attended until February, 1947. During my attending this school I posed for Paul privately at his studio located in the Wesley Memorial Church Building located on Auburn Avenue. On two or three other occasions I posed for Paul. On the last occasion I posed for Paul I was still in my posing position and was sitting in a straight or regular chair and Paul kissed me. I enjoyed him kissing me but I reminded him he had a wife and son. I left shortly afterwards because I did not want to get involved with a married man. That was just before I left to go to New York. I was very much in love with Paul at the time and when I came to New York I wrote him everyday and told him about the school I was attending. We corresponded and Paul told me he loved my letters. Before coming to New York, Paul told me of being a prisoner of the Germans. He told me of his plans in painting and of fixing his home. The last time I received a letter from Paul was about two weeks before Mrs. Refoule was murdered. I answered this letter and told him how much I loved him and how I wanted to be with him forever. I was pretty proud of this until I found out you have it [meaning the letter]. I wrote Paul one letter after the murder which was self explanatory. I felt that I was alive and his wife was dead. What I felt like is that he must hate me for what happened. Paul never said to me that he loved me.

This statement indicates that a student was in love with her teacher. What this adds to the murder investigation is hard to say. The police took the statement seriously.

The one student and two models with whom the police really wanted to talk were no longer at the art school and no longer even living in Atlanta. How such individuals could be involved in the murder was hard to comprehend, but they could tell a great deal about Paul Refoule's sex life, which was the main interest of the police now. The murder investigation was fast becoming an investigation into that aspect of the life of an artist and his models. The police maintained this was the key to solving the murder of Peggy Refoule. The evidence thus far did not appear very convincing. On June 3, 1947, the police secured the following statement from former art student Pat Sue.

I started to school at the High Museum of Art in Atlanta, Georgia on September 10, 1945. Mr. Paul Refoule was an instructor in art there at the school. I was a student in the class at which Mr. Refoule was the instructor. A few weeks after I had been in class, Mr. Refoule walked up to me in the hall one day and asked me to do some posing for him in his private studio in downtown Atlanta. He wanted me to pose for a portrait of myself which he was going to paint. I made frequent trips to his studio and posed for the portrait. I did not pose in the nude. I posed wearing my pants and a brassiere.

On the second posing I did for him, in his studio, he kissed me. I posed at first on Thursday, Friday and Saturday. He made love to me at each sitting. After that, I posed on Saturdays for him. Since we belonged to the same church, we would go to mass on Sunday and then go to his studio. Each time we went to the studio, he made love to me. During the time I was posing for Paul Refoule, he asked me to marry him. He told me that he would divorce his wife if I would marry him. He said that if I would marry him, we would travel around Europe doing painting and would probably wind up in Orleans, France. I was very much in love with Paul Refoule, but being realistic, I felt it would never be possible for me to marry him. I had to consider my parents. Other things led me to believe the marriage was not probable. Paul told me on several occasions that his home life with his wife was unhappy.

On one occasion, when I refused to have normal sexual intercourse with him, Paul kissed me all over my body and placed his tongue in my privates. I was partly clothed at the time. He stayed there with his tongue in my privates for approximately three minutes. He asked me if I liked it and I said I didn't think so, not really. He did it again but I was very embarrassed. This was the only time he did this. I posed for him some more after that. He made love to me on another occasion after that incident, in a normal manner. The affair I had with Paul Refoule went on from September, 1945, until sometime in January,

1946. The time Paul Refoule placed his tongue in my privates, we were in his studio at the Wesley Memorial Church. It was sometime during the time he was working on the murals at the Taj Mahal Bar at the Cox-Carlton Hotel, or shortly after he finished working on them. I never knew or had never heard of anyone putting their tongue in anyone else before that time. He did not ask me if he could do it but rather just went ahead and did it. Since that time, and since I have been married, my husband borrowed a book, Rennie McAndrew's *Love and Sex Technique* and I learned that this was done and there was a paragraph in the book which described the whole process. During the time I was having an affair with Paul Refoule he gave me a nice handbag with a handkerchief inside. He gave me some scarfs for my birthday.

Paul Refoule came to Florida and met my mother. I was married in August, 1946, and returned to school in September. My husband is stationed at Ft. Dix, New Jersey. I have seen Paul Refoule just casually since that time, to speak to him and have a casual conversation. He told me that he hoped that I was happy. On May 16, 1947, I received a telegram from my husband stating that he was going overseas and asking me to come to New Jersey. I went to New Jersey and learned that he had sent me the telegram to get me out of Atlanta during the investigation of the death of Mrs. Refoule to keep me from being investigated. He knew about my affair with Paul Refoule. On Thursday morning after Mrs. Refoule was killed on Wednesday, Elaine, a girl friend of mine, came to school and was very nervous and upset. We went out and got in a friend's car and listend to the radio reports of the murder. I have not heard from or seen Paul Refoule since his wife was killed. This is all I know about the case.

The police were anxious to talk with two models at the High Museum of Art who had posed privately for Paul Refoule. One was living in Florida, where on June 10, 1947, Captain Bradford interviewed her.

Question: Did you go to the High Museum of Art?
Answer: I didn't go there. I modeled there.
Q: What kind of modeling did you do?
A: Nude.
Q: What we want to do is a little embarrassing to us and it is more embarrassing after we came down here and found that you are married.
A: Yes. I understand that.
Q: How long did you model at the High Museum of Art?

A: Not more than six weeks.

Q: Did you model at Wesley Memorial for Paul Refoule?

A: Yes.

Q: We want to know the relations he had with you and the other model.

A: I got to know Pat Sue, one of the students at the school. She asked me if Paul Refoule tried to make love to me when I was posing for him and I said yes. I was surprised that he did this, but I went on modeling for him, but it was a struggle all the time. Seems to me like he was a happy-go-lucky fellow but was unhappy with his home life, but since he was a Catholic he could not get a divorce. That is the impression he gave me.

Q: Did the other model, your friend Martha, ever have any conversation with you as to her relations with Paul Refoule?

A: Well, she just had the same trouble that I did. He always messed around and told us all his troubles. She is married now.

Q: In his statement Refoule said he had intercourse with you.

A: Well . . . once.

Q: Did he ever try to do it by mouth—or did he just try to have intercourse?

A: Just the intercourse business.

Q: Your name is Carolyn. The other girl's name is Martha. Did he have the same with Martha?

A: I don't know you will have to ask her.

Q: How many times did Refoule make advances toward you?

A: Every time I went there.

Q: You always went to see Refoule alone?

A: Always. Except that once Pat Sue and I thought it would be fun to go over there together and see if he would make advances to both of us. He thought it was a good joke. We all laughed about it. The next time I went to pose for him he told me how much he loved Pat Sue.

Q: He told you that he was in love with Pat Sue?

A: Yes.

Q: Did he tell you that he had been with Pat Sue in any other way than the natural way? French?

A: He never did say.

Q: Did he ever kiss you down there?

A: Not down there.

Q: To what extent did he work himself up with you?

A: He kissed me all over my body but didn't kiss me down there. He kissed me on the ear.

Q: Did he kiss you on the breast?

A: Yes, and all over, but never down there.

Q: Did you ever meet Mrs. Refoule?

A: I was working at the studio in the nude one day when she came by to see him. His wife didn't seem to think anything about it. I thought she was very gracious.

Q: How old are you?

A: 18.

Q: How many times were you at the studio posing for Refoule before he had this intercourse with you?

A: Gosh, I don't know. Three times, or something like that.

Q: Did he make a pass at you the first time you went over there?

A: Yes.

Q: You just tell us all you can about it.

A: There is not all that much to tell. He made passes at me. I told Martha about it. He asked her to pose for him. She knew what to expect. I told her how he messed around and everything. She told me she had the same experience. He just seemed to like models.

Q: Was it commonly known that Paul Refoule was a sex-pervert?

A: Well . . . the girls seemed to know. I mean Pat Sue and the other girls who modeled for Refoule. There was a lot of talk. You see I bruise very easily so I want to say that one day I went to school with a bruise on my leg and one of the girls came into the restroom when I was dressing and asked me where I got the bruise. I didn't say anything. She said: 'modeling for Mr. Refoule, eh?' So; they all knew.

Q: Did you ever go out to Paul Refoule's house? Ever pass there or see it? Did he ever talk to you about building a new home?

A: I never was at his house. He just told me about his experiences during the war and about how unhappy he was with his wife. He said something about he wished he could build a house but I can't go into any detail. I remember vaguely about a house. The only time I was out with him was the time he took Martha and I out to the Cox Carlton Hotel to see the mural he had done there. He was just talking and talking and seemed to be in heaven to be sitting there between two girls and it didn't seem to matter to him that he was in a public place and that he had painted a mural there and that people probably knew him.

Q: Did you ever model for Refoule at his studio at night?

A: No. We worked in the mornings or afternoons. I remember

Pat Sue saying something about posing for him in the evening. When the dean at the Art School found out he was going to write Pat Sue's mother.

Q: Is posing at night a violation of the school rules?

A: No. Not for models. I wouldn't know about the students. I was not a student. Just a model.

Q: There is something else I want to ask you about. It has come to our attention and is commonly known among several students that we have talked to, and that is the 69 Club. Do you know about the 69 Club at the High Museum of Art?

A: 69 Club? What kind of club is that?

Q: Made up of students and instructors.

A: No, I don't think I ever heard of that.

Q: When did Paul first talk to you? When was the first time he started telling you how unhappy he was?

A: I met him at the High Museum when I was modeling for a painting class and these women in the class were telling me what wonderful workmanship Refoule did and what a wonderful man he was and that kind of thing. I think all the women in the class were kind of taken with Paul, him being French and all. He came into their painting class that day and looked at me and said—'Oh lovely!' So after class I saw him talking to Pat Sue and I heard her mention my name. He came over and asked me if I would like to pose for him. He started telling me when I went out for a sandwich, the first day I posed for him, about what an unhappy marriage he had.

Q: What did he say about his wife?

A: That he was unhappy being married to her, but that he was Catholic and there was the boy.

Q: Did he ever mention of anyway to dispose of her to you?

A: No.

Q: Did he ever tell you that he loved you?

A: Oh yes, several times.

Q: What did he say about it?

A: Oh, he didn't talk in the way of getting married or anything. It was just talk with him. I am sure I am not the only person he told that.

Q: In other words, when he said he loved you he didn't necessarily mean that he wanted to marry you.

A: Yes.

On June 12, 1947, Captain Bradford took a statement from the other model, Martha, in Atlanta.

Caroline, my girl friend and I, came up to Atlanta from Florida in January 1946. When we got to the railroad station, we started calling numbers furnished by the Travel Aid Society for a place to stay. We found a place and rented an apartment on Techwood Drive from Mrs. Hern. She was a widow. Caroline wanted to find work playing the piano and I wanted to find modeling work. I had done some fashion modeling and was interested in that. We went to an agency but the only request for models they had was at the High Museum of Art. We went out there and talked to a man out there about a job. He said they had fashion modeling, bathing suit modeling, and nude modeling. He said the nude modeling paid $2 an hour, considerably more than the others. Caroline went to work but I decided to think about it for a few days. I went out one day to the school and told them that I would do bathing suit modeling. A very nice lady out there told me they needed another model for a life class there at the High Museum. Caroline had told me that no one there paid any attention to the models being nude, that it was very business like, so I accepted the job.

I started modeling nude that day. The class I posed the most for was one for older women, and Mr. Shute's wife was one of them. Mr. Shute was the instructor. Mrs. Charles Nunnally was also in the class. Mr. Shute was the instructor in that class. Paul Refoule never taught that class. Once I was on a break and Paul Refoule came up to me and asked me to pose for him in his private studio. He said he would pay me the same salary as the school. I told him if I had time, I would pose for him. Caroline had posed for him before I did. She had told me that she had a struggle with Refoule when she posed for him and said that I may have one also. She said he would make advances towards her and that she would have to resist him. I went to pose for Paul Refoule for the first time in February, 1946. The first time I posed for him he was very nice. It was very pleasant. The second time I went to pose for him he tried to kiss me. He was strong, although he doesn't look very strong. He kept trying to get me to kiss him. I told him we had better get back to work.

Paul Refoule told me about being overseas in a prison camp. He was painting a watercolor picture of me. The last time I went to the studio he kissed me on the shoulders and neck and on the mouth. I told him that I was very much in love with my husband. He said that he was very unhappy with his wife. He begged me to have sexual intercourse with him. I refused. He was upset, for he was ready for intercourse, but I refused to yield to his advances. I started to leave and he grabbed my

The Fox Theatre

Fulton Tower, Atlanta's Long-time Jail

The Ansley Hotel
Like the grim structure pictured above it, this one-time fashionable hotel has been demolished.

Banker Henry Heinz (*right*) and
Mayor William B. Hartsfield.

Mrs. Henry Heinz
arrives at the Fox
Theatre for a Met-
ropolitan Opera
performance.

Accused killer Horace Blalock
shows investigators where he threw
the gun used in the Heinz murder.

Rainbow Terrace

Curious sightseers descend upon Rainbow Terrace, the palatial residence
of Mr. and Mrs. Henry Heinz.

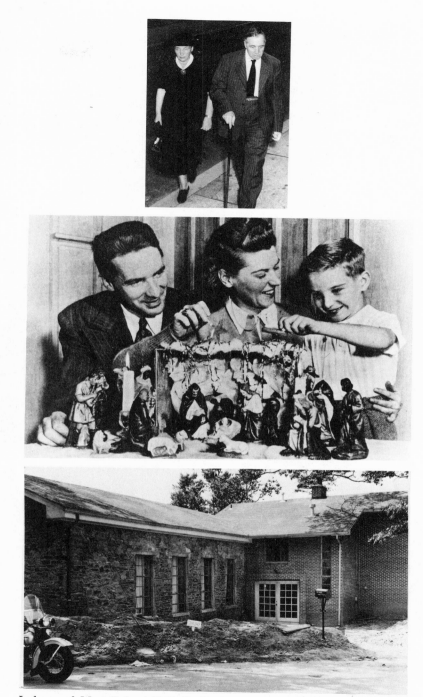

Judge and Mrs. Robert Refoule (*top*) approach the Federal Building in downtown Atlanta for the hearing of their son's suit in 1947. In happier days, Paul, Peggy, and Jon Paul Refoule (*middle*) are shown assembling a crèche at Christmas 1945. The just-completed Refoule home on Howell Mill Road (*bottom*) is shown shortly after Mrs. Refoule's murder.

AA051 A.LSA60 NL PD=ATLANTA, GA 20=

BARBARA LEVINE=

NATIONAL CONCERT AND ARTISTS CORPORATION 711 FIFTH

AVE NYK=

YOU WILL HAVE ALL TEXTS AND TRANSLATIONS OF GOETHE SONGS

BY MONDAY SORRY FOR THE DELAY REGARDS=

JOHN GARRIS=..

APR 21 REC'D

Telegram sent by opera singer John Garris shortly before he was murdered.

Capt. Cal Cates (*left*) and Supt. E.I. Hilderbrand, who figured prominently in the investigations surrounding Atlanta's most sensational murders.

John Garris in costume for one of his roles in Metropolitan Opera performances.

Terminal Station, the site of which is now occupied by the Richard B. Russell Building, at which the Metropolitan Opera cast arrived in Atlanta and from which all but one of its singers departed on April 21, 1949.

hands and held them and kissed them. He told me that I was beautiful. He told me that I was sweet. Very reluctantly I yielded to his pleadings. But just that once.

I never went back to the studio after that. The only time I was ever out with Paul Refoule was the time he, Caroline, and I went to the Cox Carlton Hotel for a drink. Paul had just completed the murals there. We went down to the bar and had one whiskey sour a piece. He took us on home and as we got out of the car, he kissed us both goodnight. This is all I know about the case.

On Friday, June 13, 1947, one month after the Refoule murder, a man walked into the Tampa, Florida, police station and screamed at the desk sergeant:

"Who am I? Who am I? I have committed a murder!"

The police checked the man out and searched his briefcase. It was crammed with clippings and data concerning the Refoule case. The man turned out to be a mental case.

At 1:30 p.m. Paul Refoule went to Atlanta airport to meet his parents. They had come from France to visit him and their grandson. While at the airport Refoule was taken into custody by Fulton County police officers and arrested on a warrant charging him with committing the act of sodomy. Paul Refoule spoke with his parents briefly after they arrived, and was then wisked away by police officers. The elder Refoules (whose command of the English language was sketchy) were driven to the Alston home by members of the French community in Atlanta. Everyone was in a state of shock. Refoule was interrogated by police officers from Friday afternoon until Saturday night—a period of some thirty hours. The police held Refoule in one room and brought in other people and questioned them separately and together. Bill Gray and two other art students were questioned for ten hours as police tried to persuade them to tell about an alleged all-male party held at the Refoule home on May 12, 1947. The only information the police had on the supposed party came from the anonymous note.

Elaine was questioned and so was Pat Sue. The evidence of the indictment charge of sodomy came from Pat Sue's statement that Refoule had performed an unnatural sex act upon her at his private studio. Assistant Chief Fitzgerald and Captain Bradford brought Refoule and Pat Sue to the same room and questioned them together.

Bradford: I believe this is the girl you had told us about you had been with at the Wesley Memorial Church studio?

Refoule: Yes.

Bradford: This is the girl you knew as Pat Sue; who was an art student and who modeled for you?

Refoule: Yes.

Bradford: This is the girl you said you put your mouth in?

Refoule: Yes.

Bradford: Is Mr. Refoule, here, the one that you have made a statement about going with you in an unnatural way at the studio?

Pat Sue: Yes.

Bradford: On this particular time you stated that Mr. Refoule went with you in an unnatural way by placing his mouth in your privates?

Pat Sue: Yes.

Fitzgerald: Did you do that, Mr. Refoule?

Refoule: I don't remember, but if she says 'Yes,' she is telling the truth.

Bradford: So; you admit going with her in this unnatural way?

Refoule: Yes, that's right.

Bradford: You said that after two or three minutes of this operation that you asked him to stop?

Pat Sue: Yes.

Refoule: (interrupting) I don't think it was that long.

Bradford: The lady said it was two or three minutes.

Pat Sue: It was sort of an incredible short time.

Refoule: Well, I think it was a very short time.

Bradford: I believe you stated that upon another occasion, you gave Miss Pat Sue a nice handbag. Is that correct?

Refoule: Yes, that's right.

Bradford: That was on another occasion, wasn't it? Did you give her anything at the same time you gave her the bag?

Refoule: I think there was a handkerchief in the bag, or something like that.

Bradford: What kind of handkerchief was it?

Refoule: I don't know.

Bradford: Was it a white handkerchief?

Refoule: I think so, but I don't know.

Bradford: What kind of handkerchief was—

Pat Sue: (interrupting) I think this is stupid! What difference does it make what kind of handkerchief it was? (pause) It was a white handkerchief with a little embroidery on the corner of it.

Bradford: Is that right?

Refoule: Yes.

Pat Sue: I still have the handkerchief, that is why I remember.

Fitzgerald: Paul, did you ever ask Miss Pat Sue here to marry you? In any conversation which you had with her?

Refoule: Yes.

Fitzgerald: Paul, just how did you figure on marrying her when you were married to Peggy? How were you planning to marry Pat Sue, if she would have married you?

Refoule: I don't know. That was very vague. I could always divorce.

Fitzgerald: Did you ever in your conversation with Miss Pat Sue say anything about your home life?

Refoule: Yes, I certainly did.

Fitzgerald: Did you tell her it was pleasant or unpleasant?

Refoule: I think I told her sometime it was pleasant, I think I did.

Bradford: What did you say to her, Mr. Refoule?

Refoule: I don't know. It was two years ago.

Fitzgerald: How long did you stay in Florida when you went down to visit Miss Pat Sue?

Refoule: I stayed one night and one morning.

Fitzgerald: Now on that trip down there, did you ask Miss Pat Sue to marry you?

Refoule: I don't know. I guess so.

Fitzgerald: Well, did Miss Pat Sue turn you down flat?

Refoule: Yes.

Bradford: You never did tell your wife you went down there, did you?

Refoule: No.

Bradford: Did you tell your mother-in-law, or any of your in-laws?

Refoule: No.

Bradford: Now then, Paul, at the time you were trying to get Pat Sue to marry you, is that the time you wrote your parents in Orleans, and told them how unhappy you were with Peggy?

Refoule: I think it was about that time.

Bradford: Was it along about the same time that you got a letter from them that stated for you not to leave your son over here?

Refoule: I don't remember. I know sometime I wrote that to my family and I remember once my father said that be very careful and not do anything, to be patient, things would be all right.

Fitzgerald: Paul, how long was it after you were in Florida before you saw Miss Pat Sue again?

Refoule: I think I saw her when she came back from school. It was probably January of 1946.

Fitzgerald: Now, did you talk to any of these girls after Pat Sue told you she was going to get married to this man in the service, did you say anything to any of the other students in regard to whether you could keep her from getting married?

Refoule: I don't think so.

Fitzgerald: You don't recall that?

Refoule: No, I didn't know the name.

Pat Sue: Why should he?

Refoule: I didn't even know the name of Pat Sue's husband.

Bradford: You just knew that she was fixing to get married, is that correct?

Refoule: No.

Pat Sue: At that time he didn't know.

Refoule: I learned that she was already married.

Bradford: She was already married and you weren't supposed to know her?

Pat Sue: What are you trying to get at? Are you trying to mess us up or something?

Bradford: No, I am not trying to mess you up.

Pat Sue: Look, I was married last August. Paul didn't know about the marriage but he probably learned about it later.

At this point Pat Sue was excused. It should be remembered that all the girls who had been involved with Refoule, with the exception of Elaine and the girl from New York, were now married and were very reluctant to have themselves associated with the case or the police. The police were constantly assuring all of them that if they would cooperate and give statements, their names would be kept out of it. Thus, in all their statements the girls are rather distant toward Refoule and put all the blame for the affairs upon him, thinking they were giving the police what they wanted to hear and keeping themselves out of the investigation as much as possible. It is interesting that when Pat Sue was confronted face to face with Refoule, she was much more sympathetic toward him and that past memories affected her. It becomes rather obvious that the reason none of the girls took Refoule seriously was that none of them was convinced that *he* was serious; that he was unhappy at times in his home life but was not really very likely to part with it. The police viewed the situation in a similar way but with a different twist, for they were convinced that Refoule would not divorce his wife, mainly because he was Catholic and because of his son, and they looked upon Refoule as a man in a trap, who to escape from his trap committed murder.

By Friday night everyone was released and sent home except, of course, Refoule, who was under arrest for sodomy, and Elaine and Bill Gray. The police wanted to find out something more concrete from these three, or otherwise they were stuck with a sodomy indictment on the basis of Pat Sue's testimony—which was something against Refoule. In a lengthy talk session the police were to make one final effort to find some link between the murder and Refoule and these two art students. Hours of questioning and going over the same data again and again did not change the statements of anybody.

That night the police made a second trip to Atlanta airport. This time they met a man they had hired from Florida who had an apparatus called a "truth machine" that could, beyond a shadow of a doubt, scientifically determine whether or not a person was telling the truth. This so-called truth machine was what would later be termed a lie detector. Since Atlanta did not have a machine, the Fulton County police hired a Mr. Keen (that was his name, for real) to fly up from Florida with his apparatus. Mr. Keen, dressed in a blue suit, brown shoes, and white socks, got off the plane with his invention under his arm. It was wrapped in brown paper and all tied up with white string. It was heavy, and Mr. Keen puffed along carrying the machine. He would not allow another soul to tamper with it.

On Saturday, June 14, 1947, Elaine, Bill Gray, and Paul Refoule all took lie detector tests. The operator was not satisfied with the first tests, so he administered second tests, and a third series of tests. This went on for hours, until everyone was dead tired. When the test was done, Mr. Keen walked out and held an extensive press conference, somewhat to the consternation of the Fulton County police.

Mr. Keen stated: "I am convinced Paul Refoule was not telling the truth when he answered 'No' to the question: 'were you responsible for the death of your wife'?"

Mr. Keen did not comment on the truth or falsity of the tests administered to the two art students. This would require further study of the tests, he stated. But Mr. Keen did go into great detail with the press about his new machine, and all the reporters hovered over it—this new, infallible machine which could tell the truth from a lie. Since the beginning of time, investigators had wished there was some means by which the police and the courts could separate positively truth from untruth. With this grand machine it was now scientifically possible, or so Mr. Keen claimed. The lie detector was something new. People believed it to be infallible. If the lie detector had suspicions about whether or not Refoule was telling the truth, this was the strongest evidence most people needed that he was not. There are no easy solutions in gathering evidence or easy ways to make people tell the truth. The police in this instance accepted a new, untried invention too readily. In this era it was thought to be the greatest boon to detective work since Sherlock Holmes. But in the Refoule case it was badly misused to make the suspect appear guilty.

The police returned to questioning Refoule—telling him that he had flunked his truth machine test. He might as well confess and tell them that he killed his wife. This line of questioning continued until Saturday afternoon, but Refoule did not change his story. After thirty hours he was allowed to see his attorney, Hal Lindsay, who immediately got Refoule released on bail. The bond was set at $10,000, which was put up by the Alston family.

PAUL REFOULE CHARGED WITH SEX CRIME

That headline appeared in *The Atlanta Constitution* on Sunday, June 15, 1947. It was accompanied by no less than five pictures of Paul Refoule: his being arrested at the airport, entering the Fulton County jail, being fingerprinted, searched, and finally gazing from behind bars. The story was splashed all over both Atlanta newspapers, and in fact it appeared that the two papers were running some kind of contest to see which could write the most compelling headlines. The stories pointed out that Mrs. W. Ott Alston, Refoule's mother-in-law, had put up the $10,000 bond and stated also that she and her mother, Peggy Alston Refoule's grandmother, were offering a $1,500 reward for the solution of Peggy's murder, stating: "We are bereft of police aid and see an effort under way to railroad an innocent man to the electric chair."

On that Sunday afternoon the Alston home suffered the same fate that the Refoule home had suffered on previous Sundays. The ghoulish drove out to stare, and speculate, and walk around. The numbers of people coming to the Alston home were much fewer than those who had besieged the Refoule house, but they were loud and they hollered from their cars. The elder Refoules were staying there and did not know what to think. A reporter stopped Mrs. Alston before she could get inside the house when she was returning from church and asked her what she thought about the latest turn in the case. She replied that "she didn't know what to think."

Members of the French community of Atlanta came to the Alston home and worked there in shifts: shooing people away, answering the telephone, and translating developments for the elder Refoules. The Alston home received a continuous stream of abusive and obscene phone calls.

The police stated to the press that Refoule's unnatural sex life was something he admitted during one of the earlier questioning sessions (this referred to the so-called unnatural act with Pat Sue) but was not brought out previously because "they were afraid it might cloud over the murder investigation."

Chief Ellis stated to the press that "other persons do not get away with this, and I see no reason why he should go free." It became rather obvious that the police, unable to gather sufficient evidence to charge Refoule with the murder of his wife, were forced to settle for the lesser, gamier charge.

The Georgia legal definition of the charge of sodomy is the "carnal knowledge and connection against the order of nature, by man with man, or in the same unnatural manner with woman." The charge of sodomy against Refoule was based solely on the incident which occurred at his downtown studio with Pat Sue two years before. The accusation concerning an all-male party at the Refoule home on the night of May 12, 1947, was not part of the indictment but was printed in the newspaper as though it were a fact—the papers failing to note that said allegation lacked either substance or proof and was nothing more than rumors spread by the police when they received the unsigned note which made the charge. However, those who read the newspaper accounts believed that the charge of sodomy against Refoule stemmed from the so-called May 12 party. The police released to the press much of their gossip gathered in countless interviews. Atlanta matrons were titillated by what they read. None could ever recall reading about such goings-on in Atlanta before. It was all so new, so strange, so radical—but *exciting*. Few even knew what sodomy meant, had never read such a thing in the newspapers before, and asked their embarrassed husbands over dinner to explain it to them.

The aftermath of the Refoule slaying created more public interest than the murder itself. Indeed, the murder and investigation thereof, was forced into the background. The foreigner's love life captured Atlanta's imagination like nothing in years. Amateurs advanced their theories on street corners, on buses, and in barber shops. People spoke of little else.

A virtual orgy of letters inundated the press and the police following the disclosures of June 15. The Fulton County Police Department received 188 letters concerning the Refoule case in the period from June 16 thru June 25.

Why not try the truth machine on Peggy Refoule's mother, Mrs. Alston? She is so all fired sure Refoule isn't guilty. Can she account for her time from 1:30 to 5 p.m. the day of the murder? Maybe there is something between her and Refoule. It smells fishy to me.

We are wondering, as probably thousands of other Georgians are wondering, what has happened to the Refoule case? There are numerous questions in the minds of the public such as: why is Mrs. Alston protecting Refoule in the face of all of the admissions that he has made regarding her daughter? Are the rumors true that Mrs. Refoule was not the real daughter of Mrs. Alston? [*Editor's note:* No.] What age woman is Mrs. Alston? Is it possible that she is infatuated with Refoule? Has Mrs. Alston's home been searched for the missing jewelry? Who is the woman Refoule wanted to marry and take back to France? These are but a few of the questions that people are asking daily. The public feels that the lid has been clamped on tight on this brutal business—but why? [The letter was signed "Georgia taxpayers."]

Have read lots about the Refoule 'murder mystery' and it looks like to me that Mrs. Alston, mother of the murdered Mrs. Refoule, might be mixed up in the affair. Why is she doing so much talking and furnishing bail for her murdered daughter's husband, who is being suspected? Something funny. [Unsigned.]

In spite of the criticism from the family of the late Mrs. Refoule which was announced over the radio today in the latest bulletin on the case, the public congratulates you on the splendid job you are doing.

A civic club in southwest Atlanta wrote the following letter which was signed by a large number of its members:

The people of Atlanta and Fulton County know that Mrs. Refoule's husband murdered her and/or had someone to murder his wife. Why does the mother-in-law take up for this queer French guy if she cares what happened to her daughter? We shudder when we think of the murders in our home city that have never been correctly solved and the murderer given justice. When we think of our good friend Mr. Henry Heinz horrible death, and yet the real murderer was never arrested. A little prowling Negro was railroaded through our courts. If the real murderers were brought to justice and given the electric chair or hanged we would not have so many of these awful murders in our city.

The mayor of Georgia's fifth largest city wrote the following:

I am keeping up with you in this Refoule murder and I am hoping to see everyday that you have solved it. I just want to tell you one thing about this case: the way it was performed just don't look like an American act to me, and you know foreigners do things different in butchering a hog or a human. And too it seems to me that as neat as this job was done it was by a very much of a man or either two people. Keep checking Refoule's friends. They are a sorry lot.

The pastor of one of the largest Baptist churches in the South wrote:

Let me sincerely commend you for the courageous and intelligent way you are prosecuting the Refoule case. We need more policemen like you in Fulton County and in places of public trust.

A Fulton County superior court judge wrote:

I wish to compliment the Fulton County police for their courage and fearlessness in handling the Refoule case. Having been assigned some unpleasant tasks myself, I can sympathize with you. I am glad to know that we have a good police department, when, they see others 'cow-towing' to the untouchables, permits their sense of civic duty and public responsibility outweigh other considerations. The department is to be commended for rendering our community valuable service.

A lawyer wrote:

I want you to know that you and your fellow officers have done a good job so far in the Refoule case. I find most other people feel the same way. My writing this letter was prompted

by the statement of the Alston family regarding the work of
the police department, which I feel they well know is not true.
It makes me wonder—do they have something to cover-up?
Keep up the good work in spite of the obstacles.

And a public school teacher:

> We are indeed praying for you. Any traveler in France knows
> that many of the Catholic men in France practice horrible im-
> moralities with boys as well as women. I know all about the
> Catholic pressure and the Alston's family pressure to defeat the
> police investigation and so I say "you all are brave and fine
> men."

At this point both God and prayer are abandoned and the
letters become unprintable: a basketfull of letters written
with crayon; words cut from the newspaper and pasted on post
cards. The letters continued to pour into police headquarters
and into the editorial offices of the newspapers. No letters
either to the papers or the police came in support of Refoule.
However, a crusty Atlanta physician wrote the following letter to the editor of the The Atlanta Constitution. The letter
was not printed.

> Even one accustomed to the tabloid tactics of some of our
> well known Eastern newspapers had to shiver when the Sun-
> day, June 15, 1947, issue of The Atlanta Constitution reached
> his eyes. Since when is the accusation of a man for the "crime"
> of sodomy fit material for a streamer on the front page of a
> great Southern liberal newspaper? Is it because Georgia law
> says sodomy is a crime and carries an automatic life sentence?
> If that outrage is truly Georgia law, then your writers would
> have something to crusade against. They would have their
> work cut out for them, and could spend less time digging into
> the past of Paul Refoule in the most merciless journalistic cru-
> cifixion of recent years. Is it because your writers believe it an
> important clue in the murder of Paul Refoule's wife? Then they
> have committed a double sin, that of accusing a man of murder
> before he is ever [indicted] and of prejudicing the minds of
> countless readers and future jurors. They have screamed the
> premises that (1) Mrs. Refoule was killed by a sex fiend, (2)
> that Paul Refoule is a sex fiend, (3) therefore—they ache to
> print the obvious conclusion. The only flaw is that the judg-
> ment that we are supposed to read between the lines is abso-
> lutely invalid conclusion. Or is it that they actually think that
> sodomy is a sensational and rare piece of news, and that a man

guilty of such a thing is the lowest sort of human being? If that is the case, then for the sake of truth and fair-play please print this: In spite of what Georgia law may state, an "abnormal" act between man and woman is not sodomy. Variations in the relationship between man and woman are exceedingly common, and are not to be confused with "perversions" which imply such grossly abnormal acts as sadism and masochism. Let's not fool ourselves. If we jail everyone who practices "variations" let alone adultery, we may not have many persons left on the outside. At any rate, the testimony of the woman in the case as to "unnatural" acts by Refoule, has nothing to do with sodomy. But if Georgia law insists that it does, why isn't the woman as guilty as Refoule? Everyone ignorant of the subject should read Havelock Ellis' *The Psychology of Sex*. This advice especially applies to newspaper writers who bring such subjects to thousands of readers at random.

On June 18, 1947, the Fulton County Police Department received a letter from Paris, France. The letter was from a Prisoner of War Association. The group did not know to whom to address the letter, so they presented it to the American Embassy in Paris and requested it be forwarded to the proper authorities in America.

The Chairman and members of the Committee of the "Amicale de l'Oflag X11 B' [POW's association] beg to draw your Excellency's attention to the case of their comrade Paul Refoule who for several years was their fellow prisoner and who was not repatriated until 1944, after an attempt to escape which unfortunately failed when he was caught at the Swiss frontier. We beg to state that while Paul Refoule was in Mainz he always behaved in an honest, loyal and straight forward manner. He was also an artist of talent, and very fond of his art. He was in no way addicted to perversion or similar vices. Such vices could not have passed unnoticed by people who shared Paul Refoule's room for many months. We should be most thankful of you if you would forward this letter to the judge who is investigating the case at or near Atlanta, Georgia.

The letter was signed by the eight members of the committee, one of whom was a general. If the letter was ever seen by Refoule or any members of the press, it is doubtful. It was never printed in the newspapers; nor were any members of the French community in Atlanta ever aware of the letter.

The growing animosity between Refoule and the police which had been building ever since the murder now exploded in a rash of charges and countercharges. Refoule greatly feared the police. He wanted to cooperate with them in every way, less they think his lack of cooperation concealed guilt. The three separate marathon interrogations lasting 15, 24, and 30 hours must be a record in the annals of police investigation. Obviously such a police procedure could not have been possible without the willing compliance of Refoule. Nevertheless, that the police would even consider such a procedure, and follow it, says a great deal about police practice at the time. But it was a different era and the police could do things then that they cannot do today. Many people insist that the change in police procedure has created a situation where the guilty are not apprehended and crime increases. Doubtless, Paul Refoule would not agree.

Whereas Refoule feared the police and felt uneasy at finding himself in a difficult situation in a strange country, the police, the public, and the press came to hate him. This is an inescapable conclusion. All the fears and terrors of the time found a scapegoat in Paul Refoule. All the ugliness that had submerged in the years since the Heinz killing surfaced once again. People hated in the Heinz case because it involved a person of wealth. People hated in the Refoule case because it involved an individual married to a person of a prominent family, who happened, coincidentally, to be French, Catholic, and an artist. It was just too much for a Southern Protestant community caught up in the shifting social changes and boom years following World War II. People were terrified. The world was changing too fast. They did not know what to think. Somehow hating Paul Refoule made the world appear simpler than it was. It was something to hold onto, this hate. Another rather unusual letter to the police expressed it well:

> Several months ago an article in the Sunday edition of one of the daily papers in the society section told about the Refoule's plan for remodeling the old Howell Mill. It was a full page article, or longer, and included several pictures of the young couple and of the mill. Here was a Frenchman married to a lovely wife, related to a prominent family in the community, with an interesting profession, an established paying position, settling down to security. Following World War I a great many of our soldiers returned with a thorough dislike (in some instances amounting to hatred) of the French; the same opinion, I regret to say, has been expressed following World War II.
>
> I think it would be wise if the police investigated the follow-

ing theory—a disgruntled, frustrated war veteran or student, not necessarily in Refoule's classes, but close enough to have knowledge of his classes and maybe a man unable to secure a home or prevented by circumstances from marrying, as a person who might be involved in the murder. I don't think Mrs. Refoule was the prime object. He was striking at the Frenchman by destroying his home life. I think this crime was planned far enough back that the killer did not think the threads of continuity could be picked up.

The writer of this letter was also anonymous, but he/she was well aware of the bitterness which existed at the time against Frenchmen, a hatred and bitterness that was being proved by events. Whether the letter has any other significance to the case is pure speculation.

On July 3, 1947, *The Atlanta Journal* carried the first in a series of articles with screaming headlines concerning an increase in sex crimes in the city. The articles were accompanied by strong editorials saying that all sexual perverts must go to prison. As it turned out, the so-called sex crime increase was all a myth. The people of the city were gripped by fear and housewives began to suspect every individual walking down the street of being a dirty old man and quickly rushed the kids indoors and called the cops to report the presence of a sexual pervert in the community. The city went on a binge of hysteria. The fear was there, embedded in the era of time and place, but the Refoule case had pinpointed it, brought it to the surface. It was now summer. People get testier and ultimately more violent in hot weather. But the bitterness generated on all sides by the police investigation of the Refoule case was just beginning. It would become more intense as the summer and hot weather continued.

Tuesday, July 8, 1947. Through his attorney, Hal Lindsay, Paul Refoule went into the U. S. District Court in Atlanta and asked the federal court to issue an injunction to prevent further illegal detention or questioning and at the same time entered a $50,000 damage suit against Chief Ellis, Assistant Chief Fitzgerald, Captain Bradford, and three other Fulton County police officers who had been closely involved in the Refoule case. For the first time, Refoule, upon this occasion, issued a public statement.

I have been accused of murder by the police. This charge is not true and the police know it is not true. They know that reliable witnesses have accounted for every minute of my time on the day of the murder. Instead of accepting this proved fact and making a real search for the murderer they have resorted to the old Nazi trick of accusing a person of sexual perversion if they cannot prove him guilty of some other crime.

The police received an anonymous letter accusing me of sex perversion. This letter was written by a person who may have known the layout of my home. Instead of taking fingerprints of this person from the letter (and he was perhaps the murderer) they smudge up the letter with their own fingerprints and broadcast the accusations contained in it. I am not guilty of murder. I am not guilty of sodomy. I have never confessed to either. I have never said that I did not love my wife.

The damage suit was based on the due process section of the 14th Amendment of the United States Constitution. Refoule declared that the police had violated his civil rights as a U. S. resident. He named 33 points of conspiracy and 60 overt acts in his charges of brutality of a deliberate police campaign of slander, of their refusal to let him have either interpreter or attorney during questioning. He said the police issued false and fraudulent statements which poisoned the mind of the public against him while they were conducting a perfunctory investigation of the murder. Refoule charged that in the May 19 questioning at his Howell Mill Road home he had been struck in the face by Bradford with the sashcord and forced to stand under strong electric lights until he collapsed with exhaustion. Also on this occasion, he claimed, he was repeatedly struck, jabbed, stepped on, elbowed, jerked, grabbed, vilified, cursed, and generally mistreated by his interrogators. He stated that he was forced to stand while being questioned and was not allowed to take his coat off, although the weather was very warm. Refoule maintained that the officers produced pictures of his wife's body and forced him to look at them, all the time accusing him of the murder and trying to get him to confess. Refoule charged that during the interrogation Captain Bradford handed a pistol to him and said:

> You have murdered your wife. Why don't you take this and kill yourself?

And the Assistant Chief (Fitzgerald) told him that if he would confess to the murder they would help him to prove that he was insane and that he could then go back to France. In the questioning at the courthouse on May 25, Refoule charged that he was given similar treatment and that the rope which the police had recovered from the tree on Peachtree Creek that afternoon was put around his neck like a noose and that a police officer twisted the rope around his neck and hit him in the face with the end of the rope. He claimed also that the police told him that if he did not confess to the murder, he would be prosecuted upon a charge of moral perversion, for which he would receive life imprisonment. Refoule also charged in his lawsuit that he was always taken into custody at night, that the police never had a warrant, and that a fake sodomy warrant issued by a justice of the peace was used to threaten him. This police harassment caused him to lose his job at Oglethorpe where he was making $160 a month, $40 a month from the High Museum of Art, and a $100 a month doing paintings and murals on a private contract basis. The Fulton County police officers issued a blanket denial.

JUSTICE DEPARTMENT CITES SEX INDICTMENT: REOPENS REFOULE DEPORTATION PROCEEDINGS

Under that screaming headline on Thursday, July 17, 1947 *The Atlanta Journal* quoted a high justice department "source" which said that because of Refoule's sodomy indictment the department was looking into the possibility of deporting him! The story was somewhat of a hoax. As of yet, Refoule had been convicted of nothing, nor even tried. He had been indicted on a sodomy charge by the Fulton County grand jury, but the case had yet to come to trial. No one appeared to be pushing to bring the case to trial, either.

Due to a continuous stream of vicious and obscene telephone calls, Mrs. Alston had her telephone disconnected. Other relatives and friends came forward to add to the reward to apprehend the killer of Peggy Refoule, and the reward reached a total of $2500, the same as in the Heinz case. The reward was never paid.

The hearing in federal court was set for July 21. The case was put off until July 29 when the defense in the case asked for more time. Spectators had waited in line at the court building most of the night and were already filing into seats in the spectators gallery when the case was postponed.

Wednesday, July 30, 1947. The temperature in Atlanta that day reached 95 degrees by afternoon. In the unairconditioned court room, the temperature was not any cooler. Hundreds of spectators crowded into the building and, those who could

make it, into the courtroom. Everybody came—housewives
with babies, summer school students playing hooky, young
matrons wearing big straw hats, and a scattering of farmers
in overalls looking for a place to spit tobacco juice.

Refoule and his lawyer entered the building by a side entrance and managed to elude the crowd outside. Inside they
had to go up in the regular elevator, and there they were be-
siged by a crowd of screaming teenage girls. Wherever Refoule went, hordes of young girls would follow, much as
though Refoule were some kind of teenage idol or Hollywood
celebrity. Getting off the elevator, a young girl ran up and
touched Refoule on the arm, swooned, and then ran off holler-
ing excitedly: "I touched him! I touched him!!"

The elder Refoules, Paul Refoule's parents, appeared at the
trial. They were not as fortunate as their son in arriving at
the court building for there was some mix-up by the driver of
the car which was bringing them, and for some reason they
were let out in front of the court building instead of at the side
entrance; consequently they had to fight their way through
the crowd of eyeballers clustered in front of the court building. The Refoules were dressed in black and were very somber
and dignified. Mrs. Refoule wore a big black hat and black
shoes and black gloves, and Judge Refoule walked stiffly with
a cane, having suffered a leg injury in France in World War I.
They were a striking couple, and their regal appearance mollified the mob sufficiently for the crowd to move back and
make room to form a path that allowed the Refoules to enter
the building. But there were catcalls and the ever-present
photographers. The Refoules were very much alone. It was an
ordeal for them to have to endure, particularly Mrs. Refoule,
who spoke practically no English. She glared at the hollerers
and jumpers in the crowd which surrounded her and wondered, no doubt, if she had arrived in the land of Oz.

Inside the courtroom, Judge Refoule was introduced to the
court and bowed stiffly before the judge. The presiding judge
had warned the spectators they had better keep quiet, he
would brook no outbursts; so many had to supress their
giggles as Judge Refoule bowed to the court. Paul Refoule and
his parents sat at one table with Paul's attorney; the police
officers sat at a table opposite with their attorneys.

Procedure took up the activities for most of the first day.
Both sides had many long affidavits that had to be included in
the record. In the afternoon the defense called many wit-

nesses—practically everyone who had been interviewed by the police in the Refoule murder investigation. Refoule was suing the Fulton County police for damages and also the bonding companies which had put up bonds for the police. The bonding companies were practically hysterical. The one insuring Captain Bradford wrote him the following letter:

> At your special insistance and request, Maryland Casualty Company executed your official bond as Fulton County police officer effective August 1, 1946 in the penalty of $1,000. As a result of the execution of this bond, Maryland Casualty Company has been sued by Paul Refoule in the District Court of the United States for the Northern District of Georgia for damages in the penalty of our bond. This is to advise you that we are expecting you to hold Maryland Casualty Company harmless for any loss, cost or expenses as a result of the execution of this bond. This is to advise you that in the event any judgment is rendered against Maryland Casualty Company in this case, we will expect you to pay the same.

The motto of this company, as stated on their letterhead, was: "Protect Yourself Against Unforseen Events." Although it was an out-of-state company, the bond was executed through the branch office located in Atlanta. After all the letters from the public telling the police to hang Refoule and what a great job they were doing, this letter to Captain Bradford came as something of a jolt.

Refoule's lawsuit was certainly no joke, and the police did not take it as such. In light of all that had occurred in the Refoule case, the lawsuit had to be looked upon as more than a mere harassment suit. The county attorney and his assistant vigorously defended the five Fulton County police officers accused by Refoule.

Judge Refoule had enough after the first day in court and caught a train for New York that night, and from New York immediately sailed back to France. He had pressing business at home for France was beset with strikes and shortages and a constant change of governments. He wished also to leave the scene of the trial and the oppressive Southern heat. All this together had been too much for the courtly old gentleman. His only comment to the press upon leaving was, "This is a foreign country to me. It has foreign habits and strange customs. I don't know what to think."

The trial continued for several days. The presiding judge in the beginning ruled out testimony on Refoule's love life and sternly told the tittering crowd in the courtroom, "You may now be excused if you so desire. I don't think the proceedings will be of much interest to you from here on out."

Elaine had already told how she had been relentlessly questioned and how the police promised her she would be let off if she would testify against Refoule. Bill Gray testified that the police threatened him and held him incommunicado demanding that he confess to being a sexual pervert. He testified also that the police went to the home of his estranged wife and told her that he (Gray) was a homosexual and tried to force her to make a statement detailing his sex perversions. The allegation in the anonymous note to the police concerning a sex party at the Refoule home on the night of Monday, May 12, 1947, was refuted by Major Durkin, who stated to the court that he and his wife had dinner with the Refoules that night and there could not possibly have been any such party. Many of the art students who testified at the trial stated that the police constantly referred to Refoule as being a man as "guilty as hell" and that they "were going to see that he did not get away with anything."

As the trial in the suit reached its last day, the tide began to turn. The protest and the hate-Refoule mail began to diminish. By the last day the courtroom spectators and reporters had all but vanished. The passions aroused over the Refoule case had about ebbed. Now the police found themselves getting the brunt of public ire. The trial pointed out that indeed the police had overstepped their bounds in their relentless investigation of Refoule. Public pressure and journalistic sensationalism had no doubt pushed the police into excesses that they would have not otherwise fallen prey to in the ordinary murder case and then deserted them. It is very poor policy for the police to bend to public prejudice. It always backfires, and it was doing so now in the Refoule case.

Refoule's attorney had a good case and he presented it well. The legal system created sympathizers for Refoule when the police and press had not. The press, beginning to sniff the change in opinion, began to back off from its former militant stand and began to chide the police for the behavior of their investigators in the case. During the trial, *The Atlanta Constitution* carried an editorial abhoring the behavior of spectators and the carnival-like atmosphere outside the court building and the rather harsh treatment afforded the Refoule parents on opening day. But the newspapers in their zeal had undoubtedly helped create this climate of opinion, this appalling behavior.

The police were not well represented in the courtroom. The county attorneys did their best, but they were so outraged by Refoule that their legal judgment was blinded and they had a difficult time being rational as they presented their defense.

What was the true picture of police practice in the Refoule case? Was Refoule subjected to the treatment he maintained in the suit, or was his affidavit somewhat exaggerated?

All the files and recordings of the case are still available. And they are mountainous. From a close study of these files it appears doubtful that Refoule was actually subjected to any physical threat or harm; that he was constantly subjected and intimidated by oral threats, there can be no doubt. The investigators in the case tape-recorded (the use of tapes was another police *first* in the Refoule case) many of the sessions they held with Refoule and the others. They did this in the hopes of building a murder case against Refoule, but the tapes today do quite the opposite, for they record in exact detail the voices, the words, and the statements of all involved. The eerie sound quality of nearly forty years ago is there on the twirling reels, and there can be no doubt that the police practice in the case was just as Refoule stated. Upon this point, there can be no doubt.

The important point about the police investigation here is that the police and the suspect began to hate each other. Their positions became rigid and polarized, and from two extreme points of view there was no retreat. Neither could really think rationally after awhile nor communicate, and both retreated into armed camps of hate. We see such things happen today. Among groups and among some police there grows and ferments an abiding hatred that can only lead to excesses on the part of both and to the detriment of each. It is not today, nor was it at the time of the Refoule case, a situation which pits the good guys against the bad guys. A retreat to such positions is disastrous.

Most thoughtful people today with knowledge of the Refoule case believe that Refoule was relentlessly persecuted by the police. While this is certainly true, we believe this study of the case creates more understanding of why the police acted as they did—at the same time fully aware it does not excuse such action.

The particular police department involved in the Refoule

case lacked the personnel and experience to handle the case. They were under enormous pressure from the press and the public to reach a quick solution of the case and bent much too easily to the pressure of both. They let their dislike of the suspect influence their investigation of the suspect's involvement with the murder.

Paul Refoule's behavior was influenced by the fact that he considered himself to be guilty of the murder of his wife. Certainly not in the physical sense, but more in a moral or religious sense. Probably Elaine described it best in her statement when she said that "underneath Paul loved his wife and the brutality of it all shocked him out of his mind." This appears to be a very clear observation. Here was a marriage that was undergoing some rough times. The husband was unhappy and had affairs with other women and thought about a divorce—but before anything is resolved one way or the other the wife is brutally murdered. It is a harrowing situation. The husband is overcome with shock and grief—and then guilt, a guilt that grows as what happened begins to sink in. This Catholic Frenchman attempts to purge himself of this guilt by confessing over and over again everything about his life, but which certainly does not include murder.

The problem was that Refoule was confessing to a policeman and not a priest. This made quite a difference in the South of 1947. But it is true, too, that Refoule had to tell the police everything to keep from becoming the prime suspect. But the police did not know who murdered Peggy Refoule, nor did Refoule know who murdered his wife. Neither did anyone else, it would seem.

In October of 1947, Paul Refoule had some good news for a change. The federal judge issued an injunction forbidding the Fulton County police from questioning Refoule further about the case unless he was placed under arrest for murder. It was a moot point, however; the police had not bothered Refoule since he filed the suit against them.

In November of 1947, Paul Refoule had some bad news. At the request of Solicitor General Paul Webb, who said he was unable to bring a key witness to Atlanta (the art student, Pat Sue), the morals charged against Paul Refoule was *nolle prossed* by the Fulton County superior court. Pat Sue had left the state to join her husband, who was still in the service, and refused to come back to Atlanta to testify; and the court was reluctant to force her to do so. After all the hue and cry this testimony of Pat Sue's was the only evidence against Refoule on the sodomy charge, and there was nothing the authorities could do but drop the case. They were secretly relieved for they had no case and the last thing they wanted was to go to trial. Refoule issued the following statement:

During the bereavement, humiliation, mental, and physical suffering which I have striven uncomplainingly to endure since the death of my dear wife on May 14, 1947, her mother, and grandmother and other members of my wife's family have stood loyally by me. Knowing that at the time of my wife's death I was teaching my art class at Oglethorpe University miles away and that I could not and would not have done the murder, they employed counsel for me. Each promptly made and signed statements of such pertinent facts as were within his or her knowledge. Many other persons, some of whom were friends, others acquaintances and still others who had been strangers to me until that time, did likewise. Motivated solely by a desire to see justice done, they have remained unshaken in their adherence to truth and doubt as to my innocence of the murder now exists only in the minds of those to whom the facts have not been made available, or who will not take the trouble to inform themselves.

This morning the sodomy charge against me was dismissed upon motion of the solicitor general over the objection of my counsel and in the face of my demand for trial which has been on file for many weeks. While I appreciate this action by the solicitor, my demand for trial stands and upon expiration of the present and next succeeding terms of Fulton Superior Court, my counsel will ask for the judgment of acquittal to which I shall be entitled under the law. In his statement to the court, when he presented his motion for dismissal of the charge against me, the solicitor stated that law enforcement officers have my confession in their files. Anyone familiar with methods then in vogue in interrogations by the police, but since, I am told, much modified and improved by court actions, will understand that, when threats and physical violence are employed, there is no such thing as a confession and no statement so obtained can be used in evidence. Had this absurd charge been tried before a jury, I feel confident that there would have been a speedy acquittal.

To those who, at personal sacrifice of time and often their own expense, have lent their assistance, to those who have written and spoken their words of cheer and confidence, to *The Atlanta Journal*, which had endeavored to present the facts fairly and accurately, my father, my mother, my small son, and I give thanks. To us, these are America.

One of those whom Refoule was thanking for lending assistance was Atlanta author Margaret Mitchell. She had spoken out publicly on Refoule's behalf and had pleaded with her former colleagues at *The Atlanta Journal* to report the Refoule case less sensationally.

The authorities had the last say. Since they knew they had no chance of conviction, they refused to bring the case to trial. In the minds of many people Refoule was still guilty. He had been denied the right to prove himself innocent.

At this point, Refoule was too ill for further protest. Shortly thereafter he entered the hospital and underwent two operations for kidney stones and hernia. While he was in the hospital, doctors discovered that he had a cancerous lung and removed it. Two weeks later he was suffering from pneumonia.

RELEASE

On February 13, 1948, Paul Refoule went into a coma and died. It was but one day from being nine months after the death of his wife. Thus ended a troubled life of adventure and story-book romance set amid a background of war and its aftermath. Paul Refoule was a man of the era. He was a victim of the times in which he lived.

People who knew Refoule felt that he was so weakened by all that he endured at the hands of the police that nothing could have saved him. At the time of his death, the suit for $50,000 against the Fulton County Police Department was still pending.

There was much bitterness engendered by the Refoule case. For many, even death did not free Refoule from public denunciation, and there was widespread comment that Refoule's priest should be made to take a lie detector test, to prove Refoule guilty! For minds so encased in prejudice, Refoule *had* to be guilty of this crime. They could never believe otherwise. The bitterness toward the Alston family and their friends, of Refoule's friends, and of the artistic and intellectual community in Atlanta was just as intense. The aftermath of the case remained a part of the Atlanta scene.

But very quickly times move on and things change. Two years after the Refoule case, the two Atlanta newspapers were merged into a single corporation. This altered reporting procedure in such cases. There was no longer the keen competition between two papers to see which could get the more sensational stories. Reporting of such crimes became more balanced, and this helped a great deal in future cases. The Refoule case had an enormous effect upon police procedure in the community and was one of the principal reasons that the Fulton County Police Department was dismantled upon implementation of the Plan of Improvement in 1952.

This leads us back to where we began: Who murdered Peggy Alston Refoule? To this day most Atlantans don't really know what to make of the murder of Peggy Refoule. It was, and remains, one of Atlanta's most baffling murder mysteries. Even when all the sensationalism regarding the investigation of Refoule and the attendant publicity is discounted, the case itself is certainly not your run-of-the-mill homicide. There are several theories concerning the case.

SUMMATION

First of all, some people still believe that Refoule was somehow implicated in his wife's death, and that if he was not the actual killer he was engaged in a conspiracy to murder his wife. After a prolonged and extensive review of the case—which involved interviewing countless numbers of people—there remains no evidence linking Refoule with any kind of conspiracy; and any impartial investigator must conclude that those who still insist on implicating Refoule will not or cannot separate in their minds the act of murder from what is, to them, a peculiar life-style and/or profession, and probably for some the two can never be really separated. The fact is that there is no evidence linking Paul Refoule with the murder.

Secondly, many people feel that the murder of Peggy Refoule was committed by someone who was unknown to either her or her husband, and that the motive was burglary, as in the Heinz case. They point out that had the police spent as much time looking for this person or tracking down the items stolen from the Refoule home as they did in investigating Paul Refoule's sex life, they would have come up with the murderer. This is a legitimate point. However, we believe it can be said for the police that they did not exclusively limit their number of suspects to Refoule. Every person who could have possibly been considered a likely suspect was investigated by the police in the beginning or after the death of Refoule. As late as 1957 investigators of the solicitor general's office traveled to Philadelphia, Pennsylvania, to interview a person who might be considered a suspect. But critics point out that when the police started investigating Refoule they turned their attention away from a search for the missing jewelry—which was the best evidence in the case. If the motive for the murder was burglary, the murderer would have tried to sell the stolen items eventually. It is true the rings were very distinctive. But it is also true that many police departments were on the lookout for the missing rings and none ever turned up. Maybe the murderer was so frightened by the uproar of the case that he hid them away somewhere and never tried to get rid of them.

Critics lambast the police for failing to search the house for fingerprints, as was done by Atlanta police in the Heinz case. The police answer to this was that the house was so overrun by people that such an effort would have been futile.

A very strong case can be made for the burglar theory. It has been supposed that Mrs. Refoule finished her ironing and went outdoors, returned, and surprised the burglar and he killed her because she could identify him. An extension of this theory is that the murderer had the house under surveillance for a long time and that when the guests left that day and Refoule departed, the killer knew that Mrs. Refoule was alone, entered the house and killed her, and then burglarized the house. The house was so constructed that a person looking in the windows could see practically everything. The Refoules had moved into an area frequented by lovers along the dirt road in back of the house. It should be pointed out that although the dirt road along the creek was used as a lovers' lane, there were no reports to the police of anyone being molested or attacked in the area either before or after the Refoule murder.

Most investigators do not believe that Peggy Refoule was murdered in the house but that she finished her ironing, decided to go for a stroll along the creek bank, and was waylaid and then strangled to death by being hung from the tree. Since the body was found in the creek, it is far more likely she was killed near the creek. It just does not seem probable that she could be murdered in the house and then removed from it. Certainly she was not dragged from the house. And if she was murdered there and removed by automobile, then it would have been a very risky thing for the murderer not to be observed. But if she was murdered along the creek bank, then the slayer had to come up to the house afterwards (probably while the victim was hanging from the tree branch) and burglarize the residence. Then, how did he get the sashcord? If it was a part of the left-over clothesline, it means he had to have been in the house before the murder. Maybe he had stolen the items from the house prior to the murder and had returned to the scene for some reason. Could the reason be to lie in wait near the creek and surprise and sexually assault the owner of the rings? This does not appear likely, for although the victim's underpants were removed, she was not raped.

Thirdly, some people believe that the person who wrote the anonymous letter accusing Refoule of being a sexual pervert killed Peggy Refoule. An elaboration of this theory is that the murderer hung the clothesline in the tree after the slaying to make Refoule appear guilty. If an examination of the case reveals nothing else, it makes plain that the Frenchman was hated. The question is: Was he hated enough by one person so much that this person killed Peggy and then tried to frame Refoule for the murder? This seems a rather bizarre assumption. The fact remains that the murder was committed on May 14 and the rope was not found until May 24, ten days later. During that time many police officers had gone over the area but the rope was not discovered, even though it was hanging from a tree branch over the area only eight feet from the ground.

Was Peggy Refoule killed by hanging? Even if we knew the answer it probably would not solve the case. Most investigators think the rope was the real murder weapon, that the victim was strangled by being hanged from the limb of the tree. This conclusion is based on the evidence that the tree limb showed that it supported considerable weight and that the mark on the victim's neck indicated upward pull.

Some people believed that the person who wrote the anonymous letter was somehow a member or in-law of the Alston family. This certainly is not very likely. There were many rumors circulated that Peggy's brother and mother were somehow involved with Refoule. This absurdity doesn't bear even repeating, except that it was discovered in investigating the case that many people still firmly believe it.

If anyone, indeed probably the only person closely involved in the case, emerges nearly 40 years later as a heroine, it would have to be Peggy's mother, Mrs. Alston; for regardless

of the most vicious public opinion and police pressure, she refused to be swayed or intimidated; and if she had not believed
in Refoule's innocence, it is doubtful that anyone in Atlanta
would have. It is also an inescapable conclusion that (1) had
Peggy Refoule's mother not believed in Refoule's innocence
and spoken up for him and (2) had not Refoule been teaching
at the time of the murder and had an airtight alibi, he would
probably have been lynched. Not to consider lynching a possibility is to inaccurately read the signs of the times and to
underestimate the fear and hatred generated by the Refoule
case.

Finally, can we rule out the writer of the anonymous note
as being the murderer? Quite frankly, we cannot. We can say
only that it is not probable. Most likely the person who wrote
the note was a person, like countless others of the time, who
was swept up in the hysteria which surrounded everything
concerning Refoule. It is even possible that the note writer
sincerely believed in what the note said, i.e., he honestly
thought or had heard that Refoule was a sexual pervert and
that being such probably killed his wife. If the note, taken in
context, can therefore be considered honest and not a ploy of
some nature, then, as far as the murder is concerned, it becomes unimportant.

Unfortunately a review of the Refoule case raised more
questions than it answers. One would think that after nearly
40 years, an impartial investigation of the facts and an interview of people involved would turn up a generally agreed
upon chain of events.

It is logical to assume that Peggy Refoule was murdered
incidental to and preceding or following a burglary of her
home. Whether she was murdered in her home or along the
creek bank becomes beside the point, for it was not a Cain-
Abel homicide but a murder committed because the victim
could identify the burglar. If this is what occurred, then all
the other doubts in the case must arise from the temper of the
times—that is within the life and times of Paul and Peggy
Refoule—and the foreign, Catholic background of the main
person involved. It is interesting that of all the people in the
neighborhood the hand of fate reached down and touched the
artist and his wife. To put it simply: If Mr. Refoule had been
Mr. Rice, a bank executive, who was a traditional Southern
Protestant who lived in a typical house of the time with vene-

tian blinds and lace curtains, his wife would have had less chance of being murdered; but he was not, and he chose to live in an unconventional house (for the time and place) and to follow a different line of work; so, in this context, his life and work probably did contribute to this tragedy. Whether or not it was because of this or was premeditated, remains a mystery to this day. Whatever, the killer is still unknown.

The Refoule home suffered the same fate as the Heinz house. Nobody wanted to live in the murder house. The Alston family, anxious to be rid of it, had a difficult time disposing of it. The home changed hands several times and suffered much personal and architectural abuse. Some twenty years after the murder, a very lovely lady, herself an artist, gained possession of the house and restored it in a way fitting the plan and design that Paul Refoule had in mind. The present owner wonders if the young couple who once had a vision of converting an old woolen mill into a home, should they come back to the present day, would they be pleased with the house? Probably so, very much.

It is not a fallacy to conclude that because Paul and Peggy Refoule were people very much ahead of their time their lives were plagued by tragedy, and the Refoule case is an absorbing revelation of how much our institutions and Atlanta has changed in the years since. At the time of the Refoule murder, Atlanta was little more than a small town in the heartland of the Bible belt.

The atmosphere of Atlanta is quite different today. Paul and Peggy Refoule would feel very much at home. Living in their old mill house, which is now engulfed by suburbia, they would be, but for another day, a charming middle-aged couple who would no doubt find the Atlanta of the 1980s a very exciting place in which to live, for they were a part of all that is now present-day Atlanta many years ago.

1947. The Refoule case. These were the times that we look back to nostalgically and fondly recall as the good old days. It comes as something of a shock to realize that the rose garden was not without its thorns.

4

Farm Wife Jeanette Reyman

The homicide rate in Atlanta and the nation reached all-time highs in the years immediately following World War II. In 1946 Georgia had one of the highest homicide rates of any state in the nation. In 1947 Atlanta led the nation in having more murders per capita than any other United States city. On the outskirts of town, along lonely streets, and in placid neighborhoods, women no longer went out unescorted and carefully kept their windows locked and their doors bolted, day and night. In Buckhead, the hardware store that sold the clothesline to Paul Refoule was now selling guns to many of his neighbors. Two lurid murders had terrorized Atlanta and made people afraid. The first of these murders was the strangulation death of Peggy Refoule and the second was the bludgeoning to death of Jeanette Reyman.

In February of 1947, Mr. and Mrs. Raleigh M. Reyman had moved from their home in Winchester, Indiana, and settled in Bogart, Georgia, a small town some 60 miles from Atlanta on the highway from Athens to Atlanta. They had bought an old farm and were in the process of erecting on a part of it a tourist court, which was a modest predecessor of today's motels. At 8 o'clock on the morning of June 25, 1947, the attractive, blonde Jeanette Reyman got into the family pickup truck and drove to Atlanta. Her errand was to purchase supplies for the restaurant and motor court she and her husband were building in Oconee County.

Jeanette Reyman had a busy shopping day in mind as she drove to Atlanta, but awaiting her in the city was a bizarre death, a brutal slaying that would erupt into one of the state's most sensational murder trials, and yet remain a clouded mystery to this very day. The death of Jeanette Reyman was all the more shocking because it followed by only six weeks the slaying of Peggy Refoule. Investigators would find many strange parallels in the Peachtree Creek murder and the death of Mrs. Reyman.

Both women were slain on Wednesday afternoons, both women were the same age and rather similar in appearance, and both women had one young son of approximately the same age. Peggy Refoule died from stangulation and Jeanette Reyman by bludgeoning. The feet of both victims were bound together, Mrs. Refoule's by her shoelaces and Mrs. Reyman by one-half-inch hemp rope. In addition, Mrs. Reyman's wrists were bound together behind her back with rubber insulated wire. A portion of both women's underwear was missing when the bodies were found, and Jeanette Reyman had been raped. The slayers of both women were bold to the point of being foolhardy. Perhaps the most pronounced similarity in the two cases is that both murders remain unsolved.

At 10 o'clock on the morning of June 25th, Jeanette Reyman reached Atlanta. She made purchases at various stores and then had lunch. She was last seen at 2:30 p.m. at the Sears store on Ponce de Leon Avenue, where she made a purchase in the housewares department. When Jeanette Reyman did not return to Bogart that night, her husband and brother went to Atlanta searching for her.

At 5 o'clock on the afternoon of the 25th, a black pickup truck pulled up in front of the Standard Coffee Company at 247 Moreland Avenue—just as the employees of the company were leaving for the day. Two employees noticed the truck and thought it might be someone making a delivery to the coffee company. They noticed a heavyset man of medium height get out of the truck and walk around to the rear of the truck, adjust and tighten some ropes, then walk away. About a half an hour later two more employees of the coffee company left the building and noticed the truck. One man said he saw blood coming out of the end of the truck but that his companion only laughed and said that it was just red paint and that he had been reading too much about murder in the newspaper lately. When these same employees returned to work the next day and found the same truck parked in front of their building, they grew suspicious and began to investigate. In the rear of the truck, they discovered the body of Jeanette Reyman.

When police arrived on the scene, they discovered that Mrs. Reyman's body had been wrapped in a green quilt, which was now blood soaked. The restaurant stools she had purchased the day before had been piled on top of the body. The keys to the trunk (a large traveling trunk in the back of the truck) were missing, as was Mrs. Reyman's pocketbook. She had left Bogart the day before with $85 in cash, two blank checks, and a $15 money order. The checks were used to buy supplies for the restaurant, but she should have had most of the cash with her. It appeared as though robbery might possibly be a motive for the slaying. The police went over the truck carefully for fingerprints, but were ultimately unable to produce anything that was significant.

Since the victim's pocketbook was missing, there was no way to identify the body. All the police had to go on was the truck with an Indiana license plate. The husband and brother of the victim were having breakfast at a diner on the highway from Athens. They had spent most of the night searching for Mrs. Reyman, and then returned to Bogart about daylight to see if she had returned. When they discovered she had not, the two men drove again to Atlanta. After stopping for breakfast, they heard over the radio that the body of an unidentified woman had been found in Atlanta near the Sears store. They knew that Jeanette had been in that vicinity the day before. They drove rapidly to the police station in Atlanta. At the morgue, Raleigh Reyman identified the body as being that of his wife.

The Reyman slaying was the first big case to break within the city limits of Atlanta after Herbert Jenkins had become chief of the Atlanta Police Department. Coming on the heels of the much-publicized Refoule case, the murder had wide press coverage.

A reorganization of the detective department within the Atlanta Police Department was one of the first official acts of the new chief. Under the reorganization, the detective force was divided into five squads or specialties—all under the overall direction of Detective Superintendent E. I. Hilderbrand. The number one squad was the homicide group under command of Lieutenant Coppenger, a veteran homicide expert. It was he who was in charge of the investigation of the Reyman case.

It was quickly determined that Jeanette Reyman was not killed where the body was found, but that the truck had been merely parked there after the murder had been committed. The first thing the police tried to do was locate the murder scene. Miles of area, stretching over two counties, were covered by detectives and police officers who rode in cars and walked on foot in an attempt to discover the spot where Mrs. Reyman met her death. But to no avail. Detectives fanned out over the city and talked with everyone who saw Mrs. Reyman that day. They determined that she knew no one in Atlanta except business acquaintances. The police questioned people in both Bogart and Athens in an attempt to find out something about the Reymans. All the reports indicated that the couple was well liked and had a fine reputation in the community where they lived—although they had been in the area only a short time.

An autopsy upon the body of Jeanette Reyman indicated that death was caused by a blow to the head that completely crushed the left side of the skull. The medical examination also bore out the fact that Mrs. Reyman had been sexually assaulted.

A man reported to the police that he saw a pickup truck similar to Mrs. Reyman's turn off Ponce de Leon Avenue into a side road described as a perfect lovers' lane. The man reported this happened late Wednesday afternoon. A search by police of the area failed to turn up the murder site. A Marietta, Georgia, man, in town on business the day of the 25th, told police that he had seen a heavyset man driving a truck bearing an Indiana tag around 5 o'clock on Wednesday afternoon. He said he noticed the truck had an Indiana license plate and that it looked very much like one he had sold about a year ago. The man was alone in the truck driving along Forrest Road near Sears. Scores of Atlanta police and detectives joined in searching the wooded area in the vicinity, and casts were made of tire tracks found in the area for matching against the tire tracks of the death truck. But once again, these efforts were to no avail. The police were unable to pinpoint the crime scene.

A clerk at the Sears store, the last person known by police to have seen Mrs. Reyman alive, insisted that she was accompanied by a heavyset man who advised her regarding several purchases. He said the two people were together and left his department together.

Police determined that Mrs. Reyman had been married once before, and that her son was born of that earlier union. The police began a search for her former husband, who turned up in California, where he was then living. It was determined that he had never been in Atlanta.

SUSPECTS QUESTIONED

A twenty-year-old dishonorably discharged army man was arrested for an attempted assault upon a young female employee of Western Union. She was going home on the streetcar late at night when the man followed her off the streetcar and stuck a gun in her back and tried to force her into an alley. She cooly replied that she knew a better place, and as they walked along they were soon in front of the young woman's home. The young lady began screaming at the top of her voice and kicking her would-be assailant in the shins, and the man quickly fled. The young woman's brother came running out of the house and the two of them jumped into his automobile. They pursued the assailant for several blocks and then leaped from the car and tackled him. The two sat on top of their prey while someone sent for the police; then they awaited the bluecoats' arrival and took the man into custody. The young lady stated she was tired of women being assaulted and murdered, and she was determined it was not going to happen to her. It just made her mad, she stated. Upon investigation by police it was determined that the former service man had nothing to do with either the Reyman or Refoule murders.

Police questioned a heavyset man concerning the Reyman slaying. The police had received a tip that such a person had been seen driving the Reyman pickup truck the day of the murder. The suspect was located and taken in for questioning on Thursday, July 3, 1947. On Friday, he was questioned in a 14-hour session by police. During the course of the questioning, officers were able to place the man within four blocks of the spot where the body was found—within an hour after the pickup truck was abandoned.

The man was identified as William Autry, a white male, aged 43, a cook in a local bakery. On Thursday he had been identified by the Marietta businessman as the person seen driving the pickup truck with an Indiana license tag. The Marietta man had picked Autry out of a lineup at the police station. He was not entirely sure of the man's identity from the full-face view of the lineup, and the Mariettan asked officers to have the man turn so he could get a profile view. As soon as this was done, he made his identification, sure that Autry was the man. Another witness viewed Autry in the lineup, and he told police that he was sure that Autry was the man he had seen driving the Reyman truck the day of the murder.

The police had a murder warrant drawn up against Autry but did not charge him with the murder—mainly because they had no other evidence except the identification by the two witnesses to link Autry with the murder. Police determined that Autry had been married twice, for the second time just recently, and members of his first wife's family said he frequently visited her home after the divorce over her protests. They supplied police with information they said was brought out in the divorce suit charging that Autry had many girl friends, and "quite a way with women." Autry insisted that he was innocent and said that he would take a lie detector test—such tests being much in the headlines since the Refoule case. Autry stated he would cooperate with the police in every way.

On Monday, July 7, Autry was allowed to call his wife and attorney. Since the previous Thursday he had been held virtually incommunicado while the police tried desperately to tie him with the murder. On Tuesday, the press was allowed to interview Autry. This was the same day that Paul Refoule filed his suit in federal court against the Fulton County police. The effects that the Refoule case would have upon police procedures, for the present and in the future, were beginning to be felt.

Autry stated to the press that he had done absolutely nothing wrong and was innocent of the murder charge. He said that the police had treated him all right and that he had not been abused physically. But he complained he could not call his wife or attorney until today and had not been allowed to shave. Autry said that he was born near Covington, Georgia, and had been in Atlanta working as a cook and a baker for the past 27 years—except for the time he spent in the army, seven months during World War II. He stated that he used to work near the police station, and some of the policemen had been very nice to him. He said that he had nothing on his conscience and that he was worried about his wife and mother. Autry's attorney stated to the press that he was filing a writ of habeas corpus to get Autry released. Autry's wife said she and her husband had just returned from a four-day honeymoon trip to Asheville, North Carolina, when the police picked up her husband. During the honeymoon, Mrs. Autry recalled there was no mention by her husband of the Reyman case and that he was not nervous on the trip, did not read the Atlanta newspapers, and slept well. He did not act like a man with something on his conscience. Mrs. Autry had her own ideas about why her husband was being held on suspicion of murder. She said there was another man who wanted to marry her before she married Autry, and she was positive this was the man who phoned the tip to police which first implicated her husband in the murder. It was just jealousy. Mrs. Autry developed this theory when she realized that nobody charged her husband with the slaying or with suspicion of murder until Autry married her.

Detectives checked and rechecked the information that caused them to detain Autry in the first place. There was absolutely no firm evidence linking Autry with the case, and in the face of a writ of habeas corpus filed by Autry's attorney, the police released Autry from custody. He was never charged with the murder.

On July 17, 1947, detectives Sikes and Mullen, who had been assigned to the investigation of the Reyman case the week before, took into custody a 29-year-old taxicab driver named Glenn Robinson. The detectives learned that Robinson had formerly been a resident of Athens, where he worked as a carpenter. He had been employed by the Reymans some months before in helping in the building of the motor court and restaurant at Bogart. In that week, the officers made five different trips to Athens and Bogart, interviewing witnesses who knew both Robinson and the Reymans. In these trips they felt they had learned enough about Robinson to book him for suspicion in the Reyman murder. The cab driver had long been a suspect in the case, but he gave the police a good alibi for the afternoon of June 25, the day of the slaying. By hard work detectives Sikes and Mullen had broken the alibi and determined that Robinson was not driving his taxicab that day between the hours of 1 and 5:30 p.m. as he stated to the police the first time he was questioned. The inability to substantiate his alibi was the most damning evidence against Robinson and would remain so throughout the investigation of the murder.

INDICTMENT

On July 25, 1947, Glenn Robinson was indicted by the Fulton County grand jury for murder in connection with the death June 25 of Mrs. Jeanette Reyman. Robinson had spent a week in jail before the indictment was issued. The formal charge of murder was lodged against him just minutes before a scheduled habeas corpus hearing demanding Robinson's release was to be held. Immediately after the murder charge was made the habeas corpus hearing was dismissed, and Robinson was held in Fulton Tower jail without bond.

Detectives Sikes and Mullen stated that there were three major breaks that led to the action. The first of these was the apparent breaking of an alibi which had purported to show Robinson was on duty in his cab on the afternoon of the slaying. Originally a cab company official had stated that Robinson had been working during that period; however, a signed statement from the owner of the cab company stated that company records showed that Robinson was off duty from noon the day of the murder until 5:30 p.m, which would have allowed him time to kill Mrs. Reyman.

The second break in the case was the discovery of bloodstained khaki pants in the Robinson home. The detectives stated that the suspect had previously denied owning a pair of khaki trousers. On a second search of Robinson's home the officers found a pair which had just been returned from the cleaners. Stains on the waistband of the pants were analyzed by Dr. Herman Jones, head of the Fulton County Crime Laboratory, and declared to be human blood stains.

The third and most dramatic break was the identification of Robinson by a person who said he saw the man with Mrs. Reyman the day of the slaying. This was the clerk at the Sears store who waited upon Mrs. Reyman and sold her two kitchen knives. The clerk picked Robinson out of a lineup as the man who accompanied her to the store that day. In actual fact, the investigation of Robinson was far from complete, but the action of Robinson's attorneys in seeking a writ of habeas corpus had forced the police to either indict him or release him as a suspect.

When confronted with the evidence, Robinson admitted to the police that he did not drive his taxicab the day of the murder, as he had previously told police. He refused to say where he was during this time. In fact, during all the interrogation of Robinson, he behaved exactly the opposite from Paul Refoule. He answered most questions put to him by the police with a curt yes or no and volunteered no other information; to some he replied, "I don't know."

TRIAL

On September 15, 1947, Glenn Robinson went on trial for murder. The defense asked for a change of venue in the case. Robinson's lawyers claimed that their client could not possibly get a fair trial because of all the unfavorable newspaper accounts of the case. The motion for a change of venue was denied by Judge Frank Hooper. The first bitter exchange in the trial between Solicitor General Paul Webb and Defense Attorney Al Henson came over the testimony of G. D. Hawks of Bogart. Mr. Hawks was a witness for the state. He had worked with Robinson on construction of the motor court. He testified that Robinson said on three occasions that he liked Mrs. Reyman and sure would like to have sexual relations with her. Henson objected to this testimony, but Judge Hooper allowed it when Webb stated that the state would prove that the slaying of Mrs. Reyman was a sex crime.

The husband of the murder victim was the second witness for the state. He testified that Robinson was employed by him in building the tourist court for a period of sixty days. He testified that Robinson knew his wife and that Robinson drove him (Mr. Reyman) to Winchester, Indiana, upon two occasions. Mr. Reyman said he had never had any trouble with Robinson and that he quit working for him voluntarily—Robinson just did not show up for work one morning and Reyman did not hear from him again. Mrs. Reyman's brother testified upon cross-examination by the defense, that he never noticed any undue attention paid to Mrs. Reyman by Robinson. Mr. Reyman had testified to the same thing earlier. Mrs. Robinson, wife of the defendant, and their three small children were in the courtroom at all times. The children were attractive and well behaved. The jury could not help but notice. The Robinsons were also expecting a fourth child, as Mrs. Robinson was obviously pregnant.

When the trial was resumed after the luncheon recess, the clerk at the Sears store identified Robinson as the man he saw with Mrs. Reyman in the housewares department between 2 and 2:30 p.m. on June 25. He testified that he sold Mrs. Reyman two kitchen knives. He noticed her companion because he discussed with her the good qualities of hollow ground knives. He said they were in the department about five minutes. The Marietta businessman testified that he noticed the pickup truck in which Mrs. Reyman's body was found because it was similar to one he himself had owned. He said he only caught a glimpse of the driver and picked out Robinson as the driver. On cross-examination Defense Attorney Henson confronted the Mariettan with the testimony at a coroner's inquest when he identified William Autry as driver of the death truck. The Mariettan said that he had picked Autry out of the police lineup and was never positive that he was the driver. He further admitted he could not be positive Robinson had been the driver.

As the trial of Robinson entered its second day in Fulton superior court, the courtroom was jammed by the largest crowd ever to try and get into a murder trial. Robinson was accompanied again in court by his wife and three small daughters.

Dr. Herman Jones identified a pair of trousers which the state claimed were worn by the taxi driver as having been stained by human blood. Dr. Jones stated that the victim had been sexually assaulted. Then, Detective Sikes took the witness stand. His appearance provoked a lively exchange between defense counsel and Solicitor Webb. Judge Hooper instructed both lawyers not to exchange words directly. Detective Sikes was on the witness stand for one hour. Most of the time was spent in replying to the defense counsel's charge that he had arrested Robinson to get his name in the newspapers. Sikes denied this. He stated that he questioned Robinson as to whether the latter owned a pair of khaki pants, which the Sears clerk Monday had said were worn by a male companion of Mrs. Reyman. Robinson denied owning such a pair of pants. He further testified that he then returned to Robinson's home and found Mrs. Robinson packing a trunk. Mrs. Robinson voluntarily started through the trunk, looking for khaki clothing, and there was discovered a pair of khaki pants, which Dr. Jones identified as bearing human bloodstains.

Cross-examined by Defense Counsel Henson, Sikes denied

that he had grilled Robinson severely without giving him an opportunity to see his counsel or his wife. Sikes stated that Mrs. Robinson visited her husband a day before he had been placed in jail.

The trial of Robinson took its most sensational turn on the third day when a defense witness identified another man in the courtroom as being the person who parked the death truck in front of the Standard Coffee Company on Moreland Avenue. M. A. Manus was testifying to the court that he had identified a former suspect as the driver of the truck in which Mrs. Reyman's body was found. Defense Counsel Henson asked: "And when is the last time you saw this man?" Mr. Manus replied: "I reckon it was in the courtroom this morning." The audience murmured in surprise. Defense counsel then asked that a man he identified as William Autry, the same man who was questioned by police for several days in the Reyman case, be brought into the courtroom. A tall man wearing a blue suit was brought to the railing and stood uncomfortably as the crowd in the courtroom gaped at him. It was Autry.

"Is this the man you saw leave the truck?" defense counsel demanded.

"Yes sir, that is the man," Mr. Manus replied positively. Autry was then led from the stunned courtroom. It was a typical "Perry Mason" maneuver and the crowd enjoyed the stunt. The judge rapped for order. Defense counsel then made a motion for a direct verdict of acquittal. He said that all the evidence presented by the state thus far was purely circumstantial and that it was insufficient to convict Robinson of the brutal crime, even had he accompanied Mrs. Reyman to the Sears store on the afternoon of her death. Judge Hooper overruled the motion.

The state rested its case. The defense immediately called three Sears clerks to the stand and they all testified they had seen Mrs. Reyman around noon on the day she was slain and that she was alone. Lt. Coppenger, head of the homicide bureau, told the jury that three persons identified Mr. Autry as the man who parked the bloody death truck.

A woman dressed in black appeared in the crowded courtroom carrying a loaded pistol in a cellophane bag and demanded that she be allowed to testify. She claimed to have seen two men in the Reyman truck and stated she had to carry a pistol because the two men had made threats against her. She had followed the trial avidly, but the judge told her sternly that if she made any further disturbance, he would have her permanently ejected. No effort was made to relieve her of her weapon!

J. D. Farlow, official of the taxicab company which employed Robinson, testified he left Robinson shortly after 1 p.m. on June 25 near the Kimball House Hotel. He stated he saw Robinson again about 5:30 p.m. the same day, and then cruised about in a cab with Robinson until about 9:30 p.m. Robinson showed no signs of emotional strain, he testified.

Robinson then took the stand in his own behalf. He denied emphatically that he knew anything about the slaying of Jeanette Reyman. "I am not guilty," he said. "I have a wife and kids and have no time for other women. I worked that day until 2:30 p.m. and then got another man to work for me while I went to the Kimball House and took a bath. I then went to Crump's Restaurant where I met my nephew and his wife. I spent an hour with them, talking about going into the army. I left Crump's about 4:15. I knew nothing about the murder until the next day. I had worked for the Reymans and liked them." Defense Counsel Henson then closed the case for the defense.

Solicitor General Webb, although he had closed for the state earlier, asked to be allowed to offer another witness. His request was granted and he put Roy Chandler, a clothier, on the stand. Chandler surprised the defense by testifying Robinson called for his new cab driver's uniform close to 6 p.m. on June 25, the day of the murder. Chandler said Robinson, dressed in a khaki uniform and apparently in a hurry, came into his shop and took the uniform off the rack, went to the rear of the shop, put on the new uniform, and walked out.

On the following day, the state asked for the death penalty without a recommendation for mercy for Glenn Robinson. The state asked the jury to show Robinson the same mercy that was shown Mrs. Reyman when she was brutally slain.

The defense had a lengthy summation. Robinson's attorney declared that the precipitant test for blood could not be relied upon after such stains had been submitted to dry cleaning and steam pressing, and that the trousers·in question had been cleaned twice before they were examined. Defense counsel attacked the testimony of Dr. Herman Jones to the effect that the Fulton County Crime Laboratory was several years behind—but quickly apologized upon receiving a frown from the bench and an objection from the state. Robinson sat impassively throughout the entire trial, his face a mask. When witnesses gave damaging testimony, he showed not the slightest emotion. His wife and three young daughters sat in the courtroom every day.

The murder case went to the jury at 9:40 a.m. on Friday, following a full week of testimony. At 3:30 p.m. the panel came out and the foreman told the court that the vote stood eight for guilty with recommendation for mercy and four for outright acquittal. The four who stood for acquittal, the foreman declared, had said they would not change their minds until a certain place froze over. The judge then sent the jury back to continue its deliberations and strive to reach an accord, and at this time the defense moved for a mistrial. The motion was denied.

Two hours later the court summoned the panel to the courtroom again and found the jurors still divided. Judge Hooper then declared a mistrial and dismissed the jury. As the jury stood, eight of the twelve men who heard the cab driver tried for the murder of Jeanette Reyman favored conviction with a life sentence. Such a sentence would have been mandatory on the court on a verdict of guilty with a recommendation for mercy. The other four jurors held out for acquittal.

ORDEAL PROLONGED

On October 21, 1947, Glenn Robinson went on trial the second time for the murder of Jeanette Reyman. Judge Frank Hooper, who presided at the initial trial, was again presiding. Detective Sikes was the first witness for the state. He testified that Robinson had been picked out of the police lineup as the man seen with Mrs. Reyman when she was at the Sears store. Sikes stated that a Sears clerk had identified Robinson and that Robinson turned pale but kept silent when the clerk put his hand on Robinson's arm and said: "That is the man."

Defense Attorney Henson cross-examined Sikes and asked him if he had ever seen anybody accused of murder who did not turn pale. Sikes said he thought he had not but insisted that accused prisoners generally made immediate denials.

Henson then brought out that Sikes began the investigation which resulted in Robinson's arrest 20 days after the crime—after other detectives had made other investigations.

The second witness to take the stand was Raleigh Reyman. He gave essentially the same testimony he gave at the first trial. The second trial got off to a late start when defense attorneys sought to have Judge Hooper issue a subpoena requiring the police to produce statements allegedly incriminating other defendants besides Robinson with the murder. Henson charged the police possessed sufficient evidence to bring four persons to trial. Judge Hooper took the request under advisement. Start of the trial was also delayed when a surprising number of prospective jurors declared themselves opposed to capital punishment. Whether or not this was because of moral conviction or the desire to escape from jury duty would be hard to say.

Two carpenters who had worked with Robinson in the construction of the tourist court at Bogart testified Robinson had lusted after Mrs. Reyman. The witnesses were J. D. Hawks (who testified at the first trial) and Leonard Roberts. They said Robinson had expressed a desire for Jeanette Reyman as she passed them while they were at work. At the second trial Robinson was again accompanied by his wife and three daughters.

On the second day of the trial attorneys for Robinson made a motion asking for a direct acquittal in the case, claiming the state had failed to establish in what county the crime actually had been committed. Medical examination of the body had shown the victim had been criminally assaulted more than once. Physicians said that she had died from three heavy blows on the head, probably inflicted by a wrench or some similar instrument. Now obviously all this did not occur in front of the Standard Coffee Company. But where? Twigs, leaves, and honeysuckle vines found on the victim's body and clothing indicated to investigators she died in a swampy area. This posed a puzzle that the police, in spite of Herculean efforts, had been unable to solve. The description of the crime scene fit at least a dozen places around the Atlanta area. But the exact murder site could not be located. To add to the confusion, police officers discovered the truck Mrs. Reyman drove to Atlanta from Bogart had been filled with gasoline when Mrs. Reyman left Bogart. When found on Moreland Avenue, the gas tank was empty, indicating it had been driven considerably farther than she would have gone on the shopping tour. Nevertheless, Judge Hooper overruled defense counsel's motion for a mistrial.

After four days of testimony the case went to the jury at two in the afternoon. After seven hours of deliberation the jury reported to the court that they were hopelessly deadlocked. Judge Hooper dismissed the jury and declared a mistrial. The jury foreman stated that after many ballots the vote never varied from the 7 to 5 vote from the beginning of the deliberations. Judge Hooper, in his charge to the jury, stressed the necessity of the state's proving beyond a shadow of a doubt the guilt of Robinson before they could return a verdict of guilty. Since much of the evidence was circumstantial, Judge Hooper said if there was doubt in the juror's minds they must bring in a verdict of innocent. Seven jurors thought that Robinson was guilty, one less than in the previous trial.

On December 3, 1947, Glenn Robinson went on trial a third time for the slaying of Jeanette Reyman. The case was much like the other two trials. One new development emerged in the strategy of the defense. After stating that he could prove that Mrs. Reyman had been previously married to a man named Poole and she had resided in Atlanta in 1942, Defense Counsel Henson cross-examined the slain woman's husband, Raleigh Reyman, about his wife's life prior to her marriage to him. Reyman denied his wife had at any time lived in Atlanta. He insisted that the fatal journey here June 25 was the first time she had ever been in Atlanta alone. She had come to Atlanta with him several times to purchase supplies for the Bogart tourist establishment, however. The state contended Robinson was the only person in Atlanta Mrs. Reyman would have allowed in her truck. Henson was trying to prove that she knew others in Atlanta who might have killed her.

Judge Virlyn Moore presided at the trial. He decided to hold night sessions because opposing counsel were unable to agree on releasing the jury nights. Another reason was the scarcity of hotel rooms, for the jury had to spend Tuesday night on cots on the mezzanine at the Robert Fulton Hotel. By holding night sessions, the judge expected to complete the trial the following day. The jurors could not endure many nights on those cots.

Witnesses at the night session included Dr. Herman Jones, who said he found blood spots on Robinson's trousers. He admitted, however, that the same spots could have been as much as seven years old. Another witness was a storekeeper, who stated that the day the truck was found, Robinson came into her store, nervous and excited, and bought a package of cigarettes. She said that several days later he returned and wanted to know if anyone had seen the driver of the murder truck.

Other witnesses were D. N. Stephens, who saw the murder truck on Forrest Avenue the day of the murder but could not positively identify the driver; M. E. Van Sant, Moreland Avenue clerk, who saw a man park the truck in front of his store and walk up the street; and L. W. Clyburn, investigator, who described a wooded area near Sears where the state contended the crime was committed. Solicitor Paul Webb placed Detective E. O. Mullen on the stand, and Mullen testified how he and Detective Sikes had found a pair of khaki trousers in Robinson's apartment which Robinson refused to identify as his own until shown his initials on them. E. D. Carden, a clerk at the Sears store, testified he had sold Mrs. Reyman a paring knife and a butcher knife around noon the day she was murdered. He said Robinson was with her at the time. He later identified Robinson in a police lineup. G. D. Hawks and Leonard Roberts, carpenters, who worked with Robinson at one time building the Reymans' tourist court at Bogart, testified that Robinson had made remarks to them about how much he wanted Mrs. Reyman.

On the following day the jury, after spending another bad night on cots, heard the summation from the opposing lawyers. Solicitor Webb, in his final closing argument, said that there was a chain of evidence which linked Robinson with the death of Mrs. Reyman. Webb said that Mrs. Reyman was a stranger in Atlanta; two witnesses testified Robinson had expressed an "unholy desire" to have her, and other witnesses had identified Robinson as being with the murdered woman, had identified the truck, and had destroyed his alibi. Webb attacked Defense Attorney Henson's effort to convince the jury that if it did not think Robinson deserved the electric chair, it should not convict him. If the jury in a circumstantial case does not recommend mercy, the judge can sentence a man convicted of murder to life imprisonment. Webb made it clear that he felt that the jury should give Robinson the electric chair or, if not that, life imprisonment.

Robinson again took the stand in his own defense. "I am not guilty of this charge. All I know about the murder is what I read in the newspaper." Robinson spoke in the same quiet, lifeless fashion which had marked his appearance at all three trials. He gave a detailed account of his actions the day Mrs. Reyman was slain. He said he went to work about 6 a.m. that day, drove a cab in company with J. D. Farlow from 8 to 11 a.m., went to get uniforms at 11 a.m., and was told he would have to wait 30 minutes until they were ready. He said he waited for the uniforms and then went to the Kimball House Hotel, where he shaved and took a bath. About 3 p.m. Robinson said he joined his nephew and niece at Crump's Restaurant after which he went to the cab office where he stayed from 5 to 5:30 p.m. He said he spent the evening until 9:30 p.m. driving with Farlow, ate at Crump's, then returned to the Kimball House for the night.

"Gentlemen, I am looking for my wife to be confined any minute. I have three kids and I have spent five months in jail for something I am not guilty of and I would appreciate it if you gentlemen come back with a verdict of not guilty," Robinson concluded.

The defendant took the stand shortly before the defense had rested its case. Several rebuttal witnesses were placed on the stand in an effort to impeach Robinson's alibi. The state argued that although the actual murder scene of the crime was in doubt, the fact that the slain woman's body was found in Fulton County made it proper for the trial to be held in the county. Webb told of Mrs. Reyman's moving to Bogart last January from her home in Indiana and said it was the state's contention that she was the type of woman who would not have picked up a man unless she knew him as she did Robinson. Webb said that it was reasonable to assume that Robinson joined Mrs. Reyman on pretext of getting a ride back to Bogart to his wife and children.

Defense counsel insisted the jury could have more than a reasonable doubt as to Robinson's guilt. Henson described testimony of some of the state witnesses as being "highly questionable, to say the least." Despite the lateness of the hour, the courtroom remained crowded, spectators on the edge of their seats. One elderly woman on the front row removed her shoes to rest her bare feet.

THE VERDICT

Late that night the case went to the jury. After some two hours of deliberation the jury returned its verdict in the case. The jury acquitted Glenn Robinson of the charge of murdering Jeanette Reyman. After five months and three trials, Glenn Robinson was a free man.

A monumental effort was made to convict Glenn Robinson for the death of Jeanette Reyman. Three juries remained unconvinced. One of the factors that influenced the jurors was: Why should they convict Glenn Robinson for the death of Jeanette Reyman when Paul Refoule was going free? To many people of the time, this was logical thinking. What appears today to be somewhat more logical is that the Atlanta police probably made the same mistake in the Reyman case as the Fulton County police made in the Refoule case. One person who thought so at the time was the head of the homicide squad, Lt. Coppenger. He did not believe that Robinson was guilty of murder. Detective Mullen, who arrested Robinson, was convinced that the taxi-cab driver was the culprit. In fact, detectives do not always agree on the guilt or innocence of a suspect in a homicide case, and unlike fictional murder mysteries, some homicides appear to be void of any rational solution. We should point out, however, that while no professional investigators now feel that Refoule was guilty of the murder of his wife, there is a rather evenly divided opinion among them concerning Robinson and Jeanette Reyman. Some think he was innocent. Many believe he was guilty.

What is interesting is how the two murder cases were tied so closely together. Robinson was able to take advantage of the way the police abused Refoule and use it to his own advantage. The courts were beginning to hand down decisions that restricted the way the police had investigated murders in the past. And it was a time of change and social upheaval. The defense counsel who represented Robinson in all three trials stated that he felt that Peggy Refoule and Jeanette Reyman were probably killed by the same man, and this would certainly exclude both Refoule and Robinson.

In 1947 the city of Atlanta had 91 homicides—the year of the Refoule and Reyman murders. In contrast, Milwaukee, a city of comparable size, had only four murders. But in this era Southern cities often had more homicides than Northern cities. The poverty, the racism, the heat—these were factors that made murder more likely.

Of the 91 homicides in Atlanta in 1947 nine victims were white persons and 82 were blacks. Black murders led because at the time the South refused to face the fact of treating black murder seriously and still followed the ancient custom of treating such homicides as "just another Negro killing." This caused the South to reap an inevitable crop of black homicides in the period following World War II, and was one of the contributing factors to the rise in the number of homicides in this turbulent era. Because in this period white juries almost invariably treated more or less lightly the crime of murder when it was confined to the Negro race, the homicide rate in this type of crime remained high.

During the same months of the investigation into the Refoule and Reyman murders, the grand jury indicted Frank Bryant, a black man, for the slayings of three other blacks. Bryant quarreled with John Jackson, a man living at Bryant's address on Farrington Avenue, and then shot him to death. When Louise Jackson, John Jackson's wife, attempted to come to the victim's aid with a butcher knife, Bryant shot and killed her. Then, Nancy Barnes, mother of Louise Jackson, arrived on the scene and she in turn was killed by Bryant. Bryant next started up a nearby street where he met Willie Barnes, husband of Nancy Barnes, and started shooting at him. Barnes ran but turned and shot back at Bryant. One shot broke Bryant's arm. When police arrived on the scene, Bryant was in the act of picking up his pistol with the other hand. There were several eyewitnesses to the killings and there was no doubt that Bryant was guilty of the murder of three people. The case was never tried. The charge was reduced to manslaughter and Bryant received six months probation. Whether or not the person committing this particular crime received the punishment commensurate with the crime, which of course he did not, is beside the point. The fact is that a dual society looked upon homicides within those separate societies in quite a different manner.

During this same period, James Ward Sims, a black male, aged 17, was accused of assaulting a white nurse in her home on Richardson Street. Sims had previously entered guilty pleas on two indictments charging him with larceny of an automobile and burglary from a house. He received a total of 25–30 years on those charges, but he refused to enter a guilty plea on the criminal assault charge of the white nurse. He maintained he was innocent. He was placed on trial on this charge, and the trial lasted one afternoon. He was found guilty by a jury after a half hour's deliberation of criminal assault and sentenced to die in the electric chair!

The aftermath of World War II, economic instability, boom times, a growing population that was on the move, and racism—all these factors contributed to a rise in the homicide rate in Atlanta and in the nation in the years 1946 to 1947. There was a growing awareness among police officials that ancient approaches of handling homicides would no longer suffice in the future.

5

Opera Singer John Garris

In the late 1940s Atlanta turned out to be a jinx town for the Metropolitan Opera Company. On the 1948 tour, a train wreck outside the city marooned most of the company's property effects, and the curtain went up on *Carmen* with the stars wearing makeshift costumes. In 1949, Patrice Munsel was shaken up and badly bruised in a traffic accident on her way into the city from the airport.

A sense of impending doom hung over the entire company when the opera season opened in Atlanta on April 18, 1949, but the cast was in top form when it sang *Otello* at the Fox Theater on that Monday night. John Garris sang the role of Cassio. In the last act when Cassio is stabbed by Iago, he cries out as he falls:

I am maimed forever—
Help, ho! Murder!
Murder!!

On Tuesday night, Garris sang the part of Laerte in *Mignon*. His masterful performance in the first act brought accolades from the audience and rave reviews from the press.

John Garris was noted particularly for his Wagnerian roles and had won wide acclaim for his rendition in *Die Meistersinger*. He had sung with the San Francisco Opera Company for several seasons before joining the Met.

Garris was regarded as one of the Met's most promising new tenors. The husky, six-feet-tall singer was thirty-six years old and was a native of Frankfurt-on-Main, Germany. His German name was Hans J.K. Gareis, but when he came to America, he adopted the Anglicized version and became John Garris. It was by the latter name that he was known throughout the music world as a man with a great deal of talent and a promising future.

When the 1949 season concluded with a performance of *L'Elisir d'Amour* on Wednesday evening, Garris was present as a member of the audience instead of as a featured singer. At 7:45 on the following morning, a workman on his way to work in downtown Atlanta discovered the singer's body in a dismal, rain-soaked alley at the rear of 305 Marietta Street.

John Garris had been shot in the region of his heart by a single bullet which entered directly below the left underarm. His body lay straightened out on its back, the legs almost carefully crossed at the ankles. It was attired in dark flannel trousers and a white shirt. Very little blood was noted in the vicinity where the body was found, which led police to theorize that the handsome tenor had been shot elsewhere and that his body had been taken to the alley.

Later, Garris' coat was found about two blocks away, carelessly thrown on the top of a garbage can. Police theorized that Garris had been killed somewhere else and the body was dumped in the alley; then as the car sped away the coat was thrown from the car. There was no bullet hole in the coat. None of the slain singer's valuables was touched by the killer or killers. His wallet, which contained twenty dollars and jewelry and personal papers, was found intact. An alien registration receipt bore the Germanic identification "Hans J.K. Gareis."

Atlanta police telegraphed Memphis police to hold all passengers on the special opera train when it reached Memphis. The train had been scheduled to leave Terminal Station at 3 a.m., but it did not get underway until after 5 a.m. It was reported that Garris boarded the train before midnight, but then got off again. He never returned, but when the train departed no one on board noticed his absence.

HIS LAST DAY

On his last day in Atlanta Garris had lunch at the Biltmore Hotel. Although the stars of the opera troupe stayed there, many of the lesser performers stayed at the YMCA. At 2:30 p.m. on Wednesday, Garris placed a call from the Biltmore to a member of the troupe at the Y. He placed no more calls that day from the hotel and received none. At 3 p.m. Garris was supposed to meet Miss Herta Glatz, a contralto with the Met cast, to attend a tea in the hotel for some of the members of the cast. At the last moment he called Miss Glatz at her room and begged off, explaining that he had a headache. When he met Miss Glatz before that evening's performance, he told her he had napped and slept well, and he seemed to be in very good spirits. The two singers were joined for dinner by a local opera buff, Mrs. Rosalie Mayer, after which the three of them attended the opera together. A member of the opera troupe saw Garris at the theater and talked with him. He followed the performance with great interest and was in a good mood. Miss Glatz and Garris left the Fox Theater together right after the last curtain at about 11 p.m. and went by the Biltmore to pick up their luggage. Mrs. Mayer drove them to the Terminal Station, where they arrived around 11:45 p.m. Garris went in search of a red cap while Miss Glatz sat in the car with Mrs. Mayer. Garris soon returned with a porter, obtained his and Miss Glatz's luggage, thanked Mrs. Mayer for her kindness, and left.

The two members of the opera troupe went to their separate cars, Miss Glatz to Car 12, Garris to Car 13. Garris had told Miss Glatz that he intended to write a letter to a friend in Los Angeles, with regard to a German-English translation which he wanted to send to a New York agency. Garris and Miss Glatz were planning a concert tour together after the Met season, and the New York agency was pressing both to submit certain translations for the tour. Miss Glatz went to her car and wrote a letter concerning the matter.

According to the porter of Car 13, John Garris seemed to be in a hurry, and he gave the porter his luggage stubs and the money for the red cap, saying that he was going to the rear car to play cards. No member of the troupe recalled seeing Garris playing cards. Miss Glatz said he did not mention it to her, and she stated that he never played cards. The porter took care of Garris' two suitcases and topcoat, putting the larger suitcase in the men's room, the smaller one on the lower berth assigned to Garris. The porter did not see Garris again after that. He noticed during the night that the berth was not occupied, but assumed that Garris was in another car still playing cards.

When Miss Glatz had finished her letter she went upstairs to the main concourse of the station to mail it. On her way back to the train she met Garris, who showed her his letter which he was on his way to mail. He went upstairs to the station and Miss Glatz returned to her car. She did not see John Garris again.

In Memphis, Lt. M.M. Coppenger and other detectives from

the Atlanta homicide bureau were interviewing members of the Met chorus and ballet and the stage hands. They interviewed several members of the company who stated the last time they saw Garris was about 12:55 a.m., Thursday, in the parking lot in front of the train station, where several members of the cast were getting into an automobile to go for sandwiches, when Garris approached the car and wanted to go along. Since there were already six people in the car, it was decided after some conversation that Garris could not be squeezed in and so the car drove off and Garris was last seen walking away from the station toward downtown. Edwin Johnson, the Met's general manager, and Max Rudolph advised Lt. Coppenger that they were on the platform at the train station at 3:30 a.m. and that they did not see Garris anywhere in or around the station, and that he had not attended a party given for the artists of the opera company following the last performance.

One of the assistant stage managers stated that he was walking toward town after midnight looking for a place to eat, when Garris overtook him and they discussed the best place to eat at that time of night. As they passed the Western Union office Garris told him that he had to send a telegram, and the two separated. The stage man stated that he walked on and found a restuarant and that after eating he retraced his route to the railroad station. He did not see Garris again.

Garris went into the telegraph office and sent a wire to his agent in New York, assuring her that all texts and translations of songs for the concert tour would reach her by Friday. The person on duty later remembered Garris because he asked him how to spell some of the words in the telegram. He said that Garris was in a very normal condition and that he appeared neat and was wearing a sport coat but no top coat and had his hat pushed back on his head. He seemed to be perfectly calm. The man stated that Garris was in the office about fifteen minutes and that the telegram went out a few minutes before 2 a.m. He was the last person known to have seen John Garris alive.

When news of the slaying broke, many theories were discussed throughout Atlanta. The case quickly revived memories of the Refoule and Reyman cases. People were betting that this one also would go unsolved. The Atlanta police were determined to solve the case, and probably spent more man-hours working on it than on any other single homicide which had ever been committed in the city. Pressure built quickly for an early solution.

Opening night of the Met in Memphis found white-socked Atlanta homicide detectives mingling with the black-tie audience. While Jerome Hines sang on stage:

> *Do not murder! For thus is writ:*
> *"He who sheds another's lifeblood,*
> *Such shall be his doom!"*

detectives backstage circulated behind props and curtains in the hope of picking up a clue to the murder. Members of the company were being questioned behind the backdrops and in the dressing rooms to find out what they knew about Garris' movements in Atlanta and what possible motive there might be for someone to take his life. During the intermission the audience talked more about John Garris than they did about the night's performance of *Lucia di Lammermoor.* The backstage police work was not done quietly, and several performers threatened not to continue unless the police got out. When a confrontation developed between the singers and the cops, it appeared for a while that there would be no second act that evening, at least with the curtain up. Edwin Johnson rushed around backstage soothing ruffled feelings and requesting the police to please work more quietly.

Following the performance, the police concluded their questioning of the members of the opera company. Lt. Coppenger and his men returned to Atlanta and the Met went on to its next stop on the tour. The Memphis interrogations gave the police some information concerning Garris' movements that proved helpful; however, no vital clues were unearthed.

John Garris had no relatives in the United States. News of the singer's death reached his parents in Frankfurt while they were attending a performance of the opera *Gotterdammerung.* The stunned parents, Josef Gareis, 73, and his wife, Maria, 70, asked to have the body cremated and the ashes returned to Germany.

BACKGROUND

Police learned that Garris' career had been a stormy one. After studying at the Frankfurt Conservatory of Music, he made his debut as a conductor at age 19. When Hitler came to power Garris fled to Greece, where he stayed until 1941. He earned a living by singing over the radio. Ultimately he worked his way to the United States and succeeded in arranging an audition at the Met, but was unable to obtain a post as a conductor. Although he had never studied voice, nor knew a singing operatic role, he tried out and was accepted eventually at the Met as a singer. Out of his salary he paid for singing lessons, soon winning wide acclaim as a recitalist for his perfect intrepretation of German *Leider*. The singer lived at 362 West 57th Street in New York City, where he shared an apartment with Lutz Peter, a drama coach. The latter, born Uhnfelder, was also from Frankfurt.

Lutz Peter was in Los Angeles at the time of Garris' death, but he returned to New York when he was informed of the murder. Detectives from Atlanta flew to New York and questioned him closely, but they learned little of value.

In New York music circles many persons recalled Garris as a debonair, charming man on the stage. When the curtain fell, however, it screened his private life. Tenants in the building where he lived described Garris as an unassuming and quiet neighbor. The woman who lived in the apartment directly above his said that she and other tenants frequently turned off their radios so they could enjoy the singing of Garris and his guests.

Lutz Peter told investigators that Garris was a modest person with a quiet disposition and that he had no enemies. Peter said that he had last seen Garris on Sunday just before the Met tour began. He said he was to have met Garris in Los Angeles when the Met tour reached there. Peter said that when Garris reached the United States in 1941 he had seventy-five cents in his pocket. Garris went to live with Peter, who coached him in all of his opera roles and advised him on his career. The coach added that Garris had been engaged to his sister, Lottie Uhnfelder, but that she had died in a concentration camp during the war. Peter had no idea who could have killed Garris, and he felt that jealousy or envy as a motive for the killing was not likely because Garris was such a likeable person.

Meanwhile, Atlanta detectives established an interesting lead. They learned that a hotel reservation had been made in the name of John Garris for Thursday night in Dallas, Texas. This indicated that Garris had changed his original plan to accompany the cast to Memphis, where he had no roles to sing, and instead planned to go directly to Dallas, the next stop on the tour where he was slated to sing. If this were the case, then why did Garris place his luggage aboard the Memphis train? And why did he tell no one of his plans to skip Memphis? It was not unusual for members of the company, when they were not scheduled to sing, to skip certain cities of the tour. If Garris had decided at the last minute not to go to Memphis, he still could have planned to send part of his luggage on with the opera special after returning to the train and retrieving his small overnight bag. But if he were planning to go directly to Dallas, he had not made any train or plane reservations.

BEAUTIFUL AND RICH

As soon as Lt. Coppenger returned from Memphis, he boarded another plane for Dallas. There he drove to an exclusive residential neighborhood and stopped at an impressive, Spanish-style mansion. This was the home of the young woman who claimed Garris had wired her to meet him at a Dallas hotel on Thursday night. The girl lived with her parents. She was 21 years old and a striking beauty with green eyes and red hair. She was very rich. She told Lt. Coppenger that she was madly in love with John Garris and had fallen for him when she was studying voice in New York the year before. She had seen him at the Met and had gone backstage to meet him and ask for his autograph. She said that after they got to know each other, he asked her for a date. They continued to see each other until she returned to Dallas, and thereafter she wrote him almost every day. A month before, she had received a letter from Garris telling her he would be in Dallas in April. Two weeks later she got a long distance call from the singer saying that he would be in Dallas on Thursday, April 21st. The young woman said she waited all that day to hear from Garris, but the hours passed without a call or a message from him. She was worried but did not know what to do. She turned on the radio and heard the news of Garris' murder.

Coppenger questioned the young beauty for three hours. She stated that during the time she knew Garris in New York, she had encountered no one who might have had reason to harm him. He had been attractive to women of all ages, she reported, and his feminine fan mail had been huge. Although girls had swarmed around him for autographs, he apparently had never become entangled with any of his feminine admirers. It began to appear more and more that the entire scenario of the murder—including culprit, motive and actual commission—centered on Atlanta.

Meanwhile in Atlanta, detectives continued to search for a late model green Buick sedan which had been seen circling the area near Marietta and Thurmond streets, N.W., during the early morning hours on the day of the murder. A man and a woman were reported riding in the car, which returned to the scene after daybreak. A warehouse watchman told detectives he overheard a shot near the entrance to the alley at around 3:30 a.m. Thursday—four hours before the body of the singer was discovered. Another night watchman and a taxicab driver reported to police that they saw the green automobile circling the area at that time. Detectives also were checking on reports of a restaurant operator in the area who stated that a man answering Garris' description came into his restaurant with several other persons early Thursday and left a short time later.

Dewey Wrenn, who lived only a short distance from the alley where Garris' body was found, told police that he heard a pistol shot sometime Thursday morning. He said that he remembered switching off a light and going to bed at 12:30 a.m. but could not recall how much time elapsed before he heard the shot. Wrenn stated to detectives that on the Monday or Tuesday before the slaying he had seen an automobile pull up to the curb near his house. He remembered the car because of its smart appearance and because it bore an out-of-state license plate. In the car was a man and a very attractive woman. The car remained there for awhile and then drove off. Detectives expressed doubt that Garris was in an automobile when he was shot, since there were no visible powder burns on the clothing or body. They pointed out that an automatic pistol fired at such close range would have left powder burns.

Atlanta police next got their first big break in the case. South Carolina authorities arrested a suspect driving a gray sedan with no license plates. The suspect was identified as Grover "Tojo" Pulley, a white male, aged 44, a parole-jumping convict from North Carolina who once had been convicted for murder. The pistol in Pulley's possession was a 9-millimeter automatic of Belgian make. Police in Clinton, South Carolina, found in Pulley's car a stained pair of trousers, an army blanket splotched with dark spots, and a $10 bill with dark brown smears.

Dr. Herman Jones of the Fulton County crime laboratory drove to Clinton to make ballistics tests of the gun. Police learned that Pulley was in Atlanta the night Garris was slain with a 9-millimeter bullet apparently identical to the bullet found in Pulley's pistol. Earlier in the investigation Dr. Jones had announced that the death slug came from a .38-caliber pistol—almost exactly the size of a 9-millimeter bullet. Dr. Jones fired six bullets from Pulley's pistol in Clinton and then left immediately for Atlanta to make a microscopic comparison of those slugs with the bullet which had been removed from the body of John Garris. A quick, superficial comparison of the test bullets with the bullet removed from the body of the slain tenor indicated that they bore a strong resemblance, but a more thorough examination would be necessary.

PRESTIGE OF MET

Meanwhile, Clinton authorities held "Tojo" Pulley on open charges after he admitted having served 17 years in a North Carolina penitentary for murder. North Carolina authorities confirmed that Pulley had jumped parole a year earlier. The patrolman who arrested Pulley in Clinton stated that the Belgian automatic found on Pulley was rather unusual, and he reported that he had found one cartridge in its chamber, two more in Pulley's pocket, and a full clip of 15 cartridges in his car.

Police learned that John Garris was not highly paid by the Metropolitan Opera Company and that up to the time of his death his greatest recompense was the glamour and prestige which surrounded his singing career. Officials of the Met were not sure that there was enough money in the slain singer's bank account to defray his funeral expenses. His friend Lutz Peter was making arrangements to travel to Atlanta to claim the body. The singer had requested that in the event of his death his body be cremated.

Atlantã police could not determine positively if the bullet which killed Garris had been fired from the gun of "Tojo" Pulley. The bullet taken from the body of the murder victim and the test bullets fired by Dr. Jones were forwarded to the FBI in Washington for analysis. An Atlanta man notified police that he knew Pulley as "Harvey Perkins" and that Pulley visited his home in Atlanta on Saturday, April 16, 1947 and remain there until 7 p.m., Wednesday, April 20th. The man told police that Pulley told him that he was going to North Carolina. The man stated that he did not know Pulley's background or his real name until he saw his picture and read a story in a local newspaper.

At this point in their investigation of the slaying, police conjectured that John Garris was killed as he strolled along the railroad tracks before the opera special pulled out of the train station Thursday morning. The probable motive, they believed, was that he had unwittingly surprised burglars attempting to break into a printing establishment near where his body was later found. Police records showed that burglar alarm calls sounded twice Thursday morning to the Montag Printing Company building on Marietta Street at the approximate time the singer was killed. Night watchmen in the area reported hearing a shot about 3:30 a.m.

Police found an assortment of burglary tools in Pulley's car. The case against him was building. But up until this point it was all circumstantial. The one piece of evidence that could really incriminate Pulley was the pistol. If the test bullets were the same as the death bullet, the police would then have a good case against Pulley. However, it was their opinion that he had not acted alone. Detectives felt that at least two men were involved in carrying the husky 175-pound opera singer from the place he was killed into the rough, rain-drenched alley. The ground under Garris' body was dry, indicating that it had been placed there before the pre-dawn rain started.

On April 25, 1949, the autopsy on the body of John Garris was completed. The results of the autopsy led police to believe that the victim died trying to defend himself against his killer, for the completed autopsy revealed Garris was fatally shot as he crouched on his knee in a defensive position. The evidence clearly indicated that Garris was shot as he rested on his right knee holding his left arm up in what could have been an attempt to fend off his attacker. Scores of tiny cinder fragments were embedded in the singer's right knee. This meant that the shooting could have occurred near the special train on which Garris was scheduled to leave Atlanta. It certainly meant that Garris was killed in the vicinity of the railroad tracks. The only area in the vicinity of the alley where

Garris' body was discovered in which cinders were found in profusion was the railroad right-of-way on which the special train was parked. The autopsy revealed that the body had abrasions on the left hand. It was also noted that Garris' right trouser leg was ripped and torn in the area of the right knee. An analysis of the contents of Garris' stomach confirmed that he had eaten shortly before he was murdered.

Governor Herman Talmadge announced that the State of Georgia would offer a reward of $1500 for the conviction of Garris' slayer. The police had asked the governor to post the reward after they found themselves in a maze of false leads and unfounded rumors. Admitting that the investigation of the case was at a standstill, they asked the governor for assistance.

Atlanta was abuzz with conversation concerning the slaying of John Garris. Everybody had a theory. The police were waiting for the report from the FBI in Washington concerning the bullets from Pulley's gun. Garris' body was still in the morgue awaiting the arrival of Lutz Peter from New York. In the interim, the case was the major topic of conversation. People wanted to know if, as some theorized, Garris was fatally wounded in the railroad yards, how did he manage to thread his way in the dark through a confusing network of railroad tracks to the alley area several hundred yards away where his body was found? And how did the supposedly dead or dying man's sport coat come to be placed on a garbage can several hundred yards farther to the north?

The FBI reported that the bullets fired from the Pulley gun by Dr. Jones did *not* match the bullet removed from the body of John Garris. The big break the police had hoped for did not materialize, for without the incriminating bullet they had no case against Pulley.

Chief Herbert T. Jenkins of the Atlanta Police Department, who was personally overseeing the investigation, paid a call upon his friend Ralph McGill, editor of *The Atlanta Constitution*. As a result, McGill wrote the following editorial for the next morning's edition of the paper.

> Atlanta police are under an uneasy national spotlight as they endeavor to solve the slaying of Metropolitan opera tenor John Garris. Already one major theory has collapsed and police are now working on other but less tangible leads. We trust they will continue their efforts without letup until the mystery kill-

ing is solved. We do not have many unsolved murders in Atlanta and Fulton County, but those remaining in that category seem invariably to be the ones which attract the widest attention. There are reports that certain information which might be of value in solving the Garris slaying has not been made available to the police. Persons who possess information about the crime or information concerning the movements of the slain man prior to his death owe it to the community to divulge their knowledge to authorities. And they should not await a formal request. Delay simply gives the killer or killers a greater chance of escape. Every new report appears to increase the mysterious circumstances surrounding the slaying. Police need help, the help of anyone having information which might shed light on the numerous dark spots of the case . . .

This editorial appeal for help produced scant results.

On April 27, Lutz Peter arrived in Atlanta to claim the body and make arrangements for returning it to New York. In an emotional statement to the press he commented that it was his belief that his friend had been murdered by someone who was known to Garris. Peter said Atlanta police had not questioned him or asked his opinion about the case. The small, slightly-built dramatics coach added he was anxious to meet detectives and give them his views of the case. Peter cited the pleasant expression on Garris' face and the carefully laid-out position of the body as his reasons for believing this. He added that perhaps an hysterical admirer or fan had killed his friend.

THEORIES AND SPECULATION

Lutz Peter arrived in Atlanta by automobile with his brother, Alfred Uhnfelder, of Richmond, Virginia, and Miss Marie Wier, of New York. The latter was an old friend of Garris. Peter said that an admirer of Garris had offered a burial spot in a New Hampshire cemetery for the body, but that the singer's parents had requested the body be returned to Germany. The following day the body of John Garris was taken to Macon, Georgia, and cremated.

Following six days of extensive investigation, Lt. Coppenger announced that police had been able to account for the tenor's movements up until shortly after midnight of the past Wednesday. Coppenger assigned detectives to comb all-night restaurants in the hope of finding someone who observed Garris between midnight and the time the first of the opera specials pulled out for Memphis at 4:18 a.m. Detectives carried pictures of Garris as well as of Pulley on the rounds of restaurants. Coppenger also ordered pictures of the two men to be shown employees of the train station and night watchmen in the area. He said police still had a considerable amount of investigating to do and that detectives were running down other clues in the mysterious slaying.

Lutz Peter was questioned by Lt. Coppenger for three hours. He told Coppenger that he had no idea who could have killed Garris. His comments to the press about Garris being killed by someone known to him had been mere theorizing, he explained.

Police then received an anonymous telephone call placed locally from a man who would not identify himself. He said the police should check out a Virginia divorcée who was a close friend of Garris and had followed him to Atlanta.

Upon checking, police discovered that Mrs. Frances Tyler of Middleburg, Virginia, had been a friend of Garris for several years. She denied that there had ever been any romantic interest between herself and Garris, adding that she had met Garris in New York some years ago and they had become friends. She had last seen Garris in Washington, D.C., during the Easter season, and she said on Palm Sunday she had gone to the National Cathedral where Garris was among singers on a special Holy Week program. She insisted however that she had never been in Atlanta, and could throw no light on the mysterious slaying. She stated that she had been shocked to read of the tragic death of her friend.

Next, detectives located the restaurant where Garris ate his last meal. They learned also that Garris had eaten at this same restaurant on Monday and Tuesday. Garris talked with the wife of the manager about leaving an autographed picture of himself to be hung in the restaurant. She had talked to Garris on Monday and Tuesday but she had not worked on Wednesday or Thursday; other employees, however, stated that Garris was in the restaurant sometime after 2:30 on Thursday morning. No one could remember whether Garris was with someone or alone. Tipsters frequenting all-night restaurants, hotels, and the like thought Garris "met the wrong man" during or immediately after going to the restaurant. Persons with criminal records were known to frequent certain late-hours restaurants. Coppenger felt that had Garris left the restaurant with a local person, other local persons would have seen them, and at least one of them, to get in good with the police, would have come forward to identify Garris' companion. Coppenger felt it was all conjecture, and he did not think much of this theory.

Atlanta police next learned that about 36 hours after John Garris' death a women whose maiden name was Jean G. R. Gareis was shot to death in upper New York state. A startling and fascinating similarity existed between the two murders. Both victims had formerly used their full first names, two middle initials, and the same surname. The name "Gareis" was certainly not a common one in the United States, and for a person with a lively imagination it could appear as if someone bore a grudge against members of the Gareis family or their survivors. Jean G. R. Gareis, the 25-year-old wife of the Reverend George Hetenyl, an Episcopal priest, had been killed by a single pistol shot. The victim in the slaying had fled Nazi Germany just before World War II. The murder was unsolved. Was there some connection between the two murders or just a weird coincidence? There was no hard evidence either way, but the police thought it was simply that, a weird coincidence.

Ten days after the slaying the Garris case had bogged down. To the dismay of the police all the effort generated in an attempt to find the slayer seemed to be getting nowhere. Tojo Pulley was still considered a prime suspect, but the police had yet to locate anything that definitely tied him to the homicide.

Lt. Coppenger was checking out-of-state automobiles reportedly in Atlanta the morning of April 21st. Reports of a green sedan circling the area at Marietta and Thurmond streets, near where the body was found, produced no definite information. Other similar reports led detectives up blind alleys.

Coppenger flew to Los Angeles to interview various members of the opera company. He took a statement from Ramon Vinay, a member of the Met company who had sung the title role in *Otello* in Atlanta. Police had discovered that Vinay had checked out of the Biltmore Hotel at 7 a.m. the day that the body was found. Vinay was one of the few Met members who did not accompany the troupe to Memphis. When interviewed by Coppenger, Vinay stated that he did not go to Memphis because he was not scheduled to sing there and that he and his wife went by train directly to Dallas. Vinay insisted that he had no knowledge of Garris' plans. As far as he knew, Garris was planning to go on to Memphis with the cast. The last time he saw Garris was at the opera performance Wednesday night in Atlanta.

Coppenger also questioned the members of the company who stayed at the YMCA during the opera company's stay. He located the individual whom Garris had called early Wednesday afternoon from the hotel. The man told Coppenger that Garris wanted some technical data concerning his forthcoming concert tour, and he said the singer had made no reference to any plans for going directly to Dallas. Lutz Peter was now staying in Los Angeles and Coppenger checked him out with people there. He interviewed people who had written letters from Los Angeles to the Atlanta police saying the police should check on the activities of Lutz Peter. It appeared that Peter, in direct contrast to Garris, was the type of person who made many enemies, and these enemies were very anxious to cast suspicion on him for the murder of Garris. Was it possible that someone had a grudge against Peter and vented it by murdering Garris? Several people whom Coppenger interviewed implied this, but it was all theory. No one had any hard evidence.

Washington, D.C., police notified Atlanta police that they had a man in jail who insisted that he knew a certain person who had threatened Garris' life, and that this individual was the type of person who carried out his threats. An Atlanta detective flew to Washington and interviewed the man. It developed that he knew nothing about the slaying or about Garris except what he had read in the newspapers. He was an artful liar, however, and it took relentless questioning to break down his story and uncover that it was all just a hoax, a device he hoped might help him get out of jail.

NEW LEADS

On May 19, 1949, the probe in the slaying of John Garris took a sensational turn. A nineteen-year-old girl from Richmond, Virginia, named Alma Johnson, *alias* Mary Smith, was taken into custody by Atlanta police for suspicion of involvement with narcotics. She was arrested following a tip to police that she knew something about the Garris case. Alma Johnson claimed that she had met Garris three years earlier in Charlotte, North Carolina, and she named him as the father of her baby. She identified pictures of Grover "Tojo" Pulley as her escort in Atlanta the night of April 20, 1949. Miss Johnson said she and Pulley and another couple arranged a meeting with Garris near the railroad tracks shortly before the opera specials left for Memphis. The object of the meeting, Miss Johnson maintained, was to persuade Garris to help care for the child. A fight ensued, during which Garris removed his coat. During the fight, Pulley shot Garris. After Garris was shot, Miss Johnson said, the first thought was to carry him to the hospital. Then, realizing that he was dead, they placed him in the alley. She stated to police that she crossed his legs and attempted to fold his arms.

It made an interesting story and was hailed by some as a break in the Garris case. Very careful checking by police, however, revealed that the story Miss Johnson told was imaginary. Police ascertained that her real name was something else and that she lived in Gainesville, Georgia. Authorities in Gainesville were looking for her on a lunacy warrant. She had previously been in a mental institution. During the time she was held by police and was telling her story, she was also undergoing withdrawal from drug use.

Lt. Coppenger then interrogated Pulley concerning the woman's story. He readily admitted going with her when he was in Atlanta, but said that her story concerning Garris was merely an attempt on her part to get back at him for leaving her in Atlanta. He stated her story was a pipe dream and that she was a "hophead."

On July 8, 1949, a Fulton County coroner's jury was empaneled and heard all the evidence thus far amassed in the Garris case. There was strong testimony at the hearing concerning the bullet. Dr. Herman Jones insisted that the bullet removed from the body of Garris came from Pulley's gun, and although the FBI did not agree with him, Jones had brought in three other experts who did agree that the bullet and comparison bullets were from the same weapon. Mainly on the basis of Dr. Jones testimony, the jury recommended that Pulley be returned to Fulton County and held for further investigation on the charge of murder. But because of the conflicting testimony and the fact that the experts could not agree about the bullets, Pulley was never brought to trial for the murder of John Garris. Lt. Coppenger, whose knowledge of the case was the most extensive, firmly believed that Pulley did not kill Garris. Dr. Jones felt strongly that Pulley was the culprit.

The Atlanta Police Department received a great deal of mail concerning the John Garris case. Many tips and leads came to the police over the telephone. All of this information was carefully checked by Lt. Coppenger and his men. And it all led nowhere.

On April 24, 1950, the Met came to Atlanta for the spring season. But the murder of John Garris the year before hung over the opera season like a dark cloud. Lt. Coppenger once again talked with members of the company but learned nothing new. In the past year Coppenger had worked on the Garris case relentlessly and had finally determined to his own satisfaction the singer's whereabouts in the hours preceding the murder.

Lt. Coppenger felt that Garris, returning to the train station, by chance happened upon something and/or saw something that he should not have seen, and was killed for this reason. Coppenger thought it quite possible that Garris was mistaken for someone else and the slaying could have been a mistaken-identity slaying. In order not to have the homicide associated with whatever was happening there, the murderers carried Garris' body several blocks and then left it where it was found. If Garris had been murdered by an individual whom he met in or around the restaurant, then the singer would have been robbed and the body left where the murder was committed.

There was much speculation that Garris had arranged to meet someone beforehand and left the train in order to do so. But testimony of several members of the opera troupe put holes in this theory. Garris would have gone with other members of the company in the automobile, had there been room, when he left the train to go out for a late meal.

The big speculation in the Garris case centered around the assumption that someone followed Garris to Atlanta for the purpose of killing him. If this were true, then why did the killer wait until the last moment and how did he know where to find Garris unless he was stalking him?

If before his death, John Garris called out the lines from *Otello*:

Help ho! Murder! Murder!!
there is no one who has come forward to say he heard it.

Lt. Coppenger interviewed and had detectives in other cities interview many people who had much to say concerning John Garris. He was highly thought of and well regarded as an artist and musician, and the fact that he could sing in five languages made him a valuable asset to the Met.

One of the most productive interviews was with Mrs. Herta Adler, wife of Dr. Justin Adler, of Memphis, Tennessee. It revealed information about John Garris which, in the context of the times, was shocking and sensational. In the long run, however, although it brought into focus possible new motives for the murder, it did not effect a solution.

Official police notes of the interview record that Mrs. Adler stated that she was originally from Frankfurt and that she had known John Garris in Germany for fifteen years. At that time he and Peter Uhnfelder (Lutz Peter) were "sweethearts," and they were together constantly. John Garris had an automobile upon which he had the initials *L. U.* painted on a door. It was commonly known, she said, about the conduct of Peter Uhnfelder and John Garris, and even in those days Garris did not care anything for the female sex because he was "madly in love" with Uhnfelder. She said the stories which had appeared in newspapers about Garris being engaged to Uhnfelder's sister were all wrong; they were, she claimed, an attempt by the latter man to "put up a phony front." Mrs. Adler went on to say that Uhnfelder left Germany first, followed by Garris, and that their departure resulted both from a dislike of Nazism and a frantic desire to avoid the rounding-up of "undesirables" which was then underway.

Mrs. Adler added that in 1946 when John Garris was in Memphis with the Met tour he stayed at her home. In talking about Uhnfelder, the singer mentioned how very much he missed him since he had been on the road. She asked him why Uhnfelder was not traveling with him, and Garris replied that the Met would not give outsiders permission to travel with the tour.

Statements given to the police by other German emigres contained essentially the same information. The police had received tips from anonymous sources from the time of the slaying that there was a sexual aspect of John Garris' nature which could have been a factor in his murder.

As late as 1955, the Atlanta Police Department continued to get tips concerning the murder of John Garris. These anonymous phone calls implied that a taxi driver with a certain cab company knew something about the murder, but they did not identify the individual by name. Detectives interviewed a number of people but could come up with nothing concrete. Again, in 1963, the Atlanta Police Department received an anonymous call from a man who refused to identify himself. This informer stated that he had overheard a conversation indicating that a particular cab company employee had certain information concerning the murder of John Garris. Extensive investigation led police to several individuals who provided information, but nothing of a conclusive nature was established.

The murder of John Garris remains unsolved.

The Refoule case had a profound bearing on the investigation into the murder of John Garris. Many more elements were present in the latter case to make it even more sensational than the Refoule investigation, but this time both the authorities and the press scrupulously avoided any "Gestapo-like tactics and yellow journalism" in the investigation into the tenor's death. The Garris investigation could have been quite a show had the police and the press wished to make it so. Indeed, the investigation into the murder makes it a case of classic dimensions because it illustrates how improved police methods and practices had become in the short, two-year period from 1947 to 1949. In retrospect the opera singer's murder is most significant because of what *did not* occur in the course of the investigation and reporting of the case.

The Garris case brought to an end the series of unsolved murders which plagued Atlanta in the era following World War II. It is interesting, and probably significant, that the bizarre murders of Peggy Refoule, Jeanette Reyman, and John Garris made them victims not only of homicide, but victims too of the unsettled and changing times in which they lived. All had been intimately affected by World War II, and the people closest to them had been affected by the war. It is quite likely that the lives of the murderers themselves had also been altered in some manner by World War II. While this of course is not the entire explanation for the slayings, it is most certainly an important factor, for if there had been no war the Refoules would probably never have left France or the Reymans their native Indiana, nor would John Garris have fled the Nazis in Germany. Their lives were changed by the events of the time in which they lived, and this contributed to their untimely deaths.

It is unlikely that a lone homicide would ever again arouse in Atlanta the interest which the Refoule, Reyman, and Garris cases provoked. The reasons for this are varied. The Garris case, coming two years later, did not arouse the intensity of interest of the other two cases. Times were changing.

Of course the primary concern of people about these cases was because the crimes were never solved. Even had they been solved ultimately to the satisfaction of everyone, which is highly unlikely, given the trend of the times, interest still would have been intense. In the absence of a confession or eyewitness, it is very doubtful that these cases could ever be solved to the satisfaction of everyone. There were too many elements involved that were a part of society at the time. These cases were not just homicides. They were a part of the social fabric, and are now a part of the social history, of everyone who lived through that era. Housewives read about the death of Peggy Refoule after finishing their ironing and thought: "That could be me!" Small-time crooks read about "Tojo" Pulley and thought the police might next try to pin a murder rap on them. Leaders of the community thought that these unsolved murders were certainly giving the community a bad name. The newspapers and radio brought the news close to everybody. The crimes, in some way and manner, appeared to touch everyone.

6

28 Young Blacks

The murder of children is the most heinous crime imaginable. The multiple murder of more than two-dozen young blacks in Atlanta in the years from 1979 to 1981 rocked the city, made the nation quickly aware of Atlanta's plight, and focused worldwide attention upon the missing and murdered children's cases. Almost simultaneously with the disappearance of the victims or the discovery of their bodies, the cases were catapulted into instant prominence. The unsolved murder cases which had occurred in Atlanta in the years following World War II had absorbed the minds and emotions of the people of Atlanta, and to a lesser extent of the people of the state and region. But the cases of the missing and murdered black children and young adults which occurred following two decades of profound social change in the country, and especially within the city which more than any other had orchestrated that change, gained immediate international notoriety. Certain complex homicides of the past occurred in social environments undergoing ardent social alterations, and in effect acted as harbingers of more that was to come. Perhaps it is no happenstance, then, that the multiple murders of young blacks took place in Atlanta and that at that point in time they most likely would not have occurred anywhere else.

In the last week of July 1979, the bodies of Edward Smith, aged 14, and Alfred Evans, aged 13, were discovered less than 150 feet apart in a dumping area in southwest Atlanta. Smith had died from a single gunshot wound, and the bullet had passed through his body and was not recovered. Investigators believed that he had been shot at another location and his body dumped where it was later found. Medical examiners assumed that Evans died from asphyxiation, but the body was too decomposed for the cause of death to be determined.

In any year, Atlanta will have from six to a dozen homicides of black children. These cases are normally solved and a relative is most often charged with the murder. These are domestic homicides in which the killer is known to the victim, and the victim is nearly always related in some manner to the killer. It is the type of homicide that began with Cain and Abel and is the kind of homicide that, as we have said a number of times before in this survey, police investigators have to deal with daily. There was no reason for the police to assume that the murders of Edward Smith and Alfred Evans, whose bodies were discovered in the hot and humid July heat of an otherwise tranquil Atlanta summer, would in time become the first and second names of murdered Atlanta children on a seemingly endless list.

On October 21, 1979, nine-year-old Yusef Bell left his apartment in downtown Atlanta near the stadium to go on an errand for a neighbor. On November 8 his body was discovered in an abandoned elementary school near his home. He had been strangled. Three days before the discovery of Bell's body the skeletal remains of 14-year-old Milton Harvey were discovered in East Point. Harvey had last been seen a month earlier riding his bicycle near his northwest Atlanta home.

Atlanta police then had in their files four unsolved murder cases of black children. For a period of four months no other cases were added, but in March of 1980 black children again began being reported either missing or murdered. By July, 12 black children had been found murdered, and none of the cases had been solved.

In this period of time, among the families of middle and low-income blacks living in the predominately or all-black neighborhoods of southeast and southwest Atlanta, it came to be believed that some evil and sinister force loose in their communities was "snatching" and murdering their children. Their children were the hope of the future. Now some person or some thing was threatening and taking them away. The black communities of Atlanta became rife with fear, suspicion, and paranoia. The people were up in arms. They were further frustrated in their plight because they had no leadership. The civil rights groups in the city that had in the past always represented black aspirations had been unable to foresee what was happening in Atlanta and to Atlanta's children.

In June, Camille Bell, the mother of Yusef Bell, gathered the mothers of seven other black children who had been slain and called a press conference. She stated that a person or persons unknown were killing Atlanta's children and the elected officials and law enforcement officers were doing nothing to stop it. The mothers demanded some action on the part of the police department. The mothers organized themselves into a Committee to Stop Children's Murders. The guiding force behind the committee was Camille Bell. Out of the frustration and despair of the neighborhoods where the murdered children lived was created an organization dedicated to doing something to stop the killings. Like other groups before it, Camille Bell's organization was born on the wings of helplessness and the sure conviction that there was nothing else that could aid black people threatened by this new and bewildering phenomenon.

Commissioner Lee Brown and the other top personnel within the Atlanta Bureau of Police Services were severely stung by Camille Bell's charges. Most of them did not believe that a sinister killer force was murdering black children. They thought it was the "usual" pattern of homicides with which the city always had to contend. But Camille Bell was stirring things up and others were feeling the heat. Mayor Maynard Jackson voiced confidence in the police department, but he promised to step up the murder investigations.

But all of the cases remained unsolved. The consensus in most black neighborhoods was that the Atlanta police couldn't catch a bad cold. Confidence in the police department in Atlanta, which had always been high, was fast eroding. This was an intolerable situation for a black city administration and police force whose two top commanders were black. The people within the community who in the past had been most supportive of the black leadership of city government were openly criticizing that government and holding it up to ridicule. This was a situation which white-led governments had had to deal with for years—this aspect of the political process which eventually falls upon those who exercise political and police powers within a democracy.

SPECIAL TASK FORCE

On July 17, 1980, Commissioner Lee Brown ordered the creation of a Special Task Force on Murdered and Missing Children. Its sole responsibility was to find out who was killing young black Atlantans. Eventually the task force would have its own separate building on West Peachtree Street in the shadow of downtown Atlanta's most impressive sky-scrapers. It originally consisted of four members but a year later it had 175 members, including state investigators and representatives from other metro-area police departments. Assisting the group was a 40-member FBI team.

Whether the Special Task Force was originally set up to handle what the police deemed to be a stymied murder inves-tigation problem or to deal with a political problem will no doubt be debated for years to come. The evidence for now would appear to indicate that the task force was set up to handle what was perceived to be a political problem. The first commander of the task force and the personnel working there were not seasoned investigators nor even detectives, but per-sonnel from the police department's crime-prevention unit. Shortly after the formation of the task force a number of in-vestigators who had worked on murder cases in other cities were invited in to assist.

A number of psychics, some invited and some not invited, also came to Atlanta to assist the police. It is not exactly clear why the task force thought it necessary to bring them in ex-cept as a gesture to try to give the impression to the public that the police were on the job. It is a pretty well-believed myth on the part of the public that psychics in the past have helped the police catch killers. Their dismal failure to do so in Atlanta will perhaps prod the public into not believing in their inviolability in future cases.

To understand why the task force thought it necessary to bring in outside investigators is more complex. There was no doubt some thought that the case might be a classic jack-the-ripper type and that any police officers who had dealt with a case like that would be helpful. However, it would seem that there was a more overriding political consideration.

In the beginning it was suggested here that one way to un-derstand the entire phenomenon of the missing and murdered children's cases is to view it in the afterwash of years of seg-regation—upon the public, the police, and the murdered vic-tims.

It takes years of training to develop a good homicide detec-tive. It means serving a number of years in the uniform divi-sion and then more years of work in vice and larceny—some twenty years of police preparation for a detective to accurately size up murder scenes and develop the contact with informers to supply him with meaningful information. As the Atlanta Police Department was segregated until the early 1960s, only a small number of blacks were beginning to attain this status in 1979, and some of them had left the department to join the Fulton County Police Department when it was formed in 1975. Many of the white detectives who had worked on complex murder investigations in the past had retired by 1979. Generally speaking, the homicide division, like the entire police department, was a young department; neither had experience in dealing with a case of this magnitude. Thus the need for outside assistance. Police officials who would fly into town for a few days and offer advice and then depart were probably more helpful to the police working on the cases than it appeared at the time. We have to constantly keep in mind that cases of this magnitude occur only about every 25 or 30 years, so they in fact become a learning experience for the police as well as for the public.

Whether or not the task force was formed as a public relations arm of the police department, the police certainly had a difficult political problem on their hands. The black public, just emerging from years of segregation, had never experienced anything like this. Following World War II the white public of Atlanta had never experienced anything like the murders and investigations that then stormed across the scene. Much of the black community of Atlanta in 1979 was about where the Atlanta white community had been in 1947–'49 in dealing with this kind of murder investigation. The main similarity is that both had to deal with developments at different points in time with something that was an entirely new experience. The times were different and the aspects of the cases were not the same, but the reaction of both communities in both periods of time was one of fear—fear of the unknown, fear of what was happening to them.

REWARD MONEY

Public and police officials decided that the best way to deal with the political problem was to make some sort of headway in solving the cases. Mayor Maynard Jackson made a public plea for reward money to be offered. Various businesses and individuals immediately came forth with a $100,000 reward to anyone giving information leading to the apprehension of the killer or killers. Mayor Jackson went on television with the hundred thousand dollars in front of him. The idea was that somebody had to know something about some of these murders and the lure of money would smoke out the culprit.

Whatever the intent, the result was disastrous. The task force was flooded with thousands of calls. Everybody who had caught a glimpse of the $100,000 had also, they were sure, caught sight of the culprit. Many investigators feel that the rush to try to collect the reward money on the part of the public so inundated the police with irrelevant information that any hope of finding the murderer at that point was lost.

In spite of the efforts of an ever-expanding task force, by the time of the 1980 presidential election 17 black children had disappeared and 13 of them had been found murdered. With the election out of the way, national media interest became intense. Camille Bell was being interviewed by reporters from everywhere.

With the release of American hostages by Iran and the inauguration of a new president, the full focus of the nation's attention was turned upon the murders in Atlanta. Atlantans felt, like the former American hostages in Iran, that they were being held hostage by the killing of their children. Everyone hoped and prayed for a quick solution to the murders.

The winter and early spring of 1981 in Atlanta had to be among the worst that any community had ever endured. Assistant Chief Morris Redding, a seasoned police investigator, had been placed in charge of the Special Task Force. The Georgia Bureau of Investigation and the Federal Bureau of Investigation had entered the case. The FBI's presence was an unprecedented action because the FBI lacked jurisdiction. This renewed activity, while not immediately productive, coincided with the finding of ten more bodies. Several of those victims had been missing since 1980; consequently, the bodies were in very bad condition, some to such an extent that the cause of death could not be determined. The bodies turned up in rivers, in wooded areas, and in vacant lots. Whereas the first bodies had been discovered within the Atlanta city limits, later bodies turned up in Fulton, DeKalb, Cobb, and Douglas counties. By the first of June, 26 black males and two black females ranging in ages from seven to 27 years of age had been added to the task force list. Since the end of March five bodies had been found, and these individuals were considerably older than the first victims. Practically no investigators working on the cases thought that they were all related. A majority of the younger children on the list were from poor and broken homes; they were street-wise and were accustomed to doing all kinds of odd jobs to earn a dollar. Generally, they were small for their ages, as were the few adults on the list; in some cases the latter were also mentally slow. None of those on the list appeared to have resisted their attacker or to have been given drugs or alcohol prior to their deaths. None had been sexually assaulted. The police were severely hampered in investigating the cases because there was no apparent motive for the killings.

In 1973 police in Houston, Texas, had dug up a number of bodies of young white boys who had been murdered and buried by Elmer Wayne Henley. In 1978 John W. Gacy, Jr., murdered 33 boys and young adults and buried them in the walls of a house in Illinois. Twisted and thwarted sexual desire appeared to have been the motive for those killings. In Birmingham, Michigan, in 1977, mysterious killings claimed the lives of seven white children. No one was ever arrested for any of the Michigan killings, but at least four and maybe more were thought by police officials to be related. Many investigators believed that the Atlanta murders most resembled the cases in Birmingham, Michigan.

POSSIBLE MOTIVES

From the very beginning it was felt by many blacks and by some whites that the killings in Atlanta were racially motivated. Blacks were being assaulted in Buffalo, New York, and Vernon Jordan of the Urban League, who was a native Atlantan, had been shot in an ambush attack. It was natural to assume that these killings could be of a racial nature. Black parents warned their children to be aware of strangers in general and of whites in particular. Young blacks were on guard so as not to be snatched by white vigilantes. Many thoughtful persons, considering the "unreconstructed" people they knew and pondering the vaunted resurgence of the Ku Klux Klan, realized there were certainly some people who were so warped as to murder the objects of their hatred. But as more victims kept turning up it became evident to nearly everyone that the motive was not racial and that the killer very likely was not white.

When the Center For Research In Social Change began to function in the late sixties, one of its first conclusions was that the police needed to place more reliance on scientific analysis. Certainly no one can accuse Commissioner Brown or anyone else on the police investigative team for not relying on the latest up-to-date scientific methods available. Some 150,000 individuals in selected Atlanta neighborhoods were reached by computerized telephone messages from Brown and mothers of the victims. The calls asked for clues in the cases and gave the persons contacted the opportunity to tell what, if anything, they knew about the cases. Computers were used to make electronic searches for links between cases and to match certain data with particular cases. The FBI attempted to lift fingerprints from the bodies, a very difficult procedure that local police departments are unable to execute. Samples of the soil and of fibrous material at the crime scene were painstakingly gathered and sent to the state crime lab for analysis. More than 1,300 tips were sent out for further analysis. Police and volunteer firemen carried pictures door-to-door throughout the city of missing and slain children. Police took pictures of persons attending funerals of the children on the chance that the killer might derive some ghoulish pleasure out of that aspect of the tragedy. A number of persons were brought in for questioning by the police task force and other metro police departments.

All of which cost a great deal of money. Money to pay for police overtime, money to pay for electronic surveillance, and money to pay for a host of other expenses incurred by the Special Task Force. Besides the money spent by Atlanta and by Fulton and DeKalb counties, as well as the cost to the federal government of keeping a 40-man FBI team in the city, the federal government made available $3,300,000 for the investigation and for mental health treatment of children who had suffered emotional problems stemming from the slayings. The involvement of the federal government to such an extent was unprecedented in what theretofore had always been regarded as a purely local matter. The city was grateful for the assistance, and it is not unrealistic to suppose that considerable violence or other upheavels would have occurred without it.

Not only public money but private money was an essential

part of the investigation. Money from businesses and individuals was received from all over the country. Charity benefits by Frank Sinatra, Aretha Franklin, and Sammy Davis, Junior, and an increase in the reward fund from $100,000 to $500,000 by a gift from former boxing champ Muhammad Ali were but a part of vast sums of money contributed or raised by well-known personalities, school children, big corporations and ordinary citizens. Money poured into City Hall, the Southern Christian Leadership Conference, and the Committee to Stop Children's Murders. The money was used to pay funeral expenses for the victims, to contribute financial assistance to the families of victims, and to provide for recreational activities for Atlanta children during the summer of 1981.

There was almost as much talk and speculation about the money raised as there was about the murder investigation. Certainly no other investigation had ever before in history brought forth such an outpouring of money. People wanted to know if the money was being spent wisely and for the proper purposes. This is another question that will be debated for years to come, if for no other reason than that nobody really knew how much money was actually contributed. Camille Bell's Committee to Stop Children's Murders was severely criticized by many for the way it handled donations. It appeared, however, that if mistakes were made, they came about primarily because the committee had grown so much faster than anyone had anticipated and because the members were unprepared for handling the responsibilities thrust upon them.

"HELPERS"

Money, psychics, dog-trackers, detectives who worked on other renowned murder cases, famous persons, and reporters from all over the world flowed into Atlanta. The Atlanta Bureau of Police Services was chastised for not having a press officer to handle the flood of media folk. The department's response was that it had barely enough resources to handle the unprecedented demands of the investigation and the media would have to fend for itself. A spokesperson eventually was designated to handle press inquiries, but much of the official word from the department continued to come from Commissioner Brown.

On the heels of the press followed a band of young people

from New York who called themselves the Guardian Angels. They were an unofficial group organized to protect users of New York's crime-plagued subway system. Their presence in Atlanta was not welcomed by Atlanta police or by the residents of Atlanta's inner-city neighborhoods. The Guardian Angels came and went, but their coming to the city sparked the formation of a citizen-defender organization in the low-income Techwood Homes area. One would-be leader of the latter group announced plans to arm volunteer vigilantes with baseball bats. In response, the police insisted that no person or group would be permitted to arrogate unto itself any portion of the police function.

Members of the task force and FBI agents interviewed hundreds of people who in some way had aroused suspicion. A number of suspects looked good, but in time further investigation caused the leads to fizzle.

Many ordinary residents of Atlanta were working either to solve the children's murders or to prevent future slayings. Every Saturday morning groups of citizens gathered at various checkpoints throughout the city to search for clues to the missing children. Other people became block parents and members of parent patrol groups and kept an eye out for all neighborhood children. These groups operated separately from the Committee to Stop Children's Murders. Some were under the auspices of city government; some were merely community-wide efforts to help protect the city's children.

The outpouring of money, offers of assistance, and expressions of sympathy continued to be received from around the world. One of the more tangible results, and one which did an inestimable amount of good, was a cost-free week on the Caribean island of Guadeloupe, which was made possible by Club-Med Inc. The international resorts firm flew several groups of 20 black children to the resort of the privileged. The week of sun, swimming and frolic—a totally new experience for most of the youngsters—caused them to return home with sparkling eyes and only vague reminders of the series of horrors which had caused the hot school-free summer months to loom portentiously over their parents and Atlanta's officials.

NEW DEVELOPMENTS

The tenseness which had gripped Atlanta into the late spring of 1981 was momentarily alleviated on June 4 when police officials announced with great fanfare that a suspect had been questioned in connection with the death of 27-year old Nathaniel Cater, whose body had been fished from the Chattahoochee River a few days earlier. In an unusual departure from established procedure, Public Safety Commissioner Lee Brown identified the suspect as Wayne B. Williams, a 23-year-old black man. Attention had been focused upon him since early on the morning of May 22, when a police stakeout under a bridge over the Chattahoochee had heard a loud splash nearby. Calling to a colleague on the road leading to the bridge above, he asked whether a car could be seen. The latter ascertained that one was moving slowly in his direction; when it was stopped a few minutes later the driver identified himself as Williams. FBI agents and police interrogated him, but had no basis for placing charges. It was not until two days later that the body of Cater, the city's 28th black murder victim, was recovered from the river.

A police recruit recalled later that a pile of clothing was in the back of Williams' car when he was stopped near the bridge, but no attention was paid to it at the time. Subsequently neighbors reported that the next day the suspect was seen removing several boxes from his home. Williams was questioned by the FBI, but after several hours he was again released. He remained under constant surveillance, however, a circumstance of which he seemed to be aware but which did not keep him from leading police on several high-speed chases around Atlanta.

Finally, on June 14, Wayne Williams was arrested and charged with the murder of Nathaniel Cater. Police stated that evidence in the form of hairs and carpet fibers collected from Williams' home and car showed "no significant microscopic differences" from evidence found on Cater's body *and also on the bodies or from the sites where the bodies of other victims had been discovered.*

Soon Williams was charged also with the death of Jimmy Ray Payne, whose body had been found in the Chattahoochee on April 27. In that case, as in others, the cause of death was determined to be asphyxiation by means unknown.

A possible clue to the puzzling fact that no evidence had been uncovered to indicate that any of the victims had struggled to save their lives was found in one of many newspaper stories dealing with the tragedies. In it the reporter quoted a member of an emergency rescue crew with whom the suspect often hung out as saying that Williams sometimes sprayed his playful companions with Mace, an aerosol compound with temporarily-disabling qualities.

As the evidence against him continued to mount, there appeared to be more than a passing chance that the accused man would be charged with several more of the young blacks' murders.

Who was Wayne Williams? The answer is not easy, for police and local newspapers reported that he appeared to be many things: a brilliant high school student who became a college drop-out, a radio station operator and free-lance photographer, a procurer of talented young blacks for supposed television appearances, a preparer of his own inflated resumés who delighted in proximity to the powerful and famous, a hustler who created illusory successes upon a foundation of disguised failures, and a man who found the limelight in which he gloried only in the pitiless and destructive publicity which could lead to the permanent loss of his freedom—or even of his life.

The unprofessional, even frivolous, manner in which police officials handled the headlong rush to identify Williams even before he was charged with a crime caused them to be severely criticized. *The Atlanta Constitution* joined the chorus on June 24 with a stinging rebuke captioned "Let The Circus End."

> Wayne B. Williams has been arrested and charged with the slaying of one of the 28 young blacks whose deaths have plunged this city into the depths of fear and tragedy. Even with Williams behind bars, the investigation goes on.
>
> The slayings and the investigation have occurred in a circus-like atmosphere that has given our city an international black eye. The investigation and arrest of Williams also were carried out under the most bizarre of conditions. Around-the-clock open surveillance of the suspect, law suits, press conferences, high level meetings with the governor—all these things have given the investigation a kind of surreal movie-like aura.
>
> It is time now to end the movie spectacular. It is time to let the wheels of justice grind without an attendant carnival. Wayne Williams is behind bars. But in the American tradition, he is presumed innocent until and unless he is proven guilty.
>
> It is time for law enforcement officials to end leaks about evidence in the case. It may also be time to stop worrying about

who pressured whom to initiate the arrest and set the prosecutorial system in motion.

Let the show-biz atmosphere dissipate. Let the kooks and cranks clear out. Let the official press conference (in which no announcements are made and no questions are answered) come to an end. Let the criminal justice system take over, and without further hindrance, let justice be done.

Mayor Maynard Jackson attempted to calm the general agitation by noting that "We must be ready to turn *to* each other and not *on* each other." He agreed with an official of Atlanta's Coca-Cola Co. who said "The sorrow has been unparalleled, but the unity has been unprecedented." The mayor went on to say that despite the tragic killings, Atlanta was still a boom town. "The impact of the killings on the economy," he added, "has been negligible."

Atlanta, despite such soothing words, must have been perceived by many millions of persons around the world as having suffered a notable diminution of its once-proud image. The sparkling New South city of towering skyscrapers and feverish growth, the inheritor of the steel-and-magnolia tradition of the Old South, was undoubtedly scarred from two years of trauma, but its staunchest admirers believed its wounds would not be fatal. Eventually, when justice had taken its ponderous course, it would again be hailed as "The city too busy to hate" and "The world's next great city." Until then Atlantans could be grateful that, for whatever reason, the shocking series of black murders seemed to have stopped.

If the tragedy of Atlanta in the 1980s can awaken people everywhere to an awareness of the harsh realities of life in the closing years of the twentieth century, and also equip them to cope more effectively with the challenges thus confronted, the victims of the senseless series of murders will not have given up their young lives entirely in vain. Already it is apparent that no murder or murder investigation has ever before touched the lives of so many people. In an age of instant communication, each new development in the seemingly-endless stream of murders was carried via satellite throughout the world. Eventually a shocked and impatient public reluctantly realized that cases of this type do not lend themselves to quick and speedy solutions.

7

The Aftermath

The Heinz, Refoule, Reyman and Garris murders had a profound impact upon police practices in regard to homicides because they were never solved to the satisfaction of everyone, if solved at all. Since these murders involved prominent victims who led unusual lives, and the cases received wide publicity, and because television did not exist at the time, they provided a certain interest, even entertainment, for everyone. These murders occurred in a period of upheaval that led to changes which affected everybody. However, this was not the only backdrop. There was also the background of a rising incidence of homicides within the community, and these four murders were used by the press to highlight the rising number of homicides. These murders made compelling reading and the general public became aware, for the first time, of changing conditions within the city insofar as the homicide rate was concerned.

The public would never have become aroused had not prominent people been killed, and as long as murder was largely confined to the inner-city, mostly-black population of the community, there were few demands that something be done to bring the homicide rate down. But the murder of important people made people *aware*. Once people were made aware, then, they began to realize that the high homicide rate was due mainly to generations of segregation, poverty, and police and public neglect. Therefore, these particular murders became more than just mere homicides; they became the basis of social awareness and, ultimately, police change. Had these murders never occurred, it is very doubtful that the larger community would have become as exercised as it did over the number of homicides within the city. But people who were never aware of a knife-killing within an upstairs room off a back alley across from the downtown railroad tracks were touched by the murder of Henry Heinz in Druid Hills and

Peggy Refoule in Buckhead. The complacency of the very private, untouched worlds of these two havens had been forever disturbed. The people who lived in these neighborhoods were galvanized into taking action which would prevent further intrusions into their private refuge. But once aroused, the people of the community would go on and insist that the police and press work for a more civilized community. The deaths of Henry Heinz, Peggy Refoule, Jeanette Reyman, and John Garris became the impetus which led to public concern which in turn led to startling changes in police practices in regard to homicides.

The following figures indicate the number of homicides, the number of these homicides which were solved, and the number of victims who were black and white in a given period of years. The chart, in some years, indicates more cases solved than homicides for the year. This is because some crimes solved in a particular year were murders of a previous year.

HOMICIDES IN ATLANTA

Year	No. Of Homicides	No. Solved	VICTIMS	
			No. of Whites	No. of Blacks
1944	69	88	13	56
1945	91	87	15	76
1946	97	82	10	87
1947	91	83	9	82
1948	76	78	2	74
1949	88	87	9	79
1950	101	106	15	86
1951	83	83	9	74
1952	102	96	15	87
1953	74	75	4	70
1954	85	79	10	75
1955	79	81	14	65
TOTAL	1036	1025	125	911

These figures cover the period from the end of World War II up until the mid-fifties. It indicates a rising homicide rate during the latter war years. A chart from the Depression years and just afterwards would indicate a similar pattern—

a rising homicide rate during the Depression and reaching a peak in the years immediately following.

In the peak year of 1946, 97 homicides occurred in Atlanta. Afterwards, for the following two years, there is a drop each year until 1949 when the rate goes up slightly, and in 1950 when it jumps, way up, and then goes down again in 1951. A probable explanation for the rise in the years 1949–'50 is the recession and outbreak of war in Korea, but of course the homicide rate will reflect many factors and this is only conjecture. It is interesting that it shows a rise in the 1949–'50 period. After 1950 the homicide rate in Atlanta dropped steadily throughout the early 1950s and then leveled off at an average of about 86. Remarkably, the number of homicides in Atlanta never again went over 100 until 1964. The year 1952 shows a jump. This is misleading. On January 1, 1952, the city of Atlanta extended its limits and took in a large area that practically doubled the size of the city's boundaries. Therefore, the figures for 1952 include statistics for an area twice the size of previous years. What is surprising about this chart which indicates the number of homicides in this period is that even after the city of Atlanta doubled its size and increased its population by addition (*not* including growth) by some fifty thousand people, the homicide rate declined considerably from what it had been in the 'thirties and 'forties.

There are two reasons which have already been mentioned that partially explain this phenomenon: In the first place, the several sensational murders in the 1940s (and there were others besides those mentioned) led to public awareness and support for the press and police to do something about the problem. Secondly, the 1940s were a time of war and social upheaval which contrasted sharply with the period of the rather placid and serene 1950s. And, thirdly, there were profound and far-reaching changes in police procedure.

The courts began to take a stern look at the methods employed by the police in homicide investigations, and cases based upon station-house confessions and continuous grilling of suspects began to fall apart in the courtroom. In order to secure convictions the police had to find other means of establishing guilt in murder cases. Mainly the police had to establish a strong case against a suspect before they arrested him. This led to new procedures. It also meant hard work and longer hours on the part of police detectives.

The national press had been very critical of police procedure in both the Refoule and Reyman murders. It concluded that the Fulton County force made no real effort to find the true killer in the Refoule case, and that detectives merely asked workmen known to have been in the area prior to the murder: "Did you murder Mrs. Refoule? Well . . . No? Do you know anyone who might have?" etc. etc., and *Newsweek* stated that Atlanta police "stumbled over each other" in investigating the Reyman case.

This criticism led to further changes and innovations. The detective division of the Atlanta police force was further upgraded and divided into specialized squads to deal with all types of violent crimes. But no matter how good the organization or the physical set-up, nothing can be done about homicides unless competent men providing outstanding leadership are doing their jobs. In Atlanta, under Mayor Hartsfield and Chief Jenkins, and most importantly Detective Superintendent Glynn Cowan, the Atlanta Police Department developed in the 1950s one of the finest homicide divisions of any police department in the world.

With the implementation of the Plan of Improvement in 1952 the old Fulton County Police Department was merged with the Atlanta force. Residents outside the city limits were impressed with the way Atlanta police were now handling homicides, and were keenly observant that the homicide rate in Atlanta was declining. The bitterness of the Refoule case lingered, and Buckhead residents were only too glad to come under the protection of a police department dedicated to do something about homicides.

The Heinz, Refoule, and Reyman cases mark the end of an era in homicide investigations. Social changes occurred in our society which altered the nature of homicides and the quest for their solution.

We cannot hope to abolish homicides. Murder has been going on since Cain and Abel. It is not likely to cease anytime soon. The problem which faces society today is an attempt to control homicides as much as possible.

We now live in a world very different from Cain and Abel. We live in a world very different from the America of the 1930s, 1940s, and 1950s. Our lives no longer follow the patterns of the past, nor do our homicides. The only thing that is the same is that the killing continues.

The homicide rate in America today is on the increase, not only in our cities but in the suburbs and smaller towns and hamlets. Homicides which in the past were mostly committed in the inner city now occur everywhere. Events have made people knowledgeable. As the Heinz and Refoule murders touched people of another era, widespread coverage of murder by the media has alerted everyone to the increasing number of killings occurring in our society today. As Atlanta in another time learned, today everybody knows what is going on. The reaction, thus far, has led primarily to an increase in weaponry. People fear the increasing violence of our times. We are told and read constantly of people being murdered in the course of a stick-up or robbery. People do not feel safe. The idea has flowered that people will kill you for no reason. People purchase guns because they do not feel safe.

Since the latter 1960s, an increase in the purchase of guns parallels an increase in homicides. While purchasing a gun makes an individual feel he is less likely to be assaulted and murdered, statistics do not bear this out. As the number of guns in private hands climbs, the homicide rate soars.

It is obvious that the elimination of handguns by itself would not abolish homicides. The 1930s were a time of economic depression. For the poor, firearms, unless stolen, were hard to come by: They simply did not have the money to buy guns. But in the 'thirties the homicide rate was inordinately high. As you go back and read through case after case from this period the one striking common denominator that comes across on the fading crumpled pages of the police reports is that, even without guns, if a person is determined to kill, he will find the means of doing so. People were stabbed to death with ice picks, but technological advance has virtually eliminated this weapon. Victims were hacked to death with axes. Household and pocket knives were favorite murder weapons. They severed jugular veins, penetrated hearts, ruptured kidneys, ripped out intestines, and partially succeeded in hacking away heads in an orgy of blood and guts that often made crime scenes look like meat processing plants. A hunk of concrete, bricks, and a variety of rocks of varying size, weight, and design were bashed over people's heads and crushed their skulls and converted the human body into a bloody pulp. We think of murder in the 'thirties being committed by tough talking crooks firing handguns. It was this way on the screen,

but not often in real life. In the era of hunger and want and
fear and lynchings and electric chairs, homicides were committed by whatever means handy and had about them an
aura of intensity that surpasses even the killings of the present day.

The violence of the period was vented upon the police as
well as the ordinary citizenry. While making a routine drunk
arrest at a downtown tavern, an Atlanta policeman was murdered when a man stabbed him with a knife. The assailant
was ultimately arrested and died in the electric chair. A policeman tried to arrest a Negro man who was assaulting a
Negro woman with a knife. While making the arrest the
black prisoner slashed the officer and nearly severed the jugular vein and cut him severely on the shoulder. The officer was
off-duty and on his way home and walking from the police
station when he happened upon the situation in the street.
The woman was screaming and called out to the policeman
for help. He rushed toward her and took hold of his assailant
and jerked him away from her. When the assailant cut him,
the officer knocked the man down with his pistol, putting the
gun out of commission. The man continued to fight with him
and the officer beat him over the head with the pistol until he
was subdued. Although badly wounded, he walked the man
two blocks to the police station and locked him up before seeking medical attention.

But citizens suffered even more. Atlanta police were called
to investigate a homicide. They viewed the body at the funeral home, for the police had not been called to the scene
when the murder was committed. This happened often in
those times. The victim had a cut under his left eye and his
face appeared as if it had been hit with an iron pipe or battered with brass knuckles. The victim also had a 1½ inch hole
in the back of his head and neck. After much checking, the
police managed to locate the crime scene and several witnesses. Everybody stated to the police that the victim fell off
the porch during an argument. The police interviewed the individual who was having an argument with the victim and
were told that the man just fell off the porch. The eyewitnesses backed up the man's story. The police calculated that
the victim fell about 10 feet from the porch to the ground. The
ground was free of sticks and stones and could not have made
the hole in the victim's head. It was obvious that the man had

been brutally murdered. The police talked with numbers of people. No one would incriminate anyone else, for whatever reason. No relatives came forward with any information or demands that the police "do something." The homicide did not make the newspapers. The people concerned had no interest in finding the culprit. The police lost interest. No one was indicted for murder.

This was a typical homicide of the time. They nearly always occurred for no good reason, over nothing; they still do. A quarrel among persons is ended when one of the individuals is murdered. It begins as a case of assault which ends in homicide.

In a case of simple assault, there is even more indifference on the part of the people involved. There was a case of the period when two men got into a quarrel at the factory where they both were employed. At the end of the day tempers had not abated and the two men went outside to settle the argument. A fight ensued and one man pulled a gun. He shot the other man in the abdomen and when the man turned to run away from the gun, the man shot him again in the backside. Both bullets were fired at close range. The bullet which hit the man in the abdomen went clear through the man's body, fortunately by-passing all vital organs on the journey. The second bullet did not go all the way through, but miraculously it also did not penetrate any vital parts of the body. The injured man was given first aid and sent to the hospital. He quickly recovered and was back at work. The man who shot him was not off the job even for a day. Why? The man who was shot said it was just an argument and he was not mad anymore. No, the man who was shot did not wish to press charges or prosecute. Besides, he had sold the gun to his assailant in the first place—on credit! But it was a case where, had either of the bullets varied in the slightest, the man would have been a homicide statistic. Was it not probable that, having used his weapon once, the man would use it again? But there was nothing that could be done. It takes a corpse to arouse people, and, as we have seen in this era, even that often did not excite people very much.

The way homicides are occurring in the present day reminds us of the bloody 'thirties and 'forties all over again. The main difference now appears to be in a change of attitude and in the choice of weaponry. It is now handguns that commit the most homicides and while other means are still employed, none are as much used as firearms. The same cavalier disregard for human life exists, however. Just recently in Atlanta a young expectant mother closed her eyes and fatally wounded her husband after he handed her a cocked .22-caliber pistol and dared her to shoot him. When the police arrived on the scene the young woman told them that she and her husband had an argument over his going down to the Tenth Street area and that during the argument the man kept hitting her and when she began crying and saying that he had hurt her, he became really angry; when he handed his wife the gun and dared her to shoot him, she closed her eyes and pulled the trigger. Her husband, shot in the chest, died in a hospital operating room. There were no witnesses to the murder, but police tended to believe the wife's story. In the old days if a wife had shot her husband she would have told the police it was an accident, that the gun just happened to fire accidentally as her husband approached threateningly. But a new generation has developed a new approach to homicides. They no longer devise elaborate ruses denying guilt—at least in homicides which are the result of a domestic argument. Homicides which are the result of assault and/or robbery are quite a different matter. But an argument between husband and wife which results in the murder of one or the other is all very casual nowadays. Premeditation, planning, intense hatred are all definitely a thing of the past. The police, by talking to the individual, usually determine quickly the facts in the case. The young mother-to-be in the above-mentioned case was routinely indicted for murder. The story attracted scant attention from the media. It was all very matter-of-fact.

A really vicious murder of the 1940s type occurred in the Atlanta metro area a few years ago. A young businesswoman vanished from a shopping center parking lot without a trace. Five days later her bound and gagged body was found covered with leaves in an adjoining county. The killer was traced to Texas. Previously he had tried to use the victim's credit cards and to cash one of her personal checks. When apprehended by the police the killer admitted his guilt. He said that he did not intend to kill her; he had intended only to steal her automobile and credit cards. He stated further that he was on heroin and morphine at the time it all happened. In the 'thirties killers often told police they murdered because they were drinking and did not remember. Harsh and Gallogly pleaded this line. Horace Blalock robbed and murdered to play the "bug." Nowadays all the murderers are on drugs and don't plan to kill and don't remember if they do kill. This aspect of the homicide story has not changed; there is merely a shift of emphasis on what the individual states is his reason or excuse for committing murder. It is doubtful that alcohol, playing the "bug," or drugs are often the cause of homicides, regardless of what the murderers say.

The killer of the young businesswoman was returned to Cobb County to be tried for the murder. The case had received wide publicity and at the time the young woman's body had been found, sight-seers had rushed to the scene in ways reminiscent of the now-legendary Refoule murder. One would expect the murder trial to draw a large crowd. But before the case-followers could even gather up their sewing work and brown-bag lunches, the most sensational would-be murder trial in Atlanta in years was concluded. In a dramatic courtroom scene the 27-year-old murderer entered guilty pleas to charges of murder, kidnap, rape and armed robbery. He was sentenced to four consecutive life terms plus three more years for stealing the victim's car. He would be eligible for parole in seven years, but considering the charges against him, gaining parole in that length of time seemed unlikely, but not impossible. No one had been sentenced to the electric chair in Georgia in a number of years, but it was no doubt still possible and since only a jury could sentence a person to the electric chair, the defendant in this case decided to take his chances with the judge.

In the old days nobody ever copped out in a case like this. The more guilty a person was in a homicide case, the more determined he was to try and beat the rap with a jury. But for a variety of reasons the sensational, headline-grabbing murder trials appear to be a vanishing spectacle.

The homicide rate at present is going up, not down. Three factors, and no doubt many others, are basic to the general upswing in murder. One is the cheap, readily-available handgun. The second is technological advance. Improvements in the field of communication, especially the advent of television, have changed everyone's life, and television has probably played a villain's role in causing the murder rate to accelerate. The third reason is social revolution and war.

The first of these factors concerns firearms. Although we live in an era of generally rising prices, the overall cost of a handgun is less now than it was in the thirties. Guns are in great supply and available at relatively low cost. Every time a national figure becomes a homicide victim, there is a movement to restrict the manufacture and sale of handguns, a movement which wanes in momentum rather quickly. Even though there was great demand for a ban on the sale of guns following the assassinations of national figures in the 1960s, there are many more guns sold to private individuals now than there were then.

Approximately 80% of some type of firearm is responsible for all homicides. Virtually all homicides which are the result of assault and/or robbery are committed with a handgun. Few robberies are carried out by the robber demanding the money from the cash register at the point of a knife. It is always a gun, or the *threat* of a gun which is a factor in hold-ups. Without the presence or the threat of the presence of a gun, there would be far fewer deaths as a result of robbery. The person who is a homicide victim as a result of a robbery is far more likely to be innocent of any wrong-doing than the person who is killed as a result of a quarrel in a domestic situation.

The latter situation is the traditional or Cain-Abel type homicide wherein the victim is a relative or friend of the assailant. In our society today, robbery resulting in a murder is armed robbery. It is doubtful that the would-be thief without his firearm would be nearly so bold and audacious. And even in street crime when the victim is robbed, if the robber is armed with a knife and the victim is slashed, the victim's chances of recovery are far greater than if his assailant had been armed with a revolver and had used it. There is little rationality for the continuing widespread availability of firearms. Yet there are more guns available for killing people than ever before. How can such a situation exist in a supposedly civilized society and, because of the guns and killing, are we becoming less civilized day by day?

Nothing is done about all these lethal weapons in our midst because there is no public pressure for action. If the press and the police had widespread public support, the gun problem could be solved. People say that a law outlawing guns would be of no use because it would not be enforceable. But if the police had the support and a law, then guns could be removed from the hands of those most likely to use them to commit homicides. There is no demand to do away with firearms. Everybody who has a gun is determined to keep it. Indeed, people are paranoid on the subject of guns, and the killing continues. Even in the wild west things always got so bad that a sheriff would get elected to office with strong support of the community to "do something." The first thing the new sheriff did to make the community more civilized was to have everybody do away with their gun belts. Today we have returned to the wild west mentality, and things may have to get worse before they can get better. A society which is fearful of violence and places its trust in guns becomes more violent and then more fearful—a dizzying merry-go-round of guns and death.

If we take an historical view of homicides, things do not appear quite as bleak. Since the time of Cain and Abel, people have become more civilized and are less prone to kill one another. We are much superior to medieval times, when people were hacked to death at random. Literally nobody was safe. But comparing our society with past times is not entirely flattering. Most other aspects of medieval times are no longer prevalent in our present-day society. Certainly we face many problems in our world today, but they are mostly the problems of modern times created by modern man. Homicides are a rather ancient link with our medieval ancestors. We should have disposed of them long ago, but have not.

Technological innovations, in direct contrast with our medieval links, also contribute to the high homicide rate. The coming of the automobile brought an upsurge of ride-rob types of homicides in the 1930s. Probably the most significant technological advance which touches everyone and contributes to an increase in homicides is television.

Television begins to look like a possible culprit or suspect when one takes a very close look at the individual homicides of the present time. Eliminating homicides which occur incidental to a robbery and concentrating solely on the Cain-Abel type of killing, one is immediately struck with an emerging pattern. There is in these murders a certain flipness, one might say cuteness, wherein the perpetrators of these crimes appear to be acting out something which to them lacks little semblance to reality, and their bravado and their posing appear to be an imitation of what they may have seen on television. There is a very strong indication nowadays that when one person shoots another he does not really believe the bullet is going to fire and kill the person. He has seen so much killing on the screen, he is so attached to his handgun—for reasons that neither he nor society fully understands—that when pushed so far he takes the gun and kills. Afterwards the killer does not say anything. People used to plead and carry on afterwards and say over and over again that they did not mean to do it. Today most likely they will not say anything. Or if they do say anything they will very carefully give accurate details and facts about everything that had happened. The closest they come nowadays to the old "I didn't mean to kill him" routine is a quiet and rather rueful "I didn't 'know' that it would kill him." From the actual killing, through the time of interrogation, even to the appearance in court, the accused of today very often acts as he has seen others act—as if he is giving some kind of performance which is expected. Maybe it is not correct to blame television for a more casual attitude toward homicide. It could merely be the trend of the times. But what has affected more the times in which we live than this marvelous technological development?

Maybe social revolution and war. In times of social unrest and war, the homicide rate always goes up. In the 1960s the homicide rate began going up as civil rights demonstrations and anti-war protests accelerated. The period of the Depression saw an increase in homicides, as did the turbulent years after World War II. There seems to be a similarity between the period of the late 1940s and the 1970s. The rise and pattern of homicides in both periods is similar. If they were similar, then we should have seen a leveling-off of homicides in the latter 1970s. But we live in more complex times and things never repeat themselves exactly, especially homicides. With all the guns in circulation and the continuing changes in the way people live, it is doubtful the homicide rate will decline very much in the 1980s unless concerted action is taken at a governmental level.

One area that is of particular importance is the field of scientific advancement in police investigative procedures. There has not been enough advancement in the field of detective work in recent years. A great deal of money has come into police work lately, but most of the new resources have been spent on sophisticated weaponry—from Mace to helicopters—

but very little has been spent on basic research. And this is critical in detective work. When homicides began to increase in the thirties, scientific analysis, for the first time, came to be used in the investigation of murders. The two major developments in chasing culprits came with the perfection of ballistics tests and fingerprints. The development of technology to the point where it could be determined if a certain bullet was fired from a particular gun has had an enormous impact on police work. When a person is shot, the bullet becomes a vital piece of evidence; it cannot be retrieved by the perpetrator. Conversely, if a person is stabbed to death it is far more difficult to link the murderer with the crime unless the weapon is recovered. Thus, bullets have become a vital piece of police procedure and have been used as strong evidence to bring guilty persons to justice.

Fingerprints are probably the best scientific advancement thus far in the field of detective work. It is still quite often the major means of linking a particular suspect at a certain crime scene. One would imagine that, considering all the publicity and knowledge of fingerprints among the general population and especially the criminal society, that would-be murderers would take precautions not to leave fingerprints behind. But, as we have seen, most murders today are not planned. The perpetrator does not intend to kill, and if he does kill he does so as a by-product of some quarrel or disagreement. The murderer is shocked as much by the killing as the victim. He does not think about fingerprints, or, perhaps with the emerging flipness in regard to murders, does not even care.

Some criminal investigators feel that the fingerprinting method should be extended to cover the entire population, and that the FBI should have everyone's fingerprints on file. This raises cries of restrictions on the non-criminal population that should not be placed upon them. More than likely, however, it will inevitably be necessary.

Scientific investigation desperately needs to go beyond ballistics and fingerprinting. Murders, as we have seen, often become very difficult to solve unless the individual is caught in the act, or unless there are eyewitnesses. It is almost impossible to conceive of the number of police man-hours spent upon investigating the Refoule and Reyman cases. Or of calculating the cost to the tax payer. In those days the police would drop everything else to work on a sensational murder case, but because of crime in other areas and of the varied demands made upon police today, this is no longer possible. There are not enough man-hours. The investigation of a homicide today is severely restricted because of the time element and the press of other cases. The police are burdened with other duties. No one any longer has the time to reflect about a homicide because one case is constantly interrupted by additional killings. It is, too often, an emergency room procedure. There is no time to think about or work out the jigsaw pieces of the latest homicide puzzle. Thus the police need improved scientific means to help speed up the investigation of murders.

The time of day, the day of the week, and the month of the year have a distinct relationship to homicides. The most popular hour for killing is Saturday night between 8 and 12 midnight. These same hours on Friday night are almost as dangerous. The next most likely day to be killed is Sunday, but this includes, of course, the Saturday night carry-over. There are three times more homicides on Friday, Saturday, and Sunday than on the other five days of the week. Monday is a slow day for murder, and Tuesday the least deadly day of the week. If couples need to have heated arguments, they should always plan them for early Tuesday afternoon. Wednesday and Thursday, in the past, were rather slow days but are picking up considerably, and as the work week continues to contract it is quite possible that Thursday will become as deadly a day as Friday. In Atlanta and other Southern towns in the 'forties and through the early 'fifties, it became a common practice for all the stores to close around noon on Wednesday in order for employees to have a half-day off. The homicide rate in this era rose somewhat on Wednesday afternoon and evening. Is it only a coincidence that the Refoule and Reyman murders occurred on Wednesday afternoon?

So much for being murdered Monday through Sunday. How about January through December? The following figures list the number of murders, by months, which occurred in Atlanta in the period from 1944 to 1956.

Month of the Year	Number of Murders in that Month from 1944–1956
JANUARY	77
FEBRUARY	71

MARCH	92
APRIL	101
MAY	76
JUNE	101
JULY	107
AUGUST	117
SEPTEMBER	111
OCTOBER	85
NOVEMBER	74
DECEMBER	106
TOTAL	1118

The figures indicate that from a medium rate in January, the incidence of murder drops in February to its lowest point of the year, begins to rise slightly in March and higher in April, and then dips downward in May. This indicates a slightly higher rate of murder in the spring months over wintertime. But it is nothing compared to what happens in the summer months. The murder rate begins climbing in June and peaks at the hot point of the year in July and August. Even the advent of air conditioning has had little impact on the murder rate. Quite obviously, people most inclined toward murder do not live in air-conditioned apartments and houses. In September the murder rate goes down once again, but the rate in September is still higher than in June. From October through February the murder rate is generally downward but does take a spurt upward in December. In recent years, there has been an increase in murders in late November. As the length of the Christmas season expands, the murder rate climbs upward.

A community which is experiencing a higher murder rate in January and February over past years might as well resign itself to a whopper year of killings because it is almost certain that if the rate is climbing over past years in the slow months, in all likelihood it is going even higher by mid-summer.

Where a person is killed remains a pretty stable statistic. People have always been more likely to be murdered in their homes than at a place of business or on the street. Nearly always when a person is killed in the home, he was killed by a relative or a friend.

Cain-Abel killings occur in the home. That is why murders

which deviate from this pattern become so difficult to solve. People could not believe that Henry Heinz was killed in his home by someone unknown to him. The Reyman murder did not occur in the home. This is a possible reason for believing that the person who murdered her was not known to the victim. We still do not know whether Peggy Refoule was murdered in her home, but in any case it was in the vicinity. This, in the eyes of the police, made the husband suspect.

Contrary to popular belief, being murdered on the street is no more likely than in the past. The jump in the number of homicides is very real, but this increase is a reflection of people being murdered in their residences, rather than on the street. People murdered at their place of business shows only a slight increase. More cash registers are being robbed than ever before, but a murder seldom occurs as a result, and when it does it is more likely to be an accident than anything planned.

In Atlanta, during the period of 1930 through 1960, a black person was five times more likely to become a murder victim than a white person. This did not change much in the 1970s. There is in the 1980s an increase in white victims but also an increase in black victims. The rate is pretty much—with perhaps a slight increase among the percentage of blacks—what it was in the past. Therefore, all past efforts to do something about black killings have accomplished little.

Insofar as murder and level of income are concerned, there again appears only very slight changes over the years. Homicides committed in high-income areas and involving prominent people still get the most attention and publicity, although they occur very seldom. There is a decrease in homicides in high-income groups and a very sharp decline in Cain-Abel killings within this group. Well-off people are not murdered with the frequency that they once were. It would appear to be bad news for the mystery writers.

Of course, the largest number of murders, those which receive the least attention and least publicity, are those involving people in the lowest income group. Poor people have always been the most prone to get killed, and their rate of increase is still the highest. There is an increase of murders among people of the middle-income group. The increase is not as great as among the poor, but when we consider that murders in the high-income group are declining, even the small rise in murders in the middle class should be considered significant. Practically all of these killings are of the Cain-Abel type.

If a person is concerned about being murdered, the safest place for him to be is on the street on a Tuesday afternoon in February. The time and place most likely for a person to be murdered is in his second-floor walk-up home on a Friday and Saturday night in late summer. Unfortunately, pinpointing the location of homicides does not lessen their occurrence. It does provide some interesting sidelights of changing patterns of homicides.

The murders of President Kennedy, Martin Luther King, Jr., and Robert Kennedy in the decade of the 1960s somehow ripped away the veils of mystery and intrigue that have hovered over homicides of the past. The television medium made everyone feel what it was like to be a part of a murder. Before, it had always been the family and friends of the victim who suffered, but television allowed everybody to suffer. For the first time society experienced what the families of Henry Heinz and Peggy Refoule and countless other families had experienced. We then realized what the relatives of these people could have told us long before—murders are not much fun.

Any police detective who has spent years investigating homicides would agree. The one thing that any police detective has a hard time understanding is the public's fascination with murders. To them, investigating murders is a grueling, unpleasant job. A police detective learns very quickly the lack of value placed upon human life. He wonders as he examines blood-drenched bodies, interviews stony-faced or hysterical relatives, and follows an often haphazard court procedure if there will ever be any end to all the killing.

Police detectives who work every day at the job of solving homicides are greatly concerned at the increasing frequency with which they are committed. They feel generally that people who murder are nowadays let off too lightly. In many instances, those who are convicted of murder get off with light sentences or even probation, whereas in the past they would have gotten twenty years or life. Some investigators firmly believe that the re-institution of capital punishment is the only solution to making a dent in the rising murder rate. Others believe that even the chair, if it were revived, would not be the deterrent that it once was. People who commit murder, they argue, are nowadays totally unaware of or unconcerned about the consequences of their acts. However, practically all detectives are united on one point: They firmly favor a stiff gun-control law. It is interesting that the day-in and day-out viewing of what guns can do to the human body makes this rather hardened group become appalled at the continued increase in the number of guns in the hands of citizens.

Some detectives say that if you were to eliminate all cops, judges, parole officers, and courts, it would have a highly negligible effect upon the homicide rate. As one seasoned Atlanta detective put it: "People were being murdered before I came on the job, people are being murdered now, and people will be murdered after I am gone."

In Atlanta, in another era, because of a variety of factors, the homicide rate was reduced. We have covered the events and factors which brought this about. We will add quickly that even then murder was not abolished, but the homicide rate was brought lower than it had ever been before and was stabilized for a rather lengthy period. It is therefore a fact of the past that when the public is aroused, the press is alert, and the police vigilant, society can reduce the number of killings occurring in a given locality at a particular time.

Many people feel that an increase in homicides can be dealt with only by harsh measures and a return to capital punishment. But more than likely this would lead only to more taking of lives and would make our society more violent and less civilized. A look at how one community, Atlanta, responded to an increase in homicides in a past era of upheaval and social change can be instructive to the problem of the present day. The response of the police and public to the Refoule killing was not exemplary, but the police and the community learned from that experience and as a result went on to do something about future investigations of homicides. Police effort should be toward newer methods and a turning away from, and not a return to, past methods. If we are willing and determined to make the effort, we can do something about the problem without a resort to violence. If we do not make the effort, murders in growing numbers will continue to plague all of our lives.

Credits for Illustrations

The author acknowledges his indebtedness and his appreciation to the following sources for the illustrations indicated:

Skyline of Atlanta—Atlanta Chamber of Commerce.

Fox Theatre, Fulton Tower, Ansley Hotel, Mrs. Henry Heinz, Rainbow Terrace, and Terminal Station—Atlanta Historical Society.

Henry Heinz and Mayor William B. Hartsfield, Horace Blalock—*Atlanta Weekly.*

Judge and Mrs. Robert Refoule, Refoule home—*The Atlanta Journal-Constitution.*

Selected GEORGIA Histories

A HISTORY OF ROME AND FLOYD COUNTY, by George M. Battey, Jr. $25

A HISTORY OF SAVANNAH AND SOUTH GEORGIA, by William Harden. Two-volume set.   Each, $25; set, $45

AMERICUS THROUGH THE YEARS, by William B. Williford. History of cotton town and railroad center. $15

ELBERT COUNTIANS IN OUR COUNTRY'S WARS, by William F. Jones. One county's sacrifices to the protection of our freedoms. $25

GEORGIA AS COLONY AND STATE, by Amanda Johnson. Georgia's social, political, and military history. $25

GEORGIA: UNFINISHED STATE, by Hal Steed. A nostalgic tour of Georgia highlighting the few pockets of Old South culture remaining in an awakening giant. $10

HISTORICAL BACKGROUND OF DOUGHERTY COUNTY, GEORGIA, 1836–1940. $14.50

ILLUSTRATED HISTORY OF ATLANTA, by E.Y. Clarke. Nineteenth-century Atlanta depicted in quaint illustrations. $4

RECONSTRUCTION IN GEORGIA, by C. Mildred Thompson. *The* authoritative source on the subject. $15

THE DEAD TOWNS OF GEORGIA, by C.C. Jones, Jr. Interesting account of now-vanished towns and villages. $10

THE FIRST HUNDRED YEARS. A SHORT HISTORY OF COBB COUNTY, IN GEORGIA, by Sarah Blackwell Gober Temple. $25

THE FIRST ONE HUNDRED YEARS OF TOWN PLANNING IN GEORGIA, by Joan Niles Sears. Important discussion of the various plans used in the layout of Georgia's major cities and early towns, with illustrations. $15

THE GLORY OF COVINGTON, by William B. Williford. An illustrated visit to the stately antebellum houses of·a Georgia city and the people who lived in them. $12

TOMOCHICHI, INDIAN FRIEND OF THE GEORGIA COLONY, by Helen Todd. Biography of the Indian chieftain whose friendship made possible the success of the English outpost. $7.95

(On mail orders include $1 postage. Georgia residents add 3% state sales tax and, where applicable, 1% MARTA or local option tax.)

CHEROKEE PUBLISHING COMPANY
P. O. Box 1081   Covington, Georgia 30209

With Mitzi Green, pianist Edgar Fairchild, George Balanchine and, at far right, producer Dwight Deere Wiman at a rehearsal of *Babes in Arms* (1937)

Playing the score of *I'd Rather Be Right*. Standing are producer Sam Harris, Larry, Moss Hart, George S. Kaufman and George M. Cohan (1937)

Taking a bow on the stage of the Met with Marc Platt and Mia Slavenska after conducting the premiere of *Ghost Town* (1939)

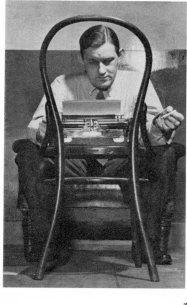

John O'Hara rewriting a scene for *Pal Joey* (1940)

With Larry, working on *Pal Joey*

Ray Bolger relaxing at a *By Jupiter* rehearsal (1942)

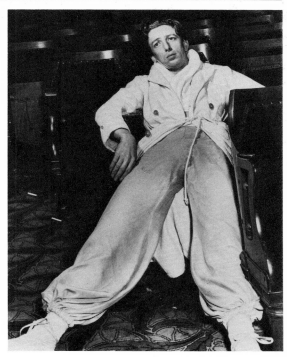

Max Dreyfus at his farm (circa 1942)

With Oscar at a rehearsal of *Oklahoma!* (1943)

Catching a bouquet after conducting the 2000th performance of *Oklahoma!* (December 4, 1947)

The oak tree and house at Black Rock Turnpike (1944)

Ethel Merman and Irving Berlin rehearsing *Annie Get Your Gun* (1946)

Governor Robert Kerr
welcoming Theresa Helburn
and me to Oklahoma City
in November, 1946

With Oscar in the Public Garden, Boston, reading the reviews of *Allegro* (1947)

HY PESKIN

With Dorothy and Oscar and Dorothy Hammerstein at the Hammersteins' farm in Doylestown (1948)

JOHN SWOPE

Writing "Bali Ha'i" at lunch in Josh Logan's apartment (1949)

With conductor Salvatore Dell'Isola, Barbara Luna, Mary Martin and Ezio Pinza listening to the playback of Columbia's cast recording of *South Pacific* (1949)

At my surprise birthday party at Rockmeadow (June 25, 1950)

Giving Mary a farewell present onstage after her last Broadway performance in *South Pacific,* June 1, 1951. Josh Logan and Leland Hayward are on the right.

One special pleasure I derived in composing the score for *Chee-Chee* was a musical joke that I used toward the end of the second act. As the son of the Grand Eunuch was being led off for his emasculation operation, he was accompanied by a triumphal march, in the middle of which I inserted several bars of Tchaikovsky's *Nutcracker Suite.* I found it gratifying that at almost every performance there were two or three individuals with ears musically sharp enough to appreciate the joke.

But no matter what we did to *Chee-Chee* it was still a musical about castration, and you simply can't get an audience at a musical comedy to feel comfortable with such a theme. If I learned anything from this experience, it's that if there's a basic problem with a show—and *Chee-Chee*'s was as basic as you can get—no amount of beautiful scenery, theatrical effects or musical innovations can hide it. We opened in New York late in September 1928 and were greeted by a barrage of critically ripened fruit, though there were a few posies tossed at the music and the imaginative way it melded into the story. The production remained on Broadway for exactly thirty-one performances, and achieved the distinction of having the shortest run of any musical I've ever written.

Including *Chee-Chee,* I had composed twelve theatre scores in four years—ten in New York and two in London. Since successes outweighed failures by about three to one, I was able to be somewhat philosophical about my latest disaster. I had developed enough self-confidence in a field notably lacking in this quality to realize that failures are an inevitable part of the game, and that they need not prove fatal if you learn from your mistakes. If you don't, you have no business being in the theatre—and you won't be for long.

Having achieved a certain amount of fame, I found myself at about this time meeting a number of people who did a good deal to alter my social life. I was single, I played the piano, I was presentable. Basically, I was the same person I'd always been, but now that I was a minor celebrity I found myself constantly being invited to parties given by a mixture of high and café society. I loved every minute of it. I don't suppose there's a person in the world who doesn't enjoy receiving compliments on his work, and these people were extremely appreciative of my accomplishments. Nobody ever complained about my piano playing (which had never improved), and my hosts seemed to feel some kind of special distinction just because the composer of "Manhattan" or "My Heart Stood Still" was playing his very own songs on their very own Spanish-shawled Steinways. As my friend Adlai Stevenson once said, "Flattery is all right if you don't inhale." Knowing the vagaries of a profession in which all too often you are only as good as your last success, I was delighted to enjoy—without inhaling—whatever adulation came my way.

Because of this never-ending flow of social dinners and parties, I did something none of my bachelor friends did: after a suitable period of mourning for *Chee-Chee,* I reciprocated the many invitations I had received by throwing my own party in mid-December of 1928 at the Park Lane Hotel. There were over a hundred people from the theatre, the arts, and what used to be called the Four Hundred, and it was such a social event that newspapers carried feature stories about it. Oddly, considering all the glittering, witty and talented guests, the only incident about the evening that I can still remember was the meeting between my father and Mayor Jimmy Walker. Because Walker had one of the most familiar faces there, Pop's idea of a joke was to put out his hand and say, with feigned sincerity, "I'm sorry, but I didn't get the name."

Despite rumors at the time, the failure of *Chee-Chee* was not the reason for the breakup of the Fields, Rodgers and Hart partnership. As a matter of fact, there never really was any breakup, because Larry and I later worked with Herb again on two shows and three movies. But after *Chee-Chee,* Herb was getting other offers, and so were Larry and I, and it was perfectly understandable that we take advantage of the best available opportunities.

Early in 1929 I received a call from a producer named Alex Aarons. Aarons was the perceptive chap who a decade before had given both George Gershwin and Vincent Youmans their first opportunities on Broadway. With his partner, Vinton Freedley, he had presented a string of Gershwin hits since 1924, including *Lady, Be Good!, Oh, Kay!* and *Funny Face.* Larry and I knew and liked both Alex and Vinton, and we had always hoped that someday we might get together with them professionally as well as socially.

What Aarons had in mind was making a musical of a play by Owen Davis called *Shotgun Wedding,* with Davis himself doing the adaptation. Owen, whom I knew as a man of great humor and kindness, had won a Pulitzer Prize for his drama *Icebound,* but what interested Larry and me even more was that his comedy, *The Nervous Wreck,* had recently been turned into a hugely successful musical for Eddie Cantor called *Whoopee.*

Owen's story, which was renamed *Spring Is Here,* was not particularly strong, but coming after *Chee-Chee* it seemed the epitome of wit, charm and dramatic skill. Frankly, it was just one more bit of fluff dealing with flirtations among the "Tennis, anyone?" Long Island social set, and it took the entire evening to unscramble a plot that was hard to find in the first place. The reader may well ask what had happened to those daring, innovative musicals that Larry and I were supposed to be dedicating our lives to create. The answer is that we didn't write our own stories. When Herb Fields wrote

Dearest Enemy or *Peggy-Ann* or *A Connecticut Yankee* we were right there with him, but by 1929 the only other trailblazing musical—and the one that towered over everything else during the decade—was Oscar Hammerstein and Jerome Kern's *Show Boat.* No other librettists besides Fields and Hammerstein seemed concerned with anything really fresh and imaginative, and Oscar certainly had no need of another lyricist for his scripts. Since Larry and I simply could not wait around for the odd chance that something novel and worthwhile would turn up, we had to accept the best offers we could get. Hence, *Spring Is Here.*

Back in January 1928, on the opening night of *She's My Baby,* I had met an imposing gentleman named Jules Glaenzer who had come backstage to congratulate Bea Lillie. Jules, who was the vice-president of Cartier's, not only loved the theatre but enjoyed even more giving parties for people in the theatre. It wasn't long before I became a member of what was known as the Glaenzer Party Set. Jules and his beautiful young wife, Kendall, had made their series of parties famous for bringing together social registrants, business tycoons and theatrical luminaries in an atmosphere of good talk and music. Though he was a wonderful host, Jules could at times be autocratic. Whenever one of his guests sang or played, he made such a point of there being absolute quiet that he became known around town as "Shush" Glaenzer. It's hard to believe that anyone would have to shush people while Gertrude Lawrence was being accompanied by George Gershwin, but the Glaenzers always made sure there was a steady flow of champagne, which had the unfortunate habit of loosening tongues at the wrong moments.

Jules and Kendall had a lovely house on the beach at Westhampton, and I was often invited there for weekends, as were other composers, including Gershwin. I'll never forget one August day when George sat down at the piano, a lean, swarthy, intense figure totally absorbed in his music, yet equally aware of his audience and the effect he was achieving. It was the first time I'd heard *An American in Paris,* and like everyone else I was captivated by the vividly evocative work. When I told George how much I admired it, he looked surprised and said, "I didn't know you were like that."

"Like what?"

"I didn't think you'd like anybody's music but your own."

Coming from anyone else, this remark would have been insulting, but George always said what was on his mind and expressed himself in such an innocent way that you knew no offense was intended. His appreciation of his own work was equally innocent. Once when we were both at a party near Westhampton, the orchestra played a new Gershwin number from a current show. When I told him that I thought it was a great tune, he simply replied, "Yes, isn't it?" Actually, it would have been impossible not to love all of Gershwin's music, and he had the added ability to perform his works at the piano in such a way that they always took on a special glow. No one could ever play a Gershwin tune like Gershwin himself, and I can still clearly recall those steely fingers racing through "Fascinating Rhythm" or lovingly caressing the notes to "The Man I Love."

One weekend when I was with a few friends at Jules's Westhampton place, Dick Hoyt, a member of the Glaenzer Party Set who lived nearby, invited us to fly back to New York on Sunday in his private seaplane so that we could all attend a party at the Glaenzers' apartment. This was early in 1929, when flying in any kind of a plane was a major adventure, and we were happy to accept.

Never having flown before, I felt tremendously stimulated by the flight. We landed in Port Washington Bay, and Dick had his car meet us and drive us to town. When I arrived at my parents' apartment, where I was still living, it was too early to dress for the party. Still keyed up by my aerial adventure, I did something I rarely do. I walked over to the piano and began improvising a melody, which to my surprise sounded good. Later I played the tune for Jules at the party. He became so enthusiastic that when Alex Aarons arrived he insisted I play it for him. When I finished, Alex leaned over, kissed me on the forehead and said, "This has got to be in our new show."

The next day Alex had me play the music for Vinton Freedley, and it almost caused the end of the Aarons and Freedley partnership. For reasons he never bothered to explain, Freedley simply didn't want the song in the show. I later was told that after I left, the two men fought furiously about it, but somehow Alex got his way and the tune was included in the score of *Spring Is Here*. Larry wrote one of his most affectingly ardent lyrics for it, and Lillian Taiz and John Hundley introduced "With a Song in My Heart."

Recalling the writing of "With a Song in My Heart" brings up a subject that is a touchy one to most people in the arts. I have always cringed at the word "inspiration." It is simply impossible to create something solely as a result of the stimulation of a single experience. I firmly believe that the single experience, whatever it is, becomes part of the totality of one's personality, and it is this personality that expresses itself through whatever medium the individual uses. My first plane ride did not inspire me to write "With a Song in My Heart," any more than a near traffic accident had inspired me to write "My Heart Stood Still." It is the excitement of the event combined with the excitement of having a job to do combined with one's background combined with one's talent that results in the song, painting or novel. I've never believed that after a man has an affair with a beautiful girl he is inspired, almost as a reflex action, to dash to the nearest piano, canvas or writing desk and pour out his emotions in a lasting work of art. The affair simply becomes part of the man's experience, which in turn helps form his personality.

In my own case, I found emotional stimulation in music when I was very young by listening to my mother play the piano. There was further excitement when my grandparents introduced me to opera, and going to the Broadway theatre was even more fascinating. But what compelled me to express myself through music was never a single stimulus; rather, it was a great number of them, combined with heredity, environment and a certain native ability. Later, increased activity and technical knowledge contributed to the proficiency I gained through the years.

One other element was also influential: the encouragement of people whose judgment and values were important to me. Because my parents loved theatre music and nurtured my love for it, I found myself going in that direction because of my desire for continued parental approval. This also gave me the impetus to work harder so that I might feel worthy of that approval.

Along with the popular misconception about "inspiration" is the concomitant one that anyone involved in the arts must be unbalanced, since creative work and logical behavior are somehow considered mutually exclusive. One evening at a dinner party a woman of apparent intelligence kept asking me questions about my working habits. As I described them I watched her expression change from skepticism to utter disbelief. It was incredible to her that I liked working in the morning because I felt fresh after a good night's sleep, or that two highballs made it impossible for me to work at all. I could see that she wasn't buying any of it, so I finally blurted out, "Look, I've been lying to you. I never get to work before two in the morning, I have to be blind drunk before I get any kind of idea, and on top of the piano I always place a small naked girl." I don't think she bought that line, either, because she suddenly stopped talking to me.

In 1927 Alex Aarons and Vinton Freedley had a theatre built for them on West Fifty-second Street which they called the Alvin, derived from the first syllable of each man's first name. Alex had a suite of offices on the top floor, and Vinton had his just below. Partly because of the argument over "With a Song in My Heart," I became much closer to Alex than to Vinton. Alex, whose father, Alfred Aarons, had been both a composer and a producer, was a bald, bespectacled man with a great fund of jokes and an enormous love for music. Almost every afternoon at five he made a ritual of meeting in his office for cocktails. Usually we were joined by Alfred Newman, the music director for all the Aarons and Freedley shows. Apart from being a fine musician, Al was a wonderfully warm and gregarious person, and for a time the three of us were almost inseparable. Actually, it was really six of us, since these five o'clock sessions were generally the prelude to dinner with Alex's wife, Ella, Alfred's wife, Beth, and my future wife, Dorothy.

Working on *Spring Is Here* was far more rewarding for the congeniality of the company than for any creative accomplishments of our run-of-the-mill show. Even the spotlighting of the brilliant duo-piano team of Vic Arden and Phil Ohman was a familiar attraction from the Aarons-and-Freedley Gershwin musicals that had gone before. Probably the only unusual aspect of the production was that we signed a Hollywood leading man for the starring role. Glenn Hunter was boyishly handsome and personable and had scored a success in a film called *Merton of the Movies,* but he did have one drawback as a musical-comedy actor that went undetected on the silent screen: he couldn't sing a note. Originally we had intended to give him the chief ballad, "With a Song in My Heart," but one rehearsal was enough to make us change our minds. After an emergency conference we decided to give the song to the vocally talented John Hundley, even though he played the role of the hero's rival. Glenn had only two numbers, one of which was "Yours Sincerely." The piece was created in the form of a letter set to music, and he recited the lyric with the orchestra carrying the melody.

When *Spring Is Here* arrived at the Alvin in March 1929, it was greeted by an enthusiastic press. To my surprise, it was pointed out that we had an amusing, if conventional, story, a youthfully energetic company, and a score that was variously described as "graceful," "tuneful," "beguiling," "lively" and "lovely." Once the notices were in, coupled with the appeal of our Hollywood star, we fully expected a lengthy run. But *Spring Is Here* ran only three months—which was all it really deserved.

Every year Jules and Kendall Glaenzer spent a number of months in Paris, where Jules attended to the affairs of Cartier's home office. Soon after *Spring Is Here* opened, they insisted that I join them in Paris for a party at which they would introduce me to their European friends. The fact that I agreed to cross the Atlantic just to go to one party gives a pretty good idea of the kind of life I was leading in those days. On arrival in Paris I rented a small apartment in the Hotel Astoria, an unassuming but charming hotel facing the Arc de Triomphe. The party itself, at Restaurant Laurent in the Champs Elysées gardens, was a posh affair, and the account in the Paris *Herald* was crowded with an eye-popping guest list, including members of both theatrical royalty and real royalty. The following day I set off for the Riviera for a few days in the April sun, and upon my return to Paris I threw a party for the Glaenzers at the Ritz with just about the same guests as the ones who had been at their party for me.

With my appetite for party going and party giving thoroughly sated, I sailed home on the *Olympic,* the same ship I had taken following the African adventure with my parents. The *Olympic* was my favorite ocean liner. I loved its paneled staterooms and its elegant Ritz restaurant, where passengers who did not wish to eat in the regular huge dining room could enjoy the finest French food, wine and service at any hour of the day. The ship made a fare reduction for those of us luxury lovers who dined at the Ritz, and we were billed separately.

In the summer of 1929 I came to a difficult decision. I was twenty-seven years old, financially independent and yet still living with my parents. They certainly weren't restrictive, nor did they interfere with my life in any way, but I felt strongly that the time had come for me to live alone. Just as Queen Victoria needed a room of her own, I needed a place of my own. Moving out was painful for all of us, but my mother and father never said a word against my leaving. Nevertheless, I knew that Mom in particular took it hard, since she had remained with her parents even after she was married; I'm sure she found it difficult to understand why anyone who was single would want to live independently. Now, for the first time in almost thirty-three years of married life, my parents would finally be alone.

The apartment I chose was on the nineteenth floor of the Hotel Lombardy on Fifty-sixth Street, between Lexington and Park avenues. It had three good-sized rooms and an enormous terrace. There was only one other apartment on the floor; it was similar to mine but facing in the opposite direction. I didn't find out who lived there until after I had moved in. One morning the hotel manager called me into his office to show me a letter he had received from the occupant, who turned out to be the novelist Edna Ferber. Miss Ferber, then spending the summer in Europe, voiced strong objection to the hotel's renting an apartment on *her* floor to a songwriter. She was sure there would be wild parties every night, to say nothing of my banging away at the piano all day. The manager confessed that he didn't know quite how to placate the lady and asked if I had any suggestions. Of course, the mere fact that he brought the matter to my attention may have been his way of warning me that now that I was living on the fashionable East Side I'd better learn to mend my debauched West Side ways. Still, I could understand his concern, and I calmly told him that all he had to do was to let me know the day before Miss Ferber was due back from her trip, and I was sure I could smooth all the lady's ruffled feathers.

When the day came, I had masses of flowers sent to Miss Ferber's apartment with a card reading "From your Nearest Neighbor." The following evening, just as I opened my door to go out, Miss Ferber opened hers and we met in the hallway. She was so overcome by my gesture that she threw her arms around me and told me how delighted she was to have me living next door. Then, to my amazement, she began berating me for not having bothered to get in touch with her when we had both been staying at the same hotel in Colorado Springs the previous year. My protestations that I did not know her at the time and that there was no one to introduce us made not the slightest impression. I suppose this was her way of telling me that she liked me, but I found it perplexing. Over the years I was to discover what a truly indecipherable woman Edna was—demanding, loving, funny, angry, generally impossible, but always a loyal and dear friend.

Spring Is Here may not have been good for more than one season, but Aarons and Freedley apparently liked our work well enough to sign Larry and me for their next musical. Called *Me for You,* it was also written by Owen Davis. The story was all about a wealthy roué, played by Victor Moore, whose daughter, Betty Starbuck, has no idea that her old man is a bootlegger. To keep Betty away from her boyfriend, district attorney John Hundley, Victor has his seagoing partner, Jack Whiting, become her legal guardian for a month, and everything gets straightened out when Betty and Jack fall in love.

At least this was the story we started with. The idea of dumpling-shaped, mild-mannered Victor Moore as a rumrunner seemed so incongruous, at least during rehearsals, that we all thought it a brilliant stroke of casting. When we reached Detroit for the first stop in our tryout tour, however, we quickly realized that all the clever dialogue and funny routines just weren't going over. It didn't take long for us to discover the flaw: audiences simply would not accept lovable Victor Moore in the unlovable role of a smuggler, nor did they care much for a story that ended with the heroine ditching a district attorney to marry a lawbreaker.

What to do? We had a score that the audiences seemed to like, a talented cast, and attractive scenery and costumes. Now, if this were a Hollywood backstage musical, the director would gather the cast and crew together and say, "Listen, kids. We've got lots of talent and some sure-fire numbers and some beautiful sets and costumes. All we have to do is change the story. So if we all work real hard, I know we'll have ourselves a great big smash." So everyone works real hard and they have themselves a great big smash. But real backstage life is not to be confused with the Hollywood version—except that in this case we did exactly what they would have done in the movies. The only trouble was that for reasons beyond our control, the show did not turn out to be a great big smash.

After two weeks in Detroit, Aarons and Freedley closed *Me for You* and we all returned to New York. But not before the producers had already hired two new librettists: Paul Gerard Smith, who had performed a similar salvaging operation on the Gershwin show *Funny Face,* and Jack McGowan, the co-author of *Hold Everything,* one of the previous year's biggest hits. Together, the two men worked frantically to fashion a story that would at least utilize whatever cast members, songs, sets and costumes we decided to keep. Now the story had Victor Moore playing a lovable cook who works aboard a yacht which, unbeknown to its owners, is being used for smuggling. Leading man Jack Whiting now became a more acceptable hero as a Coast Guard officer, and Betty Starbuck, while still in the show in a major comic role, was succeeded by Barbara Newberry in the romantic lead. We even found a spot for a skin-and-boneless dancer named Ray Bolger who had previously appeared only in one or two Broadway revues.

For some reason our revised musical was called *Heads Up!* when we opened in Philadelphia on October 25, 1929. Shortly thereafter we were faced with a problem that no amount of script changes could solve. On the day before the opening, Alex Aarons came charging down the aisle of the Shubert Theatre with the staggering news: "Boys, you can forget about the show. You can forget about everything. The bottom's just dropped out of the market!"

None of us was rich enough to be badly hurt by the Wall Street crash, but there was no question that until that fatal day everyone had been living through a period of unbelievable affluence. I remember a young elevator boy in my hotel telling me one afternoon, "Well, Mr. Rodgers, I did pretty well in the market today. I just made a thousand dollars." Overnight everything had changed, and like every other business, the theatre was going to be in for a long, painful period. It certainly was not the right time to open a large, expensive musical production, but after spending so much time and effort and money, there was no thought of turning back. Despite Alex's emotional outburst on the day of the crash, we were all victims of that compulsive attitude that makes the show the only thing that really matters. We simply could not allow our world to come to an end, no matter what was happening in the real world.

Despite the blanket of gloom that hung over the country, *Heads Up!* had a well-attended first night in Philadelphia, and our Broadway opening at the Alvin received a warm greeting from the audience. By and large the press was encouraging but we were all well aware that, particularly now, rave reviews were no harbingers of financial success. Surprisingly, the show didn't do badly and ended its run with 144 performances.

Two songs from *Heads Up!* still mean a good deal to me. One was "Why Do You Suppose?," an uptempo number with a lyric that had fun comparing the mating habits of animals and humans; the other was "A Ship without a Sail," which had an unusual construction, at least for 1929. I have already mentioned the fairly rigid "AABA" or "ABAB" thirty-two-bar form. For this ballad I divided the refrain into twelve-, eight- and twelve-bar sections, thereby achieving a mild breakthrough with an "ABA" form. It was still thirty-two bars, of course, and I don't suppose many people noticed it, but I enjoyed getting away even slightly from the accepted strictures of songwriting. When I first played the melody for Larry, he said it sounded like a barcarole. Since the show had a nautical setting, the idea of comparing one's lovesick emotions to a ship without a sail was a particularly felicitous notion and Larry developed it into one of his most beautifully crafted lyrics.

Heads Up! didn't do much for any of us, except possibly Messrs. Moore and Bolger. To give you some idea of what passed for humor in those days, I remember one line Victor had that always brought down the house. When the smugglers took over the yacht, one of them poked Victor in the ribs with his pistol and asked him if he knew what a mutiny was. "Oh, sure," piped Victor, "it's a show that they give in the afternoon."

Once the initial shock of the Wall Street crash began to wear off, most people confidently expected that conditions would soon begin to improve. President Herbert Hoover, that starched, well-meaning symbol of probity, reassured the country that business and industry would soon turn the corner, and of course we all wanted desperately to believe him. Indeed, at the close of 1929, Broadway could still offer a remarkably varied assortment of over forty plays and musicals to entertain or bore the public.

Many of us, however, were not convinced that prosperity was just around the corner. We knew that we were in a precarious business. Nobody *had* to go to the theatre. In the world of entertainment, it cost a great deal less to see a movie or a vaudeville show—and it cost nothing at all to stay home and listen to the radio. With the market continuing to slide at a rapid pace, we couldn't help but worry that our world was in danger of being destroyed.

Still, during this period of vain hopes and dire fears, Larry and I were incredibly lucky. No sooner had *Heads Up!* opened than we received two important offers in rapid succession. The first came from Charles B. Cochran, who was in New York for the opening of his imported London hit, Noël Coward's *Bitter Sweet,* which had been unveiled six nights before *Heads Up!* He told Larry and me that he had seen nothing on Broadway that he wanted to produce in London. What he did want was an original show with a score by Rodgers and Hart, but this time he thought it should be a book musical instead of a revue. Not an operetta like *Bitter Sweet* but something in a more contemporary vein, yet equally imaginative and pictorially appealing. If Larry and I could come up with an outline for a suitable story, he'd put a librettist to work on it right away.

Bitter Sweet, which was told in flashback by an elderly woman reliving her youth, was a great vehicle both for the American actress Peggy Wood, who originated the role in London, and for the British actress Evelyn Laye, who played it in New York. Cochran wanted our new show to provide an equally strong starring role for Jessie Matthews, that charming singer and dancer who had introduced "My Heart Stood Still" in *One Dam Thing After Another.* Since a musical requiring an actress to play both a young girl and an old woman had recently proved so successful, Larry and I hit upon a variation that we felt would be equally effective in revealing Jessie's talents. Our idea was that to gain publicity, a girl in her early twenties passes herself off as a woman in her sixties whose youth has been preserved through the science of modern cosmetics. Complications arise when the young man she loves balks at the prospect of marrying a woman more than twice his age. Because the girl is an aspiring actress as well, Cochran could also indulge in his penchant for elaborate spectacles that didn't have much to do with the story but did impress theatregoers. We called the show *Ever Green.*

Cochran had returned to London by the time we finished the outline; soon after we sent it to him, he wrote us that he thought it would work beautifully. There would, however, be a delay; because of the uncertain economic outlook and because he was already committed to produce Noël Coward's *Private Lives* early in 1930, he had decided to postpone *Ever Green* until the late spring.

If it hadn't been for this postponement, Larry and I would probably never have had anything to do with the second offer we received at about the same time. Understandably, the mere fact that the offer came from Florenz Ziegfeld would have elicited a firm "No, thanks" after our unhappy experience with *Betsy.* But in the closing days of 1929 it was not the time to refuse any reasonable proposal. I couldn't afford to wait for the stock market to recover or for Cochran to start work on the new show for one compelling reason: on December 7 I became engaged to Dorothy, and I knew that within months I would have to face many new responsibilities. Even before the crash, the theatre was a risky place in which to earn a living, and now I was planning to get married at the beginning of what could be a severe, prolonged depression.

Larry and I talked it over and agreed to do the show for Ziegfeld. Our enthusiasm for the venture, called *Simple Simon,* was stimulated almost exclusively by the fact that Ed Wynn was going to star in it, and we were both crazy about him. Ed was an original; there's never been a comic like him before, nor will there ever be again. He wore clownish costumes, made up silly puns, dreamed up zany inventions, and looked on the world with a wide-eyed, childlike innocence that made everything he did seem uproariously funny.

The first time we met Wynn was when we went to his apartment one evening to discuss ideas for the production. He lived on East End Avenue, and I remember that his son, Keenan, who was then about fourteen, was also at home. Basically a shy, retiring man, Ed overwhelmed us with his warmth and sympathetic understanding when we told him of our previous experience with Ziegfeld. We went home that night thoroughly convinced that no matter what our problems with Ziegfeld might be, Ed would be on our side.

And he was. But Ziegfeld was too much for Ed, who, as the co-author of the book with Guy Bolton, had enough problems of his own. Bolton was then the most prolific librettist on Broadway, but *Simple Simon* didn't win him any new laurels. It was little more than a tailor-made tale for the star, in which Wynn played a Coney Island newsstand owner who falls asleep and dreams about such Mother Goose characters as Cinderella, King Cole, Jack and Jill, and Snow White. The idea was as ridiculous then as it would be today, except that Ziegfeld's stage designer, Joseph Urban, turned the production into a spectacularly attractive show. And there was Ed Wynn. All he had to do was come out and say, in that comical lisp of his, "I love the woodth," and the audience would go wild.

Late in January 1930, after the Boston opening, Wynn came up with an idea for a musical scene in which he would accompany Lee Morse, one of the featured singers, but not on any ordinary piano. Ed designed it so that it could be mounted on wheels and he could ride it like a bicycle, with the girl sitting on top. This later became one of his standard routines. All that was required from Larry and me was a new song, which we wrote one afternoon at the Ritz-Carlton. Called "Ten Cents a Dance," it was rushed into rehearsal just as soon as the ink was dry.

The first evening the song was to be performed, Ziegfeld, in an unprecedented show of friendliness, invited me to sit with him in the audience. Wynn, the bicycle-piano and Lee Morse made their entrance and were greeted with applause. Everything would have been fine except that Miss Morse had had a few too many and couldn't remember either the words or the music. It was a distressing, dispiriting introduction for a new song, and Ziegfeld was so enraged that he fired Lee immediately. To replace her he hired a slim blond singer named Ruth Etting who had just closed on Broadway in Ruth Selwyn's short-lived *9:15 Revue.* Miss Etting had made a great impression in this show belting out Harold Arlen's first hit, "Get Happy," and we were sure she would be equally effective with our song. By now we had left Boston, and since there were no New York previews, the first opportunity Ruth had to sing the ballad before an audience was on opening night. She scored such a resounding hit that thereafter "Ten Cents a Dance" became her musical trademark.

Larry and I were particularly proud of this taxi-dancer's lament because it may have been the first show tune to express the emotions of a person caught up in one of the more unsavory areas of employment. Certainly it was influential in expanding the themes of torch songs beyond the "My Bill—My Man" threnodies that were concerned only with women being mistreated by their men. Later the same year, in fact, Cole Porter was emboldened to deal with the ultimate sordid profession in his bitter exhortation of a streetwalker called "Love for Sale."

Although Ziegfeld never faltered in his admiration for "Ten Cents a Dance," he was strangely hostile toward one of our other songs in *Simple Simon* and insisted that it be dropped. A few months later we added it to the score of the Cochran musical, *Ever Green,* and "Dancing on the Ceiling" easily became the most popular number in the show.

Ziegfeld scheduled *Simple Simon* to follow *Bitter Sweet* at his lavish Ziegfeld Theatre. I cannot recall the opening-night audience reaction, but in going through the press notices I find that the reviewers all loved Ed Wynn but were scathing in their appraisal of the libretto. "Dull," "cumbersome," "banal," "humorless" and "grim" were some of the terms used. The critics were also divided about the score; only one reviewer, Burns Mantle in the *News,* mentioned "Ten Cents a Dance," which he described as "particularly effective." It may come as a surprise that *Time* magazine called "I Still Believe in You" "one of the best tunes Rodgers and Hart ever wrote," and *Variety* proclaimed "Send for Me" the "hit number" of the show.

Of course this wasn't the first time that critics praised songs that were quickly forgotten, and virtually ignored the ones that later continued to be performed. Rereading reviews such as these makes it easy to scoff at the judgments of play reviewers. But critics are not seers. They simply react to what they are hearing for the first time, and their reactions vary just the way most people's do. Of all the elements they must comment on in reviewing a show, music is probably the one that most strongly resists interpretive appraisals. Music produces an emotional response, and it is little wonder that the terms used to describe it are often imprecise. Perhaps this is because most critics are not musicians—but for that matter, neither are most of the people in the audience. The difference is that the critics' views are in print and are likely to influence vast numbers of people. Because of this responsibility, in addition to the fact that there are usually over a dozen songs in a show, I have always thought that reviewers should have access to the entire score, either in the form of sheet music or records, before they cover a production. At least familiarity should give them a greater understanding of what has been written and why. I venture to say that my ear is at least as well trained as any theatre critic's; yet, unless the music is extremely simple and childlike, I wouldn't dare to pass judgment on a Broadway score on the basis of only one hearing. I don't think anyone can come away from a score after listening to it for the first time with a feeling much more specific than that the music is either good or bad. It is only after repeated listening that a person can appraise the individual songs with any degree of analytical judgment. Critics, however, are called upon not only to comment on music and lyrics after only one hearing, but also to make intelligent observations about every other area of the production. And of course they must never equivocate. Every time I read in a review that a score is weak or tuneless, I am amazed that a writer, after a single hearing, could make such a rash and damaging statement. I can never help wondering if such a judgment might not be entirely different if the critic had the opportunity to become familiar with a score before rendering his verdict, the way critics of "serious" music do.

Sometime following the opening of *Simple Simon,* and after displaying what I thought was admirable patience, I paid Ziegfeld a visit to ask him for the long-overdue royalties for the score. Upon telling the secretary that I wanted to see him, I was asked to wait in the outer office. So I waited— and waited. After an hour I began to get the idea that the Master knew very well why I was there and that he was counting on me to give up and leave. People kept going in and out of his office but I was prepared to stick it out if it took all night. I must have been there for about three hours when I suddenly recalled that Ziegfeld had a reputation for being terrified of an organization of theatre writers called the Dramatists Guild. Since Larry and I were members of the Guild, Ziegfeld had to sign what was known as a minimum basic agreement, and part of this agreement contained the clause that writers must report to the Guild if a producer failed to pay royalties on time. Once a producer was reported as being in arrears no other Guild writer—which meant virtually every writer in the theatre—could work for him until he paid up. It didn't even require any court action—simply a meeting of the Dramatists Guild Council to render its decision to act in behalf of the writer.

By now thoroughly fed up with Ziegfeld's waiting game, I told the secretary that I'd had enough and that her boss would next be hearing from the Dramatists Guild. The minute that message was relayed, the doors to Ziegfeld's office flew open and the producer came out with his arms outstretched and a broad smile pasted on his face. Without even the formality of asking me what I had come to see him about, he sent for his bookkeeper and told him to make out checks to Larry and me for whatever amount was owed us. If it hadn't been for that magic name, "Dramatists Guild," I don't think we would have collected a dime.

As mentioned earlier, my reason for taking on *Simple Simon* was chiefly motivated by the decision Dorothy and I had come to late in 1929. One evening while we were having dinner at Montmartre we found ourselves discussing our future together as if it were the most inevitable thing in the world. I don't think there was even a formal proposal. Suddenly the seriousness of what we were saying hit us, and without even finishing our dinner we went bounding out of the restaurant to Dorothy's house to break the news to her parents.

Parents always seem to have a strange way of knowing things like this even before they are told. As soon as we walked into the Feiners' apartment, and without our saying a word, Dorothy's mother dashed across the room to tell us how happy she was. Her father, never the most voluble member of the family, said little, but at least he didn't look unhappy. The following night there was a repetition of this mind-reading act when I went to see my parents, who were by now living at the Gotham Hotel. I no sooner had said, "I have some great news for you—" when Mom completed the thought, "You're engaged to Dorothy Feiner!"

With both pairs of parents apparently happy, the only problem arose over what kind of wedding to have. The Feiners wanted a large affair and I wanted a small one. So we compromised: there would be a small group at the ceremony—just the immediate families and close friends—which would take place at the Feiners' Park Avenue apartment, but there would also be a large engagement party to proclaim the coming event. It was held in the Ballroom of the Park Lane Hotel on Sunday, the twelfth of January, with Emil Coleman's orchestra providing the dance music.

The wedding itself took place on March 5. The service was performed by that impressively leonine man, Rabbi Stephen S. Wise, who had also married my mother and father, my brother and his wife, and Dorothy's brother and his wife. Morty was best man, and Larry Hart and Herb Fields were officially "ushers," though there really weren't enough people there for them to ush. While it's an old saying that all brides are beautiful, mine was the most beautiful of all, and in the past forty-five years I've never found any reason to change my mind.

Not wishing to spend our wedding night in a hotel, Dorothy and I boarded the S.S. *Roma,* bound for Italy. That night we had champagne and caviar all by ourselves in our stateroom, and then retired with the heady thought of how romantic it would be to awaken the next morning far out to sea. When we got up the next morning we found that we were still tied up at the North River dock. There had been some engine trouble and the ship didn't sail until midafternoon.

Naples was our first stop, just as it was on the first trip Larry and I had taken to Europe almost four years earlier. My return to the fabulous Bertolini's Palace Hotel was even more thrilling now that I had my bride with me. After a few days in Naples we took the night train down the Italian coast and across the Straits of Messina on the train ferry to Sicily, and proceeded to the ancient city of Taormina. The hotel we stayed in was a converted monastery and we slept in what had once been a monk's cell, but the awesome sight of the Mediterranean on one side and Mount Etna on the other was ample compensation.

From Sicily we took a ship to Cannes, where we stayed at the Carlton Hotel, all luxury, style and rich food. That's where I discovered that my wife loves to gamble. As for me, I simply have the wrong temperament. If I lose, I translate the loss into the cost of a pair of new shoes; if I win, I feel as though I were taking money that doesn't belong to me.

London, our last stop, gave me the opportunity of getting back to work. Charles Cochran was now ready to proceed with his production of *Ever Green,* and I had arranged with Larry, who was then traveling through Germany, to meet us in London. Since we would be working in the city, it seemed impractical to live in a hotel, but after looking at a number of service flats, including those in St. James's Street where Larry and I had previously stayed, I discovered that what had once seemed comfortable and attractive when I was a bachelor now looked dingy and cramped.

One of the friends I had made through Myrtle d'Erlanger on my last trip to London was Beatrice Guinness. At dinner one evening Beatrice told Dorothy that her daughter, Zita James, owned a house at 11 York Terrace, right on Regent's Park. Since Zita was then away on a prolonged trip, Beatrice was sure that she would be happy to rent us her house for as long as we liked.

Dorothy and I took one look at the place and promptly fell in love with it. It was a charming Regency-period town house, exquisitely furnished, with a lovely view of the park from the rear windows. There were even three sleep-in servants. But what really sold us was that Larry could move in with us and have the entire top floor to himself. It was a perfect arrangement: he would have his privacy and we would have ours.

Or so we thought. The first evening Larry was with us, we heard a persistent ringing of our front door bell after he had gone to his room. We opened the door to discover a strange woman frantically pointing to a stream of water flowing out of a drainpipe on the top floor. It didn't take long to discover what had happened: after turning on the water in his bathtub, Larry had promptly forgotten about it when he became absorbed in a book. Fortunately, no damage was done to Zita's lovely house.

Dorothy and I had expected to have our breakfast alone, but Larry was always in the dining room waiting for us. Then we discovered a tiny library and arranged to have breakfast served there. Still, Larry had no trouble finding us and invariably showed up in need of a shave, wearing a stained bathrobe and smoking a big, black, smelly cigar. But once I'd explained to him, as diplomatically as I could, that Dorothy and I preferred privacy at this time of day, Larry good-naturedly left us alone.

Dorothy had good reason for being especially sensitive at this time. After visiting a doctor whose name was—on my honor—Beckett Ovary, she received confirmation of what we both suspected: she was pregnant. At the beginning there were no unexpected ill effects and Dorothy's normal round of activities was completely unhindered. As for housekeeping, she had no problems once she mastered the intricacies of British currency and remembered, among other things, that a sweet was a dessert and a biscuit a cracker. Dorothy taught the cook to make coffee in the American way, and our English friends, who were used to the thin beverage that was always brewed a day before, loved to sample Dorothy Rodgers' special brand.

As I knew they would, Myrtle d'Erlanger and Dorothy took to each other immediately, and the entire d'Erlanger clan made sure that we were, quite literally, royally entertained. One evening at a large gathering at the home of Lord Louis and Lady Edwina Mountbatten, my host eased me over to the piano and asked me to play. Presently a slim young man came over and sat on the piano bench beside me. He surprised me by asking to hear such musical esoterica as opening chorus numbers and verses to obscure songs, and was even familiar with tunes I didn't know. I had no idea who he was, and expecting him to be a well-known composer whom I should have recognized, I was startled to be told later that my knowledgeable friend was the Duke of Kent. Obviously I was born to be chummy with the British royal family.

Benn Levy, who is best known today as the author of *Springtime for Henry,* was the librettist whom Charles Cochran had chosen to write *Ever Green.* As before, C.B. was a pleasure to work with, and Levy turned out to be a congenial and diligent collaborator. The only problem was that Cochran again found it necessary to postpone the show, this time until the fall. With the score almost completed and with no further reason to remain in London, Dorothy and I and Larry returned to New York.

Home for the newlywed Rodgerses was my apartment at the Lombardy, though it was not to be for long. Shortly before my marriage I had received a call from an executive at Warner Bros. offering an attractive contract for the services of Rodgers and Hart as movie songwriters. With the advent of "talkies," Hollywood had naturally discovered that the best way of showing off the marvels of film *and* sound was to specialize in stories that could not be made as silent movies. Which of course meant stories with songs. Since there were few songwriters then in Hollywood, the major studios went on the hunt for all the best-known Broadway and Tin Pan Alley writers they could find. What they offered was hard to refuse. They put people under contract for a specific number of years, gave them handsome salaries and comfortable offices, and in general provided the kind of security that could not be found in the theatre even during its most prosperous years.

Our arrangement with Warner's called for Larry and me to write the scores for three musical films. What made it especially attractive was that the agreement also included the services of Herb Fields as scriptwriter. Though we enjoyed working with other writers, up to this time Larry and I had never had the kind of theatrical successes or creative stimulation that we'd enjoyed with Herb. Now we were being offered a fresh opportunity for all three of us which, we hoped, might rekindle something of the spirit that had marked our early Broadway endeavors. Apart from *Fifty Million Frenchmen,* which Herb had written with Cole Porter, none of our recent musicals had done well. Maybe what we needed most was simply a change of scenery which might also help our work for the stage. And there surely could be no quarrel with the money. From every point of view except one, the Warner Bros. contract was highly attractive.

The exception was Dorothy. Her pregnancy was beginning to give her extreme discomfort and she did not feel well enough to travel to California. Though I had to go where my work took me, our leave-taking wasn't easy, both because of Dorothy's health and because it was the first time we'd be separated since our marriage.

After settling in at our hotel, Herb, Larry and I were driven to Burbank, where the studio was located and where we were to meet Jack Warner, the most prominent of the four brothers who owned the company. Warner, who was having lunch with his aides in the executive dining room, was a slim, dapper man who looked very much like a movie version of a gambling-casino owner. He gave us a flashing smile, and then proceeded to speak in the thickest Yiddish accent I'd ever heard. "I dun't van't none of your highbrow sunk-making," he warned us as his smile quickly vanished. "Music mit guts ve got to heff—sunks mit real sediment like the 'Stein Sunk' and 'Mit Tears in Mine Eyes I'm Dencink.' "

My God, I thought, could this really be the powerful Jack Warner? Then I noticed that the half-dozen or so men around the table all had their backs to us, and their sides and heads were shaking as if they were laughing uncontrollably. I realized that this was Warner's idea of a joke. Ever since the first self-made merchants and nickelodeon owners had gone West to organize film studios as movie-manufacturing plants, there had been a steady stream of gags about the illiterate immigrants who had created a new world of entertainment in and around Hollywood. Samuel Goldwyn and his celebrated Goldwynisms had become a universally accepted model of the breed, and Warner, apparently a bit self-conscious about the image, enjoyed assuming the caricature for the entertainment of his staff. I can't say I thought the routine exactly side-splitting, but from then on Jack and I got along fine. He furnished Larry and me with a luxurious office, and even made sure we had a secretary. No one gave us any idea what a lyricist and a composer were supposed to do with a secretary, and after a day or two we persuaded the studio to assign her to someone else.

Initially, the film that Herb, Larry and I worked on was to have starred Marilyn Miller, but for some reason the feminine lead went to Ona Munson, with Ben Lyon and Walter Pidgeon as her romantic rivals. The picture, *The Hot Heiress,* was so called because it was about a riveter (Lyon) who accidentally tosses a bolt into the boudoir of an heiress (Munson), and then falls in love with her when he arrives to put out the fire.

Though the story was puerile, we rather liked the idea that it used music not for spectacle, but naturally, as if the songs were part of the dialogue. However, *The Hot Heiress* was hardly a notable screen debut. We ended up with only three songs in the final print, and neither they nor the film created any stir.

I can't say that I learned much about moviemaking during this first visit to the West Coast, but I was fascinated by the process of putting a story, particularly a musical, on film. In those days, for example, there was no such thing as prerecording, and every time someone sang, the entire studio orchestra had to be on the set. What interested me most of all, however, was the work of the film editor, which, though unappreciated by the average moviegoer, is of enormous importance in determining the finished product.

One of the pleasantest aspects of this trip to Hollywood was not only that Dorothy eventually felt well enough to join me but that she even coaxed my parents into taking the trip with her. We all returned to New York in mid-August—and within a month I was forced to leave again. This time it was a call from C. B. Cochran. *Ever Green* was proceeding well, but Larry and I were needed in London for rehearsals. A transatlantic crossing was certainly not advisable for Dorothy, and once more I was forced to make a trip without her.

Saying good-bye to someone you love is always hard; saying good-bye to Dorothy at this time was extremely difficult. Her pregnancy was again causing her great distress, and I was leaving for a job that would keep me away for at least two months.

On shipboard Larry, as usual, kept himself occupied at the bar. I spent most of my time working on the piano manuscripts while sitting in a deck chair, since it would have been embarrassing to play the piano in a public room. This not only helped pass the time on a dull ocean trip, it also gave me more leisure once I arrived in London. But the problem was what to do with all that leisure. I was just plain miserable without Dorothy, and full of self-blame for doing the kind of work that would keep me away from home for such a long period. Under the circumstances there was little anyone could do to make me feel much better.

But many people tried. My mother and father came over for a visit, and my English friends helped enormously. The d'Erlangers and their group had all grown fond of Dorothy during our first trip, and their concern for her health was obviously so sincere that it helped ease the pain of our separation. Noël Coward again proved a loyal friend, and Cochran did everything he could to make me feel comfortable. Of course he was well aware that I was chafing to return home, but there was no way I could leave before the out-of-town opening. And that—in Glasgow—was still a month away!

In the meantime the Cochrans, who always seemed to know when I needed morale-boosting, took care of my weekends by inviting me to their summer home in Egham, an imposing mansion with heavy mid-Victorian furniture and glorious gardens and trees. The only trouble with the place was that there was just one bathtub and loo for everyone to fight over.

Cochran also showed extreme solicitude for my opinions on everything to do with the show, even including the costume designs. In fact, from the standpoint of mutual cooperation and admiration, I can't recall ever having worked under such pleasant circumstances.

One night after a rehearsal, C.B. took me to a prize fight which turned out to be one of the strangest events I've ever witnessed. The referee wore white tie and tails, and most of the audience was dressed formally. Except for an occasional muted cheer, the spectators sat in deadly silence, which made the sound of leather against flesh seem even more cruel. The whole evening had the unmistakable aura of the upper classes getting uninvolved pleasure from two members of the lower classes beating each other up, and it rather soured me on the British sporting scene.

Early in October I left for Glasgow alone to attend orchestra rehearsals, since, unlike in America, the Scottish orchestras rehearsed for days before a performance. The trip north was horrendous. It took ten bumpy, sleepless hours to get there, and once I arrived I had to endure a period of almost mind-numbing loneliness. During the day I could occupy my time with orchestra rehearsals, but at night there was nothing to do but have dinner alone, take in a movie or a show alone, return to a depressing hotel and be in bed by ten.

A week later the *Ever Green* company arrived. As the hotel was part of the railroad structure, it was necessary only to get a porter to carry the bags into the hotel through its rear lobby entrance, but for some reason Larry couldn't be convinced that the hotel was right at the station. After huffing and puffing at a cabdriver, he managed to get the confused man to load his luggage and drive him around the corner to the main entrance on the street.

The dress rehearsal of *Ever Green* went exceedingly well and proceeded to disprove one of the theatre's ancient saws that a good dress rehearsal means a poor opening-night performance. Cochran had assembled a truly sumptuous production, with colorful scenes depicting such locales as the Albert Hall in London, a *Folies-Bergère* type of revue in Paris, an elaborate street fair in Neuilly, and even a religious ceremony in Catalonia, Spain. What helped immeasurably was that our revolving stage, which was being used for the first time in Britain, worked without a hitch or even a sound.

Jessie Matthews scored exactly the kind of triumph Cochran had hoped for. Her naïve charm, gossamer dancing and liquid voice won praise, even adoration. It was *Ever Green* that led to Jessie's movie career, in which she reigned as the queen of British musicals.

Initially, however, everyone thought that Cochran was taking a chance with Jessie. The British public has always been loyal to its idols, and Jessie had recently tangled with Evelyn Laye, a long-time favorite, over the affection of Evelyn's husband, Sonnie Hale, which resulted in the breakup of the marriage. Jessie and Sonnie had subsequently married, and since he was playing the male lead in *Ever Green,* it was feared that loyalty to Evelyn might turn the public against Jessie. Fortunately, these fears proved unfounded.

Our songs were also well received. "Dancing on the Ceiling," rescued from *Simple Simon,* was performed by Jessie and Sonnie all around a huge inverted chandelier that rose from center stage like an incandescent metal tree. The song itself is worthy of some comment because its creation throws further light on the unusually close collaboration between Larry and me. I had composed the music first, and there was something about it that gave Larry the feeling of weightlessness and elevation. This in turn led to the original notion of a girl imagining that her distant lover is dancing above her on the ceiling. Note that in the first two bars—on the words "He dances overhead"—the notes ascend the scale in a straight line, then descend in the third, and then suddenly leap a seventh, from D to C on the words "(ceil)ing near," at the beginning of the fourth bar:

Because the song was written in the "AABA" form, these notes are repeated in the second and third "A" sections. This is particularly effective at the end, when the leap occurs on the words "a danc(ing floor)," and then, as a variation, rises even higher on "Just for," before unexpectedly dropping a seventh for the final words "my love."

Once *Ever Green* was successfully launched in Glasgow, there was no further need for me to remain with the show for its London opening. Knowing how desperately I wanted to be with Dorothy, Cochran told me I could leave for New York whenever I wanted to. The day after the tryout opening, I took the same bumpy train ride back to London and caught the next ship sailing for New York. By happy coincidence it was the *Majestic,* that lovable liner on which, more than four years before, Dorothy and I had first gotten to know each other.

On reaching home, I was determined to remain with Dorothy until the birth of our child. But Herb, Larry and I were still under contract to Warner Bros. for two more films. Had the contract not involved the two others, I would have tried to get out of it, or at least postpone it, but with no ties of their own, Herb and Larry were anxious to get started and I simply could not walk away from my obligation both to them and to the studio.

We had no idea of what we wanted to do, but when we discussed it with the Warner people in New York there was a certain amount of hemming and hawing, and they advised us to go to California to talk the matter over with Jack Warner. I had to go, but by this time I was thoroughly fed up with assignments that meant my constantly packing and unpacking a suitcase. Before I was married I'd had one show after another on Broadway; now that I had a wife at home there didn't seem to be any work for me nearer than three thousand miles in either direction.

As it turned out, this trip to the West Coast kept me away for a much shorter period than I had expected. Even before we had a chance to bring up the subject of the new movie, Jack Warner hit us with the news that musical films, which had been a major attraction for every studio during the past year, had suddenly become a glut on the market. No one wanted to see song-and-dance movies any more. Why there should have been such a turnabout has never really made sense to me, except that there were probably so many inferior productions that they created a negative reaction against *all* musicals. Whatever the reason, it was the condition that prevailed and there was nothing we could do about it; Warner simply wanted out. We hired a Los Angeles attorney to arrange a satisfactory financial settlement for the two canceled films, and returned to New York as quickly as we could.

During the subsequent weeks I really began to feel the effects of the Depression. For the first time in many years my telephone was not jangling with offers from producers to write new shows. As in the days when we first started, it was up to Larry and me to get together with a librettist and create a story and score that would interest a producer. Herb Fields was in the same situation, and it occurred to the three of us that a show built around the crazy world of Hollywood would make a timely and amusing musical. Based in part on our own recent experience, we slapped together a piece about two kids who go to Hollywood, where the girl becomes a silent-screen star. With the sound revolution, it's the boy who makes good while the girl, as happened so often in real life, proves unable to maintain her success when she is heard as well as seen. True love, of course, turns out to be the only remedy for the girl's bruised ego. While it was an ordinary plot, we did manage to avoid one stereotype: our studio mogul was an Irishman named Dolan. In tribute to Mary Pickford, who had nothing to do with the show, we called it *America's Sweetheart.*

Now to find a producer. By the end of 1930 some of the most highly respected men in the theatre were in serious financial difficulty and there was general retrenchment all down the line. Even though Alex Aarons and Vinton Freedley had a big success with *Girl Crazy,* they were unwilling to take a chance on another musical in the same season. Lew Fields, who had a flop with *The Vanderbilt Revue,* vowed he'd never do another Broadway show—and he never did. Dillingham had been hit hard by the crash and was in virtual retirement. Theresa Helburn and Lawrence Langner of the Theatre Guild, who had just sponsored another *Garrick Gaieties* (without Rodgers and Hart), didn't think our new musical was for them. Billy Rose was just beginning his career as a Broadway showman, but he was almost as much of a credit risk as Ziegfeld—and we sure as hell weren't going to go back to Ziegfeld.

Fortunately the Broadway reunion of Fields, Rodgers and Hart did have enough appeal to win the support of one prominent producing team, Laurence Schwab and Frank Mandel. I had known both men for a long time, though we had never before been associated in a theatrical production.

Schwab, in fact, was the man who had first taken me to see Max Dreyfus on that miserable occasion when the publisher told me that my music had no value. Since then they had had considerable success, primarily with romantic Sigmund Romberg–Oscar Hammerstein operettas *(The Desert Song, The New Moon)* and breezy, modern musical comedies *(Good News, Follow Thru)* by the Bud De Sylva, Lew Brown and Ray Henderson team. They were both thorough men of the theatre who could write as well as produce (Mandel was co-author of *No, No, Nanette*), and though shrewd, careful businessmen, were extremely likable and easy to work with.

At the recommendation of Herb Fields, the producers signed a bearded, sharp-tongued director named Monty Woolley who had previously worked with Herb on two Cole Porter musicals. For the male lead there was unanimous agreement that the part was ideal for smiling Jack Whiting, Broadway's most popular juvenile, who had been in *She's My Baby* and our last musical, *Heads Up!* For the female lead we auditioned a number of actresses and then settled on a tiny, round-faced blonde with an oddly appealing nasal voice. Her name was then Harriette Lake, but by the time she emulated the show's heroine and went to Hollywood herself she had become known as Ann Sothern.

In the midst of rehearsals—on January 11, 1931—Dorothy gave birth to our first child at Lenox Hill Hospital. The obstetrician was my brother, Mortimer. Mary was a healthy, lively, generally happy baby, and naturally the brightest and prettiest little girl two nutty parents ever clucked over.

I was spared some of the more disagreeable chores of early parenthood because eight days after Mary was born I was off to Pittsburgh for the first stop in *America's Sweetheart*'s tryout tour. The reception was encouraging, and after a week we opened at the National Theatre in Washington.

In the score of *America's Sweetheart,* Larry and I had a song that was one of the few we wrote which made a passing reference to the country's economic condition. It was called "I've Got Five Dollars," and in it, a marriage proposal takes the form of an offer of, besides five dollars, such itemized possessions as six shirts and collars and a heart that hollers. The mood was jaunty and optimistic, and the use of repetitive note patterns helped convey the desired effect of a light-hearted inventory.

America's Sweetheart opened in New York in February, but received little help from a divided press, with comments ranging from "sounds like discarded cues from *Once in a Lifetime* set to music" (John Anderson, *Journal*) to "New York will clasp it to its bosom until we get back our light wine and beer" (Robert Coleman, *Mirror*). I'm not sure about that bosom-clasping but we did last the season, which in 1931 was all that anyone could reasonably expect.

Larry and I were happy to be back on Broadway after a full year's absence, but it didn't take long before the exhilaration of opening night disappeared. Having a musical on Broadway and even having a creditable run were not enough. We had to start planning our next production as soon as possible. At first we hoped to continue the newly reactivated Fields, Rodgers and Hart trio, but Herb soon got an offer to write Hollywood scripts. Larry and I tried batting story ideas around, but nothing seemed to work. Even if we did come up with something that we thought promising, there was always the problem of finding a solvent producer. Still, with Hollywood closed to us, we had no other alternative but to try to keep active and hope that something would turn up.

What did turn up was totally unexpected. During these doldrum days for song-and-dance movies, one screen entertainer, the irresistibly exuberant French singer Maurice Chevalier, had managed to appear in a succession of hit musicals. Chevalier's movies were gay, bubbly confections, usually set in Europe and directed by that master of continental comedy, Ernst Lubitsch. They succeeded when others failed, I suppose, because they were concerned with glamorous people in glamorous locales far from the troubled shores of the United States, because they offered moviegoers something a bit spicier than the ordinary domestic product—and because they had Chevalier. And just how did Rodgers and Hart fit into all this? We were the songwriters Paramount wanted for the next Maurice Chevalier picture.

12

Larry and I went to Hollywood with a contract for one picture and stayed for two and a half years. My second experience in the film capital started out brightly enough—*Love Me Tonight* is still considered to be among the most imaginative screen musicals ever made—and I derived a certain amount of satisfaction from one or two other assignments. But two and a half years? What on earth could have compelled me to devote so long a period of time to what was, for the most part, the most unproductive period of my professional life?

I could give many valid reasons why I did not head for home as soon as it became apparent that Hollywood and Rodgers were not made for each other. There was my fascination with film technique, coupled with my feeling that I could make a genuine contribution to the medium. There was the appeal of the sunbaked, affluent life that I found all around me. There was the attraction of parties and social affairs where Dorothy and I enjoyed meeting the idols, moguls and other fawned-over fauna of the area. There was the benefit of bringing up a child in a healthier atmosphere than a crowded, dirty city.

But I would gladly have chucked it all had it not been for the strongest of all chains that bind a man to a life he finds unrewarding: money. The Depression didn't last just a year or two, it lasted almost an entire decade, and the years from 1931 to 1935 were the hardest of all. A man with a family to support, particularly given the ephemeral nature of my profession, had to acknowledge the financial importance of a contract with a major studio. The arrival of a substantial weekly pay check can go a long way in assuaging dissatisfaction with working conditions—or the lack of working conditions.

Moreover, during this period the New York stage was hard hit by the country's economic woes, so whenever I began longing for the sweet misery of sweating over a bar of music at two in the morning during a hectic rehearsal in New Haven, I consoled myself by rationalizing that Broadway had had it and that the screen was not only the most popular but also the most challenging and exciting form of entertainment in the world.

At first I didn't have to do any such rationalizing. It really looked as if I had made the right decision in going West when I did. If a film of the quality of *Love Me Tonight,* I reasoned, could be created when screen musicals were in disfavor, surely when they regained popularity Rodgers and Hart would be in the vanguard. But it didn't turn out that way. Ironically, the resurgence of film musicals that began in 1933—sparked by the Busby Berkeley extravaganzas and later by the Astaire-Rogers pictures

—had almost the reverse effect on the career of Rodgers and Hart. When no one else was making musicals, we worked on one of the screen's most highly praised achievements. When everyone else was making musicals, we had a contract but no work.

When Larry, Dorothy, Mary and I arrived in Hollywood in November 1931, the director assigned to *Love Me Tonight* was George Cukor. He seemed an excellent choice, since he had worked with Ernst Lubitsch on the previous Chevalier-MacDonald film, *One Hour with You.* A week later Larry and I were surprised to learn that Cukor was out and that Rouben Mamoulian had been tapped to succeed him. Mamoulian did not seem as good a choice. A Chevalier picture needed a deft, delicate touch, and on the basis of such melodramatic offerings as *Applause* and *Dr. Jekyll and Mr. Hyde,* Mamoulian didn't appear to have this attribute. As soon as we met him, however, Larry and I quickly realized that there could be no better director for *Love Me Tonight.*

Owlish, with a thick crop of black hair and an exuberant manner, Mamoulian had a concept of filming that was almost exactly what we had in mind. Like us, he was convinced that a musical film should be created in musical terms—that dialogue, song and scoring should all be integrated as closely as possible so that the final product would have a unity of style and design. Fortunately, he was the producer as well as director of the film and had complete autonomy. One of the first things he insisted on was that I compose all the background music, not simply the music for the songs. This was—and still is—highly unusual, since film scoring has generally been left to composers specializing in the field. It is more or less stop-watch composing, with the writer creating musical themes to fit precisely into a prescribed number of frames. I had no background in this sort of work but I found it extremely challenging and fun to do, and it certainly helped in giving the film the desired creative unity.

One sequence I was particularly proud of was the scoring for the deer hunt. In it, I had to create two contrasting and intercutting themes, one— on the brass—for the pursuing dogs and horses, the other—on the strings —for the frightened deer. Mamoulian staged the entire sequence as if it were a zoological ballet.

Primarily, however, *Love Me Tonight* gave Larry and me the opportunity to work with one essential tool of the musical film that heretofore had not been properly utilized: the camera. In almost every musical, the camera would be set up, a boy and girl would be stuck in front of it, and it would photograph them while they sang or danced. It was all done within the limits of one prescribed locale. What we had in mind was not only moving the camera and the performers, but having the entire *scene* move.

There was no reason why a musical sequence could not be used like dialogue and be performed uninterrupted while the action took the story to whatever locations the director wanted. Mamoulian loved the idea, and fortunately the script for *Love Me Tonight* provided us with the perfect situation in which to try it out.

Early in the picture there is a scene in Paris in the tailor shop owned by Maurice Chevalier. He has just made a morning suit for a portly bridegroom-to-be, and in expressing their mutual delight at the results, the two men are no longer able to contain their emotions in ordinary dialogue but break into rhyming dialogue:

MAURICE: The tailor's art/ For your sweetheart.
CUSTOMER: That's like poetry in a book./ How beautiful I look.
MAURICE: The love song of the needle/ United with the thread,
        The romance of the scissors . . .
CUSTOMER: So Claire and I could wed.

With the musical mood established in rhyme, Maurice exclaims, "Isn't it romantic?," and suddenly the music takes over. Following the verse ("My face is glowing, I'm energetic,/ The art of sewing I find poetic"), the refrain finds Maurice anticipating marriage to an adoring and subservient wife who will scrub both the floor and his back, cook him onion soup and provide him with a huge family. (Incidentally, the lyric in the film is different from the one Larry later wrote for the commercial version.)

Once Maurice has finished the song, the music is picked up by the customer, who expresses admiration for the "very catchy strain." Still humming and singing, he bids Maurice good-bye and jauntily walks down the street. A passing taxi driver hears him and begins whistling the tune, which in turn is repeated by his fare. The fare turns out to be a composer on his way to the railroad station who starts writing down the music, singing each note as he goes along. With no break in musical continuity, the scene cuts quickly to the interior of a railroad car, where the composer is now busily putting words to the music. The song is overheard by a group of French soldiers who, in another abrupt change of scene, now sing the piece in march tempo as they hike through the countryside. Suddenly the camera pans away from the soldiers to a gypsy boy who is listening intently. He dashes back to his camp and plays the theme, now oozing with romantic passion, on his violin. By this time night has fallen, and in a long shot we see a nearby château with a single lighted room. The camera dollies in, and there is Jeanette MacDonald, as a lovesick princess, looking wistful on a balcony. Now it is her turn to be affected by the music she hears coming from the gypsy camp, and she expresses her longing for an unknown prince in armor who will kiss her hand, bend his knee and be her slave.

Thus, from a tailor shop in Paris to the sidewalk, to a taxi, to a railroad car, to a country road, to a gypsy camp, and finally to a château far from the city, one song is used to provide the romantic link between hero and heroine, even though they are miles apart and have never met.

Another effective sequence in the film was the opening, which in quick, dramatic shots establishes the sights and sounds of an awakening Paris, all orchestrated—without an orchestra—into a steadily accelerated rhythmic pattern. This was entirely Rouben's idea; in fact, he had already used it in a different setting for the 1927 play *Porgy* (later to become the Gershwin opera, *Porgy and Bess*). Just as he had previously coordinated the early-morning Catfish Row activities, now Rouben coordinated a succession and accumulation of activities in a Paris neighborhood—workmen digging up the street, a baby crying, a woman sweeping her steps, men grinding knives, shopkeepers opening their stores, auto horns honking, whistles tooting, smoke belching out of chimneys. Every shot and sound is synchronized until the orchestra, at first almost imperceptibly, takes over for Chevalier's first song, "That's the Song of Paree." Is there any wonder that Larry and I were stimulated by a man as brilliant as Mamoulian?

Actually, our story really wasn't much—merely a satirical variation on the Cinderella and Sleeping Beauty themes—but it was perfectly suited for a variety of dramatic, comic and musical innovations. In fact, many of the techniques we used—particularly moving from one location to another during one song, and the quick cutting and undercutting of scenes—are still very much a part of moviemaking today.

Though Larry and I were primarily concerned with the cinematic quality of the score, we did not forget that having Maurice Chevalier introduce our songs would help them enormously in winning popularity. Indeed, Chevalier had already done so well in immortalizing the charms of such ladies as Valentine and Louise that we decided to write a perky little piece for him about a girl named Mimi (somehow the film's dialogue made it apply to Princess Jeanette). We also wrote four other songs that we felt confident were just right for the Chevalier delivery: a romantic title song, which both Maurice and Jeanette were to sing as solos but which, thanks to a split screen, would be made to appear as a duet; a dramatic number about life as an Apache; "Isn't It Romantic?"; and "That's the Song of Paree."

One memory that will always be with me was of the day Larry and I performed our songs for Chevalier. Unlike the luxurious office we had at Warner Bros. when we were toiling over *The Hot Heiress,* Paramount had assigned us to a cell-like cubicle on the first floor of one of their buildings. It couldn't be dignified by being called an office; if we went over to the tiny window and stuck our noses right up against the glass, we could see a patch of about six inches of sky. One day we heard a knock on the door, and there, with eyes twinkling and teeth gleaming, stood Maurice Chevalier. Everything he wore was blue—blue jacket, blue sport shirt, blue scarf, blue slacks, blue shoes—which accentuated the incredible blueness of his eyes. He greeted Larry and me as if we were old friends, told us how happy he was that we were writing the songs for his picture, and asked if we would mind playing some of them. With Chevalier practically sitting on my lap in our cramped quarters, I played the music and Larry and I took turns singing the words. Chevalier sat silent throughout, his usually expressive face without a trace of either approval or disapproval, and when we'd finished he simply rose and left without saying a word. We were stunned. The only conclusion we could reach was that he didn't like what he'd heard. Now what? Should we start all over again? Would the studio replace us with another team? And what about our reputation once it got around that Chevalier, the screen's leading musical star, had turned thumbs down?

The next morning we tried to sneak into our little room without anyone seeing us; we were certain that word of Chevalier's displeasure had already spread and that it was only a matter of time before we'd be called into the front office to be dismissed. We couldn't do any work; we simply stared at each other and at the walls like prisoners in Death Row, a feeling heightened by the cell-like atmosphere of the room. After a couple of hours the door burst open and there again stood our smiling blue boy. "Boys," Chevalier said, throwing one arm around Larry and the other around me, "I just had to come back to tell you. I couldn't sleep a wink last night because I was so excited about your wonderful songs!" *He* couldn't sleep a wink last night! Why he couldn't have told us the day before I'll never know, but suddenly the weight was lifted from our shoulders, and it was a tough job for Larry and me to conceal our feeling of relief.

Maurice and I became friends and saw quite a bit of each other socially during my stay in Hollywood. His personality was very much what it was on the screen—warm, ebullient, full of vitality. Though extremely gregarious, he was not a quick man with a dollar, which was probably a result of his poverty-stricken youth; in fact, he was the only man I've ever met who would accept a cigarette and put it in his pocket.

Jeanette MacDonald, whom I had known slightly when she was a Broadway ingénue during the twenties, had already attracted notice as Chevalier's leading lady in two films. In *Love Me Tonight* she had a song, "Lover," which, though treated as a joke and never reprised, somehow managed to catch on. Jeanette sang it in an outdoors scene while riding in a horse-drawn cart. Still yearning for an unknown lover, our lonely princess sings the romantic lyric with sincerity, except that certain words and phrases are directed to her occasionally frisky horse. As, for example:

> Lover, when you find me
> Will you blind me with your glow?
> Make me cast behind me all my—WHOA!
> Kiss me, hear me saying
> Gently swaying I'll obey
> Like two lovers playing in the—HEY!

Not many people know that Jeanette was an accomplished horse-woman, and that she insisted on doing all her own riding in the film. In the finale she was called upon to ride a horse fast enough to overtake a rapidly moving train, jump off the horse and force the oncoming locomotive to come to a halt by standing defiantly on the tracks. Our cameras were set up on a train running parallel to the one being filmed, and Jeanette had to race furiously between them. It's hard to understand why the studio allowed her to take such a risk, but she managed to get her way. It was not for nothing that she was called the Iron Butterfly.

The most lasting friendship I made during *Love Me Tonight* was with Myrna Loy, one of the most charming, witty and perceptive women I have ever known. Before getting the part of the man-hungry countess in *Love Me Tonight,* Myrna had been cast almost exclusively as an Oriental vamp, and this film gave her the first opportunity to show her rare gift for comedy. She had the best line in the picture. After the frail Princess Jeanette has fainted, someone rushes up to Myrna and asks, "Can you go for a doctor?" "Certainly," she answers, batting her large almond-shaped eyes. "Bring him right in."

Love Me Tonight served to establish Larry and me as a motion-picture team very much in the same way that *The Garrick Gaieties* had established us on the stage. It proved that a movie musical produced at a time when everyone was certain there was no market for it could be both artistically and commercially successful. It even supplied us with a bonus: "Lover," "Isn't It Romantic?" and "Mimi" became Rodgers and Hart's first song hits to emanate from Hollywood.

Unfortunately, things began going downhill almost immediately thereafter. Paramount was impressed enough with our work not only to offer us a contract for a second film but also to provide us with an outward symbol of our new eminence—a luxuriously appointed office to work in. On paper, our next screen assignment, *The Phantom President,* seemed like a welcome change of pace. It was to be a satirical musical concerned with political skullduggery during a presidential campaign, with the leading role to be played by Broadway's legendary Yankee Doodle–Song-and-Dance man, George M. Cohan.

Larry and I had never met Cohan. Though as a composer he was hardly up there with the Kerns, Berlins or Gershwins, I did admire the infectious vitality of his songs, and I had great regard for him as an actor. No matter how simple-minded or corny his shows were, he never failed to give a highly skilled, even subtle performance.

But the times had almost passed Cohan by, and he was in semiretirement when he signed the contract with Paramount for what was to be his first screen role. I'd heard that he had been promised the opportunity of doing some of the writing on the film, but a change in the studio hierarchy ended whatever verbal agreement might have been made. At any rate, neither Larry nor I had been directly informed about this, though we were aware that we had the questionable distinction of being the first lyricist and composer other than George M. Cohan himself to write songs for him.

This, coupled with the fact that Cohan seemed to feel that the studio did not treat him with the deference that was his due, produced tension right from the start. There was never anything overt, simply a curtness and a disdain that he displayed not only to us but also, with rare equanimity, to everyone who had anything to do with the picture. One just knew that he felt he could direct better than the director, write a script better than the scriptwriters, and write music and lyrics better than Rodgers and Hart. During the shooting he never remained on the set when he wasn't required in front of the cameras, but always returned directly to the seclusion of his dressing room. I don't recall that he ever deigned to grant interviews, sign autographs or speak a civil word to anyone. It was obvious that he felt miserable about making the picture and he wanted us all to know it. (After the film was completed, he did let off steam in a newspaper interview. "If I had my choice," he said, "between Hollywood and Atlanta, I'd take Leavenworth.")

Probably because of the frigid atmosphere on the set, I don't remember much about the making of *The Phantom President.* I do recall that Claudette Colbert was in it, and so was Jimmy Durante—who never called me anything but "Roger." I also know that, like *Love Me Tonight,* the picture offered Larry and me opportunities to work out our concepts about incorporating songs within the action of the story. Our most ambitious number was the presidential convention in which the entire session—including speeches by candidate Cohan and sidekick Durante, as well as the reactions of the delegates—was all set to music. We tried getting away from the usual treatment of a love song by having a trio of twittering birds sing the ballad "Give Her a Kiss" to the timid Cohan while he is sitting next to Claudette in an open-top automobile.

The Phantom President was made early in 1932 and released just in time for the Roosevelt-Hoover election campaign. I think even Hoover was more popular than the film.

A month or so after finishing work on the Cohan picture, Dorothy and I were hit with a tragedy from which it took us both a long time to recover. Soon after moving into a furnished house on North Elm Drive, we were told that Dorothy was to have a second child. This was joyous news because it meant that Mary would have a companion near her age at a time when she most needed one. Suddenly, almost at full term, Dorothy began having a series of premature contractions. Late one night she was rushed to Cedars of Lebanon Hospital, where the baby, a girl, was born but lived only a few minutes. I had never before realized how traumatic such an experience is. Dorothy was physically depleted and emotionally drained.

With two movies released at about the same time and one of them a success, Larry and I could sift through a number of offers before deciding on our next project. In dealing with a presidential election, no matter how outlandish, *The Phantom President* had given us the opportunity to handle a contemporary theme. For *Hallelujah, I'm a Bum,* the picture we were asked to do next, the theme was equally contemporary but far more daring. It was the first and probably the last musical ever made in Hollywood that concerned itself almost entirely with the problems of the Depression. During those years so many people lost their jobs, money and homes that they were forced to live wherever they could find a few yards of vacant ground. In our picture we focused on bums living in Central Park, with Al Jolson playing the part of Bumper, their leader, Harry Langdon playing Egghead, a radical who calls the police "Hoover's Cossacks," and Frank Morgan as a Jimmy Walkerish mayor who is always at least two hours late for appointments and who spends most of his time at the Park Casino. We tried to keep the score relatively light, but we were defeated by the theme. The subject of homelessness at a time when it was such an urgent national problem didn't strike many people as something to laugh and sing about.

Hallelujah, I'm a Bum was produced by Joseph Schenck at United Artists, with Lewis Milestone directing. Milestone, who had already handled such grim epics as *All Quiet on the Western Front* and *Hell's Angels,* was a highly imaginative director who shared with Mamoulian an abiding hatred of doing the same kind of movie twice.

Most of the shooting of the Central Park sequences took place at the Riviera Country Club, in Pacific Palisades. One of the unusual aspects of the filming, since there still was no technique for dubbing of music, was that a large orchestra, conducted by my old friend Alfred Newman, was ensconced right on the golf course so that the songs could be performed in their proper exterior setting. At that time, probably as a convenience to studio orchestras and to save money, the conventional method was to shoot all exterior musical sequences indoors and try to make them look as if they were being performed outdoors.

Hallelujah, I'm a Bum gave us the opportunity to expand on the innovation, already tried out in *Love Me Tonight* and *The Phantom President,* of what was then called rhythmic dialogue, though a better term might be "musical dialogue." We simply used rhymed conversation, with musical accompaniment, to affect a smoother transition to actual song and to give the entire film a firmer musical structure. It was similar to recitative in opera, except that it was done in rhythm and was an authentic part of the action.

In one scene Jolson and his buddies, street cleaner Harry Langdon and hobo Edgar Connor, are walking through the park when they hear the insistent sound of a clock ticking (which is actually performed by the orchestra). They discover the clock attached to a lady's handbag in Langdon's sanitation bin and comment on it:

> CONNOR: Tick tick tick
> That sure am slick
> JOLSON: Not so quick
> CONNOR: Tick tick tick
> LANGDON: What's that thing?
> JOLSON: It's a lady's bag
> LANGDON: The aristocratic rag
> Of a plutocratic hag . . .

When they examine the contents of the bag, Jolson finds a letter addressed to the owner—which, being in rhyme, conveniently lends itself to song. Suddenly the dialogue and the tick-tick-tick music become more agitated as the three argue about what to do with a thousand-dollar bill they also find in the bag. This leads directly into the number "Bumper Found a Grand," in march tempo, in which the news is conveyed from one tramp to another as they all try to get cut in on the money. Jolson ends the scene by addressing the crowd ("Friends, rummies, countrymen") and extolling the virtues of poverty in the song "What Do You Want with Money?"

Unlike our experience with Cohan on *The Phantom President*, Larry and I found working on *Hallelujah, I'm a Bum* almost as exciting as *Love Me Tonight*. Jolson, who I had been told might prove difficult, turned out to be a sweet man who at the time was undergoing one of his frequent estrangements from his wife, Ruby Keeler. He was completely cooperative, though it often took a little patience to corner him to get down to business.

During part of the time I worked on the picture Dorothy was back in New York visiting her parents. A letter I wrote to her in October 1932 gives an account of an unusually nerve-racking day:

> Today was one of those mad ones that made me satisfied that you were away. It started with writing, manuscripts to be done, conferences about rehearsals, orchestrations, and everything else. I had half an hour for dinner, alone, at the Derby, and then back to a rehearsal. Jolson wouldn't work because he wanted to go to the fights. I agreed to go with him if he'd promise to work with me later. So to the fights we went (terrible ones) and then to his apartment where I rehearsed him for an hour. Then to meet the boys at Milestone's house to hear the final dialogue scenes, then home. It's two a.m. and I'm pooped . . .

Late in the year Larry and I got a call from Irving Thalberg, the young production head at Metro-Goldwyn-Mayer, who offered us not only a contract but a choice of assignments. He had been greatly impressed with what we had achieved in *Love Me Tonight* and was sure that either one of two stories his studio owned could be adapted with equally effective results. One was a then popular comic novel that we would work on with its author, Thorne Smith; the other was a Hungarian play about a banker whose wish comes true when he marries an angel. Larry and I thought the Hungarian fantasy had greater screen possibilities, and with everyone's blessing we went to work with a young writer named Moss Hart who had been assigned to do the screenplay. Moss, no relation to Larry, was the co-author of a successful Broadway play, *Once in a Lifetime*, in which he had ridiculed the sham, pretensions and frustrations of Hollywood. Our experiences with *I Married an Angel*, the name of our fantasy, could easily have provided him with enough material for a whole new play.

Moss was an intense, almost Mephistophelian-looking fellow, fairly bursting with ideas. The three of us worked closely, and within a month or so completed the entire story and score. Louis B. Mayer, who was Thalberg's boss, had intended the picture as a vehicle for his newest contract star, Jeanette MacDonald, and had even lured her to sign with the studio because of his enthusiasm for the project. But when we were all finished and everything was set to roll, Mayer called God into conference and issued a royal decree: fantasies were uncommercial and he was canceling the production. The fact that he had approved the studio's purchase of the story, signed Jeanette MacDonald on the basis of her doing it and had nothing but praise for our treatment made not the slightest difference. No one could budge him, and that was the end of it.

Well, not exactly. Years later we did make *I Married an Angel* as a Broadway musical, and years after *that* M-G-M decided it would be just the thing for Nelson Eddy and—yes, indeed—Jeanette MacDonald. Thus, Larry and I ended up in the curious but happy position of being paid for the same material three times: as a movie that was never filmed, as a stage musical, and as a movie that was filmed but—from what I've heard about it—never should have been.

After working on the first *I Married an Angel,* however, we had no thought of any future monetary rewards. We had wasted our time, and it was back to the bars for Larry and back to the tennis courts for me. Moss was smarter than either of us; he returned to Broadway, where he and Irving Berlin put together a show called *As Thousands Cheer* that was one of the great revues of the decade.

My disappointment was somewhat mitigated by an event that occurred in Washington at about the same time: the beginning of the Presidency of Franklin D. Roosevelt. FDR's decisive defeat of President Hoover in the 1932 election had been a stimulant for the entire Depression-weary country. With confidence exuding from his voice, his jutting jaw, the tilt of his cigarette holder, his bright, piercing eyes, he became so much the physical embodiment of the nation's longing for optimism that it was easy to ignore the fact that he was unable to walk without crutches.

From the very start of his presidency, Roosevelt churned up and turned out a dizzying succession of ideas, programs and laws. One of the first things he did after he had taken office in March was to declare a Bank Holiday in order to stop the alarming number of bank failures. During the week-long period while the government established laws to control banking, everyone had to live on whatever cash he had on hand. Ever since moving to California, a year and a half before, I had been sending my folks a weekly check because Pop was then in virtual retirement. As soon as the Bank Holiday was declared, my father telephoned me. To my amazement, he told me that he had dutifully cashed the checks I had been sending but had never spent any of the money. Instead, he simply put the bills in a safe-deposit box, and since he was sure I could use some cash he would wire me the money. Because of Pop's foresight, I was among the few people in the country with more cash than they needed during the emergency.

By 1933 the team of Rodgers and Hart had three movies in circulation, which had, we thought, helped to evolve the screen musical into a form that was indigenous to the medium. Had *The Phantom President* or *Hallelujah, I'm a Bum* succeeded, who knows? Maybe our kind of musical would have set the standard. One thing we did know: in March 1933 Warner Bros. released a backstage movie with a series of dazzling production routines which, more than any other film, was responsible for the rebirth of the screen musical. It was *42nd Street,* and all our innovations in music-and-story integration, in using one song to carry the action through a number of different locales, in bridging songs with rhythmic dialogue were quickly forgotten. Everyone wanted backstage musicals with lavish spectacles. Our old friend Busby Berkeley, who had choreographed two Rodgers and Hart shows, had revitalized an entire cinematic form with his daring overhead shots and his ingenious kaleidoscopic effects.

Buoyed by the country's renewed interest in musicals, the M-G-M hierarchs again thought of Rodgers and Hart. This time, however, Thalberg wanted us to sign a one-year term contract rather than one for a specific film. While he could not assure us that our experience with *I Married an Angel* would not be repeated, he was convinced that with musicals once again in demand, there would be plenty of work for us. Still, Larry and I remained dubious. A term contract would put us under obligation to do exactly what the studio wanted, whether we liked the assignment or not. It also meant that if it chose to, the studio could ignore us entirely. We had known too many writers who had been sold the benefits of a term contract, only to find themselves with little to do except collect a weekly pay check. We did, however, become a bit less dubious when Thalberg told us what our weekly pay check was going to be, but what really clinched the deal was opening the *New York Times* one morning to discover that there was a total of exactly five shows then running on Broadway. What was I to do? Run home for the unlikely prospect of making it six? Suddenly I realized how hollow was my long-held belief that I could chuck Hollywood any time I really wanted to and take up where I had left off in New York.

Well, what the hell. There was bound to be work; there was certain to be a fat salary; the year would go fast enough. Besides, there was no alternative. So Larry and I accepted our sentence: one year at soft labor at M-G-M.

Our period of servitude began, surprisingly, with a bang—though not the kind I ever want to hear again. We had been given a large studio in which to work, and one afternoon while playing piano for some friends, I suddenly heard a roaring sound and a deafening crash, followed by the incredible sight of the piano moving away from me. We were in the middle of an earthquake! Luckily the studio was on the first floor of the building, and we simply dashed for the nearest window and jumped out.

Since telephone lines had been damaged and road travel was temporarily halted, I had to spend anxious, frustrating hours worrying about Dorothy and Mary. At the time we were living on Angelo Drive and when I was finally able to return home, I almost collapsed with relief to find my family safe and our house only slightly affected.

The next day I discovered that the deafening crash I'd heard was caused by a brick wall falling on an empty rehearsal hall adjacent to my studio. If the wall had fallen just a foot closer, we would have been killed. The aftershock of this experience lasted for months, and to this day the passing of a heavy truck makes me acutely sensitive to the trembling of the ground beneath.

Larry and I were under contract to M-G-M for a month before anyone knew what to do with us. At the time Howard Dietz was the studio publicity chief, though he was a good deal more than a company flack. With composer Arthur Schwartz he had written some outstanding songs for Broadway revues, including "Dancing in the Dark" and "I Guess I'll Have to Change My Plan." He was a dynamic, extremely able man who easily wore more than one hat and looked great in each one he put on.

What Howard had in mind was the screwball picture to end all screwball pictures, with a cast including every available comic on the M-G-M lot, some guest-star appearances, and a score by Rodgers and Hart. After many changes along the way, the picture was eventually released as *Hollywood Party,* with Howard serving as co-author and co-producer. For the comedians, he managed to round up Jimmy Durante, Jack Pearl, Charles Butterworth, Polly Moran, Lupe Velez, Ted Healy and the Three Stooges, Laurel and Hardy, and even Mickey Mouse.

The picture turned out to be a real hodgepodge, and by the time it was released there had been so many directors assigned to it that none was credited—or blamed. (While Larry and I were working on the film, the man in charge was Edmund Goulding, but at least three other directors had a hand in it.) We submitted about a dozen songs, but only three were retained in the final print.

One of our ideas was to include a scene in which Jean Harlow is shown as an innocent young girl saying—or rather, singing—her prayers. How the sequence fitted into the movie I haven't the foggiest notion, but the purpose was to express Jean's overwhelming ambition to become a movie star ("Oh, Lord, if you're not busy up there,/ I ask for help with a prayer/ So please don't give me the air . . .").

For some reason the scene was never used. A few weeks later we were asked to write something for a Harlem night-club sequence in *Manhattan Melodrama,* a nonmusical starring Clark Gable, Myrna Loy and William Powell. Since I rather liked the melody for the discarded "Prayer," Larry came up with a new lyric and Shirley Ross sang it as "The Bad in Every Man" ("Oh, Lord, what is the matter with me?/ I'm just permitted to see/ The bad in every man . . .").

But that still wasn't the end of the song. While under contract to M-G-M, we were also under contract to its music-publishing company, then run by a man named Jack Robbins. Robbins was so enthusiastic about the song's possibilities that he assured us that if Larry would write a more commercial lyric, he'd get behind the number and plug it from one end of the country to the other. Larry came up with the third lyric, Robbins was as good as his word, and the song became the only success we ever had that was not associated with a stage or screen musical. This is the way it began: "Blue moon, you saw me standing alone,/ Without a dream in my heart,/ Without a love of my own . . ."

One final word about *Hollywood Party.* In one scene Jimmy Durante was supposed to say, "I'm the lord of the manure," but Howard Dietz was afraid he couldn't get away with it. He telephoned the studio front office for a ruling and was advised that the line could not be used. The censors wouldn't allow the word "lord."

With the completion of our work for *Hollywood Party,* Larry and I received a few offers for individual songs from various studios. Since we had no assignment at M-G-M, the studio lent us to Samuel Goldwyn to write an appropriate ballad for Anna Sten to sing in her first Hollywood film.

Remember Anna Sten? Anyone who lived through that period and was at all aware of movie stars must recall the round-faced Russian beauty with soulful eyes whom Goldwyn chose as his entry in the "another Garbo" sweepstakes. With some of the most persistent drumbeating that ever preceded the appearance of a screen personality, Goldwyn vainly tried to make Anna a star before anyone even saw her on the screen. Perhaps it was a case of oversell, for American moviegoers did not take to her, and she left after making only a few films.

Goldwyn's idea was to launch his discovery in a new version of Emile Zola's *Nana,* in which she would be obliged not only to act but also to sing. Dorothy had to return at that time to New York for a minor operation, and I wrote to her about the new assignment:

> When I got back to Larry's house, he had already written a lyric for the tune I had for the movie. We rushed down to United Artists

and played it for Al Newman, who's conducting. Al raved about it and we took it right up to Goldwyn. Well, sweet, we've had reactions in our time, but this was the top! He yelled and screamed and phoned Sten to tell her it was the best song he'd ever heard. His parting remark was, "Boys, I thank you from the bottom of my heart!" Of course, now I'm in love with Goldwyn! You know what a fool I am for anyone who's kind to me or likes my work. Well, this guy was so unaffected and naively enthusiastic that I was really touched.

Unfortunately the song, "That's Love," never did catch on with the public, but for a while Sam had us convinced that we had come up with another "Lover." One day he asked me to play it for Frances Marion, a sweet, precious little woman who was one of Goldwyn's favorite screen writers. Al Newman was also there. When I finished, I looked up from the keyboard and was startled to see the lady standing with her eyes closed as if in a trance. When Sam asked her what she thought, she slowly opened her eyes and said, in her sweet, precious little way, "Sam, this song is the essence of Paris. I've never heard anything so Parisian in my life." With that, Goldwyn wheeled around to Newman and commanded, "Newman, in the orchestra eight French horns!"

This is the kind of story that always prompts patronizing laughter, and it is a funny line. But I think I understand what Sam meant and why he said it. It was simply his way of telling Newman to go all out in supplying the proper Parisian flavor for what he had just been assured, by a woman he considered brilliant, to be a genuinely Parisian song. He was expressing both his delight and his gratitude, and I found this kind of warm, impetuous reaction disarming.

It is unfortunate that in making fun of Goldwyn and his Goldwynisms we often forget the man's brilliance. His innate good taste was responsible for what was probably a higher percentage of quality pictures than any other moving-picture producer. He never did anything just because someone had told him it was the commercial thing to do. When Sam said, "I make my pictures to please myself," he wasn't merely mouthing a line that would look good in print; he really meant it. It's also important to remember that since he used his own money and never depended on large-company backing to finance his projects, he was probably the only really independent producer in the business. My theory about Goldwyn and his language problem has always been that since he was foreign-born and didn't arrive in the United States until he was in his twenties, his mind worked so quickly that his tongue was simply never able to keep up with it. His thinking was always far ahead of his speech.

David O. Selznick was another major film executive I got to know well in Hollywood. Actually, I had known him ever since we went to the same public school in New York. In 1933 he had just been brought over to M-G-M from RKO Radio Pictures by his then father-in-law, Louis B. Mayer. One of David's first pictures was *Dancing Lady,* a rather blatant follow-up to *42nd Street,* into which he had poured an all-star line-up including Clark Gable, Joan Crawford, Franchot Tone and, making his Hollywood debut, Fred Astaire. In our contract with M-G-M, Larry and I had signed to write only complete moving-picture scores, not individual songs, but since we had already done one song for Goldwyn, we could hardly refuse when Selznick asked us to provide a number for the *Dancing Lady* finale.

The song was to be sung by Nelson Eddy and was intended to accompany a lavish production routine all about the pell-mell pace of modern living. After Larry and I put together something we thought appropriate, we were asked over to an enormous studio where we were obliged to perform the number before King David and his retinue of sound men, cameramen, wardrobe people, publicity people and anyone else they could find who wasn't doing anything. When we finished to applause and many complimentary words, David thanked us profusely.

Feeling satisfied about the song's reception, I took the next day off to play tennis at the Beverly Hills Tennis Club. I was in the middle of a game when I was told I was wanted on the telephone, so I jogged over to the clubhouse.

It was Selznick. "Dick," he said, "I want to tell you how crazy all of us are about the song you played yesterday."

"Thanks, David."

"It's really just what we need for the finale."

"Glad you feel that way. Is that all you called me about?"

"Well, no, Dick. Er . . . as a matter of fact, I do have one thing I'd like to ask you."

"Yes, David?"

"Could you make it a little better?"

Could I make it a little better? As patiently and with as much control as I could, I explained that it's impossible to make a song "a little better." It's like making an egg a little better. It's either a good egg or a bad egg. If it's a song, that's it; good or bad, there's nothing that can be done about it. Slightly flustered, David thanked me for my elementary lesson in composition and assured me there would be no problem.

But this wasn't the end of Selznick's uneasy feeling about the song. During rehearsal the dance director, Sammy Lee, needed about eight bars of the melody to help him convey the proper rhythm to the dancing chorus. A recording was made of these eight bars and Lee played it over and over until the dancers became thoroughly familiar with the beat. One day I got a memo from Selznick reading, *in toto:* "I like your tune very much, but don't you think it's a bit monotonous?"

At this point, of course, I am expected to show what a really unappreciative boob Selznick was by revealing the name of a song that is so familiar it will prompt the reader into whistling all thirty-two bars. Hardly. The song was called "That's the Rhythm of the Day," and today even I have difficulty remembering how it goes. I guess I should have made it a little better right from the start.

And that was the way Rodgers and Hart spent the year 1933: one score for a film that wasn't made; one score, mostly unused, for a film no one can recall; one song for Goldwyn; one song for Selznick.

It's bad enough to know you're wasting your time and not accomplishing anything; what really hurts is to realize that others are aware of it too. One morning, reading the Los Angeles *Examiner,* I came across the following query in O. O. McIntyre's syndicated Broadway column: "Whatever happened to Rodgers and Hart?"

The comment scared me so much that my hands began to tremble. I was only thirty-one, Larry wasn't yet forty, and McIntyre was writing as if we no longer existed. But the phrase meant more to me than that; what had happened inside us that could impel us to accept money without working for it, spend day after day on the tennis courts or in the local bars, and simply allow our talents to rot? How could we have let ourselves be caught in this trap? What *had* happened to us?

No sooner had I read the piece than I told Dorothy that we simply had to leave Hollywood and get back to the real world as soon as possible. Then I telephoned Larry. The item had hit him exactly the same way, and he was perfectly agreeable to my doing what I could to get us out of our contract. Without even tentative plans for the future, I called our agent and told him I didn't give a damn how he did it, but that Larry and I wanted out. The agent did what he could, but for reasons unknown the studio flatly refused to let us go.

Possibly motivated by our desperation at having nothing to do, Thalberg signed us up to write the score for his next movie, *The Merry Widow,* which would star Maurice Chevalier and Jeanette MacDonald. Actually, he didn't sign "us," he signed Larry, since Franz Lehár had written a pretty fine score without any help from me. But because Larry and I had one of those "whither thou goest I will go" contracts with the studio, the lyrics were officially credited to "Richard Rodgers and Lorenz Hart."

There's no question that Larry was a highly adaptable lyricist, but Viennese musical pastry was simply not his dish and he loathed every minute of the assignment. What made it even tougher was that the only thing Larry and Ernst Lubitsch, the movie's director, had in common was their fondness for big black cigars. Though he was the acknowledged master of gaiety and sophistication, Lubitsch was an autocrat on the movie set, with a decidedly Teutonic approach to film making. He insisted that Larry be punctual for all meetings, and that his lyrics be submitted on neatly typewritten sheets. He took it as a personal affront when Larry would show up late and fumble through his pockets for scraps of paper on which he had scribbled the lyrics. Still, Larry did manage to turn in his usual creditable job, and many people have sung his words to "The Merry Widow Waltz" and "Vilia" without realizing that he wrote them.

And what was I doing all the while Larry was working on *The Merry Widow?* Tennis. I was doing tennis.

Eventually our contract ended, and Dorothy, Mary, Larry and I packed up and went home. On my final day as an employee of Metro-Goldwyn-Mayer, I thought it only polite to say good-bye to Irving Thalberg, who had, after all, thought enough of us to sign us up originally. I drove over to the studio, went directly to the cottage on the lot in which Thalberg worked, gave the receptionist my name and in a few minutes was ushered into Thalberg's office. There I found the producer seated at a conference table with five men flanking him. I walked over and said, "Larry and I are leaving today and I just wanted to say good-bye." Thalberg looked up with an uncomprehending, glassy stare on his boyish face, and I suddenly realized that he hadn't the faintest idea who I was.

This incident vividly demonstrated to me the kind of dehumanized, impersonal world that existed under the factory system the studios then maintained. To Thalberg, we were all faceless, anonymous cogs. Whenever we were needed, all he had to do was press a button and we'd hop over to help turn the company's wheels. I had no definite plans when I left Hollywood that day but I was sure of one thing: I would never again tie myself down to this kind of spirit-breaking situation.

I'd like to emphasize, though, that my feelings about Hollywood had nothing to do with moviemaking *per se.* My dislike was solely for the system of binding a creative person to a particular studio for a particular length of time. What an appalling waste of money, time and talent! Brought up on the old-fashioned idea that people should only earn money because they work for it, I found it impossible to adjust to this unpressured, indolent existence. Everyone said the same thing: Don't knock yourself out, enjoy life, get some sun on your face, brush up on your tennis game. The living was so easy that it was unbearable.

I know that there were many writers in Hollywood during those years who were constantly and gainfully employed. But, perhaps for reasons of insecurity, studio moguls always seemed to have a certain antipathy toward people from the Broadway theatre. They used us when they had to, but they were never really happy about our being there. For our part, I don't suppose there were many Broadway writers who were happy about being there either. He never told me in so many words, but Jerry Kern must have been miserable in Hollywood, and I know Oscar Hammerstein was. The people who succeeded in moving pictures—and I'm talking primarily about lyricists and composers—were those who did not have an extended background in the theatre.

Part of our adjustment problem was that we were used to writing complete scores of anywhere from a dozen to twenty songs. In Hollywood they thought a score was four or five songs. Or they would only need one. They also had the sneaky habit of comparison shopping. They'd ask three or four writers for a song and then would choose the one they liked best. So far as I know, I was never involved in any of these little competitions.

In a way, I have always had a feeling of gratitude toward M-G-M. If its management had tossed Larry and me only a few more crumbs, we might have been lulled into staying longer, and that would have been the end of Larry Hart and Dick Rodgers. I'm sure I would have ended up as a neurotic, a drunkard or both.

13

For months Dorothy and I had been dreaming about going home, but when we got there we found that we didn't have a home.

Three years earlier, soon after Mary was born, we had moved to larger quarters at 50 East Seventy-seventh Street, an apartment building that was actually part of the Hotel Carlyle. When we were on our way to Hollywood, we had subleased the apartment to an elderly couple, and since they'd taken such good care of it, when they left after about a year we felt emboldened to sublease the place to an affluent, newly married couple. Naturally we had advised them when we would return, but to our astonishment they were still there when we arrived. The girl had had a baby some weeks before and they simply did not want to leave. In fact, when we walked in early in the afternoon the young mother was fast asleep. I'll never forget the look on Dorothy's face when she saw the woman in her bed.

What was even worse was what they had done to our home. Despite our request that there be no animals, they hadn't been able to resist buying a puppy, who in turn couldn't resist using the legs of our tables and chairs for teething or relieving itself all over our carpets. A tray with glasses had been dropped, and there were liquor stains and pieces of glass everywhere. Chewing gum was stuck under the chair arms, vases and china pieces were broken, the walls were covered with fingerprint marks, and some of our drapes were torn. Even our dining-room table was ruined because their butler had used it as an ironing board on which to press the master's trousers. Welcome home, Dorothy and Dick!

One remark I shall never forget. Dorothy took one look at the kitchen —filthy stove, grease marks on the walls, dozens of unwashed dishes piled in the sink—and raged into the bedroom to confront our reclining tenant. "Yes, I know," the young lady replied sweetly, "I went in there once and never went back."

The only thing to do was to move into a temporary apartment—which we luckily found right in the Hotel Carlyle—and exert whatever pressure we could to get these Kallikaks out. When we finally did, we were then faced with the huge task of cleaning up after them. Dorothy looked at the mess around her and blurted, "Oh, I wish there were one magic place that I could go to and say, 'There it is—you fix it.'" Instinctively I came up with the logical question: "Why don't you start a business like that yourself?" Eventually Dorothy did exactly that: a year and a half later she founded Repairs, Inc., whose function was to serve as a single agency that would hire skilled craftsmen to repair any kind of broken or damaged objects.

But in the spring of 1934 the main task for me was to repair my own damaged career. Mine and Larry's. We made calls and we saw people, but things were just as bleak as we had feared. A few shows were running— the Moss Hart–Irving Berlin revue *As Thousands Cheer;* Jerry Kern and Otto Harbach's *Roberta;* a Shubert-sponsored *Ziegfeld Follies;* Leonard Sillman's first *New Faces* revue—but between March and June not a single new musical opened on Broadway, and the prospects for the fall weren't encouraging. Lew Fields was no longer producing shows, Terry Helburn and Lawrence Langner of the Theatre Guild were tied up with long-range plans for a Gershwin musical based on the play *Porgy,* Schwab and Mandel had split up, as had Aarons and Freedley (though Freedley was continuing alone), and Ziegfeld was dead. But the Shubert brothers were still active and a new flock of producers had come into prominence while we were away. There really was nothing else for us to do but dig in, make the rounds— and hope.

The offer that did materialize was from a totally unexpected source, and once again from Hollywood. While working on the one song for Sam Goldwyn, I had become friendly with his production chief, Arthur Hornblow, Jr. Possibly because Arthur's roots were in New York—he had been a playwright and an editor for *Theatre Magazine,* which his father had founded—he was particularly sensitive to the plight of theatre writers in Hollywood. He had recently left Goldwyn to become a producer at Paramount and he offered Larry and me the chance to write the score for his first musical, which was called *Mississippi.* W. C. Fields was to star in it, along with a new singing hero, Lanny Ross. Neither Larry nor I was exactly thrilled at the prospect of returning to Hollywood so soon after leaving, but it was our only firm offer and we needed desperately to get back to work. Besides, as we kept telling ourselves, it would only be for five or six weeks.

Feeling guilty about leaving Dorothy alone to supervise the renovation of our apartment, I rented a house in Rye, New York, for her and Mary for the summer, and by July I was back in the land of make-believe. No sooner had I arrived there than I received news that made me want to turn around and go home: Dorothy was pregnant again.

As for the actual writing assignment, however, things really couldn't have been better. "This is the first time since *Love Me Tonight,*" I wrote Dorothy early in August, "that I have felt satisfied with myself. This appears to me to be a complete, well balanced score with three good tries for popularity, a couple of amusing musical sequences, and plenty of musical material for the camera. I'm really excited about it. Fields will be excellent, but my one doubt is Ross. Perhaps careful direction will do something for him."

Those "three good tries for popularity" were "Down by the River" and "Soon," which made it, and "Roll, Mississippi," which didn't. Two out of three wasn't bad predicting.

Actually, there *was* a third song from *Mississippi* that became popular but it wasn't written until I returned home. As soon as Larry and I were safely back in New York, Paramount got a new studio boss. He took a hard look at the film's rushes, decided that production on the film be halted at once and that, at Arthur Hornblow's suggestion, Lanny Ross be replaced by Bing Crosby. I couldn't quarrel with his judgment so far, but then the new studio head decided that the Rodgers and Hart score would have to be scrapped and that an entirely new one was needed. Hornblow didn't simply object; he told the man that if our score was thrown out, he'd walk out, and apparently this was enough to guarantee that our songs remained. It was also enough to guarantee that Arthur Hornblow and I would remain lifelong friends.

But there was still another problem; now it was decided that Bing needed another number. Without returning to California, Larry and I wrote it in New York, made a recording of it, and mailed it to Hornblow. The song was—and turned out to be—"Easy to Remember."

Shortly after our return to New York, I bumped into Harry Kaufman on Broadway. He was an amiable but shrewd theatre man who was then the actual producer of the Shubert brothers' musicals. The brothers had hired him as something of a good-will gesture, since they were well aware of their reputation as tough men to work for, and they felt that Harry might attract people who otherwise would have nothing to do with them. Harry, who had just produced the *Ziegfeld Follies* and *Life Begins at 8:40,* two highly regarded revues, asked me if I had anything in mind that the Shuberts might be interested in.

I sure did. While Larry and I were in Hollywood during our last trip, we had read in a trade paper that RKO, having recently completed *The Gay Divorcee,* was looking for something new for its dancing stars, Fred Astaire and Ginger Rogers. Since we both had long wanted to write a score for Astaire, we naturally started talking about what kind of story might be suitable for him. Astaire had made his fame as both a ballroom and tap dancer, and it seemed to us that he might be receptive to a story that would allow him to demonstrate his skill in a different area. So we began tossing ideas around, and eventually came up with the saga of a former vaudeville song-and-dance man who composes and performs a modern ballet with a classical ballet company. There would be some kidding of the ballet form, and of course Fred would become involved with the glamorous ballerina before returning to the cute little trick he really loved. We called it *On Your Toes.*

Larry and I wrote a two-page outline and two or three songs, and then invited Fred to our rooms at the Beverly Hills Hotel to try to sell him on the idea. He was receptive to it but ultimately turned it down; he was afraid his public wouldn't accept him in a role that would not allow him to wear his trademark attire of top hat, white tie and tails.

When I told Kaufman about *On Your Toes* and our meeting with Astaire, he said he thought the story had the makings of a great musical, but he had another dancer in mind. All he had to say was "How about Ray Bolger?" and I knew it would all work out. This spidery, sparkling dancer, who was then appearing in *Life Begins at 8:40,* had made a great hit in *Heads Up!,* and there was no question that he was a perfect choice for the lead. On the strength of the story outline and Harry's enthusiasm, Lee Shubert put the show under contract and gave Larry and me an advance against royalties.

Once we had finished the dialogue and about half the songs, we auditioned the material for Lee Shubert. I had been warned that holding an audition for Shubert was an experience, and indeed it was. His leathery face, protruding nose and slicked-down black hair gave him the look of an Indian chief, and his impassive, stony stare could easily wither the bravest of the braves. But that wasn't the worst of it; I was going through the third number in the score when I heard an odd sound, and I looked up. Lee Shubert was fast asleep, snoring peacefully.

Obviously Shubert was somewhat less than fired with enthusiasm for the project and did nothing to get it going. Whenever I asked about it, he would insist that he was planning to get started very soon, and that I should just be a little patient. Since so much was riding on this project, I was extremely apprehensive. Larry and I had been away from Broadway for four years and we could not allow this chance to slip away. Besides, it wasn't just *any* show; this was all ours—lyrics, music *and* story by Rodgers and Hart.

On March 5, 1935, our fifth wedding anniversary, Dorothy and I received a beautiful gift: our daughter Linda. Mary, who was then four and in the kindergarten of the Brearley School, was excited and a bit confused about the birth and the anniversary occurring on the same day. She was acting in a play performed by her class and proudly announced to one and all that her mother had just had a baby and couldn't possibly come to see the play because she was getting married.

While Larry and I were being kept dangling by Lee Shubert, we got a call from our old friend Billy Rose, now a Broadway producer. Actually, Broadway couldn't hold Billy. He had a grandiose scheme to mount a production that would be part circus and part musical comedy, and had already taken a lease on the venerable Hippodrome, at Sixth Avenue and Forty-third Street, which had once been the home of the most dazzling stage spectacles ever presented. But he wasn't content merely to hire a hall; his idea was no less than to gut the entire interior of the theatre and have it redesigned and rebuilt like a circus tent, with the audience in banked seats looking down on a single "ring." All the action—story, song-and-dance numbers and circus acts—would take place either in the ring or, for the aerial acts, high above it.

Billy wasn't going to stint on a thing and was getting the best designers, directors and writers available. Jimmy Durante and Paul Whiteman and his Band would be in the show, and his agents were scouring Europe for the greatest jugglers, tumblers, clowns, animal acts and trapeze artists they could find. It was, he assured us, going to be the most mammoth attraction of its kind, and appropriately, he was calling it *Jumbo*.

Billy's request that Larry and I write the score came at a particularly opportune time. By now it was clear that Shubert had no intention of producing *On Your Toes*. We had taken it to another producer, but work could not begin until Shubert's option had run out. We still had qualms about Billy, since we remembered all too well that he had never paid us for our last assignment for him, but his enthusiasm was so infectious that we agreed to do the show without even seeing the script.

As befitting the super-showman that he was, Billy seldom thought along conventional lines. For his story, he went to Ben Hecht and Charles MacArthur, the co-authors of *The Front Page* and *Twentieth Century*, who had never before written a musical-comedy book. Though he was certain that they would come up with a plot that was fresh and different, what they produced was another Romeo and Juliet variation, in which the daughter of one circus owner falls in love with the son of his bitterest rival. It was, however, convenient enough for the purpose, though there was scarcely any actual collaboration between the librettists and the songwriters.

The official billing for *Jumbo* read: "Entire Production Staged by John Murray Anderson." Actually Murray, who had been so helpful ten years before in putting on *Dearest Enemy*, was primarily concerned with the physical aspects of the production—the scenery, lighting and costumes—and didn't really care much about the story or the way the songs fit it. I recall once just before the show's opening when he took me backstage to demonstrate the workings of a huge, complicated lighting switchboard. "Each one of the lights is controlled by its own special switch," he explained. "It's all pre-set. All you have to do is just touch a switch and you get exactly the lighting effect you want." Then he started to giggle. "See this little yellow one here?" he said, pointing to a tiny toggle switch at the far right of the board. "Do you know what that's for? That's for the book." A single light switch was all the plot of the musical meant to him.

For the man who *would* be concerned with the book, Billy hired a director whose experience heretofore had been solely in nonmusical plays. George Abbott was a tall, sharp-featured ramrod of a man who, more than anyone else, was responsible for tying all the disparate elements of the production together. *Jumbo* was the beginning of what would be a number of fruitful associations between Abbott and Rodgers and Hart.

Like many people in the theatre, Billy Rose had a vision that far exceeded his finances. By the time the show opened—after many delays— it had cost in the neighborhood of $340,000 (most of it supplied by Jock Whitney), which I think was a record up to then. Billy, however, never parted with a dime if he didn't have to. He even managed to get a special ruling from Equity, the actors' union, that he was not obligated to pay the performers during the lengthy rehearsal period because the show was classified as a circus, not a regular theatrical production. Billy had a curiously personal attitude about money. He hated to have anyone ask him for a delinquent payment, not so much because he didn't have the money or didn't want to pay it, but because it hurt his pride.

One of Billy's idiosyncrasies was that he would not allow any of the songs for *Jumbo* to be played over the radio, giving the reason that people wouldn't go to see his show if the airwaves were saturated with its songs. This, too, was really a matter of pride. He simply felt that his show was so great that it didn't need any further plugging from a rival form of entertainment. Pride or no pride, his decision was a serious blow to us. In our score were "The Most Beautiful Girl in the World," "My Romance" and "Little Girl Blue." We were confident that they had the potential for popularity, and eventually they did catch on, but by the time Billy had lifted his ban, the show's run was almost over and nothing could help it. The reviews were great and the production certainly gave customers their money's worth, but big, fat, colorful *Jumbo* was just too expensive to keep running and it closed after only five months.

Still, what mattered most to Larry and me was that we had returned to Broadway with a highly acclaimed show, and that despite the myriad attractions it offered, our work did not go unnoticed. No one would again have to wonder whatever had happened to Rodgers and Hart.

    *   *   *

With *Jumbo* out of the way, we could now devote all our efforts to getting on with *On Your Toes*. Once Shubert's option ended, Dwight Deere Wiman, the producer who had already expressed interest in the musical, was ready to go ahead with it any time we were.

Wiman was a curious anomaly in the frequently rough-and-tumble world of Broadway. Though he had been producing plays ever since the middle of the twenties and had already presented such hits as *The Road to Rome, The Little Show* and *She Loves Me Not,* something about him made people take him for a dilettante. He was what my mother called a "swell." He had inherited wealth, plus the manners, accent and appearance to go with it. He may have lacked that certain drive and dedication associated with producers, yet he probably had more profitable attractions than most of the more aggressive members of the breed.

Wiman liked *On Your Toes* from the start, but since neither Larry nor I had had much success in writing anything but songs, we took our script to George Abbott for advice. In addition to being a director, George had had considerable experience as a playwright, including at least two hits, *Broadway* and *Three Men on a Horse.* He told us what he liked and disliked about the script, and what he said made so much sense that we asked him not only to rewrite the book but to direct the production. He agreed, rewrote the book, and just before the show was to go into rehearsal, abruptly left to spend the winter playing golf in Palm Beach. There was no further explanation; George simply wanted to get away, and that was that. This left us in a terrible hole. We had everything and everyone ready, including Ray Bolger, so there was nothing else to do but get ourselves another director.

Our opening in Boston late in March 1936 turned out to be so bad that we knew drastic measures had to be taken. No one else could get us out of this jam but Abbott, so I sent him a telegram. He was, after all, the co-author of the show and he must have *some* concern about its success. Fortunately for all of us, he did. He arrived in Boston and saw the show, but didn't make a single note nor say a word about the performance after we left the theatre. When I suggested that Dwight, Larry and I go back to the hotel with him to talk things over, George shook his head. "Boys," he said, "there's nothing to talk over. We'll have plenty of time after we start rehearsals tomorrow. Now let's get some girls and go dancing." Which is exactly what we did.

What Abbott did the next morning was simple—and radical. Because our other director had made so many changes in his script, all George did was cut out the new material and go back to his original book. And it worked. In almost no time we were right back where we started, and from which we should never have left.

One of the great innovations of *On Your Toes,* the angle that had initially made us think of it as a vehicle for Fred Astaire, was that for the first time ballet was being incorporated into a musical-comedy book. To be sure, Albertina Rasch had made a specialty of creating Broadway ballets, but these were usually in revues and were not part of a story line. We made our main ballet an integral part of the action; without it, there was no conclusion to our story. During the dance, two gangsters enter a theatre box intent on shooting the hero at the conclusion of the ballet. Seeing their guns aimed at him, he beckons the conductor to continue the music so that he can keep on dancing to avoid being a target. Finally the police come, and the hero falls to the floor exhausted.

This ballet, called "Slaughter on Tenth Avenue," had always been part of the script, but we knew that much would depend on getting the right man to choreograph it. George Balanchine was a leading European choreographer who had worked with impresario Sergei Diaghilev and had recently settled in New York, where he founded the American Ballet Company. The previous year his company had given a highly praised recital at the Adelphi Theatre, which had led to its being signed as the resident ballet company for the Metropolitan Opera. Once Larry and I had seen his work, Balanchine was the man we wanted.

I met with Balanchine one afternoon in his studio to play the music. I didn't know a thing about choreography and told Balanchine that I was unsure how we should go about it. Did he devise his steps first and expect me to alter tempos wherever necessary, or did he fit his steps to the music as written? Balanchine smiled and with that wonderful Russian accent of his said simply, "You write. I put on." And that was the way we worked. He used the music just the way I had written it and created his dance patterns to conform. I don't think that our arranger, Hans Spialek, had to change more than thirty-two bars.

On Your Toes, and particularly his dance in "Slaughter on Tenth Avenue," made Ray Bolger a star. It didn't hurt Rodgers and Hart, either, especially as a showcase for a song called "There's a Small Hotel." It was the melody—romantic, unsophisticated, youthful—that suggested the theme to Larry of an idealized country inn with its wishing well, one-room bridal suite and view of a nearby church steeple. This was another example of his ability to convey the appeal of the simple life. There is no question that Larry was a big-city kid who thrived on the vigor and pace of Broadway, yet he could write longingly about quiet pleasures far from the razzle-dazzle world. "Mountain Greenery" was an early attempt, though it was obviously the work of a Manhattan sophisticate. More sincere was his tribute to the isolated "Blue Room" that was "far from worldly cares," or his description of "A Tree in the Park" as an oasis in the noisy city. Larry loved having people around him, but when, in "There's a Small Hotel," he wrote the lines "Not a sign of people—Who wants people?" he made you believe that a rural retreat was his idea of heaven.

The Broadway season of 1935–36 offered many good musicals. There was the colorful Howard Dietz–Arthur Schwartz revue, *At Home Abroad*, starring Beatrice Lillie and Ethel Waters; Gershwin's monumental opera, *Porgy and Bess;* the elegant *Jubilee*, by Moss Hart and Cole Porter; Oscar Hammerstein and Sigmund Romberg's romantic *May Wine;* a glittering *Ziegfeld Follies* with Fanny Brice and Josephine Baker; and a new *New Faces*, with Imogene Coca. But when the season ended, the two longest-running musicals turned out to be *On Your Toes* and *Jumbo*.

Larry and I had come back, finally, from the limbo of Hollywood. No longer would we ever have to take an assignment just for the money or simply to have our names attached to a Broadway show. More than anything else, the rebirth of our career had given us the security, both financial and professional, to do the kind of creative work that had long been our goal.

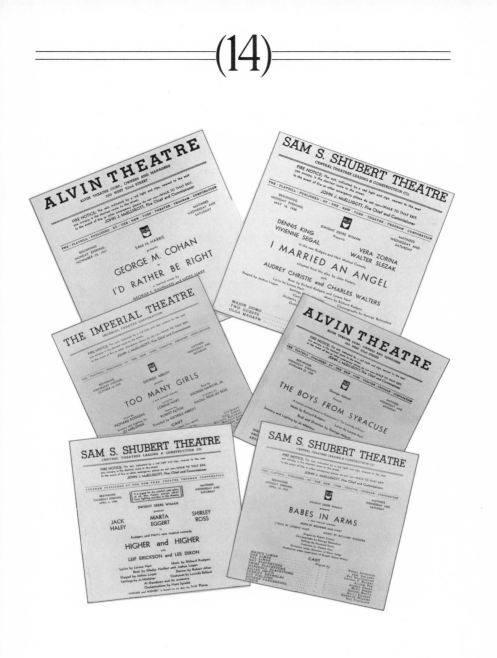

14

From the fall of 1935 through 1942 was a period of almost unbelievable productivity for Larry and me. We had ten shows in those seven years, all but one a success. It seemed as if nothing we touched could go wrong. We had the freedom to do what we wanted and the satisfaction that what we wanted to do, others wanted to see. We could experiment with form and content not only in our songs but in the shows themselves. We should have been the happiest of men in the happiest of worlds.

Most of the time, in fact, we were. Larry was never easy to work with, so nothing he did really surprised me. He'd always drunk too much. He'd always do anything to avoid getting down to work. He'd always loved staying out late and carousing until dawn. But now the years of dissipation began to show. Not in his work, of course; if anything, this was better than ever. But there were signs. Now, instead of being an hour late for a meeting, he'd be two hours late. Or he'd disappear for days. Or he'd show up and I'd take one look at him and know he couldn't begin to put pencil to paper.

At first I chose to ignore it. I was too full of the euphoria of being back on Broadway with one hit after another. We were constantly showered with offers. People who only a year or so before had been too busy to see us were now taking us out to lunch and inviting us to parties. Somehow, our renewed activity seemed to be mirrored throughout the country. Roosevelt won re-election in a landslide, and economic conditions appeared to be improving. And though some of us were deeply concerned about what was happening in Germany under Hitler, the idea of another world war still seemed remote.

Larry even went in for self-improvement at about this time—at least, his idea of self-improvement. Always somewhat concerned about his height and general appearance, he now started wearing Adler elevator shoes to make him appear taller and began taking treatments to restore his falling hair.

One of the better influences on Larry was his maid, Mary Campbell, a sharp-tongued, no-nonsense black woman who was never one to hide her displeasure at the behavior of either her employer or his friends. Among the guests at one dinner party was the glamorous black entertainer Josephine Baker. Josephine, who grew up in St. Louis but was then living in Paris, batted her eyelashes at Mary and asked grandly, *"Donnez-moi une tasse de café, s'il vous plaît."* Mary shot Josephine a look of incredulity mixed with contempt. "Honey," she said, "you is full of shit. Talk the way yo' mouth was born!"

But even Mary couldn't curb Larry's prodigal habit of inviting people to his home without a thought of how many were coming or whether he even knew them. One Sunday when Larry and his mother were at our house for lunch, Dorothy asked Mrs. Hart, "Don't Larry's parties ever disturb you?" Mrs. Hart smiled and said, "No, not ferry much. Except dot night ven Paul Viteman came mit his whole band!"

Another time, when Larry asked Lawrence Riley to dinner, the playwright asked, "About seven?" Larry's answer was "Hell, bring as many as you like."

There are many examples of Larry's generosity and his almost compulsive habit of check-grabbing. Once when I was in London, Dorothy's mother and father gave a dinner party at the Berkeley Hotel to which they invited my parents, who were visiting London at the time, and Larry. When the waiter brought Mr. Feiner the check after dinner, Larry leaped up from the table and tried to tear it out of his hand. It was slightly embarrassing, but those of us who knew Larry also knew how frustrating it was for him to let anyone else ever pay for anything.

One year, on my birthday, Larry told Dorothy and me that he was sending us "a little ashtray" as a present. The little ashtray turned out to be a bronze nude figure in the center of a large marble receptacle which must have measured nearly two feet in diameter.

Larry's generosity even resulted in a fistfight on one occasion. I hadn't seen him for about a week and had the feeling he was purposely ducking me. When we finally met for lunch, I was shocked at his appearance. He had black-and-blue marks on his face and a gash above his left eye. What had happened, he explained, was that a stranger had telephoned him with greetings from a mutual friend in California. After chatting a bit, Larry invited the fellow to his apartment for dinner. As the evening wore on, the man got drunk—which wasn't a difficult thing to do at Larry's place—and also somewhat unpleasant. Finally Larry escorted him down to the street, hailed a taxi for him and turned to go upstairs. For some reason the man suddenly started to curse and then threw a right which knocked Larry down. No one came to his rescue; a few taxi drivers in the area simply stood around watching the mayhem.

The story upset me terribly. "Oh, don't feel sorry for me," Larry said with a mischievous smile. "As soon as I got my breath I kicked the son of a bitch in the nuts and he's still in the hospital."

This was typical of Larry. First he told the story exactly as it had happened, leading me to believe that he was the one who had been seriously hurt. Only after I had expressed my concern and sympathy did he reveal the ultimate outcome of the brawl.

*   *   *

In the fall of 1936, Larry and I thought it might be challenging to try something away from either the stage or the screen. At the request of Paul Whiteman, we wrote a narrative concert piece for soloist and symphony orchestra called *All Points West*.

Though the work had only a few performances and is barely remembered today, it was a further attempt on our part to expand the scope of our writing. I had already composed extended musical sequences for the film *Love Me Tonight,* and also the ballet "Slaughter on Tenth Avenue" for *On Your Toes,* but this was something entirely different: a self-contained work, billed as a "symphonic narrative," which was created specifically for the concert hall. Whiteman conducted it at the Academy of Music, in Philadelphia, at the end of November with the Philadelphia Orchestra and with baritone Ray Middleton as soloist. After the concert was over I caught a glimpse of Paul Whiteman's score. To my astonishment it was complete with arrows and exclamation points, and in red pencil little remarks such as "LOOK OUT!" and "WARNING!"

In answer to the inevitable question about why we had written *All Points West,* I told a newspaper interviewer, "We wanted to do something with more freedom. We wanted to escape the conventions that hedge in the musical-comedy song. For one thing, you're supposed to work in your title in the first eight bars and then to repeat it at the end. If you're bursting with independence, you might add a few bars here or take away a few bars there, but the form is almost inflexible. Also we got pretty tired of writing about nothing but love."

The form of *All Points West*—and I can't recall whether it was Larry's idea or mine—was a soliloquy sung by a train announcer at Grand Central Station. In it he reveals the frustrations of a life that keeps him tied down while others are on their way to exciting, distant places. Suddenly a prisoner on his way to Sing-Sing escapes from the police and the announcer, caught in the ensuing gunfire, is killed. At last he gets his wish to go on a journey to a faraway land. Pretty sentimental and melodramatic, I admit, but it was a faltering step in a basically right direction. Later I would be able to take firmer steps, even within the confines of the musical theatre.

Sometime during the summer of 1936, while Larry and I were strolling through Central Park, we noticed a bunch of children in a playground who were making up their own games and rules. We began talking about kids and what might happen if they were suddenly given adult responsibilities, such as finding ways to earn a living. One way might be to put on a big benefit show that would turn out to be a hit. And that's the way *Babes in Arms* was born.

The idea appealed to us for a particular reason. Every musical production on Broadway seemed to be dependent on at least one big star, and we thought audiences might welcome something youthful and unassuming for a change. By casting our show with talented but largely unknown performers, we hoped theatregoers would welcome the opportunity to discover future stars themselves.

We put together a serviceable book and took the idea to Dwight Deere Wiman. Though Wiman was inclined to be lavish in his taste, he turned out to be easy to sell. I don't think the whole production cost him more than $55,000, and even with a top ticket price of $3.85, it turned a nice profit.

Actually, *Babes in Arms* was one of those shows that worked right from the start. About a week before our Boston opening in March 1937, I wrote Dorothy: "Yesterday afternoon we had a run-through of the whole piece. It still looks encouraging. Naturally, we can't be sure of our values, but as far as material is concerned, we're in excellent shape to open. The cast is holding up well and there have been definite improvements. The numbers looked very good and are nearly all set now. Dwight and everyone else, especially Larry, were very happy about the whole thing."

Most of the kids in the show were really kids. I think Mitzi Green was sixteen; Ray Heatherton, in his mid-twenties, was the oldest; and for those looking for future stars, there were Alfred Drake, who sang the title song, and Dan Dailey.

Since there was a good spot for a ballet, we again hired George Balanchine for the choreography. We had particular fun with the scene in the kids' show in which Wynn Murray sang "Johnny One Note." For some reason that I can't recall, it was performed in an Egyptian setting, but instead of going in for exotic scenery and costumes, we emphasized the do-it-yourself nature of the show by having the cast come out wearing such household appliances as towels, bath mats, coat hooks and scrub mops.

In creating a story which contained a show within a show, we had a certain leeway, since "Johnny One Note" was just a specialty number. "My Funny Valentine," however, was very much about a specific character in the book; in fact, before the show opened we even changed the character's name to Val.

"Where or When" was probably the most popular song in this score, at least during the run of the show, and it had an interesting theme that was hardly typical of a musical-comedy song. We have all experienced the psychic phenomenon of "déjà vu" at one time or another—that is, doing something for the first time and being certain that we have done it before —but Larry was the first to use it in a lyric. He and I even received letters from college psychology professors telling us they were using the song to help illustrate their lectures.

Hollywood was making noises again. This time the call came from Warner Bros., the studio for which Larry and I had written our first movie score. The picture was to star Fernand Gravet, the latest French import, and Carole Lombard, and one of the attractions was that we would again be working with Herb Fields, who, with his brother Joseph, was writing the screenplay. Larry and I had already agreed to do a Broadway show in the fall, so with no assignment to keep us in New York, we went to California in June. The picture? *Fools for Scandal.* If you remember this choice little exhibition, raise your right hand.

Larry and I wrote a complete score for the film, and since everyone was pleased and predicted great things, we returned to New York and thought no more about it. Then one day sometime in March of the following year, I received a telephone call from the head of the Warner Bros. office in New York. He said, *"Fools for Scandal* is opening at the Music Hall next week."

"Great! We'll all go and make a party of it."

"Not exactly, Dick. In fact, I'm calling you to ask you to promise that you won't go to see it."

"Why shouldn't I?"

"Well," said the gentleman from Warner's, "because if you do, there'll be a certain number of deaths. Either you'll shoot yourself or you'll shoot everybody at Warner's, and I'm not looking forward to dying so soon."

So I never saw *Fools for Scandal.* It turned out that they had cut almost every song out of the picture and had simply used the score for background music. Our only recourse was to stay away.

I recall little about this particular stay in Hollywood except for one tragic event that happened while I was there: the death of George Gershwin. The best way I can indicate how his illness and death affected me is to quote my letters to Dorothy. On July 10, 1937, I wrote:

> I don't like what I hear about George. He's had a complete mental collapse and they don't know what to do with him. They'd like to send him East to a sanitarium as they don't trust the ones out here, but he's too ill to be moved. Moss [Hart] tells me that he can't eat or even talk and is in a house which they've taken for him and turned into a hospital.

The next day I wrote:

> I'm so upset at the moment I can hardly think enough to write.
> I phoned Cedars [of Lebanon Hospital] a little after ten-thirty and was
> told that George had just died.
>
> It shouldn't have been such a shock to me as I've been in close
> touch with the situation for days through Moss, but I just can't believe
> he's gone. I've been interrupted at least five times since I started this
> by people calling up. Moss just phoned, crying so he could hardly talk.
> It's pretty tough on him as he's been very close to the family and has
> stood the brunt of all the hospital arrangements . . .

Again, in a letter the following day:

> The town is in a daze and nobody talks about anything but
> George's death. There seems to be a certain amount of mystery as to
> the reason why no diagnosis was made until the night before the
> operation, but since we don't know the details it isn't possible to have
> an opinion. It's just awful . . .

George's death left such a pall over my stay in Hollywood that I was
especially eager to return home and get started on a new project.

Engendered by the widespread cynicism that developed during the
Depression, one of the distinctive forms of musicals in the thirties was the
topical revue or topical musical comedy. The best of these never went in
for preaching or propaganda but managed to make their comments on the
conditions of the world without forgetting that the basic function of entertainment was to entertain. The Gershwin brothers had supplied the scores
for the antiwar musical *Strike Up the Band,* the presidential lampoon *Of
Thee I Sing,* which won the Pulitzer Prize as the best drama of the season,
and its less successful sequel, *Let 'Em Eat Cake.* Irving Berlin wrote the
songs for a musical about New York City police corruption called *Face the
Music,* as well as for the revue *As Thousands Cheer,* which was created
entirely in the form of a newspaper.

George S. Kaufman, the co-author of the three Gershwin shows, and
Moss Hart, the author of the two with scores by Berlin, now thought the
time was ripe for them to collaborate on the most daring political satire of
them all, and they wanted Larry and me to write the songs. Their idea was
nothing less than a musical-comedy lampoon about President Roosevelt
himself. Though Presidents had been depicted before in musicals—Cal-
vin Coolidge in our first *Garrick Gaieties* and recently Herbert Hoover
in *As Thousands Cheer*—this would mark the first time that the leader

of our country would be seen as the protagonist of a book musical.

When Hart and Kaufman outlined the idea to us, we fell in love with it right away. All four of us were ardently pro-FDR, but we were sure we could have a lot of fun sticking pins into such current phenomena as the New Deal and its alphabetical agencies, the packing of the Supreme Court, and the outlandish idea that Roosevelt would dare break tradition and run for a third term. Though we might make a few people squirm a bit, we felt that the show could be done with taste and without giving real offense. Besides, creating such a musical comedy at this time was in itself an affirmation of the freedom we had always enjoyed and had long taken for granted. Hitler, who had come to power in Germany the same year Roosevelt first took office, had already instituted repressive measures against non-Aryans and "enemies of the state." Abolition of all forms of dissent was also part of Mussolini's Fascist regime in Italy and of the aggressive military leaders in Japan. Spain was in the midst of a civil war led by Franco, with the blessing and backing of Hitler and Mussolini. In one country after another, one saw the extinction of human life and liberty. Suddenly all those who had been moaning about what had happened to us during the Depression were beginning to realize that ours was one of the few nations on earth where people weren't afraid of their leaders. We could talk against them, we could vote them out of office—and we could even put them up on a Broadway stage as the butt of ridicule in a song-and-dance show.

The idea of working with two such imaginative craftsmen as Kaufman and Hart was exciting, and the idea of doing this kind of show—which, at Dorothy's suggestion, was eventually called *I'd Rather Be Right*—was even more so. But then Kaufman and Hart told us the name of the actor they were getting for the leading role: George M. Cohan. When I heard the name I must have turned at least a dozen shades paler. Dammit, Larry and I had already had our fill of Cohan in *The Phantom President*. Didn't they know that he was a disgruntled man with no respect for anyone's work but his own? Didn't they realize what they were getting themselves into?

Moss tried to reason with me. Cohan, he confided, had nothing but the highest regard for Larry and me. It was simply that he was unaccustomed to working in Hollywood, and the studio had really treated him shabbily. This was going to be different. This would be Cohan returning to Broadway in a musical comedy after an absence of almost ten years, and he was anxious and grateful to be getting back to work. Besides, the show was to be presented by Cohan's closest friend and former partner, Sam H. Harris. Everyone knew that Sam was one of the sweetest men on Broadway and that he was just about the only person in the world who could keep Cohan in line. What's more, Cohan had only recently appeared in Eugene O'Neill's play *Ah, Wilderness!* for the Theatre Guild and from all reports had been a model of cooperation.

Well, I hated to see this opportunity going to someone else, and maybe Moss was right; maybe it *was* just Hollywood. Surely this was a great way for Cohan to cap his career, and he'd be crazy to blow it. Larry and I were also aware that we couldn't get just anybody for the part. It needed an outstanding star, and whatever we might feel about him personally, Cohan was exactly that, possibly the only one in the musical theatre who could play Roosevelt. So, heeding the famous Lee Shubert dictum, said about another actor, "Never have anything to do with that son of a bitch unless you need him," we agreed to do the show. And of course everything turned out to be even worse than we had feared.

Our first encounter took place on a lovely day early in September 1937 on the occasion of the first playing of the score for our star. Because I was apprehensive about the way Cohan would receive it, I thought it would be helpful to get away from the customary rehearsal hall or office where auditions usually take place. For the occasion my friend Jules Glaenzer kindly let us use his elegant East Side apartment, which had a living room so spacious that it contained two pianos.

All of us showed up at Glaenzer's that day—Harris, Kaufman, Hart, Larry and me—and when Cohan arrived, we seated him midway between the two pianos. I played one piano and Margot Hopkins, my rehearsal pianist, was at the other. Moss Hart did the singing. He didn't have a trained voice, of course, but he had excellent enunciation and an oddly charming way of putting over a song. All during the performance Cohan sat with his arms folded, his eyes half closed, his mouth drooping. No matter what the number, neither his expression nor his position changed. He never moved his head, smiled, frowned or said a word during the hour it took. This didn't bother me much, since I'm a quiet listener myself, but once we were finished, Cohan rose from his chair, walked over to me, patted me on the shoulder, mumbled, "Don't take any wooden nickels," and then walked out the door.

That was that. We all looked stunned. I tried to reassure the others by saying, "Maybe it will be like Chevalier," recalling the time when Maurice was equally noncommittal after hearing our songs for *Love Me Tonight,* only to return the next day full of praise. But we knew it wouldn't be, and it never was. Throughout our entire association with Cohan, Larry and I were treated with only thinly veiled patronizing contempt, and when we weren't around, we were told, he never referred to us by anything other than the sarcastic nicknames of "Gilbert and Sullivan."

One of the problems, which none of us was fully aware of before production began, was that Cohan hated Roosevelt. On our opening night in Boston he even added his own lyrics to an encore of "Off the Record" which were particularly cruel to the President. The pretext for this addition, according to Cohan, was that he objected to lyrics that Larry had written about Al Smith which *he* thought were too cruel. Actually, those particular lyrics had been discarded weeks before. The only reason Cohan put in his own lines was simply for his own ego—to show everyone that he could still beat us at our own game. Trying to make a joke of it after he sang the lines, Cohan confided to the audience—though of course for our benefit—"I'll probably get my two weeks' notice for doing that."

As soon as the performance was over, Larry and I raised hell with Sam Harris, and Cohan promised that he'd never do it again. Then, to our amazement, the next morning's New York *Herald Tribune* carried the entire story of the blowup with the following headlines:

COHAN REFUSES
TO SING LYRIC
ABOUT AL SMITH

In Boston Tryout He Cut
Lines, Put in His Own
and Writers Object to It
But All's Happy Now

"Gilbert and Sullivan of
U.S." Rewriting the Part

All hell broke loose again. Cohan was furious because he thought I had planted the story, and I was fuming over the "Gilbert and Sullivan" crack. Sam Harris prevailed upon me to try to placate our high-handed star, but there was little I could do. Luckily, there were no further incidents of this sort.

I can't say that my relationship with George S. Kaufman was much better. I'd known and liked Moss ever since our frustrating days in Hollywood writing *I Married an Angel,* but Kaufman's acerbic sense of humor never appealed to me. I was also amazed by his attitude toward musicals. Though he had been associated with some outstanding productions, both as writer and director, he had no love of music. He even told me that with *I'd Rather Be Right* he was deliberately setting out to prove that the book was more important that the songs. I'm quite willing to admit that our score for *I'd Rather Be Right* may not have been one for the ages, but it did seem a curious attitude for someone to express, especially to a composer. Anyway, Kaufman managed to convince Sam Harris that he was right, with the result that Kaufman and Hart got a higher royalty percentage than Rodgers and Hart.

I'd Rather Be Right may well have been the most eagerly awaited musical of all times. Our out-of-town tryouts were covered as if they were Broadway opening nights. Newspapers ran editorials about what a wonderful country we lived in where shows like this could be presented. Gags from the show were repeated all over town even before the official New York premiere. Perhaps expectations were too high because for the most part the reviews were not the out-and-out raves we had hoped for. Cohan, however, got ecstatic notices, and I'll be the first to admit that he fully deserved them.

Although our production was billed as "a musical revue," it did have a thin story line. A young couple in Central Park talk about getting married but the boy's boss won't give him a raise until Roosevelt balances the budget. In a dream, the boy and girl meet Roosevelt, who tries to do what he can to help. This somehow strengthens their resolve because once the dream is over they decide to get married anyway. Most of the time the show was merely a series of scenes that lent themselves to topical wisecracks and songs—a cabinet meeting, a fireside chat, a birthday party (with a dour Alf Landon as the butler) and a press conference. Dorothy's favorite lines were in Treasury Secretary Morgenthau's song:

> I'm quite a busy man right now—
> I'm Secretary Morgenthau.
> I have achieved, you must admit,
> The biggest goddam deficit!

This was part of a number called "A Homogeneous Cabinet" sung by leading members of Roosevelt's cabinet. Not exactly a catchy commercial title; nor was it meant to be. In fact, almost every song was written to express some viewpoint on major topics of the day, as revealed in such titles as "A Little Bit of Constitutional Fun," "Sweet Sixty-Five" (about Social Security), "We're Going to Balance the Budget," "Labor Is the Thing," "Off the Record" (for the press conference), and "A Baby Bond." Out of town, we had a romantic piece as the title song but this was changed before New York to an uptempo number with a political slant. Even our one remaining ballad, "Have You Met Miss Jones?," was introduced simply as one way of getting the President's cabinet to become sympathetic to the young lovers' plight.

* * *

After our experience with George M. and George S., Larry and I were anxious to return to people with whom we enjoyed working and with whom we shared a mutual respect. Our two experiences with Dwight Deere Wiman—*On Your Toes* and *Babes in Arms*—had proved so pleasant, as well as profitable, that we had made plans to do our next show together even before we began working on *I'd Rather Be Right*.

As I've already mentioned, back in 1933 Moss, Larry and I had collaborated on a screen treatment of *I Married an Angel.* One night at dinner I began telling Dwight all about the project—including, of course, the fact that M-G-M had never done anything about it. Without hearing a note or reading a word, Dwight gave us his assurance that if he could buy the property from the studio, he would present it on Broadway.

After protracted discussion, Wiman and M-G-M finally came to terms —and remarkable terms they were. The company gave Larry and me the right to make a stage musical out of all the material written for the unproduced film, provided that they would retain the right to pick up an option on the stage production for possible filming in the future. Within a week after the show opened, M-G-M did pick up the option and eventually made the picture.

For the musical stage version of *I Married an Angel,* Larry and I decided to return to the original Hungarian play rather than to Moss's scenario. Since we had recently written our own libretto for *Babes in Arms,* we felt confident that we could do at least as well with the new story.

Just as *Jumbo* had brought George Abbott into the musical-comedy field, so *I Married an Angel* was instrumental in adding another brilliant director to the ranks. Although Joshua Logan had been associated with Wiman in the past and had recently directed Dwight's highly acclaimed production of *On Borrowed Time,* he had never before directed a musical. One meeting, however, convinced us that he could handle the job with ease.

Josh Logan is a big hulk of a man with a flamboyant personality; he is also a diligent worker and a great worrier. After *I Married an Angel* had been in rehearsal for a week, he came to Larry and me and told us he was upset with the way things were going. That very night the three of us met in Larry's apartment to thrash things out. Almost every idea Josh offered made sense, and we decided to start immediately on a thorough rewrite. With his prodding, we threw out about a third of what we had written, adding new dialogue and situations, even entire scenes. All three of us took turns dictating to a secretary, and by the time we were finished, at six in the morning, we finally had a script that worked. I don't think there were more than half a dozen changes thereafter.

This show had some wonderful people in the cast. Dennis King had already had a solid career both in the classics and in operetta; Vivienne

Segal had been playing leading roles in musicals for some twenty years; Walter Slezak, like Dennis, was a highly versatile actor, with experience both in Europe and New York. But the one who stole the notices and the applause was Vera Zorina, here making her Broadway debut as the Angel. Dwight Wiman had been extremely impressed with her when he saw her in the London production of *On Your Toes*. Not wanting to oversell her, however, he cautiously mentioned that he thought she might be good in a small part in *I Married an Angel*. A little while later, when I was in Hollywood for the *Fools for Scandal* assignment, I was at a party when in walked a breath-takingly lovely young girl with a charming European accent who quickly had everyone crowding around her. The next day I sent Dwight a telegram: SMALL PART NOTHING HAVE JUST MET VERA ZORINA THATS OUR ANGEL.

In our play, we made no effort to condescend to our audience's imagination by putting the story in the form of a dream. Dennis didn't fall asleep or get bopped on the head to make it easier for people to accept the preposterous idea of a man marrying an angel. In effect, our attitude was take it or leave it; this fellow actually marries a real angel. And as so often is the case when you respect your audience, everyone was happy to go along with us.

The theme of the play was that it's possible for someone to be too good. Our angel nearly ruins her husband's life by her truthful but undiplomatic remarks. It is only when, under the expert tutelage of Vivienne Segal, she becomes devilish instead of angelic that the marriage is saved.

One of the scenes we added to the show during that all-night session was a takeoff on the Radio City Music Hall stage show which we called "At the Roxy Music Hall." It was a satirical fantasy, choreographed by George Balanchine, with a line of well-drilled Rockettes consisting solely of Vivienne Segal and Audrey Christie, and an arty underwater ballet with Zorina as a sea nymph. I haven't the faintest recollection of how the Radio City Music Hall got involved in a show set in Budapest, but in those days motivation was not among the most important factors in a musical comedy. If it worked, it worked, and this one did.

On opening night, however, it seemed to me that nothing was working. As Dorothy and I sat in the last row of the Shubert Theatre, I was certain that the show was dying before our eyes. There were only sporadic laughs and hardly any applause. During the intermission we both ran out for a drink at the nearby Astor Hotel bar—three drinks, as a matter of fact. Possibly because I was so well fortified, the second act seemed to go slightly better. Still, after the curtain I was sure we were going to have a hard time keeping it open for any kind of a run.

The next morning I picked up the *Times* fully expecting Brooks Atkinson to confirm my worst fears, and read: "*I Married an Angel* perches on the top shelf of the Rodgers and Hart musical cabinet. For this is no grinding of the Broadway hurdy-gurdy, but an imaginative improvisation with a fully orchestrated score and an extraordinarily beautiful production . . . Musical comedy has met its masters, and they have reared back and passed a Forty-fourth Street miracle." Wow! Could we have been at the same opening? Still slightly dazed, I read Richard Watts, Jr., in the *Herald Tribune:* "Thanks to a characteristically delightful score, imaginative settings, and the enchanting performance of Vera Zorina, it is a thoroughly charming musical comedy."

The afternoon papers were almost all on a par. "It has the most delightful score Mr. Rodgers has written in several seasons and some of Mr. Hart's drollest lyrics," wrote the *Post*'s John Mason Brown, who ended with: "Altogether a very pleasant and most unusual evening." Richard Lockridge in the *Sun* called it "a gay and capricious delight, full of jauntiness and grace and happy songs." To Sidney Whipple in the *World-Telegram,* it was "lavish entertainment," and John Anderson, the *Journal-American*'s critic, hailed it as "a winged wonderwork from the musical heavens of Rodgers and Hart."

In hindsight it is easy to say that I should have had more confidence, and that I should have known from experience that first-night audiences are notoriously inaccurate barometers. Those who give opinions are invariably the victims of wish-fulfilment, hoping the production will be good or bad, depending on their attitudes toward the people involved. But though I am very much aware of the many ultimate failures that are cheered passionately on opening night and the great successes that are received with coldness, I still cannot be oblivious to what I see and hear around me. Because of the first-night reception, I was certain that *I Married an Angel* was going to fail; it turned out to be our biggest hit in about ten years.

Chronology does not always give an indication of the time span during which shows are written. *On Your Toes* was ready before *Jumbo,* but was produced five months later; *I Married an Angel* was in the works well before *I'd Rather Be Right.* Hence, it shouldn't surprise anyone that the idea for *The Boys from Syracuse* came to Larry and me when we were busily involved with writing *I Married an Angel.*

That was early in 1938. We were on a train heading for Atlantic City, where we thought the fresh sea air might help to stimulate some new ideas. For some reason we began discussing Shakespeare, which led to our discovery that no one had ever thought of using one of his plays as the basis of a musical comedy.

The mere fact that it had never been done before was reason enough for us to start thinking that it should be our next project. The problems of *I Married an Angel* were pushed aside for the rest of the trip as we began tossing around titles of plays. Even eliminating the tragedies and histories, we had a pretty large field to choose from.

But one play attracted us from the start, and for a very personal reason. Larry's younger brother, Teddy, was a clever comedian best known for such George Abbott farces as *Three Men on a Horse* and *Room Service.* He was short and dark, and though he looked a good deal like Larry, he was always being mistaken for another gifted comic, Jimmy Savo.

"Why don't we do *The Comedy of Errors*?" Larry said, rubbing his hands together as he always did when a good idea hit him. "Teddy and Jimmy would be a natural for the twin Dromios." Nepotism notwithstanding, we both realized that it was an inspired casting idea, and once *I Married an Angel* was behind us, we got down to serious work on the show that eventually became known as *The Boys from Syracuse.*

When we started talking about a director for this kind of musical farce, we could come up with only one name: George Abbott. Moreover, George was so enthusiastic that he decided to produce the show himself. At first Larry and I were supposed to collaborate on the script with him, but he had it all finished before we could get started. The book was so sharp, witty, fast-moving and, in an odd way, so very much in keeping with the bawdy Shakespearean tradition that neither Larry nor I wanted to change a line.

There was one line, though, that George appropriated directly from the original play. This was the Seeress's "The venom clamours of a jealous woman poisons more deadly than a mad dog's tooth." Lest anyone unfamiliar with the classics accept this as a sentence he had thought up all by himself, George had Jimmy Savo follow it by sticking his head out from the wings and proudly announcing to the audience: "Shakespeare!"

The cast for *The Boys from Syracuse* was full of talented young people. Besides Teddy and Jimmy, we had Eddie Albert and Ronald Graham as the Antipholus of Syracuse and the Antipholus of Ephesus. There were also three notable charmers for our leading ladies: Marcy Westcott, Muriel Angelus and an energetic cream puff named Wynn Murray.

Abbott whipped the show into beautiful shape, and George Balanchine was again with us to stage the dances. It was fortunate that everything went so smoothly because Larry's disappearances had become more frequent than ever. When he was there, he worked rapidly; all we had to say was that we wanted a new line or two or a complete new verse and it wouldn't take him long to come up with exactly what was needed. Once Abbott and I were deep in conversation at a table and Larry was sitting with us. Our animated talk didn't bother him in the least; he just kept scribbling away and when he was finished he'd written the verse to "Falling in Love with Love."

Last-minute changes are fully expected in the creation of a musical, and Larry was certainly aware of how important it was to be with the show during its tryout. But when *The Boys from Syracuse* company took off for New Haven, he was nowhere to be found. Luckily, the show was so well set that no further work was needed, but how much longer could our luck hold out?

We found out soon enough, and the answer, as I had feared, was not reassuring. A few weeks after *The Boys from Syracuse* opened successfully on Broadway in November 1938, George Abbott came to Larry and me with the idea of doing a rah-rah college-football musical called *Too Many Girls*. The script was by a writer named George Marion, Jr., who had done some of the writing for *Love Me Tonight,* and though the story had originally been conceived for the movies, it was easily adjusted to the requirements of the stage. Larry and I were drawn to the idea, I suppose, because it gave us the chance to work again with talented young people who were not yet anointed as "stars." We signed Marcy Westcott, who had been in *The Boys from Syracuse,* and Mary Jane Walsh, who had been in *I'd Rather Be Right.* Our All-American backfield consisted of Richard Kollmar, Desi Arnaz, Eddie Bracken and Hal LeRoy, and our cheerleaders were led by Diosa Costello and Leila Ernst. We were back in *Babes in Arms* country again, and it was fun.

Larry, however, was no fun at all. It was almost impossible to find him when we needed him, and this time we needed him desperately. The show had many rough spots and we were constantly cutting and rearranging the songs. I vaguely remember that I came up with the idea for the opening number in the show, "Heroes in the Fall," in which the football players of Pottawatomie College lament the brevity of their tenure as campus luminaries. Since Larry was nowhere to be found, I had to supply the necessary lyric myself. This happened on a few other occasions as well.

All the major songs, however, did have lyrics written by Larry. Because our story dealt, more or less, with an institution of learning, in "I Didn't Know What Time It Was" he came up with the idea of discovering both love and wisdom, and in "Love Never Went to College" he personified love as an ignorant but all-powerful ruler. Two songs in the score even allowed us the chance to express our feelings in a light-hearted way about situations of current concern. We had already serenaded our romantically idealized city in "Manhattan," and now, in "Give It Back to the Indians," we turned things around and pointed out its blemishes. Some of the problems we touched on are still very much with us today:

Broadway's turning into Coney,
Champagne Charlie's drinking gin,
Old New York is new and phoney—
Give it back to the Indians.
Two cents more to smoke a Lucky,
Dodging buses keeps you thin,
New New York is simply ducky—
Give it back to the Indians.
Take all the reds on the boxes made for soap,
Whites on Fifth Avenue,
Blues down in Wall Street losing hope—
Big bargain today,
Chief, take it away!
Come, you busted city slickers,
Better take it on the chin,
Father Knick has lost his knickers,
Give it back to the Indians!

Larry even wrote the lines "We've tried to run the City/But the City ran away," probably the earliest admission in song that New York is ungovernable.

Our other beef was registered in "I Like to Recognize the Tune," in which we voiced objection to the musical distortions then so much a part of pop music because of the swing-band influence. We really had nothing against swing bands *per se,* but as songwriters we felt it was tough enough for new numbers to catch on as written without being subjected to all kinds of interpretive manhandling that obscured their melodies and lyrics. To me, this was the musical equivalent of bad grammar. On the other hand, once a song has become established I see nothing wrong with taking certain liberties. A singer or an orchestra can add a distinctive, personal touch that actually contributes to a song's longevity. I can't say I'm exactly grief-stricken when something I've written years before suddenly catches on again because of a new interpretation.

Too Many Girls was not one of Broadway's immortals, but it received enthusiastic notices and had a respectable run. To tell the truth, I scarcely cared; overshadowing everything was Larry, and he worried me greatly.

At about this time I was commissioned by the Ballet Russe de Monte Carlo, then the foremost ballet company in the world, to compose the score for a new work. I was particularly appreciative of the chance, since *Too Many Girls* had provided little that was creatively challenging, and I was also glad to get away, however briefly, from the Larry Hart problem.

It was Gerald Murphy, the wealthy ballet patron and artist, who first interested me in doing this score. At the time, the Ballet Russe specialized in the classics or in new works by European choreographers and composers, and Gerald was anxious to see the Paris-based company expand its repertory by adding ballets that would be completely American in theme and choreography. A young dancer named Marc Platt had an idea for a ballet based on the gold rush, and Gerald brought us together to work on the libretto. Our tale, which we called *Ghost Town,* concerned an old miner in a ghost town who tells a story to a couple of tourists about a gold prospector and his fortunes and misfortunes. As the story unfolds, the scene changes to the days of the gold rush, and at the end, the old miner turns out to be the protagonist of his story. We brought in a lot of characters, including Jenny Lind and Algernon Swinburne, and I'm afraid it was too cluttered and involved for its own good. But it was given a sumptuous production with some of the company's most gifted dancers and it did serve its purpose of introducing a native American work into the repertory. Years later the Ballet Russe would do far better with other Western ballets, most notably Agnes de Mille's *Rodeo,* but at least *Ghost Town* was the one that started the trend.

I conducted all the New York performances. What made the first evening truly memorable was that my family—Dorothy, Mary, Linda, Mom and Pop—was in the audience, beaming down on me from a box. Little Richard, who used to show off for company in front of his parents' living-room fireplace, was now showing off in the pit of the Metropolitan Opera House.

One rehearsal incident I'll never forget. I was naturally nervous about conducting the famed orchestra of the Ballet Russe, and one day, following a run-through, the first trumpeter jumped up from his chair and yelled "Rodgers!" Now I knew I was in trouble. No one yells "Rodgers!" to the conductor—and composer!—unless there's something wrong. Then, breaking into a wide grin, the man said, "Rodgers, Broadway composer, from you I expected hot licks!"

Higher and Higher, the next musical on the Rodgers and Hart agenda, was a classic example of my theory that it's impossible to redesign a show once the basic concept proves unworkable. With Vera Zorina such a tremendous success in *I Married an Angel,* it was only natural for Larry and me to attempt a musical tailored to her specific and considerable gifts. Josh Logan brought us an amusing story about a maid who is passed off as a debutante, and we thought it would work just fine.

Zorina was then in Hollywood making, among other films, *On Your Toes,* and was unable to return to New York because of her screen commitments. Perhaps we should have waited for her, but at the time it seemed best to have the play rewritten to fit someone else. Which decision led straight to disaster. The Hungarian actress Marta Eggert was chosen to play the lead, but she was an entirely different type from Zorina—for one thing, she was a singer, not a dancer—and the show suffered. It wasn't that Marta wasn't good, but the part wasn't good for her. It had taken me years to learn that a show can be altered, songs can be added or dropped, and actors can be replaced, but once the basic structure of the production is set, it is suicide to try to change it.

If *Higher and Higher* is remembered at all today it is probably not because of its cast or songs but because of a trained seal. This leads to another of Rodgers' Irrefutable Rules: If a trained seal steals your show, you don't have a show.

In the summer of 1940, two events had a profound effect upon me.

The war in Europe had begun the previous September, but apart from my hope that it would somehow end quickly with the destruction of Hitler, it did not concern me directly. For a while, in fact, there was so little military action that it was dubbed the "phoney" war, and it appeared that some kind of settlement would be agreed to. Then, suddenly, Germany began its lightning invasion of Norway and Denmark, followed by the conquest of Holland, Belgium and France. Obviously England was the next target, and news from our friends in London was not reassuring. Myrtle d'Erlanger, our closest friend over there, was so concerned for the safety of her daughter that she cabled us to ask if Zoë and her nurse could live with us for the duration of the war. Zoë was a charming, bright child, about a year older than Mary, and for the three and a half years she was with us, she was almost as close to Dorothy and me as our own daughters. It was fortunate that she came at the time she did because only a few weeks after she arrived, England was subjected to the devastating Battle of Britain.

The other event, which occurred early in September, was the death of my mother. For the past few years my parents had made a custom of taking extended vacations at the Traymore Hotel in Atlantic City. This time they had been away for about a month when I got a telephone call from my father. With a voice that was ominously unsteady, he said, "Richard, your mother's very sick." When I told him that Dorothy and I would catch the next train down, he said, "Don't rush, don't rush. It's too late."

Dorothy and I and Morty and his wife went down to Atlantic City together to bring Pop home and to be of whatever help we could. What had happened was simply that Mom had awakened in the morning, complained of a pain and suddenly died of a stroke.

At the time of Mom's death, my folks were living at the Hotel Croydon, at Eighty-sixth Street and Madison Avenue. When Pop walked into the apartment he did the kind of inexplicable thing all of us are likely to do in times of crisis. He went straight to his desk and said he had to write some letters. When I asked what letters could be so important that they had to be written at a time like this, he said he was writing to the magazines to which he subscribed advising them to change his subscription address from the Traymore Hotel back to the Croydon.

During the first few months after my mother's death, my father continued to be remarkably composed until one evening when Dorothy and I were taking him back to the Croydon in a taxi. Without any provocation he suddenly burst into tears. Neither Dorothy nor I said anything, but we knew what he was going through.

Ours was a close family and Mom's death affected us all deeply. Her understanding and sympathy, particularly at the time when I was floundering around at the beginning of my career, were something I shall always hold dear, and for which I shall always be grateful.

15

Thursday

Dear Dick:

I don't know whether you happened to see any of a series of pieces I've been doing for *The New Yorker* in the past year or so. They're about a guy who is master of ceremonies in cheap night clubs, and the pieces are in the form of letters from him to a successful band leader. Anyway, I got the idea that the pieces, or at least the character and the life in general, could be made into a book show, and I wonder if you and Larry would be interested in working on it with me. I read that you two have a commitment with Dwight Wiman for a show this spring, but if and when you get through with that I do hope you like my idea.

All the best to you always. Please remember me to the beautiful Dorothy and say hello to Larry for me. Say more than hello, too.

Faithfully,

John O'Hara

I was in Boston with *Too Many Girls* in October 1939 when the letter reached me. John and I had known each other for a few years, but it had never occurred to me that there would be a point at which our professional careers might meet. The letter was a total surprise, and a welcome one.

Since *Jumbo,* Larry and I had had phenomenal luck with most of our shows, but the problem of what to do next was constantly with us. I knew that *Too Many Girls* was not in the same league as our previous musicals, and I had certain misgivings about *Higher and Higher,* the Wiman commitment O'Hara referred to in his letter. But a musical based on O'Hara's Pal Joey stories in *The New Yorker* could be something really special. The "hero" was a conniver and braggart who would do anything and sleep anywhere to get ahead. The idea of doing a musical without a conventional clean-cut juvenile in the romantic lead opened up enormous possibilities for a more realistic view of life than theatregoers were accustomed to.

As I expected, Larry was equally enthusiastic about the project. He had spent thousands of hours in exactly the kind of atmosphere depicted in the stories and was thoroughly familiar with the Pal Joeys of this world.

Not only would the show be totally different from anything we had ever done before, it would be different from anything anyone else had ever tried. This alone was reason enough for us to want to do it.

I didn't make O'Hara wait long before sending him a telegram expressing our interest. He was then in California writing film scripts, and we had a long correspondence discussing various aspects of the project.

Almost as soon as I began writing to John, I had decided on the actor I wanted for the leading role. A week after *Too Many Girls* opened, Dorothy and I went to the opening-night performance of William Saroyan's play *The Time of Your Life*. In the small role of an aspiring entertainer was an especially engaging young man named Gene Kelly. The stage was aglow with life whenever he appeared, and his dancing was superb. The next day I wrote O'Hara that we had our Joey.

What John had in mind was not a musical based on any single story, but something that would borrow scenes and characters from a number of stories. As the plot developed, it turned out to be about Joey's affair with a wealthy woman, what she does to help him get ahead, and her ultimate disillusionment with him. Next to Joey, the show's most important role would be that of the benefactress, and since Vivienne Segal had been so right as the worldly cynic in *I Married an Angel,* she seemed like a natural for the part in *Pal Joey.* She was.

Work on *Pal Joey* began in earnest soon after the opening of *Higher and Higher.* There were problems right from the start. The Larry Hart problem I knew about, and with luck I could cope with it. But I was unprepared for the problems with O'Hara and with George Abbott, who had agreed to be both producer and director.

Strangely, though it was O'Hara who first broached the idea of a musical-comedy *Pal Joey,* he turned out to be rather indifferent, after he came East, to the creative aspects of the show. Like Larry, he proved difficult to nail down to do any work. There were periods during which I didn't hear from him for several weeks, and I couldn't even get him on the telephone. Finally, in desperation, I sent him a wire: SPEAK TO ME JOHN SPEAK TO ME. But nothing could change him, so a lot of the rewriting fell to Abbott himself—though occasionally John would drop by to make revisions of the revisions.

The problem with Abbott was of an entirely different nature. This was the third Rodgers and Hart musical produced by Abbott, and the first one that presented any differences about money. One day he informed me that he felt Larry and I were getting too much of a royalty and that we should agree to take a cut. He was never specific about why he thought so, and I told him that I couldn't understand his attitude. We parted without either of us giving in. A day or so later I saw him again, and this time he told me that he had been talking to his general manager, who had convinced him to pay us our regular royalty. I was pleased to hear this, of course, but I couldn't help wondering why George needed—or heeded—someone else's advice on such a matter.

The whole issue was curious, until two incidents gave me some inkling of the way George's mind was working. The first came at a meeting I had with Jo Mielziner, who was designing the show. When I made certain suggestions about the sets, he said, "You know, George told me to spend as little money as possible on production costs." Why? "Well," said Jo, "George hasn't got much faith in this show."

This disturbing attitude was confirmed soon afterward by Bob Alton, our choreographer, who told me that he needed two more girls for the chorus. I suggested that he call Abbott and say so. Bob did, and then relayed the startling message that George had told him that if he wanted two more girls in the chorus, he should get me to pay their salaries.

The next morning in George's office I told him about my meetings with Mielziner and Alton, and then said calmly, "George, I think you ought to give this show up. I don't think you're the right one to produce it. It's obvious that you have no faith in it, and the best thing all around would be for us to find someone else who does."

Apparently this was enough to straighten things out. Abbott may not have been wild about doing *Pal Joey,* but, by God, he wasn't about to let anyone else get his hands on it. Mielziner got the money for the settings, Alton got his two extra girls, and Larry and I never heard another word about a royalty cut.

Why George put us through all this I really don't know. Perhaps because of the daring nature of our show he thought he was sticking his neck out a bit too far. Apparently people must have told him that it wasn't commercial to do a show with such a disreputable character for a hero, and he was apprehensive about losing money on so risky a venture.

But whatever his personal attitude, the production George staged was a beauty. Nothing was softened for the sake of making the characters more appealing. Joey was a heel at the beginning and he never reformed. At the end the young lovers did not embrace as the orchestra swelled with the strains of the main romantic duet; in fact, they walked off in opposite directions. There wasn't one decent character in the entire play except for the girl who briefly fell for Joey—her trouble was simply that she was stupid.

Throughout our score for *Pal Joey,* Larry and I were scrupulous in making every song adhere to the hard-edged nature of the story. Taken by itself, "I Could Write a Book" is perfectly straightforward and sincere; in the context of the plot, however, Joey, who had probably never read a book in his life, sang it for no other reason than to impress a naïve girl he had just picked up on the street.

Because of the night-club setting of most of the musical's action, Larry and I were able to have fun writing numbers burlesquing typically tacky floor shows. We had all our chorus girls parade around with little on except headdresses representing flowers (in "The Flower Garden of My Heart") and colors ("That Terrific Rainbow"). But of all the songs, the one that has endured the longest is unquestionably "Bewitched, Bothered and Bewildered." Here we tried something that is particularly effective in comedy numbers—the contrast of a flowing, sentimental melody with words that are unsentimental and self-mocking: "Lost my heart, but what of it?/ My mistake, I agree./ He's a laugh but I love it/ Because the laugh's on me." At the end of the show, we used the melody again, but now the lyric expressed the reverse:

> Romance—finis
> Your chance—finis
> Those ants that invaded my pants—finis—
> Bewitched, bothered and bewildered no more!

There was no question that *Pal Joey* was radically different. Brooks Atkinson, of the *Times,* the most influential of all the critics and usually among the most discerning, referred to the story as "odious," and ended his review by asking, "Although it is expertly done, can you draw sweet water from a foul well?" Fortunately, other appraisers were more appreciative, including Wolcott Gibbs, of *The New Yorker,* who wrote: "I am not optimistic by nature but it seems to me just possible that the idea of equipping a song-and-dance production with a few living, three-dimensional figures, talking and behaving like human beings, may no longer strike the boys in the business as merely fantastic."

We had reason to be proud of *Pal Joey,* and despite legend that the show lacked popular appeal, it did have a successful eleven-month run, followed by a three-month tour.

But legends die hard. In 1952, when Jule Styne, who was then a producer as well as a composer, secured the rights for a revival of *Pal Joey,* he met with tremendous difficulties in raising the necessary money. At one point things looked so bleak that I pleaded with him to drop the project. But Jule had a stubborn faith for which I shall be eternally grateful, and eventually he managed to get the show on. With Vivienne Segal, looking not a day older and again playing the feminine lead, and Harold Lang now in the title role, *Pal Joey* was greeted as the freshest, most exciting musical of the season. This time the slightly gloating Wolcott Gibbs wrote: "Standards apparently have changed because up to now I have met nobody who found anything embarrassing in the goings on." Brooks Atkinson admitted that though he had been less than enchanted by the show when he first saw it, a second viewing convinced him that the musical "was a pioneer in the moving back of musical frontiers, for it tells an integrated story with a knowing point of view . . . Brimming over with good music and fast on its toes, it renews confidence in the professionalism of the theatre."

In a personal appraisal, which appeared in the *Times* on the occasion of this new production, I wrote: "Larry Hart knew what John O'Hara knew —that Joey was not disreputable because he was mean, but because he had too much imagination to behave himself and because he was a little weak. While Joey himself may have been fairly adolescent in his thinking and his morality, the show bearing his name certainly wore long pants and in many respects forced the entire musical-comedy theatre to wear long pants for the first time."

Pal Joey was the most satisfying and mature work that I was associated with during all my years with Larry Hart. And how did I follow it up? By taking piano lessons. My sight-reading had never been good, and I felt that if I didn't do anything about it now, I'd never get around to it. I also had a particular reason: I wanted to play well enough to be able to join a few other musicians from time to time to perform some of the standard chamber-music works.

My teacher was an old friend, Herman Wasserman, who was extremely helpful. I had a marvelous time practicing four or five hours a day, and it did a great deal of good not only for my playing but for my composing too. I'm afraid, however, that I never really progressed far enough to perform chamber music. Besides, after the United States became directly involved in the war, there simply wasn't anyone around to play with.

One morning early in May 1941, after Mary, Linda and Zoë d'Erlanger had gone off to school, Dorothy and I received a cablegram informing us of the death of Zoë's mother, Myrtle, in a German air raid. The news was shattering. That morning Zoë was appearing in a school production of *The Mikado,* and Dorothy and I had promised to attend. All we could think about as we saw her singing and acting on the stage was that we would soon have to tell her the dreadful news.

Later in the day, after we had returned home, we sat Zoë down and told her as gently as we could what had happened. During the entire time she just sat looking at us, betraying not the slightest sign of what was going on inside her. When we finished, all she said was, "Don't tell Linda." At such a time, this remarkable child could think only of protecting the feelings of another child five years younger.

There is little that anyone can do to console a person in such a tragic situation. By coincidence, however, Dorothy and I had recently made a decision that helped slightly to mitigate the pain: we had decided to move out of the city. Though we had always considered ourselves city people, we found that living in a New York apartment with three growing girls did make life a bit cramped, particularly since my work required me to do much of my writing at home. We had friends who had bought homes in and around Fairfield, Connecticut, and we always enjoyed the feeling of spaciousness and serenity whenever we visited them. It was close enough to the city and far enough away to give us what we thought would be the best of two worlds.

We found a place on Black Rock Turnpike in Fairfield that seemed suitably large enough for the kids to romp around in. It was a Colonial house, built on a high knoll, with fifteen rooms and five baths and situated on about six and a half acres. The house was more functional than attractive, but we decided to buy it because Dorothy and I fell in love with a tree standing in the front yard. It was a massive oak with a ninety-foot spread and we thought it the most magnificent tree we had ever seen. So in June, after the children's school year, the Rodgers family—including Zoë d'Erlanger—packed up and moved to Black Rock Turnpike. We were not to have a permanent New York address for the next four years.

During August the Duke of Kent, who was Zoë's godfather, visited President and Mrs. Roosevelt at Hyde Park. Because he was anxious to see Zoë, the Roosevelts invited the Rodgerses and their young English charge to visit them. (The invitation failed to include the Rodgers children, an omission that Mary found especially hard to endure.)

The Duke and the Roosevelts were all at Val-Kill Cottage, Mrs. Roosevelt's private house, when we arrived. I could not help but notice that the President's granite-like head and muscular shoulders and arms looked incongruous in contrast to his painfully feeble legs. When we shook hands, mine actually seemed to disappear into his. Later Mrs. Roosevelt took Zoë for a swim in her pool so that the Duke could tell us the horrible circumstances of Myrtle d'Erlanger's death. She had been killed during one of the most devastating air raids over London and her body was not discovered until four days later.

My memory of this visit will always be dominated by that remarkable woman, Eleanor Roosevelt. One incident was especially revealing. After making a graceful dive into the pool, she quickly swam to the shallow end and then bounded out of the water to join us. We were all impressed with her skill, and Dorothy commented that it was obvious she had been swimming and diving all her life. Mrs. Roosevelt beamed. "Oh dear, no," she said. "I learned to dive only recently. It was my grandchildren. They were making fun of me because I didn't know how, and I was determined to show them I could do anything they could do!"

Zoë d'Erlanger remained with us for almost three and a half years. Dorothy and I often talked about how much we would love to adopt her, but we were sure that her family would never allow it. The war was still going on when she was told that she would have to return home because her great-uncle was very ill and wanted to see her before he died. Seeing her leave under any circumstance would have been painful, but at this time it was almost unbearable. With her English nanny, Zoë had to make the perilous trip by freighter to Lisbon, then by plane to England. Dorothy and I spent many a restless night worrying about her, but fortunately she was unharmed during the journey and the remaining years of the war. Now married, with a family of her own, she is still very close to the Rodgers family and her annual visits are always happy ones.

Nineteen forty-one was the first time in six years that Rodgers and Hart did not have a new show on Broadway, and the reason, I'm afraid, was Larry.

The drinking, the staying out all night and the disappearances were increasing to an alarming degree. It was now almost impossible to rely on him to keep an appointment, and if he did, he was seldom in condition to do any work. He no longer seemed to give a damn about anything. He still wore elevator shoes to make him appear taller, but he'd given up his hair-restoring treatments and looked as if he slept in his clothes.

Larry Hart was not my responsibility except insofar as our professional collaboration was concerned. Still, because of my deep affection for him, it would have been inhuman if I didn't do what I could to help. Not that he felt that he needed help. From the start he had made it clear that he led the life he wanted and was not about to change it for anyone, though I knew it bothered him that, as he once told me, his mother was constantly nagging him to "settle down like Dick and marry a nice girl." But the fact remained that I had known him for over twenty years. We had worked together, struggled together and succeeded together, and I simply could not look the other way while this man destroyed himself.

One way I could help was with money. Larry was never in need of money, but he had no concern about it and was constantly throwing it away. I couldn't stop him from spending it foolishly or being an easy touch, but I could make it difficult. The scheme I devised was actually an idea my father gave me. It was Pop's plan to get Larry to agree to turn over to me a certain amount of money each week, which I dutifully put in a safe-deposit box in his name. What made the scheme work was that Larry had no idea where the safe-deposit box was located.

Later our friends Edna Ferber and Peggy Pulitzer recommended a wonderful man named Willy Kron to handle all of Larry's finances. Willy was far more than just a financial wizard who advised his client where to invest his money. He loved Larry and spent a great deal of time with him trying to keep him out of trouble. Larry was grateful enough to Willy to put him in his will.

There was a time when I thought psychiatry might help. Once, following a three-day drinking binge, Larry agreed to go to Doctors Hospital to get dried out. While he was there, I went to see Dr. Richard Hoffman, a well-known psychiatrist, and told him about Larry's problems. I knew that Larry would never voluntarily submit to psychoanalysis, but the doctor told me not to worry: he'd simply pass himself off as a hospital staff member and drop in to see him from time to time. He was sure that the deception would work and promised to keep me advised. That night I received a telephone call from Larry. All he had to say was, "Your witch doctor was in to see me," and that was the end of that.

I have made much of Larry's "disappearances" in this book. The logical question is, "Where did he go?" and my honest answer is, "I don't know." After our working day was over, I would go home to my family. I was never with Larry on any of his binges, though I did know that he liked hanging around Ralph's Bar on Forty-fifth Street in the heart of the theatre district. I also know that he frequently went to the Luxor Baths to get steamed out. Other than that—what he did, where he went, and with whom —I have no idea. What mattered to me, as far as our work was concerned, was that he was never available in the morning, and that when he did show up sometime in the afternoon he would be fresh from the barber, with his face heavily powdered and his eyes deeply pouched. Occasionally he might mumble something about having overslept, or having had a rough night, but most of the time he never gave any excuse. After our many years together I knew better than to press him for details.

One of the odd aspects of our partnership was that we never had a fight. Disagreements, of course, but only about work and never about anything serious. Basically he was such a sweet guy that it was impossible to be angry with him. I could be angry with what he was doing to himself and what this was doing to our relationship, but I never reached the point of issuing ultimatums or expressing my displeasure in a direct manner.

Perhaps at an early stage a confrontation might have done some good. Perhaps not. I was always so anxious to get on with my work and so impressed with the quality of work Larry produced that I was genuinely fearful of upsetting what was, to judge by the finished product, a closely coordinated, harmonious team.

One of the questions I'm most frequently asked is about our working method. This cannot be answered simply, because there were many methods. Larry seldom gave me a completed lyric; at best it would be no more than a verse or opening chorus. Occasionally he would give me a title which would suggest a melody. Most of the time I would play a completed melody for him and we'd sit around tossing titles and lyric ideas at each other. Once we agreed on the general theme, Larry would write the words and we'd have a finished song. For example, one afternoon I said to him, "Why don't we start off with a title that doesn't suggest a typical lyric, that has absolutely nothing to do with a romantic expression?"

"For instance?"

"Oh . . . 'I've Got Five Dollars.' "

As the years went on, Larry's concentration span became shorter and shorter. He could never work alone, so I knew that if he didn't show, it meant that no work was being done. During all our sessions he was good-natured and usually willing to compromise. For my part, I not only had to supply the musical themes to get him started, I also had to supply him with periodic drinks. He was a phenomenally fast worker and luckily I was too, because he could be controlled for just so many hours. Then, with little warning, he'd grab his hat and coat and be gone.

Much as I loved Larry and much as I took pride in what we had accomplished together, in the summer of 1941 I realized that the situation was becoming critical. I was thirty-nine years old, in good health and supremely grateful to be able to do the kind of work I loved, but I was linked professionally to a man forty-six years old who was compulsively bent on self-destruction and who no longer cared about his work. I *had* to think about the unthinkable: I had to think about a life without Larry Hart.

At first I felt guilty about it. Everybody thought of Rodgers and Hart as an indivisible team. People never thought of one without the other; in fact, it was almost one word: Rodgersandhart. Those who didn't know us personally neither knew nor cared if we had first names or that we were two totally dissimilar human beings. Never before had there been a writing team with such a long partnership in the history of the Broadway theatre, nor one more closely associated in the public mind.

I was even more concerned about what a break would do to Larry. He always looked on me as something of a big brother. Though he had a mind of his own when it came to the kind of songs and shows we should do, in almost every other professional area he was totally dependent on me. Pounding out songs for potential backers, auditioning singers, discussing terms, even tracking down producers who owed us money—these were always my jobs. The thought of leaving Larry was the most painful aspect of the entire situation. For the first time since the days when I was struggling unsuccessfully to get a start in the theatre, I was plagued by insomnia. I just couldn't see any way to avoid hurting someone. Still, I knew that I had to start planning for the day when Larry would no longer be able to work.

Once I began thinking of this inevitability, I was faced with the problem of finding someone to replace Larry. Who could equal his talent and also be the kind of partner with whom I could work closely and successfully? Many gifted lyric writers came to mind, but I always returned to one man: Oscar Hammerstein.

There were many reasons why I should not have thought of Oscar. He had always been part of a romantic, florid kind of theatre, more operetta than musical comedy, which was quite different from Larry's and mine. He had written his best lyrics with men of traditional, classical European backgrounds or training, such as Rudolf Friml, Sigmund Romberg and Jerome Kern. Also, I had to face the fact that he had not had a solid Broadway success in almost ten years.

But the main point was that I had absolute faith in Oscar's talent. I had seen show after show in which his lyrics were of high quality but whose productions were so stale, flat and obviously unprofitable that nothing could have helped them. I was convinced that any man who could write *Show Boat, Sweet Adeline* and the lyric to Jerome Kern's "All the Things You Are" was far from being through, that his talent was being misused rather than used up. Oscar's kind of theatre was rapidly becoming passé and mine was all too often in a rut. If we both were flexible and dedicated enough, perhaps something fresh and worthwhile could emerge from our combined efforts.

There were other considerations. Oscar was an old friend. I had known him ever since I was a kid and had even written a few songs with him. Though we did not see each other regularly, I always felt that I could turn to him if I had a problem, and I think he felt the same way about me. I was also aware that his background was not dissimilar from mine, and that, apart from the theatre we shared many similar views. Nor was it lost on me that Oscar was considered something of an anomaly on Broadway: a genuine pipe-and-slippers man who abhorred night life, had a closely knit family and was devoted to a warm, charming, attractive wife whose name also happened to be Dorothy. Thus, almost from the start the possibilities narrowed to one.

During the period that I was most despondent about Larry's condition, George Abbott asked me to read the script of a musical comedy he was planning to produce. It turned out to be another collegiate story, with some funny lines and clever situations, but this time George was not interested in a Rodgers and Hart score. He was, understandably, anxious to try his luck with a new team, though he wanted me to join him as co-producer and general overseer of the musical department. I agreed, but only on one condition: fearing that people might interpret this activity as a rift between Larry and me, I insisted that my name not be used in publicity or listed in the program credits. Because we had the libretto before we had a composer and lyricist, George and I held a number of auditions before giving the assignment for the show, which we eventually called *Best Foot Forward,* to two gifted newcomers, Hugh Martin and Ralph Blane.

I was in Philadelphia with the show during its pre-Broadway tryout in September 1941 when I unburdened myself to Abbott about my fears concerning Larry. George was even more pessimistic than I was. Almost instinctively, I picked up a telephone and called Oscar Hammerstein at his farm in Doylestown, Pennsylvania. The place was only about an hour's drive from Philadelphia, and I invited myself over for lunch the next day.

Seeing Oscar again in the surroundings of his rustic, solid farmhouse gave me a feeling of assurance that the situation could not be as bleak as I feared. Dependable, realistic, sensitive Oscar Hammerstein was the right man, possibly the only man, who not only would be understanding about my problem but would make constructive suggestions.

Over lunch I told him what was happening between Larry and me, and of my concern for the future of our partnership. Oscar listened without saying a word. He thought for a minute or two after I finished, and then said, "I think you ought to keep working with Larry just so long as he is able to keep working with you. It would kill him if you walked away while he was still able to function. But if the time ever comes when he cannot function, call me. I'll be there."

It was exactly what I had hoped to hear. Then he said something that revealed even more the kind of selfless person he was. "I'll even go a step further," he told me. "If you and Larry are in the middle of a job and he can't finish it, I'll finish it for him, and nobody but the two of us ever need know."

I left Oscar that day with enough of the weight removed from my shoulders to make me feel a bit more optimistic than I had for months.

My personal problems were real enough, but at this particular time, worrying about a songwriting partnership was quickly put into perspective by even a cursory glance at the daily headlines. A state of unlimited national emergency had existed in the United States since the previous May, and almost everything that happened in the world seemed to be moving us inexorably into a global conflict. At last others were beginning to realize what the Rodgers family had already learned in a very personal way: that the fate of the United States was inescapably linked to the fate of Great Britain.

Because of our emotional involvement, Dorothy and I were active in organizations that aided the Allies. Just three weeks prior to the Pearl Harbor attack, we were in Canada—along with Larry, Jane Froman and André Kostelanetz—to do what we could to help the Canadian War Savings drive. Since the United States was not yet on a wartime footing, it was a shock to visit a country that was. During the day we talked, sang and performed at at least half a dozen army camps near Toronto, and at night we took part in a radio broadcast. We had been on the go ever since seven o'clock in the morning and by midnight, when we caught the train back to New York, we were all exhausted but also exhilarated. As we walked through the station to our train, Jane Froman, who was so tired that I had to support her, suddenly burst out laughing. "You know, Dick," she said, "if we were getting paid to do this, we'd all raise hell!"

I remember the Canadian trip for another reason: Larry. On the night train going up he had spent almost all the time drinking himself into a stupor. After we arrived at the hotel in Toronto the next morning for breakfast, with many local dignitaries there to greet us, he got as far as the corridor outside the dining room when he got violently sick all over the floor. Dorothy and I shared a two-bedroom suite with Larry, and when we came back upstairs she went directly into his room, and for the first and only time in all the years that she knew him, let him know that she was aware of his drinking. All she said was, "Give me the bottles," and Larry, probably because he was so shocked by the order, meekly handed them over. As she was leaving the room he pleaded, "When can I have a drink?" "Tonight after the radio show" was Dorothy's no-nonsense answer.

Larry comported himself fairly well during the day and made the tour of the camps and the city hall reception without any mishaps, but by the time we reached the radio station he was in bad shape. The Rodgers and Hart contribution to the program was to read a war savings appeal. Larry read his lines all right, but I noticed that his right hand, which was holding the pages of his script, was shaking uncontrollably. After our turn was over, we went backstage and there was Dorothy, true to her word, waiting for him with a tumbler of whiskey. He drank it down in one gulp.

Once war finally came to the United States, my first thought was to apply for a commission. I took the Air Force physical examination and to my surprised satisfaction passed it. The only trouble was that because of a sudden crackdown on civilian commissions, I was never able to get one. This was a bitter disappointment, particularly because so many people close to me were either enlisting or otherwise engaged in work directly related to the war. Even my father, then seventy-two, had come out of retirement to volunteer his services examining draftees. Eventually I came to accept the fact that the best thing I could do to help the war effort was to continue doing exactly what I had always been doing: writing songs and shows that could make some small contribution to the morale of our armed forces and of the people supporting them.

At about this time a literary agent named Audrey Wood asked me to read the script of a play written by one of her clients. It was *The Warrior's Husband,* by Julian Thompson, which had been successfully presented on Broadway some ten years before with Katharine Hepburn in the leading role. The play dealt in a light-hearted fashion with the conflict between the Amazons and the Greeks and had some amusing things to say about the male-female relationship in a society in which the women dominated the men.

I thought the story could be turned into an amusing book for a musical, and Larry, who had been going through an extended depression, perked up noticeably when I told him about it. In fact, we decided to write the adaptation ourselves. I also decided that having gained some experience in the management field with *Best Foot Forward,* I would produce the new musical. But aware that I still had much to learn in this area, I formed a partnership with the more experienced Dwight Deere Wiman.

Now that I was both co-creator and co-sponsor, I had two problems. One was that I could never find Larry; the other was that I could never find Wiman. I was used to Larry's disappearing act, but Wiman's absences were a surprise. He was a very social, "clubby" man who always managed to find more time for his outside activities than for what should have been his primary concern.

In one instance this proved to be especially embarrassing. Like all Broadway shows, ours needed outside financial backing, and though it was really Wiman's job to find the "angels," I did manage to come up with one myself. This was Howard Cullman, a wealthy cigar manufacturer and patron of the arts who had expressed interest in investing in the show. Howard and I made an appointment to see Wiman in his office, but he kept us waiting for well over an hour—a breach of etiquette which, for a producer, is roughly akin to self-immolation. Fortunately for all of us, Howard had enough faith in the show, if not in Wiman, to put money in it.

Another person who helped finance the musical, which was eventually called *By Jupiter,* was Richard Kollmar, the young actor who had played the juvenile lead in *Too Many Girls.* He came into the office one day and said simply, "I hear you need thirty-five thousand dollars. If I can find it for you, will you give me credit as associate producer?" We agreed, Kollmar came up with the money, and that's how he got his start as a producer. I never did find out where he got that $35,000.

I had hoped that Larry's enthusiasm for the show would, however temporarily, keep him relatively sober, but he was less dependable than during any previous production. Weeks would go by before I'd hear from him. One day his doctor and I went over to his apartment, where we found him lying on his bed in a semistupor. We bundled him into a taxi and rushed him over to Doctors Hospital for the drying-out treatment. Now that I had him where I could keep an eye on him, I also took advantage of his confinement by putting him to work. In those days, Doctors Hospital had guest rooms that could be rented by the day by patients' relatives and friends, so I simply rented a hospital room as my office and had Steinway send up a piano. It was only after we had completed the score that Larry's doctor permitted him to be discharged. But once we got to Boston for the tryout, Larry was up to his old tricks and disappeared for three days.

Right from the start we'd had no other actor in mind than Ray Bolger for the lead of *By Jupiter.* He had scored a tremendous success in *On Your*

Toes and we were sure that his new part, that of the effeminate husband of the Amazon chieftain, played by Benay Venuta, would give even greater scope to his remarkable talent.

The production also marked the first time that I was associated professionally with John Green, then known as Johnny, who was our musical director. Johnny and I had been friends ever since he was a Harvard undergraduate; he was probably the only conductor on Broadway whose credits included leading a popular dance band, writing durable song hits (including "Body and Soul" and "Out of Nowhere"), and—years later— conducting symphony orchestras. (It was partly because of my admiration for Johnny's songs for *Beat the Band,* a 1942 George Abbott musical, that I joined George as co-producer. As in the case of *Best Foot Forward,* I took no official billing.)

Among the songs Larry and I had written for *By Jupiter,* we had thought the most popular would be the torch ballad "Nobody's Heart." The show-stopper, however, turned out to be a minor song called "Life with Father," thanks to a dance Bolger did with the sixty-year-old Bertha Belmore. Another song, "Wait Till You See Her," in which the hero describes his beloved, was well received, but after we opened in New York we decided to cut it for no other reason than that the show was running late. We didn't put it back until toward the end of the run, but despite this lack of exposure it was picked up by singers and orchestras and today is the best-known piece in the score.

By Jupiter had the longest run of any Rodgers and Hart show presented on Broadway except for the revival of *Pal Joey,* and it could have run even longer than its 427 performances if Ray Bolger had not decided to quit the cast to entertain American troops in the Far East. Since it was clear that the customers wouldn't come without him in the lead, we ruled out finding a replacement and closed up shop.

During the run, however, we did have to replace the feminine lead, Constance Moore, who had to leave because of a film commitment. We auditioned a number of girls to succeed her, but none seemed exactly right. Eventually, we found what we were looking for in a vivacious, snub-nosed singer named Nanette Fabray, but before she was picked, our endless auditions were responsible for my favorite story involving that tenacious breed known as the talent agent. One day I was walking through Shubert Alley when I was stopped by an agent whom I knew slightly.

"Understand you're auditioning for a new girl to take over Connie Moore's part," he said.

"That's right. Any suggestions?"

"Sure have. Leila Ernst would be great in the part. Remember how good she was in *Too Many Girls* and *Pal Joey*?"

"Leila's certainly a talented girl," I said, "but she's too tall for the part."

"Oh, I don't know," said the agent. "Have you seen her lately?"

At Rockmeadow in the summer of 1951

At the piano under Doris Lee's painting of *Oklahoma!* (1953)

At the television salute to Rodgers and Hammerstein, which was carried by four channels on March 28, 1954

MILTON GREENE

Rehearsing the New York Philharmonic for a concert of my music in 1954

MARGERY LEWIS

Cutting the cake at our 25th Wedding Anniversary Party on March 5, 1955

Marilyn Monroe with an admirer on the same evening

At the recording session of the album I conducted with the New York Philharmonic in December, 1955

Rehearsing Julie Andrews for the television musical *Cinderella* (1957)

With Richard Kiley, Samuel Taylor, conductor Peter Matz, Diahann Carroll, Don Chastain, Bernice Massi and Mitchell Gregg at a rehearsal of *No Strings* (1962)

During the liturgical concert at Manhattanville in preparation for *The Sound of Music* (1959)

TONI FRISSELL

Mary

Linda

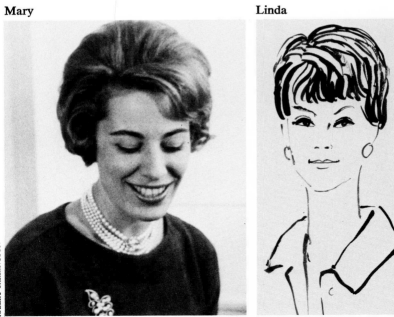

ROBERT CARRINGTON

DAGMAR FREUCHEN

At our house in Fairfield, Connecticut (1967)

With Mayor John V. Lindsay at Mt. Morris Park on June 27, 1970

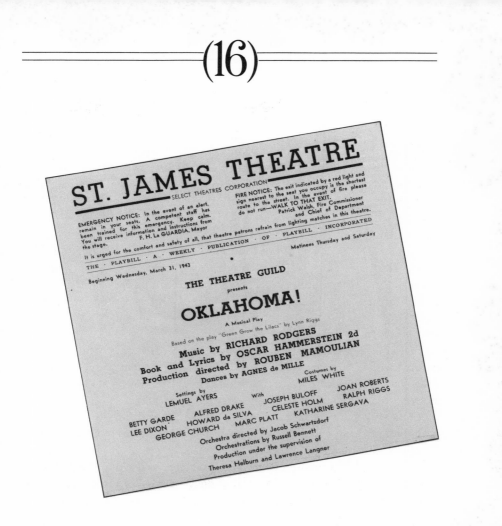

16

ST. JAMES THEATRE

SELECT THEATRES CORPORATION

EMERGENCY NOTICE: In the event of an alert, remain in your seats. A competent staff has been trained for this emergency. Keep calm. You will receive information and instructions from the stage. F. H. La GUARDIA, Mayor

FIRE NOTICE: The exit indicated by a red light and sign nearest to the seat you occupy is the shortest route to the street. In the event of fire please do not run—WALK TO THAT EXIT.
Patrick Walsh, Fire Commissioner and Chief of Department

It is urged for the comfort and safety of all, that theatre patrons refrain from lighting matches in this theatre.

THE · PLAYBILL · A · WEEKLY · PUBLICATION · OF · PLAYBILL · INCORPORATED

Matinees Thursday and Saturday

Beginning Wednesday, March 31, 1943

THE THEATRE GUILD

presents

OKLAHOMA!

A Musical Play

Based on the play "Green Grow the Lilacs" by Lynn Riggs

Music by RICHARD RODGERS
Book and Lyrics by OSCAR HAMMERSTEIN 2d
Production directed by ROUBEN MAMOULIAN

Dances by AGNES de MILLE

Costumes by
MILES WHITE

Settings by
LEMUEL AYERS

With

JOSEPH BULOFF   JOAN ROBERTS
ALFRED DRAKE   CELESTE HOLM   RALPH RIGGS
BETTY GARDE   HOWARD da SILVA   KATHARINE SERGAVA
LEE DIXON
GEORGE CHURCH   MARC PLATT

Orchestra directed by Jacob Schwartzdorf
Orchestrations by Russell Bennett
Production under the supervision of
Theresa Helburn and Lawrence Langner

Three of my Connecticut neighbors were Terry Helburn and Lawrence and Armina Langner. Ever since Larry and I wrote the scores for the Theatre Guild's first two *Garrick Gaieties,* and particularly since our return from Hollywood, Terry and Lawrence had often brought up the subject of our writing another show for the Guild. We never got down to specifics until shortly after *By Jupiter* opened, when Terry asked me to read the script of a play that the Guild had produced eleven years before. It was *Green Grow the Lilacs,* by Lynn Riggs, and I only had to read it once to realize that it had the makings of an enchanting musical. Set in the Southwest shortly after the turn of the century, with a cast of farmers and ranchers, it was a distinct departure from anything I had ever done before. I promptly told Terry and Lawrence that I wanted very much to write the score.

Of course, the Theatre Guild was assuming that they would have a musical with a score by Rodgers and Hart, since neither Terry nor Lawrence had any idea of Larry's condition. Though I knew that Oscar Hammerstein was waiting in the wings, I wanted to make one last effort to continue with Larry. I told him of my desire to do the show, sent him a script and made an appointment to meet him at the offices of Chappell and Company, our music publisher.

I was in the company's board room when a haggard and pale Larry walked in. He had obviously not had a good night's sleep in weeks, and I realized that I could no longer avoid talking about what was on my mind —that, if necessary, I'd have to be brutal to make him understand what he was doing not only to himself but to our partnership. I began by telling him I wanted to get started on the new show right away but that he was obviously in no condition to work. Larry admitted this and said that he needed a rest and was planning to leave soon for a vacation in Mexico. He was sure it would straighten him out and he'd return feeling much better.

This was nonsense; he knew it and I knew it.

"Larry," I said, "the only reason you're going to Mexico is to drink. When you come back you'll be in worse shape than ever."

Larry looked as if I had stabbed him. This was the first time in all the years we'd been together that I had ever spoken to him this way.

"We've got to work something out for the good of both of us," I continued. "I want you to have yourself admitted to a sanitarium, and I'll have myself admitted along with you. We'll be there together and we'll work together. The only way you're ever going to lick this thing is to get off the street."

Larry, who had been avoiding my eyes, looked at the floor and said, "I know, Dick. I'm sorry. But I want to go to Mexico. I have to."

I felt the blood rushing to my head. "This show means a lot to me," I told him. "If you walk out on me now, I'm going to do it with someone else."

"Anyone in mind?"

"Yes, Oscar Hammerstein."

Even the realization that I wasn't bluffing, that I actually had someone else waiting to take over, couldn't shake him. Still looking at the floor, all that Larry said was, "Well, you couldn't pick a better man." Then, for the first time, he looked me in the eyes. "You know, Dick," he said, "I've really never understood why you've put up with me all these years. It's been crazy. The best thing for you to do is forget about me."

There wasn't much more either one of us could say. Larry could no more fight his compulsive drinking than I could have thrown aside my family and career. He got up to leave and when he reached the door he turned around and said, "There's just one more thing. I really don't think *Green Grow the Lilacs* can be turned into a good musical. I think you're making a mistake."

With that he was gone, and so was our partnership.

I walked out of the board room to tell Max Dreyfus, who was waiting in his office, what had happened. But I never got there; I simply broke down and cried.

Larry did go to Mexico. When he returned a month later he had to be carried off the train on a stretcher.

As he had assured me, Oscar was ready to go to work. He read the script and saw the musical possibilities immediately. Because he was a librettist as well as a lyricist, he also saved us the problem of finding someone else to write the adaptation. And so Rodgers and Hart became Rodgers and Hammerstein.

It is only natural to feel some apprehension in forming a new partnership, especially after having worked exclusively with one man for so long a time, but because of the circumstances that brought Oscar and me together and because of the kind of man he was, I never had to go through a period of adjustment.

Our first meeting on the project that eventually became known as *Oklahoma!* took place at my home in Connecticut. We sat under the huge oak tree and tossed ideas around. What kind of songs were we going to write? Where would they go? Who would sing them? What special texture and mood should the show have?

We had many such sessions until we became thoroughly familiar not only with every aspect of the play but with each other's outlook and approach as well. Fortunately, we were in agreement on all major issues, so that when we finally did begin putting words and notes on paper—which didn't occur until we'd gone through weeks of discussions—we each were able to move ahead at a steady pace.

The first problem was, appropriately, how to open the show. We didn't want to begin with anything obvious, such as a barn dance with everyone a-whoopin' and a-hollerin'. After much thought and talk we simply went back to the way Lynn Riggs had opened his play, with a woman seated alone on the stage churning butter. For the lyric to the first song, Oscar developed his theme from the description that Riggs had written as an introduction to the scene: "It is a radiant summer morning several years ago, the kind of morning which, enveloping the shape of earth—men, cattle in a meadow, blades of the young corn, streams—makes them seem to exist now for the first time, their images giving off a visible golden emanation that is partly true and partly a trick of imagination focusing to keep alive a loveliness that may pass away . . ."

This was all Oscar's poetic imagination needed to produce his lines about cattle standing like statues, the corn as high as an elephant's eye, and the bright golden haze on the meadow. When I read them for the first time I could see those cattle and that corn and bright golden haze vividly. How prophetic were Oscar's words "I've got a beautiful feelin' / Ev'rything's goin' my way."

By opening the show with the woman alone onstage and the cowboy beginning his song offstage, we did more than set a mood; we were, in effect, warning the audience, "Watch out! This is a different kind of musical." Everything in the production was made to conform to the simple open-air spirit of the story; this was essential, and certainly a rarity in the musical theatre.

Oscar and I made few changes in the basic plot and the characters. We added the part of Will Parker, Ado Annie's boyfriend, and we made her a more physically attractive girl. For the ending, we tied the strands together a bit more neatly than in the play by having Curly being found innocent of murdering Jud Fry, rather than being given his freedom for one night to spend with his bride.

Most of the musical numbers presented no great problems. One, which every songwriter must face over and over again, is how to say "I love you" in a way that makes the song different from any other romantic ballad ever written. In "People Will Say We're in Love," Oscar hit on the notion of having the young lovers warn each other against showing any signs of affection so that people won't realize they're in love. (Larry and I had already written a different song of this kind in "This Can't Be Love," and later Oscar and I would try another variation on the theme with "If I Loved You.")

This song also demonstrates another familiar problem, especially for lyric writers. There are, after all, only so many rhymes for the word "love," and when Oscar decided to call the duet "People Will Say We're in Love," he was determined to avoid using any of the more obvious ones. After spending days thinking about this one rhyme, he called me up exultantly to announce that he'd solved the problem. His solution: the girl ends the refrain by admonishing the boy:

> Don't start collecting things,
> Give me my rose and my glove;
> Sweetheart, they're suspecting things—
> People will say we're in love.

Earlier in the story we needed a song in which Curly, who is stuck on Laurey, tries to tempt her into going to a box social with him by describing an imaginary "Surrey with the Fringe on Top." Oscar's lyric suggested both a clip-clop rhythm and a melody in which the straight, flat country road could be musically conveyed through a repetition of the straight, flat sound of the D note, followed by a sharp upward flick as fowl scurry to avoid being hit by the moving wheels:

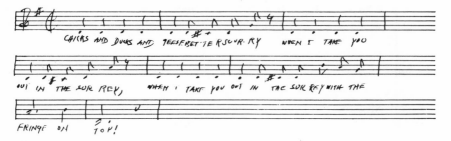

Oscar was so moved by this song that just listening to it made him cry. He once explained that he never cried at sadness in the theatre, only at naïve happiness, and the idea of two boneheaded young people looking forward to nothing more than a ride in a surrey struck an emotional chord that affected him deeply.

Though the words could be poetic and the music tender and romantic, Oscar and I were both careful in writing the score and lyrics to make the songs sound natural when sung by cowboys, ranchers and farm girls living in Indian Territory at the turn of the century. Though I had no prior experience creating melodies indigenous to this period and locale, I felt it important that the songs be my kind of music, though they could be embellished with a certain amount of regional flavoring. I remember that shortly before beginning the score Oscar sent me an impressively thick book of songs of the American Southwest which he thought might be of help. I opened the book, played through the music of one song, closed the book and never looked at it again. If my melodies were going to be authentic, they'd have to be authentic in my own terms.

This is the way I have always worked, no matter what the setting of the story. It was true of my "Chinese" music for *Chee-Chee,* of my "French" music for *Love Me Tonight,* and later of my "Siamese" music for *The King and I.* Had I attempted to duplicate the real thing, it would never have sounded genuine, for the obvious reason that I am neither Chinese, French, Siamese, nor from the Southwest. All a composer—any composer —can do is to make an audience believe it is hearing an authentic sound without losing his own musical identity.

In my judgment, the musical theatre has never had two greater lyric writers than Larry Hart and Oscar Hammerstein, yet they were as different in personality, appearance and technique as any two men could be. Working with Oscar was a brand-new experience. For twenty-five years, the only way I could get Larry to do anything was virtually to lock him in a room and stay with him until the job was finished. Oscar's working habits were entirely the opposite. I remember that when I first started talking to him about our method of collaborating, he seemed surprised at my question.

"I'll write the words and you'll write the music" was all he said.

"In that order?" I asked.

"If that's all right with you. I prefer it that way. You won't hear from me until I have a finished lyric."

And for 90 percent of the time, that's the way we worked together. Larry needed the stimulus of the music to get him started; Oscar needed nothing more than an agreement about what was required. Once Larry heard the music, he was a rapid, almost spontaneous worker, devoting little more time than it took to jot down the words. Oscar was slower and more painstaking, a characteristic partly dictated by his method of collaborating. I found no problem whatever in working this way. It gave Oscar the freedom he needed, and it helped me a good deal to have a completed lyric in front of me. It also offered me the opportunity to break away—even more than I had in the recent past—from the generally accepted "AABA" thirty-two-bar song construction. Lastly, I did not have to be with Oscar every time he got the urge to write a lyric. Since the actual creation of a melody has always come quickly to me, I was spared the endless hours I'd formerly had to spend playing nurse.

Oscar usually created his lyrics with "dummy" melodies going through his head—which he frankly admitted were stolen from fragments of other people's tunes. Often the melodies I wrote for his lyrics did not subscribe in time signature or scansion to his concept. For instance, he might have conceived of a melody in 3/4 time, but when I'd finished, it would appear with a 4/4 time signature. For some reason the change always pleased him. Though Oscar was not a musician, he did possess a superb sense of form. He knew everything about the architecture of a song—its foundation, structure, embellishments—and because we always had thorough discussions on the exact kind of music that was needed, this method of collaboration helped us enormously in creating songs that not only were right for the characters who sang them but also possessed a union of words and music that made them sound natural.

The most important member of the production staff of any musical is the director. In Hollywood, Larry and I had worked with Rouben Mamoulian on *Love Me Tonight,* and Oscar and Jerry Kern had worked with him on *High, Wide and Handsome.* Moreover, both Oscar and I realized what a magnificent job he had done on the Theatre Guild's production of the Gershwin opera, *Porgy and Bess.* A musical like ours, we reasoned, required someone who was both creative and not too steeped in the conventions of traditional Broadway musical comedy. Mamoulian seemed ideal.

But not, strangely enough, to Terry and Lawrence. Why? Because he was Russian, and they didn't think he could handle a story about the American Southwest. Oscar and I were dumfounded; my God, if he could direct a story about Negroes living in a Southern ghetto, why couldn't he do an equally good job with cowboys living in Indian Territory? Well, that was different, they said. No, it wasn't, we said. Eventually we got Mamoulian.

Because our story required dances more in the style of ballet than musical comedy, we were on the lookout for someone with a background in classical choreography. Terry had already seen *Rodeo,* sponsored by the Ballet Russe de Monte Carlo, and she raved about the work of a young choreographer named Agnes de Mille. Once Oscar and I saw it, we too felt that she would be just right to handle the dances.

These were the major people in the production end: Terry Helburn and Lawrence Langner, Rouben Mamoulian, Agnes de Mille, Oscar Hammerstein and me. With one exception, none of us had had any Broadway successes recently, and some of us had never had one. Terry and Lawrence freely admitted that the new production was the Theatre Guild's last chance to reverse its dwindling fortunes. Mamoulian had staged only one previous musical on Broadway, and that had been over seven years before. Agnes de Mille's Broadway experience was limited to one show, which had been a flop. Oscar had done nothing memorable since *Music in the Air* ten years before. I was the lone exception in this rather unpromising lineup, and this, according to those supposedly in the know, was the most convincing reason of all why our new venture had no chance of success. Because of my string of hits with Larry Hart, everyone was certain that I could not possibly do well with any other partner.

From the start, Oscar and I were determined that a musical such as ours required actors and singers who had to be right for their parts, regardless of whether or not they were box-office names. Terry Helburn, however, perhaps because of the financial plight of the Guild, felt that the only way to stage a musical was to spend little on scenery and costumes and to concentrate on established stars who could lure both backers and customers. She came up with the likes of Shirley Temple for our heroine and Groucho Marx for the peddler, but Oscar and I held fast, and after some discussion we were able to assemble exactly the kind of cast we wanted.

Auditions began in the fall of 1942. One of the first to try out was Celeste Holm, who had her eye on the part of Ado Annie. Knowing that she had a trained voice, I was surprised that she would want such a hoydenish role. I told her that I wanted to hear her sing as if she had never taken a lesson in her life and was simply a gawky farm girl. That's exactly what she did, even to throwing in a sample of uninhibited hog-calling, and she got the part.

I had seen Joan Roberts before, in a recently produced operetta Oscar had written called *Sunny River,* and she easily won out over Shirley Temple. Alfred Drake, our hero, came right out of my past, since he had been the robust youth who introduced the title song in *Babes in Arms.* Betty Garde, our Aunt Eller, was a well-established character actress, and Joseph Buloff, the peddler, had spent most of his years in the Yiddish theatre.

For the dancing role of Will Parker we cast the boyish-looking Lee Dixon, who had appeared in *Higher and Higher* and had begun his career in Warner Bros. musicals. When we signed him he told us that he had a drinking problem but that he was confident he could control it. He did for a while, but after the show opened he began drinking heavily again and tried to cover up his whiskey breath by eating garlic. The odor made things pretty unpleasant for the other members of the cast, especially for Celeste Holm, with whom he played most of his scenes. After a year and a half he left the show of his own volition.

Initially, both Rouben Mamoulian and Agnes de Mille were determined to maintain their authority within their respective domains. One of their battles was over three girls whom Agnes brought in—Bambi Linn, Joan McCracken and Diana Adams—who were all brilliant dancers and strikingly attractive. For some reason Rouben strongly objected to their being in the show. Agnes got her way, but Rouben retaliated by preempting the stage of our rehearsal theatre for the book rehearsals and forcing Agnes to use whatever other space she could find.

One day Jerome Whyte, whom we had brought over from the George Abbott office to be our chief stage manager, came over to me and said, "Sneak down into the lounge and take a look at what Agnes is doing." There was Agnes, leading her dancers through some of the most dazzling routines I'd ever seen anywhere. If something could look that great in the men's room, I had no doubt it would be breath-taking onstage.

At the beginning, Rouben Mamoulian did not have the security of command that I had remembered from our experience in filming *Love Me Tonight*. His clashes with Agnes were unquestionably a result of this insecurity, and it was further apparent when he flew into a rage upon discovering that Oscar and I had been shown the costume and set designs before he'd seen them. Gradually, though, he settled down, and his brilliance in weaving together the component parts of the musical soon became obvious to us all.

Raising the money to put on this musical was one of our biggest hurdles. Apart from the spotty track record of the people involved, there was the production itself. Who ever heard of a successful "cowboy" musical, as one prospective backer called it? Who wants to see chorus girls in long dresses? What kind of musical keeps the dancers offstage until almost halfway through the first act? Could anyone give a damn about a story whose burning issue was who takes whom to a box social? "C'mon, Dick," my friends kept saying, "go back to Larry. Give us another *Boys from Syracuse* or *By Jupiter* and you'll get all the money you need for the show."

In order to help raise whatever backing we could, Oscar and I—usually with Alfred Drake and Joan Roberts—had to tour the "penthouse circuit," playing our songs and reading from the script. One such evening was held at the palatial home of a woman named Natalie Spencer, a friend of Terry Helburn's. Her apartment was not only large enough to have a ballroom in it, it actually *had* a ballroom in it. There must have been seventy people there to see us audition our material. We even rented a second piano so that Margot Hopkins and I could play four-handed accompaniment. It was an elegant evening of song, story, bright chatter and many complimentary words—but we didn't get a penny from anyone there.

What money we did get came in relatively small figures—a thousand here, five thousand there. One day Terry Helburn got the bright notion of going to Metro-Goldwyn-Mayer with the idea of their putting up the amount still needed. Since M-G-M owned the rights to *Green Grow the Lilacs,* Terry offered them 50 percent of the profits for a $75,000 investment, plus the movie rights for another $75,000. If the show succeeded, they'd get back their initial $75,000 and then some, so the movie rights really wouldn't cost them anything, and if the show failed, it would cost them no more than $75,000, since they wouldn't have to buy the movie rights. Despite the attractiveness of the proposal, the studio turned her down.

Then Terry said to them, "Look, since you're not giving us the money, you're making it impossible for us to get backing from any other studio because you still own the rights to *Green Grow the Lilacs.* Why don't you let us have an option to buy back the rights once the show opens?" This the company agreed to do, but with the proviso that we'd have to exercise the option within thirty days after the New York opening. We did it within thirty hours.

Through our friend Max Gordon, the Broadway producer, we then approached Harry Cohn, the powerful head of Columbia Pictures, with an offer similar to the one Terry had made to M-G-M. When we auditioned the songs for him at Steinway Hall, he was so enthusiastic that he told us that not only would he get Columbia to put up the money but Oscar and I must write the screenplay. Now we were really in business; everyone knew that Harry Cohn always got Columbia to do what he wanted.

This time, however, Columbia balked. The board of directors simply refused to go along with Cohn. To show his good faith, however, Harry put up $15,000 of his own money, which was of enormous help in convincing other investors, and Max Gordon made a sizable investment of his own.

Until the beginning of rehearsals in February 1943, we used the working title of *Green Grow the Lilacs.* We had no intention of keeping it, but we were stumped in coming up with something better. More out of desperation than anything else, we settled on *Away We Go!* The idea of calling the musical *Oklahoma* was mentioned, but we were reluctant to name it after a state. If the show turned out to be a success, fine, but if it was less than a smash, it would seem presumptuous and therefore self-defeating.

Away We Go! opened in New Haven on March 11. There was no advance sale and little publicity, but the reception on opening night was phenomenal. New Haven is not New York, we kept telling ourselves, but we were so encouraged that we tossed caution aside and changed the name to *Oklahoma!* Who should get credit for the title I really can't recall; nor do I remember whose idea it was to add the exclamation mark. It was, however, too late to use the new title in Boston, our next pre-Broadway stop, so we were still stuck with *Away We Go!*

There were few changes in the production between New Haven and Boston. We took out one of the songs, "Boys and Girls Like You and Me," a second-act love duet for the hero and heroine, because it tended to slow down the action. We also changed the song "Oklahoma," the final number in the show, from a solo for Alfred Drake to a rousing chorale for the entire company.

Boston turned out to be even more receptive than New Haven. We were all still concerned, however; nothing is "in" until it reaches New York. Many a show has been ruined by complacency because of favorable reactions on the road, and many others have been ruined by too much tinkering because a critic or a stagehand thinks it needs work. Yet with this particular production I was always confident that everything was going to work out. If anything, Dorothy was even more optimistic. I remember a run-through early in March while we were still in rehearsal. There were no costumes or scenery and the only accompaniment was a piano. Some people in the audience, including Dorothy, left immediately after the performance while I spent the next few hours at a production meeting. When I got home, on the pillow of my bed was a message which read: "Darling, This is the best musical show I have ever seen. Love."

Though things were going beautifully in Boston, the Broadway savants who'd gone to New Haven were apparently unwilling or unable to believe what they saw and heard around them, and they quickly spread the word that the show wouldn't make it. There was a celebrated remark, "No legs, no jokes, no chance," quoted in Walter Winchell's column. Somehow people got the mistaken idea that he'd made it up, but he had used it merely to show how wrong the Broadway crowd had been about *Oklahoma!*'s chances. The man generally believed to have originated the line was producer Michael Todd. Everyone knew that he had left in the middle of the show in New Haven. Later he apologized to me, explaining that a friend of his was in jail in New York and he had to rush back to bail him out.

But I didn't let anything get me down. In Boston we were playing at the Colonial Theatre, just across the street from the Common. At night after each performance, Terry, Lawrence, Oscar and I used to walk back to the Ritz-Carlton, where we were all staying. Whenever one of the others would express doubts about our prospects, I'd point out—song by song and scene by scene—that it simply couldn't miss. Never before had I had the assignment of keeping up the morale of the troops, but that's exactly what I found myself doing during this period.

Our opening in New York took place on March 31, 1943, at the St. James Theatre. Just as I knew it would, the audience responded to everything. Not only could I see it and hear it, I could feel it. From the time Alfred Drake began the opening bars of "Oh, What a Beautiful Mornin' " to the last exultant chorus of "Oklahoma," everything really was going our way.

After the final curtain we all went over to Sardi's to await the *New York Times* review. As we jostled our way into the restaurant, I suddenly saw a little man break through the crowd. It was Larry. Grinning from ear to ear, he threw his arms around me. "Dick," he said, "I've never had a better evening in my life! This show will still be around twenty years from now!" And I knew he meant it.

We'd been at Sardi's a little over an hour when the phone call came from our press agent, who read us the *Times* review. Lewis Nichols, who had succeeded Brooks Atkinson as the paper's drama critic for the duration of the war, gave us our first rave. "Wonderful is the nearest adjective," he wrote, "for this excursion combines a fresh and infectious gaiety, a charm of manner, beautiful acting, singing and dancing, and a score which does not do any harm either, since it is one of Rodgers' best."

Now even the last lingering doubts were removed. We whooped it up a little more at Sardi's, and then left for the party Jules Glaenzer was throwing for the entire cast. As I walked into his apartment Jules asked me if I wanted a drink. "No, thanks, Jules," I said. "I'm not going to touch a drop. I want to remember every second of this night!" I didn't have anything stronger than ginger ale the whole evening.

Our opening night had not been sold out completely, but the rave notices in the press guaranteed that the line at the box office would start queuing up early. Oscar and I went to the theatre the next day around noon, and it was bedlam. Everyone was pushing and shoving to get to the box office. There was even a policeman trying to keep order.

Since Oscar and I had made an appointment for lunch, I asked him, "Shall we sneak off to someplace quiet where we can talk, or shall we go to Sardi's and show off?"

"Hell, let's go to Sardi's and show off," said Oscar, and we did. From the moment we walked in until we left, everyone kept crowding around us, congratulating us, hugging us, kissing us, telling us they were on their way to buy tickets—or asking us to get them some—all the while assuring us that they'd known right from the start that the show would be a hit.

I have long held a theory about musicals. When a show works perfectly, it's because all the individual parts complement each other and fit together. No single element overshadows any other. In a great musical, the orchestrations sound the way the costumes look. That's what made *Oklahoma!* work. All the components dovetailed. There was nothing extraneous or foreign, nothing that pushed itself into the spotlight yelling "Look at me!" It was a work created by many that gave the impression of having been created by one.

In addition, *Oklahoma!* had two external factors working for it. In the spring of 1943 the Broadway musical stage was not enjoying the best of health. *By Jupiter* was still running, as was *Something for the Boys,* starring Ethel Merman. So much for conventional musical comedy. In addition, there was Olsen and Johnson's raucous revue, *Sons o' Fun;* a glorified burlesque show called *Star and Garter;* a vaudeville show called *Show Time;* a new version of *Die Fledermaus* called *Rosalinda;* and an ice show called *Stars on Ice.* That was the competition. Even if *Oklahoma!* had been created less skillfully, it would have stood out in this company.

Then there was the fact that we were in the midst of a devastating war. People could come to see *Oklahoma!* and derive not only pleasure but a measure of optimism. It dealt with pioneers in the Southwest, it showed their spirit and the kinds of problems they had to overcome in carving out a new state, and it gave citizens an appreciation of the hardy stock from which they'd sprung. People said to themselves, in effect, "If this is what our country looked and sounded like at the turn of the century, perhaps once the war is over we can again return to this kind of buoyant, optimistic life."

It was also extremely gratifying to have written music for this production that people so obviously enjoyed singing. This was brought home in a very personal way just two mornings after the show's Broadway opening. My family was in the country and I had to spend the night at a hotel just off Park Avenue. I was awakened in the morning by the sun streaming through my window and the sound of children singing something familiar. I looked down into the courtyard and there was a group of kids singing "Oh, What a Beautiful Mornin'." The show had just opened and they knew the song already! What a lovely feeling it was to realize that I was reaching not only the theatregoing adults but their children as well.

Oklahoma! was more than just another Broadway success. It was an event, something that transcended theatre, music, dance or anything confined to a specific production in a specific place. I was forty at the time, with a number of hit shows behind me, but nothing had ever remotely compared to this. It was a rebirth, both in my associations and in my career.

What kept going around in my head was the title of a once best-selling book called *Life Begins at Forty.*

Everyone, it seemed, just had to see *Oklahoma!,* and people outdid themselves in making up stories about how hard it was to get tickets. I do know one story whose truth I'll vouch for. Oscar had a farmer working for him in Doylestown whose son was about to get married. The farmer wanted to give the couple a pair of tickets as a wedding gift, the idea being that they would see the show following the wedding ceremony. Of course Oscar promised to get the tickets, and asked when the wedding would take place. "The day you can get the tickets," the farmer replied.

Right from the start, there was considerable competition for the rights to record the songs from the show. None of the offers appealed to Oscar or me until Jack Kapp, the president of Decca Records, came to us with a revolutionary idea. He wanted to use our cast, our conductor and our orchestra to reproduce on records the same musical program that people heard in the theatre. It was the most exciting recording concept we'd ever heard of, and naturally we consented. From *Oklahoma!* on, the original-cast album has become a major by-product of Broadway musicals, but this was the first time it had been done.

Another first for me was that the Guild sent out a road company while the New York company was still performing. The tour began in New Haven in October 1943 and ended ten and a half years later in Philadelphia. In all, it played over 150 cities in the United States and Canada, with many return engagements. The London company, which began its stay in April 1947, was also assembled by the Theatre Guild, with our stage manager, Jerry Whyte, as the on-the-scene producer.

In 1944 the Pulitzer Committee awarded a special drama prize to *Oklahoma!* The reason for this unusual citation was that word had spread that I was to be the recipient of the prize in music, an honor that I did not feel I could accept without sharing it with Oscar. Therefore the special award to *Oklahoma!* was given as something of a compromise.

It wasn't until November 1946 that the road company of *Oklahoma!* gave its first performance in Oklahoma. Governor Robert Kerr decided to turn the event into a statewide celebration, and invited Terry Helburn, the Lawrence Langners, Agnes de Mille, Lynn Riggs, Rouben Mamoulian, the Oscar Hammersteins and Dorothy and me to participate. A private railroad car transported us to Oklahoma City, where we were met by the governor, who put us all in a surrey with a fringe on top for the ride to the hotel. That morning there was to be a mammoth parade, with no fewer than forty-seven marching bands and thousands of Indians on horseback. Just as we were leaving the hotel to watch this spectacle, however, the weather suddenly changed into a sleet storm. They canceled the parade not, we were advised, because the kids who had been let off from school might catch pneumonia, but because the horses might slip and break their legs.

The performance of the show went on that night as scheduled and was followed by a formal ball in our honor. We were also made honorary Kiowa Indians, and each of us was presented with a chief's headdress. As if that wasn't enough, a few years later they made "Oklahoma" the official state song. Our show was apparently a great morale booster for citizens of the state who had long been stigmatized by the words "dust bowl" and "Okies," and they did everything they could to show their appreciation.

On December 4, 1947, we passed the 2,000th-performance mark on Broadway, a milestone then unheard of for a musical. Since I've always enjoyed conducting my own music, I took over the baton that evening for the second act. After it was over, members of the company complained that I took the tempos too fast—and they were right.

Perhaps of all the pleasures associated with *Oklahoma!* the one that gave me the greatest satisfaction was an arrangement we made to give forty-four special matinées for the armed forces. No one paid to get in and no one was paid to work, and everyone connected with the show always looked forward to these performances.

Oklahoma! did, of course, have an effect on the musicals that came after it. Everyone suddenly became "integration"-conscious, as if the idea of welding together song, story and dance had never been thought of before. There were also a number of costume musicals, and no self-respecting production dared open without at least one "serious" ballet.

But in a broader sense I feel that the chief influence of *Oklahoma!* was simply to serve notice that when writers came up with something different, and if it had merit, there would be a large and receptive audience waiting for it. Librettists, lyricists and composers now had a new incentive to explore a multitude of themes and techniques within the framework of the commercial musical theatre. From *Oklahoma!* on, with only rare exceptions, the memorable productions have been those daring to break free of the conventional mold. Freedom is the sunniest climate for creativity, and *Oklahoma!* certainly contributed to that climate.

The world outside was still torn by devastating warfare, but my little world within the theatre in 1943 brought me nothing but happiness. Still, there was someone tugging at my conscience: Larry Hart. Following *Oklahoma!* I very much wanted to continue the partnership with Oscar Hammerstein, but it was impossible to make a clean break with Larry. I even fantasized that the shock of *Oklahoma!*'s success might provoke him to getting back to work and possibly keep him from destroying himself. Ours was a one-way partnership in the sense that while I could work with another lyricist, it was inconceivable for Larry to work with another composer.

Oscar understood my apprehension about Larry; in fact, at about this time he became preoccupied with a separate project of his own. For some years he had been obsessed with the idea of turning Bizet's opera *Carmen* into an updated Broadway musical with an all-black cast. He called it *Carmen Jones,* and following the reception of *Oklahoma!,* he had little difficulty in securing Billy Rose as producer.

Since the rest of the year found Oscar involved with Bizet, it left me free to try to work again with Larry. But what could we do? Because of the endless problems I'd had with him in our most recent shows, I was afraid of attempting a new one that would be too much for him to handle.

One day I discussed the matter with Herb Fields, and together we hit on a solution of sorts: a revival of *A Connecticut Yankee,* with Larry's dear friend Vivienne Segal in the role of Morgan LeFay. But it wouldn't be just a word-for-word, note-for-note revival of the sixteen-year-old show. It would have new dialogue and half a dozen new songs augmenting the more familiar numbers from the original. In this way, we thought, Larry would not be overburdened; it would be familiar territory for him, he'd be working with people he liked, and most important, it might prove therapeutic for him. At least that was the idea.

Larry behaved beautifully during the months we spent preparing the show. He would come up to stay at our place in Connecticut and we'd work regularly at reasonable hours. I don't think he took a drink the entire time. There was no question that he was making a genuine effort to rehabilitate himself and to prove that the team of Rodgers and Hart was still a going concern. As a result he turned out some of the most charming and witty lyrics he had ever written, including "To Keep My Love Alive," a riotous account of the way Queen Morgan LeFay got rid of all her husbands.

But once rehearsals were over and there was nothing further for Larry to do, he simply caved in. All those months of self-denial had taken a lot out of him and he could no longer resist his thirst. He had proved that he could still work, but in so doing, he had stretched his nerves to the breaking point. The night *A Connecticut Yankee* opened in Philadelphia, Larry went on a drinking binge from which he never recovered. He'd always had the habit of leaving his coat and hat in bars, and since it rained or snowed almost every day that week, this only accelerated his physical deterioration.

On the show's opening night in New York, I was so worried about Larry that I instructed two men from our company to stand near him as he weaved back and forth in the rear of the theatre. My concern was not only for his health but for what he might do to cause a disruption of the performance onstage. As it turned out, this concern was well founded. Suddenly, in the middle of the first act, he began talking incoherently to the actors, at which point the men standing near him simply picked him up and took him home.

Two days later Willy Kron, Larry's friend and financial adviser, came up to me in the back of the theatre and said, "Larry has pneumonia. Probably more like double pneumonia. He's a very sick man."

"Willy," I said, "Larry isn't just sick. He's dying."

This time, I knew, he would never recover. But we did what we could. We got him to Doctors Hospital, but all his strength had been sapped and his resistance was gone. On the night of November 22, 1943, Dorothy, Larry's doctor and I had dinner at the hospital restaurant. None of us could eat or say very much, for we all knew that the end was not far off. When we returned upstairs, a dozen of his friends were in the corridor, none saying a word. Larry was in a coma.

Since we were at war at the time, there were air alerts and practice blackouts. Suddenly the wailing of sirens broke the hospital stillness, and the entire building, except for shaded emergency lights, went dark. One of these lights was in Larry's room because he was getting oxygen. All of us stood there in the darkness outside his room, our eyes on the door. Presently the doctor came out of the room, and as he told us that Larry was dead, we heard the all-clear siren and the lights throughout the hospital immediately came on again.

We may scoff, of course, but everyone has a natural inclination to believe in signs and portents and to attribute ordinary occurrences to psychic phenomena. To those of us in the hospital that night, the lights going on again at that moment was some sort of cosmic assurance that the darkness which had always surrounded Larry had suddenly disappeared— that in death he could at last enjoy the warmth and brightness that had eluded him all his life.

17

O ne evening during the run of *Oklahoma!* I got a telephone call from Sam Goldwyn, who was at the show and was calling during intermission. He asked me to meet him at the theatre after the performance and go out for a drink. An hour later I took a taxi to the St. James just as the people were streaming out of the theatre. Sam was walking up the aisle, and when he saw me he danced over and planted a kiss on my cheek.

"This is such a wonderful show!" he bubbled. "I just had to see you to give you some advice. You know what you should do next?"

"What?"

"Shoot yourself!"

This was Sam's blunt but funny way of telling me that I'd never create another show as good as *Oklahoma!* What to do after a hit is always a problem, though the magnitude of *Oklahoma!*'s success made the problem greater than at any time in the past. Still, there was never any thought of quitting. I knew it wouldn't be easy, but *Oklahoma!* was finished. If I had become absorbed in trying to duplicate what I had just done, nothing would have been accomplished; I would have been immobilized. The only solution was to move ahead, doing my damnedest to be as good as I possibly could be, without dwelling on any of the head-turning events that had happened in the past.

The revival of *A Connecticut Yankee* was only a stopgap production which gave me a chance to catch my breath and to help postpone a dear friend's drinking himself to death. My main objective following *Oklahoma!* was to establish a strong working relationship with Oscar. But it wasn't simply a matter of deciding what show to write next. Right from the start, our partnership embraced a number of varied but related projects.

The first was publishing. Even before rehearsals of *Oklahoma!* had begun, we wanted to show our faith in the production in a very concrete way: we decided to publish the score. We went up to Bronxville, where Max Dreyfus lived, to discuss the matter with him, since he had been Oscar's publisher as well as mine during most of our careers. Max was highly receptive to the idea, and we arranged to form a company in partnership with his own company, Chappell. Thus, Williamson Music came into existence with *Oklahoma!*—which wasn't a bad way to begin. As to the name of our firm, since Oscar and I were both sons of men named William, it seemed a fitting way to pay our respects to our fathers.

Oscar and I never had any kind of agreement to continue together after we had finished *Oklahoma!,* but I felt strongly that it would be wrong— once *Carmen Jones* and *A Connecticut Yankee* were out of the way—for us to split up even temporarily. One morning I heard that Oscar's lawyer, who by then was also my lawyer, was trying to line up a new musical for Oscar to write with Jerry Kern, another one of his clients. This so upset me that I went to see the lawyer and told him how I felt.

That afternoon I had lunch with Oscar at Dinty Moore's, and he brought up the matter. I told him of my conviction that it would be a serious mistake, except in an emergency, for either of us to do anything professional without the other. Oscar was in complete agreement.

"Then we can consider this a permanent partnership?" I said.

"As permanent as any partnership can be."

And it was, for the seventeen remaining years of Oscar's life.

At first, since *Oklahoma!* was still playing to packed houses, we didn't want to step on our own heels by writing a new musical. However, we were anxious to keep active in the theatre and also to establish our names as a team. This led to our becoming producers. Dorothy had read a novel by Kathryn Forbes called *Mama's Bank Account,* and she thought it could be successfully adapted as a play. Oscar and I thought so too, and we quickly obtained the dramatic rights. To write the adaptation we chose John Van Druten, who'd had a tremendous success the previous year with a three-character comedy called *The Voice of the Turtle.* In John's skilled hands, *Mama's Bank Account* was transformed into *I Remember Mama,* which, with Mady Christians giving a memorable performance, became one of the Broadway successes of 1944.

Now that Oscar and I were in the business end of the theatre, we were expected to act like businessmen. The first step was to open our own offices, which we did at 1270 Sixth Avenue. Morris Jacobs, a feisty, highly skilled theatre pro, joined us as general manager, and remained with the firm until his retirement in 1971.

I Remember Mama made it two in a row for Rodgers and Hammerstein. Though I can't say it gave us the heady excitement of writing a musical, producing a play had its own gratifications, particularly because our first effort was a success.

It was inevitable that eventually we would receive an offer from a film studio. 20th Century-Fox, which was planning a musical remake of its ten-year-old hit *State Fair,* was interested in having Oscar and me write the score. We went to a special screening of the movie at the studio's Fifty-sixth Street office, and were immediately won over. We made sure, though, that our contract included one provision. Because of our multiple activities in

New York, we had no intention of spending an extended length of time in Hollywood, and we insisted that we be allowed to write the songs in the East. Though they found the request a bit unusual, the studio people agreed; the story, which was set in Iowa, would be filmed in California, while the music and lyrics would be written in Fairfield, Connecticut, and Doylestown, Pennsylvania.

It turned out to be a satisfactory arrangement all around. The only disagreement we had with the company was over the proper tempo for the song "It Might as Well Be Spring." I had written the music at a bright, medium tempo, and the studio's musical director wanted it done as a slow ballad. We argued the matter until the studio promised to reshoot the number if it did not go over well at a preview performance. After the preview they telephoned us to say that the song had been enthusiastically received and that it would be a serious mistake to change it. There was no point in pushing the matter any further, so we reluctantly agreed. Later, when we saw the picture, we had to admit that they were right and we were wrong.

The song itself deserves some additional comment, both on its lyric and on its music. Initially Oscar had planned to write about a girl with spring fever, but then he discovered that state fairs are held only in the fall. This gave him a far more original idea: the self-portrait of a girl who shows all the symptoms of spring fever even though it isn't spring. As for the melody, it is a good example of the way a tune can amplify the meaning of its lyric. The first lines are: "I'm as restless as a willow in a wind storm, / I'm as jumpy as a puppet on a string." Taking its cue directly from these words, the music itself is appropriately restless and jumpy. Moreover, since the song is sung by a young girl who can't quite understand why she feels the way she does, I deliberately ended the phrase on the uncertain sound of the F natural (on the word "string") rather than on the more positive F sharp:

One unusual aspect of our work for *State Fair* was that after we had completed the score, we were told that Darryl F. Zanuck, then the head of 20th Century-Fox, wanted to see us in Hollywood before shooting was to begin. Since the company had been extremely cooperative in letting us do the job the way we wanted, it would have been ungracious to refuse— particularly as we were to be guests of the studio for a week and they were even thoughtful enough to invite our wives. Obviously there must be important things that Zanuck wanted to discuss with us that required a face-to-face meeting.

So the Hammersteins and the Rodgerses got on the cross-country train and spent a week in Hollywood. The accommodations were elegant, we met friends, attended some parties and saw a few screen tests of actors who were being considered for roles in the film. It wasn't until the day before we were to return home that Oscar and I were at last summoned by Zanuck. We were ushered into his pale-green office and there he was, riding crop across his lap, sitting behind a huge desk chewing on a huge cigar. And what did we talk about? Actually, I can't recall that Oscar or I said much. For twenty minutes Zanuck held center stage as he reminisced about his recent wartime experiences in North Africa. Then, when our allotted time was over, he rose, we rose, and we were ushered out of the office. We never saw him again.

Why was Zanuck so anxious to have us travel three thousand miles to see him after we had completed our work? Largely, I think, it was a matter of pride and muscle. He had paid us a lot of money and had acceded to our working conditions, but he wanted the satisfaction of being able to make us do as he wished. It was one more example of the kind of ego-satisfying extravagance that eventually helped contribute to the downfall of the Hollywood studio system.

Publishing songs, producing plays and writing songs for moving pictures were profitable and challenging enterprises, but Oscar and I never thought of ourselves as anything but writers for the Broadway musical theatre. After spreading our wings in diverse fields, we were anxious to get back to our first order of business.

Again what interested us was an idea that originated with Terry Helburn and Lawrence Langner. In 1921 the Theatre Guild had produced a play called *Liliom* by the Hungarian playwright Ferenc Molnár. Simply put, Terry and Lawrence felt that Oscar and I could do for *Liliom* what we had already done for *Green Grow the Lilacs*.

But this time we said no. A musical *Liliom* seemed totally impossible. It was a fantasy, which always presents problems; it was set in Budapest, and neither Oscar nor I had any feeling for the locale; it had a bitter, pessimistic ending that was unsuitable for a musical; and it was a recognized theatre classic which was continually being revived without any help from a songwriting team. Besides, what about Molnár himself? It was common knowledge that he'd already turned down offers from both Puccini and Gershwin to adapt his work for the musical stage.

But Terry and Lawrence were persistent. It didn't have to be set in Budapest, they pointed out; it could be anywhere we wanted. Terry suggested changing it to New Orleans, but that didn't seem right either. Eventually, I threw in the idea of relocating the story in New England, which somehow won unanimous agreement. We could always alter the ending, of course. In the play, the dead father returns to earth and slaps his daughter, which she feels as if it were a kiss. Certainly we could strengthen the importance of the man's return in helping to give the girl a more optimistic view of life. We couldn't do much about the fact that *Liliom* was an internationally celebrated play, but we were impressed to learn that Molnár, after having seen a performance of *Oklahoma!,* had voiced his approval of Oscar and me as possible adapters.

But there was still a major problem: what kind of music to write and where should it go? How do you sing *Liliom*? Oscar and I kept reading and rereading the play, searching for clues. Suddenly we got the notion for a soliloquy in which, at the end of the first act, the leading character would reveal his varied emotions about impending fatherhood. That broke the ice. Once we could visualize the man singing, we felt that all the other problems would fall into place. And somehow they did.

Though the bittersweet fantasy of *Carousel,* the name we gave our musical, was far different from the sunny pleasures of *Oklahoma!,* we assembled the same basic team to put it together. We reasoned—rightly, as it turned out—that with *Oklahoma!* behind them, both director Rouben Mamoulian and choreographer Agnes de Mille would feel secure enough to work smoothly together this time. We also decided that we would again have a cast consisting largely of unknown actors. Armina Marshall, Lawrence Langner's wife, had heard a singer named John Raitt in California and sent him East to audition for *Oklahoma!* He was a big, brawny fellow with a magnificent baritone who would be perfect either for Curly in *Oklahoma!* or Billy Bigelow (the name we gave Liliom) in *Carousel*—so we agreed to cast him as both. Since we weren't yet ready to begin rehearsals for *Carousel,* we put him in the Chicago company of *Oklahoma!* just to keep him busy. Jan Clayton, equally unknown, was cast as the heroine.

Preparations for *Carousel* were in welcome contrast to those we'd had to undergo for *Oklahoma!* We had no money or reputation worries. I won't say that *Carousel* was easier to put together than *Oklahoma!,* but it certainly was easier for Oscar and me to work with the people putting it together. And I think they found it easier to work with us.

Again, as in *Oklahoma!*, Oscar went directly to the text of the original play for his ideas. For example, the main love duet, "If I Loved You," evolved from the following dialogue in *Liliom:*

LILIOM: But you wouldn't dare to marry any one like me, would you?
JULIE: I know that . . . that . . . if I loved any one . . . it wouldn't make any difference to me what he . . . even if I died for it.
LILIOM: But you wouldn't marry a rough guy like me—that is . . . eh . . . if you loved me—
JULIE: Yes, I would . . . if I loved you, Mr. Liliom.

The dialogue is like this throughout the scene—awkward, hesitant, slightly disconnected—as the two leading characters try to express their feelings. Oscar caught the mood in a lyric that eloquently expressed the emotions of these two young people, even having the girl admit:

If I loved you,
Time and again I would try to say
All I'd want you to know.
If I loved you,
Words wouldn't come in an easy way—
'Round in circles I'd go!

For the overture to *Carousel* I decided not to have an overture. I had become weary—I still am, in fact—of the sound that comes out of an orchestra pit during an overture. All that is ever heard is the brass because the orchestra never has a sufficient number of strings, and the audience must make a concerted effort to pick up any melody that is not blasted. Instead I tried to avoid this problem by making the audience pay attention, which I did simply by opening on a pantomime scene, with the orchestra playing a single piece, the "Carousel Waltz," rather than the usual medley. In this way we also gave the audience an emotional feeling for the characters in the story and helped to establish the mood for the entire play.

As for the "Soliloquy," which had played such an important part in our doing the show in the first place, it turned out to be an unusually lengthy number which took Oscar two weeks to write. Of course we had discussed the kind of music for the song ever since we'd begun the project, so that once I had Oscar's words before me, it did not take long to create the music.

Which brings up a point I'd like to emphasize. Whenever I get an idea for a song, even before jotting down the notes, I can hear it in the orchestra, I can smell it in the scenery, I can see the kind of actor who will sing it, and I am aware of an audience listening to it. When we began discussing the "Soliloquy" well before either of us did any writing, I asked Oscar, "How would this be for the music?" At the piano I gave him an idea—not the actual melody, but the general tone, color and emotion I thought would be appropriate. I know this helped him when he wrote the words, and it certainly helped me when I wrote the music.

"You'll Never Walk Alone," which was used in the play to give hope and strength both to the heroine, Julie, and to her daughter, has become something of a universally accepted hymn. Fred Waring once told me a remarkable story about it. His mother had died in a small town in Pennsylvania, and he went home for the funeral. It was a thoroughly miserable day, with leaden clouds hanging ominously over the entire sky. Among the musical pieces chosen for the service, which was held in the local church, was "You'll Never Walk Alone." The choir sang, the organist played and the melody ascended step by step until it reached the climax, the syllable "nev-" in the final line, "You'll never walk alone." Just as the singers hit that climactic note, the sun broke through the clouds, streamed through the stained-glass windows and cast a beam directly on the coffin. The entire congregation was so overcome that everyone, as if on cue, let out a spontaneous, audible gasp.

On the day of the first run-through of the play, I was sitting next to Oscar midway in the orchestra. For some reason I happened to turn around. There, in the back of the theatre, his coat draped around his shoulders and a monocle stuck in his right eye, sat Ferenc Molnár. We had never met before, no one had given any indication that he'd be there, and I was terrified.

"Don't look now," I whispered to Oscar, "but Molnár is sitting in the last row." We both began to sweat. Nothing looked or sounded right that afternoon. Whatever we saw was through Molnár's haughty gaze; whatever we heard was through his disapproving ears. I began making mental lists of excuses and explanations. One thing I was certain he would hate was our new ending. In order to give the story some measure of hope, we'd changed the scene to a high-school graduation in which Louise, the unhappy, frightened daughter of the leading characters, is encouraged by her dead father to heed the words of the song "You'll Never Walk Alone." Just before the ending, the girl sitting next to Louise shyly puts her arm around her, they smile, and we know that Louise will no longer be afraid. This so completely changed the spirit of the original that we awaited a humiliating dressing-down from the playwright.

When the run-through ended, I nudged Oscar. "Well, we might as well face it. Let's meet Molnár." We walked to the back of the theatre and Lawrence Langner introduced us.

Molnár opened his mouth and the monocle popped out of his eye. "What you have done," he said, "is so beautiful. And you know what I like best? The ending!"

It was better than a rave notice in the *Times*.

Thereafter Molnár came to almost every rehearsal. Only once did he express an opinion. That was after Mamoulian had directed a big scene and had jumped down from the stage to look at it from the viewpoint of the audience. As he headed back for the stage, a voice called out, "Mr. Mamoulian, please." There was dead silence as Mamoulian walked over to where the playwright was sitting. "Mr. Mamoulian," Molnár said, his face wreathed in a smile, "when you direct a large scene with a lot of people, you make it look as though there were twice as many people. You handle crowds better than any director I've ever known." Rouben beamed. "And, Mr. Mamoulian," Molnár continued, "when you have a love scene, you bring out such tenderness, such feeling. I've never known anybody who did it so well." By now Rouben was positively glowing. "But, Mr. Mamoulian" —and here Molnár's voice suddenly turned to ice and Rouben's jaw dropped—"but, Mr. Mamoulian, there is one thing I do not like. You smoke too much."

Our New Haven opening in March 1945 went well except for the scene in which we depicted a "Mr. and Mrs. God" as a New England minister and his wife. Oscar rewrote the scene and substituted the Starkeeper. The other major change was to add a reprise of "If I Loved You" in the second act because we felt it needed more music.

When one is preoccupied with a new show the work becomes so all-consuming that it tends to block out all personal considerations. I've always tried to guard against this, particularly in my relationship with my wife, because I know that Dorothy has contributed vitally to whatever success I have achieved, even though she has always had her own activities and interests. Among her accomplishments, she not only started the business called Repairs, Inc., which I mentioned earlier, she also invented a toilet cleaner aptly known as a Jonny-Mop and devised a basic dress-pattern fabric which she sold to McCall's.

Still, despite an extremely heavy schedule, Dorothy was never reconciled to the necessity of my leaving without her whenever I had to go out of town with a new production. At the time I was in Boston with *Carousel,* she wrote me a letter which, though full of warm praise and encouragement, voiced the normal reactions of a wife who felt she was being a bit shut out. This was my answer:

THE RITZ-CARLTON
Boston 17, Massachusetts

April 3, 1945

Darling,

Now I can write you because last night we had a SHOW! I'm a
very cautious kid, as you know, but there are certain bits of evidence
that cannot be refuted. Best of all, I know how I feel, and I feel that
there are many moments of extreme beauty here and that the public
will want to see and hear them.

Which brings me to your letter. It would be disingenuous to say
that I disagree with your feelings that my work is improving. There
are many reasons for this, and we've discussed most of them. But I
think it's awfully important to both of us to recognize the part you play
in my work. If the things a man writes are an expression of his personality (and they can't be anything else), then what greater influence can
his personality and his writings have than a woman with whom he has
lived for fifteen years? It's terribly important for you to understand and
remember that. It's *your* name on the program or in the newspaper,
and its meaning goes far deeper than a bow to custom. When an
audience applauds something I've done, you are certainly entitled to
a gracious nod of the head and I think you ought to do it. I recognize
and understand the demands of your own ego. You wouldn't be worth
much without it, but the next time you feel shut out of things try to
realize that you never can be, any more than Mary and Linda can ever
stop being the children of both of us.

To this testimony of devotion I set my hand and seal this 3d day
of April, 1945.

In other words, I'm crazy about you.

Dick

The Boston tryout was clouded by the death of President Roosevelt.
No one who lived through the Roosevelt years can ever forget the day it
happened, or the strangely personal loss that was felt throughout the country.

I was in the Colonial Theatre holding understudy auditions when our
musical director, Joseph Littau, crawled through the rows of seats and
whispered the news in my ear. He didn't want to interrupt the auditions,
but when word got around, everyone was so upset that we canceled them.
We were undecided about giving a performance that evening, but after
checking on what other shows were doing, we decided to go ahead. I

remember telephoning Dorothy as soon as I could get out of the theatre. We could hardly speak; all we did was cry over the phone.

Immediately following the Boston tryout I had a strange accident that put me on my back for several weeks. I was returning to my home in Fairfield via train and got off at the Bridgeport station, where Dorothy and Mary were waiting for me. Because of the war, there weren't any porters, and I had to lug my two heavy bags to my car. I suffered no ill effects that night, but the next morning when I got up I coughed. With that I felt a pain in my back that was so excruciating that I simply collapsed on the floor. I had wrenched one of my lumbar vertebrae. The doctor told me I had to stay in bed, but I wanted to be at the final dress rehearsal in New York. Dorothy drove me from Fairfield to the Volney Hotel, which was then our city residence. I was in bed for several days, and on the night of the dress rehearsal I was taken by ambulance to the Majestic Theatre. There I was laid out, on a stretcher in the middle of the center aisle, from which position I conducted the rehearsal as best I could.

The following night, the opening, I again was taken to the theatre via ambulance. The Majestic has curtains that descend from the upper boxes, and I was placed, still on my stretcher, behind the ones on the left-hand side. From this biased position I could see only part of the stage, but since I was drugged with morphine, I could not have appreciated what was happening even if I'd had the best seat in the house. In fact, so fortified was I against pain that I was also unaware of the laughter and applause, and was convinced that the show was a dismal failure. It was only afterward, when people came over to me—making me feel like an Egyptian mummy on display—that I realized that *Carousel* had been enthusiastically received.

Molnár was there, too, of course, as proud and as happy as if he had written the adaptation himself, and I introduced him to Morty. "He may be your brother," Molnár said to Morty, patting my hand, "but he is my son."

One of the most frequent questions I am asked is: "What is your favorite of all your musicals?" My answer is *Carousel*. Oscar never wrote more meaningful or more moving lyrics, and to me, my score is more satisfying than any I've ever written. But it's not just the songs; it's the whole play. Beautifully written, tender without being mawkish, it affects me deeply every time I see it performed.

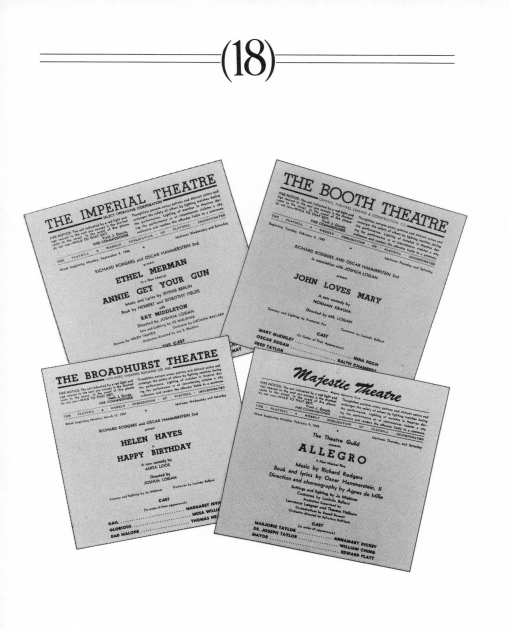

18

I cannot speak with authority about any other field, but I've always felt that a theatrical production is a success or failure the moment someone says, in effect, "Let's do a show about . . ." Given the fact that the people involved are at least competent in writing, casting and producing, this is where everything starts and ends. If the "about" is a bad idea, no matter what is done with it, the show is almost certain to fail. If it's a good idea, there have to be almost catastrophic mistakes to keep it from being a success.

One morning Dorothy Fields and her brother Herb came to see Oscar and me in our office and asked, "What do you think of Ethel Merman in a show about Annie Oakley?" Without hesitation we answered, "Go home and write it and we'll produce it." It was a one-sentence suggestion and a one-sentence acceptance. With Dorothy and Herb writing it, with Merman playing the colorful sharpshooter, there was no way the show could fail.

The idea of our writing the score was never brought up because neither Oscar nor I thought we were the right ones for it. We had been going in a certain direction with *Oklahoma!* and *Carousel,* and this did not seem to be along the same path. Besides, since Dorothy Fields was a highly skilled lyricist, she naturally expected to collaborate on the score. Choosing a composer was easy; Oscar's friendship with Jerome Kern and my near idolatry of him dictated the selection.

Kern's most recent Broadway musical had been *Very Warm for May,* which he wrote with Oscar in 1939. Although he was reasonably active in Hollywood, where he was now living, he had made it clear that he was anxious to return to Broadway if the right project could be found. We mailed him a script and I sent him a wire: IT WOULD BE ONE OF THE GREATEST HONORS IN MY LIFE IF YOU WOULD CONSENT TO WRITE THE MUSIC FOR THIS SHOW. Soon afterward we received an enthusiastic response.

Jerry arrived in New York early in November 1945, and had been in the city for three days when he suddenly collapsed on a sidewalk, suffering from a cerebral hemorrhage. An ambulance was quickly summoned. Going through his wallet, the attendant found an ASCAP membership card and called the society to say that he was taking Kern to the Welfare Island Hospital. Someone at ASCAP had the presence of mind to get in touch with Oscar, who was then with me at a meeting of the Dramatists Guild at the St. Regis Hotel. When we were notified of what had happened, we got a cab and rushed over to the hospital.

Jerry had been put in a regular charity ward, and I was frankly apprehensive of entering it, not knowing the conditions that would exist in such a place. To my surprise, it was spotlessly clean, and the fifty or so other patients—mostly derelicts and alcoholics—were all very quiet. We soon found out that the doctor in charge had already told them who Jerry was and had requested that they behave themselves. He was getting exceptionally good care, but his wife, Eva, did not want him in a public institution and insisted that he be taken to Doctors Hospital. But there was really nothing to be done for him, and within a few days he was dead.

I never knew Jerry Kern well. He wasn't really an easy person to know, partly because his wife was so overprotective. A year or so before his death I was going to the Coast, and Max Dreyfus, who had been his publisher long before he became mine, asked me to see Jerry because he had recently suffered two strokes and Max was concerned about him. In Hollywood, Eva kept putting me off, which of course only made me fear the worst. Finally, when we did meet, I was delighted to find him in good health. His mind was alert, he moved without difficulty, and we chatted beside his swimming pool for most of the afternoon.

Kern's death affected me deeply, primarily because of what his music had meant to me ever since I'd been a teen-ager scurrying up to the balcony to sit absorbed in the wonders of his earliest shows. No matter what I myself accomplished, I always felt I was continuing to build the same kind of musical theatre that Kern had helped to create. To me, the greatest gratification allowed anyone is to be able to gather a large group of people under one roof, and through words and music, impel them to feel something deeply and strongly within themselves. This was Kern's mission and he accomplished it superbly.

Once the shock of Jerry's death had faded, Oscar and I were faced with the problem of finding a composer to replace him on the Annie Oakley musical. Having already chosen Kern, we felt it was extremely important to get another composer of equal stature, and this could only mean Irving Berlin.

"We're aiming awfully high to try to get Berlin," I said to Oscar.

"What can we lose?" he answered. "The worst that can happen is that he'll refuse."

One hurdle would be Dorothy Fields's reaction, since she had already been signed to write the lyrics and Berlin wrote both words and music. Dorothy, however, was enthusiastic about bringing in Berlin, though like the rest of us, she was afraid that he would feel miffed at being our second choice.

Apparently this never played any part in Berlin's thinking. When he came to see us, we outlined exactly the kind of show it was going to be and what we wanted him to do, but our enthusiasm barely made a dent. Irving was simply not interested in writing the score for a book show. His latest had been about six years earlier, and many changes had taken place in the theatre since then. As a result of *Oklahoma!,* everyone was upholding the importance of "integration" in creating musicals, and he feared that sticking closely to the story line would inhibit him. We argued that just the opposite would be true: a good libretto could offer tremendous help in stimulating ideas for songs and in showing exactly where they would be the most effective. Still, Berlin remained unconvinced. Finally I said, "Irving, there's only one way to find out. Here's the script. Take it home, write a couple of numbers and then see how you feel about it."

That was on a Friday. On Monday morning Berlin came bounding into the office with a big grin on his face and handed over three songs. They were "You Can't Get a Man with a Gun," "There's No Business Like Show Business" and "Doin' What Comes Natur'lly." They were all brilliant, and there was no further need to convince him that he could write the songs for *Annie Get Your Gun.* In fact, he was so grateful to Dorothy and Herb for the help their script had given him that he insisted that they receive part of his percentage of the show. Generosity such as this is an exceedingly rare commodity.

Although he was justifiably proud of all the numbers he wrote for the score, Berlin was extremely sensitive about their reception. In the early days of preparation, we had a series of evenings in which his pianist played the score for all the staff connected with the production. Everyone adored the songs, of course, but at one performance I noticed that one of them had not been played. When I asked Berlin what had happened to it, he said, "I dropped it because the last time it was being played I didn't like the expression on your face. I didn't think you were happy about it and I decided not to use it."

"My God, Irving," I said, "don't ever pay any attention to the expression on my face. I love that song. I looked sour only because I was concentrating on where it should go."

That's how "There's No Business Like Show Business" almost got cut out of *Annie Get Your Gun.*

My relationship with Berlin during the preparation of the show couldn't have been better, perhaps because everything worked without a hitch almost from the very start. Everything, that is, except for the orchestrations. We were in New Haven for the tryout, and with opening night just a few days away, we spent one morning listening to the first orchestra rehearsal. I was not satisfied with what I'd heard, and I was sure Irving wasn't either.

During the lunch break, the two of us walked across the street to Kaysey's restaurant. Berlin didn't say a word until we sat down. "Well, Mr. Rodgers," he began—and I knew that when he called me "Mr. Rodgers," he was deeply troubled, "I'm very unhappy about the orchestrations." I confessed that I was, too, and after lunch I telephoned Max Dreyfus. "Max," I said, "I need Russell Bennett immediately." Russell was out of town with another show, but the next morning, promptly at ten, he was at the Shubert Theatre in New Haven. He reorchestrated the entire score, did his customary superlative job, and soon Irving was again calling me by my first name.

I had never worked with Ethel Merman before *Annie Get Your Gun.* There was no question that she was "the star," but this was an innate part of her personality and had nothing to do with anything she said or did. Throughout her entire association with the show she was totally dependable and disciplined. I suppose I've accomplished as much as I ever dreamed of in the theatre, but the one thing I've missed was hearing Ethel Merman belt out one of my songs clear up to the second balcony.

The only major problem we had with *Annie Get Your Gun* had nothing to do with the show or the people involved. The day before the scheduled Broadway opening at the Imperial Theatre, I was standing on the stage watching the crew hang the scenery when suddenly I heard a frighteningly loud cracking sound above me. One of the stagehands, with the knowledge stagehands always seem to have about such matters, ran over to me and shoved me into the wings. The steel girder holding up the top of the stage had buckled. Fearing the entire roof might cave in, we quickly cleared everyone out of the theatre, but luckily the buckled girder was the extent of the damage. Still, we couldn't risk opening the show until the building was safe.

Oscar and I rushed over to the Shubert office and told Lee Shubert, who owned the theatre, that he had to give us an interim out-of-town booking. At first he blamed the scenery rather than his theatre, but eventually he agreed to let us play the Shubert Theatre in Philadelphia while the necessary repairs were being made. There was the small matter of another show then playing at the Shubert, but Lee managed to have it transferred to Boston, and a week later we moved in. Though we had taken out only a tiny ad in the Philadelphia papers, we were sold out for our entire two-week run even before the opening. No one had to beat drums to make people flock to see Merman sing songs by Berlin in a show written by Dorothy and Herb Fields.

It was the same in New York. When the Imperial had been repaired, *Annie* scored what the press, in near unison, liked to call a bull's-eye. But how could it have been otherwise? It was a bull's-eye from the moment

Dorothy and Herb walked into our office with the idea of Ethel playing Annie.

With *Annie Get Your Gun* out of the way, Oscar and I turned our attention to producing a more modest attraction that Helen Hayes brought us. It was called *Happy Birthday,* and had been written for Helen by her dear friend Anita Loos. After its opening some of the daily reviewers loftily held that the First Lady of the Theatre was wasting her time in such an obvious trifle, but we thought it worth doing if only to give Helen a change of pace and to demonstrate her considerable talents as a comedienne. In any case, Rodgers and Hammerstein had another hit. Would it never end?

It didn't end with our next production, either: *John Loves Mary,* by Norman Krasna. It was only a fair play, but it certainly was entertaining and the public kept it going for almost five hundred performances.

On October 10, 1947, the Theatre Guild presented *Allegro,* the third Rodgers and Hammerstein musical, at the Majestic Theatre in New York. On that same day, *Oklahoma!, Annie Get Your Gun, Happy Birthday* and *John Loves Mary* were all playing on Broadway, the touring *Oklahoma!* was in Boston, the touring *Carousel* was in Chicago, and the touring *Annie Get Your Gun* was in Dallas. In London, both *Oklahoma!* and *Annie Get Your Gun* were sellouts, and within ten days Oscar and I would send out a road company of *Show Boat.*

Even now, it is hard to write calmly about this extraordinary period in my life. There was just no letup. No sooner had we stopped one project than we began another. Most of the time we worked on a number of shows simultaneously. Every day required an unending stream of decisions. Who would succeed Ethel Merman during her vacation? Which moving-picture company offer should we consider for *John Loves Mary*? What record company should we choose for the original-cast album of our next show? Could I afford the time to see the young interviewer from the Los Angeles *Times*?

Because Oscar and I were primarily writers, not businessmen, it was vital that we surround ourselves with competent people who could handle the variety of problems that were constantly arising. In addition to our general manager, Morris Jacobs, we now had Jerome Whyte supervising our shows in London, and we hired John Fearnley as casting director. Our lawyer, Howard Reinheimer, handled many of the details of our productions, and from time to time we hired others for specific jobs when they were needed.

In this way Oscar and I were more or less able to devote most of our attention during 1947 to writing *Allegro.* In fact, we were so determined to be free of the production headaches involved that we took the show to our old friends Terry Helburn and Lawrence Langner, who were eager to have the Theatre Guild sponsor it.

Allegro was the first musical Oscar and I wrote that was not based on a previous theatre production. From a practical point of view, adaptations are helpful, since they enable the writer to work from a source that already has a shape and form. But an original concept gives you a feeling of special pride, and you don't have to worry about a playwright approving or disapproving what you've done to his creation. It's all yours, and if you can pull it off, the mere fact that it's difficult to do makes the success all the more rewarding.

Still, the terms "adaptation" and "original" are tricky. In a way, everything is an adaptation. We get ideas from people we know or items we read about or events that happen to us. But whatever its origin, a musical must stand on its own. It isn't necessary to be familiar with the literary source of an adaptation; why should anyone care how faithfully a work has been changed into another form? All that really counts is the finished product itself, and its effect upon an audience.

Allegro was Oscar's idea. Originally, he had wanted to write an ambitious work about the life of a man from the cradle to the grave, and thought of making him a doctor because of his close friendship with his own doctor. Perhaps because my own father and brother were also doctors, I was immediately drawn to the idea. I also liked the questions the play raised: How does a doctor maintain his integrity when tempted by an easy practice of wealthy hypochondriacs? How can he avoid compromising his principles when he is caught up in the politics of a large hospital?

In discussing the way the story would take shape, we decided that we would have to limit the action from the hero's birth to his mid-thirties. We also realized that such an episodic story would need something like a Greek chorus to bridge the scenes, comment on the action, and talk and sing directly to the actors and the audience. Further, to avoid specific sets, we proposed suggesting various locales through lighting and different stage levels.

To achieve a smooth interflow of narrative, songs and dances, we were convinced that a single guiding hand should be in charge of every element of the production. This led us to Agnes de Mille. She is supreme as a choreographer, but to our dismay we found that she was unprepared to take on the additional chores of directing the dialogue and staging the musical numbers. Hence, we ended up with a divided command: Oscar directed the book, I staged the songs, and Agnes did what she did best. It was not a satisfactory solution by any means.

The New Haven opening of *Allegro* was unforgettable—and unpredictable. Lisa Kirk, the brightest performer in the show, had a number called "The Gentleman Is a Dope," in which, while putting down the man, she reveals how much she loves him. Lisa is a tall, hourglass-shaped girl who puts everything she has into a number, and that night she became so involved that she stepped right into the orchestra pit. The two cellists who caught her simply hoisted her back onto the stage, and she didn't stop singing through the entire accident! I don't think anyone ever got a bigger hand after a song.

There was another, even more frightening incident that night. During the second act, someone sitting on the right side of the orchestra suddenly got up and yelled, "I smell smoke!" At this the audience started to move toward the exit doors. Suddenly, from the other side of the house came the sound of an even more authoritative voice booming: *"Sit down!"* It was Joshua Logan, and when he commanded, everyone obeyed. Not sure where the smoke was coming from, I dashed out into the stage-door alley and discovered that someone in the building across the street was burning trash and that a draft was pulling the odor into the theatre. Because it was such a muggy September night, all the exit doors had been left open. By running around and closing them we let the people know that there wasn't a fire in the theatre.

In addition to the major problems of *Allegro,* an unusual one affected my department. For the scene at the college prom, which was set in the mid-twenties, everyone connected with the show thought it would be a clever stroke to have the band play "Mountain Greenery"—everyone, that is, except me. I hated the idea of dredging up something from the past for its obvious applause-catching effect, and felt that if something authentic was needed it should be by Gershwin or Berlin. Somehow, though, I was talked into it. What particularly rankled was that after our New York opening, Richard Watts, the drama critic of the *Post,* who was otherwise one of the production's greatest boosters, wrote that I'd had to fall back on "Mountain Greenery" to come up with anything tuneful in the score. What is tuneful or not tuneful is, of course, subjective, and Dick knew nothing of my objection to using the song. Still, it hurt to read such a misinterpretation.

The show got a genuinely mixed bag of reviews, ranging from the loving (Brooks Atkinson's "A musical play of superior quality") to the loathing (Louis Kronenberger's "An out-and-out failure"), with the loving very much in the majority. *Allegro* ran for nine months on Broadway and toured for another seven. Nothing to be ashamed of, certainly, but after *Oklahoma!* and *Carousel* it was a disappointing reception.

Trying to assess the musical **now**, I suppose that it probably was too preachy, as many people claimed. Audiences usually don't enjoy shows that moralize, and this one went a bit overboard in that direction. One reaction that did bother me was that some people seemed to feel that two men who had succeeded in the city were claiming that city life was no good. This was a misconception, but since it was a prevalent one I must conclude that the fault was ours for not stating our point of view more clearly. We never condemned big-city life; what we were against was the corrupting effect of big institutions. At the end of the story, the hero does leave the big city for the small town in which he grew up, but this was only so that he could work in a clinic and devote himself exclusively to healing the sick. It could have been a clinic in Harlem or in Des Moines; the locale had nothing to do with the point we were trying to make.

Of all the musicals I ever worked on that didn't quite succeed, *Allegro* is the one I think most worthy of a second chance. Some of the observations we made, particularly about what ambition does to a man's integrity, are in no danger of ever becoming dated. From time to time, various ideas for revising *Allegro* have been proposed, and though so far none has seemed feasible, I still keep hoping.

19

E̲ven if I'd been a four-year honor
student at Columbia rather than a two-year extension dropout, I doubt that
I'd ever have been a rah-rah alumnus rushing up to root for the football
team on gray autumn afternoons. But I have always had a special affection
for the college because it offered me the chance to write two Varsity Shows
which helped set the course of my future career.

In 1948 I embarked on a project that I felt would benefit both Columbia
and the cultural life of New York. For some time I'd had an idea for an
art center, and the logical place for it seemed to be at Columbia. I strongly
believed that the largest university in the largest city in the country should
have one building set aside exclusively for the arts, a place where a boy from
Mobile or a girl from Bombay could come to study painting, architecture,
music, theatre or the dance. New York is the hub of the world's cultural
activity; it has more concerts, plays, art exhibits—more of everything—than
anywhere else. We can see all these forms of artistic expression around us;
yet we still lack one central educational institution where they can be
taught. Art does not exist in a vacuum, and its various forms should not
be learned as departmentalized entities. An architect should be familiar
with music, just as a sculptor should know the difference between a tour
jeté and an arabesque. If they were taught within one building, every form
of art would be enriched by feeding all the others.

I discussed this project with friends on the Columbia faculty and was
gratified by the response. The board of trustees also reacted favorably, and
I had the backing of the then president of the university, Dwight D. Eisenhower. Given his military background, Eisenhower's genuine enthusiasm
for the plan surprised me, but even more important, he immediately got
down to specifics and threw himself wholeheartedly into our efforts to
secure financial backing. I am convinced that if Eisenhower had not resigned his position to become commander in chief of the NATO forces,
Columbia would have an arts center today.

During the period that I was working on this project, I saw the General
quite often. He was a thoroughly likable man without any pretense, and I
was delighted by his desire to help. But one thing I found odd was his
occasional naïveté, particularly in areas with which he should have been
thoroughly familiar. I remember visiting him one morning after he had been
to the theatre the previous night to see *Mister Roberts*. When I asked him
if he had enjoyed it, he said he hated it. Why? "Our boys don't talk like
that." I couldn't argue with him about the accuracy of the language "our

boys" used, since he'd been to war and I hadn't, but I couldn't help wondering what war he'd been to if such relatively mild expletives annoyed him so much.

Later, when Ike ran for President, I supported him initially but became increasingly disillusioned when he failed to take a stand against the contemptible behavior of Senator Joseph McCarthy. Weakness was not what I had expected of him, and it certainly wasn't a trait I admired in a President. Therefore, midway through the campaign, I switched my support to Adlai Stevenson. Why this change of heart by a Broadway composer was deemed so important I'll never know, but the story was carried as front-page news clear across the country. Since Ike had been such a loyal supporter of my arts-center project, I was certain that this would signal the end of our friendship.

But Eisenhower was not a small man. After being in office for two years, he invited Oscar and me to the White House for dinner. It was one of those stag dinners he enjoyed giving for twenty or thirty men, mostly industrial tycoons, and to my surprise I was seated next to him. It was a delightful dinner, Ike couldn't have been more charming, and it was obvious that he harbored no grudge. After dinner we all went into the Red Room. By then McCarthy had been censured by Congress and was no longer a threat, but for some reason his name came up in the course of conversation. Eisenhower, who was sitting some distance away, leaned forward and said, "You see, Dick, sometimes if you don't talk about things, they go away."

It was incredible to me that anyone, especially someone of Eisenhower's intelligence, could feel that by disregarding a man like McCarthy, he would simply disappear. This silent treatment didn't destroy McCarthy; it was the very vocal objections by members of Congress who had the courage to censor him that ensured his downfall. To me, Ike's attitude was on the same order as saying, "If you don't call the fire department, the fire will go out."

My efforts to establish an arts center at Columbia occupied my time for a number of years. After Eisenhower resigned as president of the university late in 1950, his place was taken by Grayson Kirk, who was sympathetic but never seemed fired with enthusiasm. The main problem, of course, was raising the necessary funds, and Kirk was nothing if not blunt. One night at a dinner party I discussed this matter with him.

"I guess a project to benefit the arts is the toughest thing to get people to support."

"No," he said, "it's next to the toughest. The toughest is dentistry."

Obviously, people in the food-packaging business or steel can be found to make contributions to studies that have some relationship to their own industries. Chemistry, medicine, business administration and engineering are where the money goes. Dentistry is too unromantic, I suppose, and art too romantic, so my dream got nowhere.

During 1948 I was also concerned about a more personal matter. Pop was still at the Hotel Croydon, but his health was now steadily deteriorating. He had been an invalid for about a year, suffering from a lingering but mercifully painless form of cancer, and died in November at the age of seventy-seven. His passing was not the tragic shock that my mother's had been. He had lived a full life, devoted to his family and his profession, and he died peacefully.

Ten years earlier Garson Kanin had told me that for a movie he had written he had used my father as something of a model for the leading character, a hard-working, unsung doctor. The picture was called *A Man to Remember.*

Though we had no new shows opening during 1948, there were many duties to occupy my time professionally, particularly holding auditions for the many cast changes that were needed for our long-running Broadway and touring companies. Naturally, however, I was always on the lookout for something new. One day I was going through a little black notebook I always carry and found a notation: "Fo' Dolla'." Did I owe someone money, or did someone owe me? And why the devil had I suddenly started writing in dialect? Very puzzling, but I soon put it out of my mind. Some days later I received a telephone call from Josh Logan wanting to know if I'd ever bothered to take his suggestion and read "Fo' Dolla'." Then I remembered; meeting Josh at a party a few weeks earlier, we'd chatted about what we were working on, and I had to confess that I still hadn't found an idea for a musical that excited me. Thereupon Josh told me about a story he'd read called "Fo' Dolla'," which was in James Michener's collection of short stories, *Tales of the South Pacific.* He thought it had the makings of a great musical libretto and urged me to read the book. He wanted to direct it and had already lined up Leland Hayward as co-producer, but if Oscar and I were interested in writing it, he thought that we could all sponsor it together.

At the time of Josh's call I was in bed again with my back ailment, so with little else to do I read not just the one story but the entire collection. I could see immediately what Josh had in mind, and after Oscar read it, he could too. I told Josh we were interested, but suggested that we secure the dramatic rights not only to "Fo' Dolla' " but for the entire book. In this way we would have the opportunity, should the need arise, of using characters and situations from other stories.

It turned out to be a wise move. A couple of months later Oscar and I were in Los Angeles for the opening of *Annie Get Your Gun,* in which

Mary Martin was appearing, and sitting beside the pool at the Bel Air Hotel one afternoon, we began discussing the show. The story of "Fo' Dolla' " dealt with a South Seas native named Bloody Mary whose sixteen-year-old daughter, Liat, has a brief but intense affair with an American naval officer named Joe Cable. The more we talked about the plot, the more it dawned on us that onstage it would look like just another variation of *Madama Butterfly*. Though we liked the story, we became convinced that it was not substantial or original enough to make a full evening's entertainment.

Since we now had the rights to the entire book, we began discussing some of the other Michener stories that could either be substituted for "Fo' Dolla' " or run parallel to it. The most likely one was called "Our Heroine" and dealt with a romance between a middle-aged French planter named Emile de Becque and a young American nurse from Little Rock named Nellie Forbush. This, we decided, had to be the main story. The contrast between the two characters and the strong appeal of their attraction to each other virtually dictated that it would be a more dramatic and unusual plot. But the surprising thing was that we didn't have to abandon our original story. The stories of Nellie and Emile and Liat and Joe could complement each other and make for a fuller evening. Later we even managed to interweave them more closely by having Emile accompany Joe on a mission behind Japanese lines.

All this was against the accepted rules of musical-play construction. If the main love story is serious, the secondary romance is usually employed to provide comic relief—such as Ado Annie and Will Parker in *Oklahoma!* or Carrie Pipperidge and Mr. Snow in *Carousel.* But in *South Pacific* we had two serious themes, with the second becoming a tragedy when young Cable is killed during the mission. Breaking the rules didn't bother us, but we did think the show needed comic leavening, so we went to still a third story for an affable wheeler-dealer named Luther Billis and added him to the cast.

By a remarkable coincidence, late in the same day that Oscar and I had replotted the script, I received a telephone call from Edwin Lester, the West Coast producer. "Dick, I've gotten myself in a jam," he said. "As you probably know, Ezio Pinza has given up opera and wants to appear in a musical. I have him under contract, but there's a penalty clause in it. The trouble is, I haven't been able to come up with a damn thing that's right for him, and if I don't find something in a hurry, I'm going to have to pay him twenty-five thousand dollars. Do you and Oscar have anything cooking that might be suitable?"

"Yes," I said, as the whole picture suddenly began to take shape before my eyes. "I think I do. I think I do."

I hung up and ran back to Oscar, who saw exactly what I saw: handsome, virile, mature Ezio Pinza, the acclaimed Metropolitan Opera basso, as Emile de Becque. After our return to New York, Oscar, Ezio and I had our first meeting at lunch in the Oak Room at the Plaza. Though we had neither script nor songs, within two hours we'd managed to accomplish two things. We had our male lead and we had saved Edwin Lester $25,000.

With so formidable an attraction we were now confronted with finding the right girl to play opposite him. We needed someone young, pretty and lively, who could sing well but not necessarily with an operatic range, and who could project the quality of believable innocence. Oh, yes, and it wouldn't hurt if she had a slight Southern accent. At the time there seemed to be just one actress who could fill that bill, and we had just seen her on the West Coast as Annie Oakley. I put in a call to Mary Martin and told her what we had in mind. She was apprehensive, however. She'd played opposite musical-comedy juveniles and leading men but, my gosh, this was Don Giovanni himself! How could we possibly expect her to sing on the same stage with Ezio Pinza? Because there was some logic in what she said, I assured her that we'd write the score without a single duet for her. Mary promised to think it over, and when she came East in July we arranged to have her listen to the five songs we'd written. She and her husband, Richard Halliday, drove to Fairfield, where they heard the songs, and promised to call us in the morning to give their decision. That evening at dinner the telephone rang. It was Mary. She said that she couldn't wait until the morning for fear that we might change our minds and give the part to someone else overnight.

As soon as Oscar and I had finished congratulating ourselves on getting the two leads we wanted, we sat down with our general manager, Morrie Jacobs, to to take a look at the budget. What we saw convinced us that we had just cast ourselves out of a show. Adding what we would be expected to pay Mary, based on her salary for *Annie Get Your Gun,* to what we were already committed to pay Pinza, there was no way that *South Pacific* could be anything but an economic disaster, no matter how long it ran. So we called a meeting, explained the situation, and asked our two stars a simple question: "How much does it mean to both of you to work together?" After only a minimum amount of consultation, both Ezio and Mary did something unheard of in the theatre: they agreed to cut their salaries and percentages in half. Thereafter *South Pacific* never had any financial problems.

Mary and Ezio worked extremely well together, and their rapport showed in their performances. Mary was a thorough professional, strong-willed and tough-minded when necessary, but always deeply concerned that whatever she did be in the best interest of the production as a whole.

Pinza, too, was a joy. The only problem was that his English wasn't always distinct, a situation that precipitated the only major fight that Oscar and I had with Josh Logan and Leland Hayward. We were in the midst of rehearsals when Josh stormed over one night insisting that Pinza simply could not be understood and that we'd have to replace him. Leland backed Josh, but Oscar and I managed to prevail upon them to give Pinza a little more time. We knew that he was working diligently to overcome the problem, and we had confidence that he would. He had to; establishing himself as a Broadway star was vitally important to Pinza at this stage of his career. His ego simply would not let him fail, and it didn't.

One decision we made early in the preparation of *South Pacific* was that we would not have the kind of choreography to which audiences had been accustomed in previous Rodgers and Hammerstein musicals. We had two strong, dramatic stories, and we didn't need extended dance routines to flesh them out in any way. With his tremendous gift for staging, Josh managed individuals and groups so well that there wasn't a static moment. He brought a feeling of movement to the entire production which brilliantly disguised the fact that its dancing was minimal and basically formless.

As I had promised Mary, she had no duets with Pinza. Her songs were colloquial, direct, sunny and youthful, whereas his were sophisticated, romantic, even philosophical. Both had pieces that said "I love you," but there is a world of difference between a Nellie Forbush who scampers about, flinging her arms in the air and radiantly declaring, "I'm in love with a wonderful guy," and an Emile de Becque who fervently reveals his emotion by describing that "enchanted evening" when a man first looks at a woman and for some inexplicable reason decides to make her his own.

Some years before *South Pacific* went into production, I was idly playing the piano at home when a tune suddenly came to me. Since this was unusual, I played it for Dorothy and my two daughters. I promptly forgot about it, but they didn't, and one day when Oscar was at the house the girls asked me to play the melody because they thought it might fit a certain scene. Sure enough, Oscar agreed that it had exactly the qualities of romantic innocence for the song Cable sings to Liat. He took the music home, wrote the lyric and called it "Younger than Springtime."

Another song for Joe Cable, "Carefully Taught," has been denigrated in some quarters because it is considered propagandistic. The fact is that the song was never written as a "message" song, though it has, I know, provided ministers of many faiths with a topic for a sermon. It was included in *South Pacific* for the simple reason that Oscar and I felt it was needed in a particular spot for a Princeton-educated young WASP who, despite his background and upbringing, had fallen in love with a Polynesian girl. It was perfectly in keeping with the character and situation that, once having lost his heart, he would express his feelings about the superficiality of racial barriers. End of sermon.

Probably the most often repeated story about my method of composing has to do with the writing of "Bali Ha'i." Unfortunately, it is another example of the wrong emphasis being placed on my so-called speed. It is true that Oscar spent the better part of a week sweating over a lyric to the song, and that one day when we were lunching at Josh Logan's apartment he handed me a typewritten sheet with the words on it. I spent a minute or so studying the words, turned the paper over and scribbled some notes, then went into the next room, where there was a piano, and played the song. The whole thing couldn't have taken more than five minutes.

But it is also true that for months Oscar and I had been talking about a song for Bloody Mary which would evoke the exotic, mystical powers of a South Seas island. I knew that the melody would have to possess an Oriental, languorous quality, that it would have to be suitable for a contralto voice, and even that the title was going to be "Bali Ha'i." Therefore, as soon as I read the words I could hear the music to go with them. If you know your trade, the actual writing should never take long.

One lyric Oscar never liked was "This Nearly Was Mine." The reason was the word "paradise." Oscar hated such cliché words as "paradise" and "divine," which have been used over and over again by hacks because they are so easy and "poetic." But though he tried hard, he was unable to come up with anything better for the lines that required three-note endings. Admittedly, the word did convey exactly the way the character felt; he *was* close to paradise, whether Oscar liked it or not.

Basically, I had the same feeling about *South Pacific* that I had had about *Oklahoma!* and *Annie Get Your Gun*. It was failure-proof. The story was honest and appealing, the songs were closely interwoven but still had individuality, the staging was masterly, and it certainly didn't hurt to have the leading roles played by two such luminaries. Even before rehearsals began, and notwithstanding Pinza's cut-with-a-knife accent, I was dead sure there was nothing wrong with the show that couldn't be fixed.

We took *South Pacific* to our two favorite tryout cities, New Haven —where we cut two songs—and Boston. After making some other changes and tightening scenes here and there, it was tied with a ribbon and ready for Broadway.

The opening night at the Majestic Theatre, on April 7, 1949, was every bit as exciting as that of *Oklahoma!* Though in the past others had given parties for the shows I'd been associated with, I'd always been afraid of throwing one myself. What if you're clobbered by the critics? Is there anything more dispiriting than dozens of people frantically trying to reassure one another that reviewers don't know what the public likes and that the show is bound to run forever? But this time I thought we could risk it, and Oscar and I booked the St. Regis Roof. Then, to show how really cocky we were, even before Mr. Atkinson's comments appeared in print, we ordered a couple of hundred copies of the *Times* to give to the guests. Fortunately our gamble paid off (Brooks called *South Pacific* "as lively, warm, fresh and beautiful as we had all hoped it would be"), and the merrymaking went on until dawn. Again I was happy to remain cold sober in order to enjoy every minute of that night.

Once launched, *South Pacific* immediately joined that rare company of such musicals as *Oklahoma!, My Fair Lady* and *Fiddler on the Roof* which are not only successful stage productions but major social, theatrical, historical, cultural and musical events. We even made it into something of a philanthropic occasion by setting aside preferred locations at every performance for people who made sizable contributions to the Damon Runyon Cancer Fund.

All that marred the show's run was the frequency of Mr. Pinza's absences. He loved basking in the adulation bestowed on him as a middle-aged matinée idol, but he never could be counted on to show up for performances. He couldn't wait for his year-long contract to expire, and the minute it was up, he was on a plane for Hollywood—where he made two of the deadliest bombs ever released.

South Pacific surpassed *Oklahoma!* in one respect. It was awarded an honest-to-God Pulitzer Prize for drama, not a consolation "special award" that had gone to the other musical. This was tremendously gratifying, and I felt especially honored because it was the first time that the committee had included a composer in the drama prize. For some absurd reason, George Gershwin had not been included in the citation when the prize went to *Of Thee I Sing,* even though every other writer of the show was. It was also gratifying that the Michener book on which we had based our musical had previously won the Pulitzer Prize for literature.

South Pacific ran for almost five years on Broadway and for a while was second only to *Oklahoma!* as the longest-running musical. The closing night was especially emotional. Myron McCormick, who'd played Luther Billis ever since the show opened, stepped to the footlights after all the bows had been taken, and with tears in his eyes announced that the curtain would never be lowered on *South Pacific.* Everyone was then invited to sing "Auld Lang Syne," after which they were supposed to file out of the theatre. But with the curtain still up, the audience apparently thought there was going to be some kind of onstage party and no one wanted to leave. After remaining in their seats for half an hour, they reluctantly departed.

Mary Martin was with the show for over two years, then left to star in the London production, which despite some critical carping ran for two years at Drury Lane. At first, however, I didn't think it would run for two weeks. Josh Logan had gone over to rehearse the company but I didn't get to London until a few days before the opening. Expecting to see a reasonable facsimile of our New York production, I was shocked at what I saw at the dress rehearsal. Apparently tiring of his original concept, Josh had so deliberately altered and rearranged the show that it no longer held together. I couldn't understand what he was trying to do, and during the intermission I made my feelings known. Josh, however, remained unconvinced.

At the conclusion of the rehearsal, Mary sent word that she wanted to see Josh, Oscar and me in her dressing room. We found her crying hysterically. Between sobs, she told us that if the show wasn't put back the way it was originally, she wasn't going to open in it. We all tried to calm her, and Josh agreed to her demand. But Mary was still uncontrollable. She was sitting facing her dressing-room mirror and I happened to be standing in a spot where I was the only one who could see her reflection. It was barely perceptible, but as our eyes met in the mirror, Mary winked.

20

The Broadhurst Theatre

FIRE NOTICE: The exit indicated by a red light and sign nearest to the seat you occupy is the shortest route to the street. In the event of fire please do not run—WALK TO THAT EXIT.
Frank J. Quayle, FIRE COMMISSIONER

THE · PLAYBILL · A · WEEKLY · PUBLICATION · OF · PLAYBILL · INCORPORATED
Week beginning Monday October 23, 1950   Matinees Wednesday and Saturday

RICHARD RODGERS AND OSCAR HAMMERSTEIN 2nd
present

KENT SMITH   BARBARA BEL GEDDES   HOWARD DA SILVA
in

BURNING BRIGHT

A New Play by
JOHN STEINBECK

Directed by
GUTHRIE McCLINTIC

Scenery and Lighting by

The Plymouth Theatre

FIRE NOTICE: The exit indicated by a red light and sign nearest to the seat you occupy is the shortest route to the street. In the event of fire please do not run—WALK TO THAT EXIT.
Frank J. Quayle, FIRE COMMISSIONER

THE · PLAYBILL · A · WEEKLY · PUBLICATION · OF · PLAYBILL · INCORPORATED
Week beginning Monday, February 13, 1950   Matinees Wednesday and Saturday

RICHARD RODGERS and OSCAR HAMMERSTEIN 2nd
present

THE HAPPY TIME

A New Comedy by
SAMUEL TAYLOR
Based on the Book of the Same Name by
ROBERT FONTAINE

CLAUDE DAUPHIN   RICHARD HART
KURT KASZNAR EDGAR STEHLI   EVA GABOR   LEORA DANA   JOHNNY STEWART

Directed by
ROBERT LEWIS
Scenery and Costumes by
ALINE BERNSTEIN

THE CAST
(In order of their appearance)
BIBI ....
PAPA .... JOHNNY STEWART
MAMAN .... CLAUDE DAUPHIN

The WILBUR THEATRE

DIRECTION : MESSRS. LEE and J. J. SHUBERT

PROGRAM WEEK FEBRUARY 20, 1950

RICHARD RODGERS and OSCAR HAMMERSTEIN 2nd
present

THE HEART OF THE MATTER

by GRAHAM GREENE
and BASIL DEAN
From the Novel by
GRAHAM GREENE

With
Ian Hunter
Rosalie Crutchley   E. J. K

Alison Leggatt

Directed by
BASIL DEAN

Costumes by

Settings by Samuel Leve

On Stage

ANOTHER JEROME PRESS
Executive Offices: 49 Portland Street, Boston, M

St. James Theatre

138 West 44th Street Theatre Co., Inc.
FIRE NOTICE: The exit indicated by a red light and sign nearest to the seat you occupy is the shortest route to the street. In the event of fire please do not run—WALK TO THAT EXIT.
Hon. George P. Monaghan, FIRE COMMISSIONER

Thoughtless persons annoy patrons and distract actors and endanger the safety of others by lighting matches during the performance. Lighting of matches in theatres during the performances or at intermissions violates a city ordinance and renders the offender liable to ARREST.

THE · PLAYBILL · A · WEEKLY · PUBLICATION · OF · PLAYBILL · INCORPORATED
Week beginning Monday, April 16, 1951   Matinees Wednesday and Saturday

RODGERS and HAMMERSTEIN
present

GERTRUDE LAWRENCE
In a New Musical Play

THE KING AND I

Music by
RICHARD RODGERS
Book and Lyrics by
OSCAR HAMMERSTEIN 2nd
Based on the Novel "Anna and the King of Siam" by
MARGARET LANDON

with
YUL BRYNNER
DOROTHY SARNOFF   DORETTA MORROW

Directed by JOHN van DRUTEN
Settings and Lighting by JO MIELZINER
Costumes designed by IRENE SHARAFF
Choreography by JEROME ROBBINS
Orchestrations by ROBERT RUSSELL BENNETT
Musical Director, FREDERICK DVONCH

The most distinctive characteristic of the theatre is simply that it's alive. A play can't be put into a can like a movie or a television program to be taken out and shown without change. Theatre exists only when there are real people on both sides of the footlights, with audiences and actors providing mutual stimulation. No two performances or audiences are ever exactly alike; it is this unpredictability that makes the stage a unique art form.

In the theatre we use the term "frozen" to denote that a show requires no further changes before the Broadway opening. But nothing that is alive can ever be truly frozen. Even after the opening, even after the show seems on its way to a lengthy run, we must always be on our guard against complacency. One of the toughest jobs is the day-to-day task of keeping the production fresh. Rehearsals are constantly held to make sure that the people who buy tickets will always get the best performance possible. Actors take sick, go on vacation or leave to accept other jobs, and replacements must be found. Last-minute crises—anything from a torn curtain to a broken toe—must be faced and overcome. Consequently, now that Oscar and I had added *South Pacific* to our other shows, as well as acquiring the rights to *Oklahoma!, Carousel* and *Allegro* from the Theatre Guild, there was no end to the problems requiring our constant attention. Much as I felt stimulated by my work, my multiple professional activities might have put a severe emotional and physical strain on me had Dorothy not made sure that I enjoyed a home life that was so well attuned to my particular personality and needs.

In 1945, having grown increasingly uncomfortable in the cramped quarters of the Volney Hotel, Dorothy and I decided to move. Our friends the Andrew Goodmans had an apartment at 70 East Seventy-first Street, but because the building was about to become a cooperative, they had made plans to move to the country. Their place was a spacious duplex with fifteen rooms, though no view, and Dorothy and I promptly fell in love with it. Since co-ops were relatively new at the time and were considered by some to be a risky investment, my lawyer was dead set against the move. He reasoned that if one owner in the building went broke, the others would have to share the responsibility of the empty apartment. I secured a list of the other owners and discovered, not surprisingly, that if anybody were to go broke, I was likely to be the first one. Probably the greatest advocate of our buying the place was my father, usually an extremely cautious man, and he helped us make up our minds. Though we feared the cost would be prohibitive, we were happy to find out that when rented apartments went cooperative in those days, the asking price was quite low. My offer was quickly accepted and we moved in that June. Twenty-six years later, when we finally sold the apartment, we realized a handsome profit. Pop would have been proud.

To describe the apartment briefly, on the main floor we had a good-sized library which led into a huge living room where my two pianos fit quite cozily. Across a large foyer was the dining room and an extra room, which we combined into one L-shaped dining room with space enough for a sofa and a coffee table. Up a short circular staircase were the bedrooms. I cannot go into details about the decorating job Dorothy did, but I do know she managed to combine style with comfort, two qualities that are not always compatible.

The social highlight of our years on Seventy-first Street was the annual Christmas Eve party. Initially these get-togethers were intended primarily for non–New Yorkers who, for one reason or another, were unable to return home for the holiday; gradually, however, they grew until in later years we found ourselves with seventy or eighty guests. There were always small gifts for everyone—Dorothy took special pains in wrapping each one individually—and omelet-master Rudolf Stanish was always on hand to whip up his specialties. But eventually these affairs became too much of a chore for Dorothy and we gave them up just before we gave up the apartment.

Between 1945 and 1949 we divided our time between our city apartment and our country house on Black Rock Turnpike. Soon after *South Pacific* opened, however, we sold the house and moved to Rockmeadow, a Colonial house with gray shingles and imposing white chimneys situated on about forty acres in Southport, Connecticut. All our summers were spent at Rockmeadow, as well as most weekends, except during the extreme cold. Dorothy and I did a good deal of informal entertaining there, and especially enjoyed competing with friends who were fellow addicts of that curiously frustrating game known as croquet.

One particular occasion will always stand out in my memory. In June 1950, a few days before my birthday, Oscar and his Dorothy were spending the weekend with us. On Sunday morning we heard over the radio that two criminals had escaped from a nearby work farm, and at lunch we noticed two strange men walking around outside our dining-room window. My wife, however, assured me that they were only friends of our caretaker.

After lunch we were sitting in front of the house when we heard the sound of police sirens coming closer and closer. Because Rockmeadow was situated in such a way that it was impossible for us to see the curved driveway, I became increasingly apprehensive. When at last a police car loomed up in front of the house, I was certain that the two strange men I had seen were the two fugitives and that soon we'd be caught in the crossfire of a shoot-out. But then I noticed something else: following the police car was a caravan of a dozen automobiles, and out of the first one jumped Mary Martin! Then more familiar faces kept appearing as people tumbled out of the other cars. They were all members of the cast and crew of *South Pacific,* who proceeded to serenade me with "Happy Birthday." My surprise was so total that it amounted to a small shock. I actually felt my knees trembling as Mary rushed up and threw her arms around me.

How Dorothy had managed the whole thing with such secrecy I'll never know. She'd arranged for our guests to go swimming in the pool, and had even marked out a baseball field for the boys. That night, also as a result of Dorothy's prearrangement, we all square-danced at a neighbor's barn to the music of a small orchestra.

Somehow Dorothy had even provided us with a full moon, and when we returned home, the kids all went swimming again. I'll never forget the sight of the lovely Betta St. John, who played Liat in the show, diving from a stone wall into the water with the moonlight shining on her. At about midnight when they all departed, they left behind one emotionally drained but terribly happy birthday boy.

In a way, *South Pacific* presented Oscar and me with a problem similar to the one we'd had to face after *Oklahoma!* opened. With the show obviously set to run for years, we saw no point in competing with ourselves by following it up with another musical of our own. Therefore we did as before: we turned to producing other people's plays, though this time we found ourselves working on two projects almost simultaneously.

The first was *The Happy Time,* which Samuel Taylor, an old friend, had adapted from a novel by Robert Fontaine. Many years before, when Sam was a fledgling playwright, the Dramatists Guild had sent him over as an "observer" to study the production of *The Boys from Syracuse* straight through from casting to opening night. This was intended to give him practical knowledge in the theatre which presumably would help him in his writing. We had never lost touch, and now when he came to us with his warm and amusing story of a French Canadian family, Oscar and I produced it and everything turned out fine.

The other production, however, didn't turn out fine at all. This was an adaptation of a Graham Greene novel, *The Heart of the Matter,* which the author had written with a fellow Englishman named Basil Dean. We opened in Boston in February 1950, just one month after unveiling *The Happy Time* on Broadway. Unfortunately, it turned out to be one of those plays that are better on paper than on the stage. We were all realistic enough to see that it had no chance on Broadway, so we closed it within a week. It is the only production I've ever been associated with that failed to open in New York.

Later the same year we tried again with another serious play, *Burning Bright,* by John Steinbeck. Like Sam Taylor, John was an old friend; we had met through his wife, Elaine Anderson, who had been an assistant stage manager of *Oklahoma!* Oscar and I had always hoped that someday we might be associated with John on either a play or a musical, and when we read *Burning Bright* we were impressed and put it into immediate production. Perhaps our admiration for the author blinded us to the play's shortcomings; in any case, we found that while we thought highly of *Burning Bright,* most others did not, and it ended its Broadway run after only two weeks.

The play also ended Rodgers and Hammerstein's career as producers of works by other writers. This was not because we'd had two failures in a row; rather, it was because we'd had five previous hits with little to show for them. There are really only two basic reasons why people produce plays: the satisfaction of presenting something of quality, and to make money. We had the satisfaction, but since our own musicals were doing so well, we discovered that once we'd finished paying our taxes as writers, there was nothing left of our profits as producers. There is just so much time and energy that anyone can devote to the theatre, and we had enough to do concentrating on the shows we wrote ourselves. Hence, thereafter we served as producers only for our own musicals—and the only reason we did even this was simply that we had assembled a highly capable staff and it was easier for us to make decisions with people we knew well than to put our fate in the hands of others.

Despite our curtailment of the purely managerial end of Rodgers and Hammerstein, we had outgrown our offices. With the number of productions we now controlled, and with the ever-increasing requests we were getting from summer theatres and amateur groups to present our musicals and plays, it was necessary to move to an office large enough for a "library," where we could store all the scripts and musical parts. In addition, we also wanted a spot where, if necessary, we could hold auditions in the privacy of our own office without the bother of hiring a hall every time we wanted to hear someone sing. Consequently, in mid-1950, we moved to 488 Madison Avenue, occupying part of the ninth floor, and remained there for fourteen years.

In addition to general manager Morrie Jacobs and casting director John Fearnley, a third major member of our staff joined us at about this time. Jerry Whyte, who had been the chief stage manager for the Theatre

Guild and who had supervised our productions in London, was now with us on a permanent basis, alternating his time between serving as production supervisor in New York and heading our producing firm, Williamson Music Ltd., in London. Jerry was probably the most able man in his field, and he was a close friend and adviser until his death in 1974.

All of the first four stage musicals Oscar and I wrote together began with a story idea, which then suggested certain performers suitable for various parts. *The King and I* completely reversed the process. For the first time in our career, a project was submitted by someone who wanted to play the leading role.

Early in 1950 we received a call from Fanny Holtzmann, Gertrude Lawrence's lawyer, asking if we would be interested in writing and producing a musical adaptation of *Anna and the King of Siam*. It had been both a popular novel and a successful moving picture, and Gertrude was convinced that it would make an appealing and colorful vehicle for her.

At first our feelings were decidedly mixed. As mentioned above, we had never before written a musical specifically with one actor or actress in mind, and we were concerned that such an arrangement might not give us the freedom to write what we wanted the way we wanted. What also bothered us was that while we both admired Gertrude tremendously, we felt that her vocal range was minimal and that she had never been able to overcome an unfortunate tendency to sing flat.

On the other hand, here was an opportunity to write for one of the theatre's genuine stars. Gertrude had a distinctive quality all her own, a sort of worldly fragility, and she had won deserved acclaim in modern, sophisticated comedies and musicals. From what we knew about *Anna and the King of Siam,* the role would mark an obvious departure for her, and this alone made the project highly tempting. But before we came to a definite decision, we arranged to see a private screening of the film at the 20th Century-Fox office.

That did it. It was obvious that the story of an English governess who travels to Siam to become a teacher to the children of a semibarbaric monarch had the makings of a beautiful musical play. There was the contrast between Eastern and Western cultures; there was the intangibility of the attraction between teacher and king; there was the tragic subplot of the doomed love between the king's Burmese wife and the Burmese emissary; there was the warmth of the relationship between Anna and her royal pupils; there was the theme of democratic teachings triumphing over autocratic rule; and lastly, there were the added features of Oriental pomp and atmosphere. Here was a project that Oscar and I could really believe in, and we notified Fanny that we were ready to go to work.

With the "I" in *The King and I* already cast, we began thinking about "The King." Since Rex Harrison had given such a splendid performance in the movie version, we got in touch with him. Though he had never before sung in a stage musical, Rex was interested and was sure he could handle whatever singing was required. We had one meeting, but unfortunately were never able to come to terms.

The more we worked on the story, the more we wanted the one actor we felt could play the king with the power and authority the part needed. Our *Oklahoma!* hero, Alfred Drake, who had just left the cast of *Kiss Me, Kate,* was unquestionably the biggest male star in the musical theatre at the time, but we were confident that he would be interested. Oddly enough, we found him hard to pin down. After considerable effort on our part, including transatlantic telephone calls when we were in London for the opening of *Carousel,* he finally agreed to meet us for lunch at the Oak Room.

Oscar and I arrived at the restaurant first and were ushered to a table for four in a corner. Presently Alfred came bursting in with an armful of scripts, which he proceeded to dump on the unused chair. Suitably impressed that he was obviously much in demand, we enumerated the reasons why he should give preference to appearing in our musical. Alfred listened intently and then uttered the words we'd been waiting for months to hear: "I'd love to do it." Unfortunately, this was followed by a "but," and after the "but" came two provisions: 1) he could not remain in the show longer than six months because he had a commitment in London; 2) following the London commitment, he wanted us to buy a particular play from Gilbert Miller and produce it with him in the leading role. This seemed a bit much, so I said, "Alfred, let's forget the whole thing. You've obviously got too much on your mind right now. We'll get together on something else in the future."

Alfred said he understood, and we parted amicably in front of the Plaza. Thoroughly discouraged, Oscar and I hopped into a cab and went directly to the Majestic Theatre, where John Fearnley was holding auditions for the part of the king. The first candidate who walked out from the wings was a bald, muscular fellow with a bony, Oriental face. He was dressed casually and carried a guitar. His name, we were told, was Yul Brynner, which meant nothing to us. He scowled in our direction, sat down on the stage and crossed his legs, tailor-fashion, then plunked one whacking chord on his guitar and began to howl in a strange language that no one could understand. He looked savage, he sounded savage, and there was no denying that he projected a feeling of controlled ferocity. When he read for us, we again were impressed by his authority and conviction. Oscar and I looked at each other and nodded. It was no more than half an hour after we had left Drake, and now, out of nowhere, we had our king. (Incidentally, I never found out what happened to Alfred's London commitment or the play Gilbert Miller controlled, but eventually Alfred did play the king for two and a half months in 1952, when he temporarily took over the part while Yul was on vacation. He gave a superb performance, as Oscar and I had known he would.)

Yul Brynner turned out to be particularly helpful with a talent he possessed that we knew nothing about when we signed him: his ability as a director. Our director for *The King and I* was John Van Druten, who did a capable job except that he lacked the kind of strength needed to direct Gertrude Lawrence. Fortunately, Yul had that strength, and when he spoke, Gertrude listened. We might have been in serious trouble had it not been for Yul.

I had known Gertie for many years, ever since 1924, in fact, when she and Beatrice Lillie made such a notable Broadway debut in *Charlot's Revue.* We had been at many parties together, and I always found her to be light-hearted and self-assured, and to embody everything that means theatrical glamour. Once she started working on *The King and I,* however, all her insecurities came to the surface.

The trouble began early in 1951 when we invited Gertrude to our office to hear the score on the day before rehearsals were scheduled to begin. Because we wanted the numbers to sound as good as possible, I had asked Doretta Morrow, who was playing Tuptim, the king's Burmese wife, to do the singing. Doretta was a dark-haired, ravishingly attractive girl with a rich, lyrical, highly trained voice, and she performed beautifully. Gertrude seemed to approve of what she had heard and I was under the impression that we all parted the best of friends.

The first day of rehearsals is always important. Everyone there is conscious that it is the beginning of a production that may turn out to be not only successful but even historic. Now, at last, after months of preparation, one gets the first taste of what the songs and scenes will sound and look like when the actors perform them onstage. Usually there is a certain amount of excessive gaiety as old friends meet and newcomers try to feel at ease, but there is a deeper feeling of genuine camaraderie, born out of unspoken knowledge that each person has a contribution to make that will affect the final results.

As Gertrude strode into the crowded rehearsal hall, Oscar and I jumped up to welcome her. She greeted Oscar warmly, waved to others she knew, and cut me dead. There could be no misunderstanding; it was obvious to everyone. What had I done? Why, on the very first day of rehearsals, would the star deliberately snub the composer and co-producer? That afternoon, though Gertrude and I were scheduled to go over the songs together, she was still giving me the silent treatment, and I made some excuse about having to be somewhere else.

As soon as I could, I talked the matter over with Oscar and we both came to the conclusion that Gertrude's unhappiness must have something to do with the audition of the songs the day before. Apparently she felt so insecure about her vocal limitations that she had deeply resented hearing her numbers first sung by someone so vocally well equipped as Doretta Morrow, and since I had been the one who had asked Doretta to do it, Gertrude simply took the whole thing out on me.

We hoped that she would soon get over this antagonism, but she didn't. As the days progressed, and despite my efforts to achieve some kind of détente, there were no signs of any thaw. It was unthinkable to replace Gertrude, so I did the only thing possible: I hired an excellent vocal coach named Joe Moon to work with her on the songs. Happily, the two got along well, and Joe's efforts showed. Still, he couldn't cure her of singing flat. Even after the show had opened on Broadway and was attracting huge crowds, audiences were noticeably uncomfortable during her singing and showed it with muffled but audible sounds.

Though I had known all along that her singing would be a problem, I also knew something else about Gertrude Lawrence: she had a radiance that could light up an entire stage. Even during rehearsals it was obvious that she would be magnificent in the role of Anna. I also felt that her intrinsic style and feeling for music would compensate for her faulty pitch, and most of the time it did. Taking no chances, though, I was careful to write songs for her that were of relatively limited range—"I Whistle a Happy Tune," "Hello, Young Lovers" or "Shall We Dance?"—while saving the more demanding arias and duets—"We Kiss in a Shadow" or "Something Wonderful"—for those singers whose voices could handle them.

In composing the score, I followed my usual custom of writing the best music I could for the characters and situations without slavishly trying to imitate the music of the locale in which the story was set. Not only would I have been incapable of creating anything authentically Siamese, but even if I could, I wouldn't have done it. Western audiences are not attuned to the sounds of tinkling bells, high nasal strings and percussive gongs, and would not find this kind of music attractive. If a composer is to reach his audience emotionally—and surely that's what theatre music is all about— he must reach the people through sounds they can relate to. I have always compared my approach to this particular score to the way an American painter like Grant Wood might put his impressions of Bangkok on canvas. It would look like Siam, but like Siam as seen through the eyes of an American artist. Any other approach would be false and self-defeating.

Even though our view of Siam couldn't be completely authentic, Oscar and I were determined to depict the Orientals in the story as characters, not caricatures, which has all too often been the case in the musical theatre. Our aim was to portray the king and his court with humanity and believability, while avoiding the disease Oscar used to call "research poison."

The King and I was the only production in which I've ever been associated with a slim, intense, supremely gifted young choreographer named Jerome Robbins. It was Jerry who devised the amusing staging of "Getting to Know You," as well as the delightfully varied entrances for the princes and princesses during the "March of the Siamese Children." But the main ballet, the one we were counting on to be the highlight of the second act, gave him great trouble during the initial stages. One morning I walked into the Broadway Theatre, where we were holding rehearsals, before anyone else had arrived—at least I thought I did. As I entered the darkened theatre I could see Jerry sitting on the steps leading from the orchestra floor to the stage, staring into space. When I asked him what was wrong he confessed that he was stumped by the second-act ballet. It was to be a climactic scene in which, like Claudius in *Hamlet,* the king would observe a pantomimed story revealing his misdeeds.

Trying to be helpful, I mentioned to Jerry that he had already created one of the funniest ballets ever staged on Broadway, the Keystone Kops chase in *High Button Shoes,* and suggested that he might consider approaching the ballet for *The King and I* from a comic rather than tragic viewpoint. Jerry said he'd think about it. What resulted, of course, was his brilliant creation of "The Small House of Uncle Thomas." While the purpose of the ballet was serious, the juxtaposition of Oriental movements within the melodramatic Harriet Beecher Stowe saga—complete with King Simon of Legree chasing Eliza over the ice—made the work both funny and touching.

We made our customary New Haven stop and listened carefully to the advice of all our friends. The most drastic suggestion came from Leland Hayward, who said we ought to close the show. Luckily, we didn't listen. The main rewriting was done in Boston. We all agreed that there was something heavy about the show—we had purposely avoided any overtly comic character—and it was Gertrude who suggested that we could perk up the first act by giving her a song to sing with the children. She was absolutely right. For the music, I went back to a melody I had originally planned for Joe Cable to sing to Liat in *South Pacific,* but had discarded in favor of "Younger than Springtime." For the words, Oscar wrote a charming lyric about Anna's pleasure in getting to know the Siamese people, which he appropriately called "Getting to Know You." It not only gave the act a much-needed lift, it also voiced a philosophical theme for the entire story. Another piece written out of town was "I Have Dreamed," sung by the two young lovers.

The King and I opened in New York at the St. James Theatre (our first time back since *Oklahoma!*) on March 29, 1951. As usual, Dorothy and I sat in the last row of the orchestra, and I had the dread feeling I occasionally get that suddenly the whole production was falling apart before my eyes. I was delighted to be proved wrong; the headlines in the next day's papers told the story without even making it necessary to read the notices: "They Do It Again" . . . "Another Triumph for the Masters" . . . "Another Great Hit for Dick and Oscar" . . . "Another Enchanted Evening." Curiously, the score received mostly offhanded comments, implying that it was little more than a satisfactory accompaniment to the play. I don't know why it took the songs so long to catch on, but thanks in part to the excellent film version, they eventually won widespread popularity.

Gertrude appeared in the show for well over a year before going on an extended vacation during the summer of 1952. According to her husband, Richard Aldrich, she was in good health the entire time she was away. She returned to *The King and I* in mid-August (Celeste Holm had been her replacement) looking fit and well rested, and was in such high spirits that she even treated me as if there had never been the slightest rift between us. After she had been back only a few days, however, she began complaining of severe pains, and her doctor recommended that she check into a hospital for tests. At first her ailment was diagnosed as hepatitis which, though serious and painful, was no cause for undue alarm. Soon, however, it became clear that she was actually suffering from a rare form of cancer which was not accompanied by a lingering period of physical deterioration. She died relatively peacefully within a week after being admitted to the hospital.

As I wrote at the beginning of this chapter, the theatre exists only because it is alive, and because it is alive it must perpetually adjust to all sorts of emergencies. The tragic death of a star casts a pall over everything, but if you believe in the theatre you know that, like life itself, it must continue. There is no alternative but to find a replacement and go on. In the case of *The King and I,* it was Gertrude's friend and understudy, Constance Carpenter. Later the part was played by Annamary Dickey and

Patricia Morison in New York, Valerie Hobson in London, Deborah Kerr in the movie, and by many others throughout the world. Each brought something special to the role, and each was certainly more vocally secure than Gertrude Lawrence. Just the same, whenever I think of Anna I think of Gertie.

21

"If you were approached to do some work for the United States Navy, we'd like your assurance that you wouldn't refuse to consider it."

"Well, of course I wouldn't refuse to consider an offer from the United States Navy."

This peculiar exchange took place during a telephone conversation I had early in the fall of 1951 with Sylvester "Pat" Weaver, then vice-president in charge of television at NBC. His curiously negative question, it turned out, was simply a matter of protocol. The Navy had approached NBC with the idea of presenting a television documentary series about its exploits during World War II, but before a definite offer could be made I had to give my assurance in advance that I would at least consider composing the score. One simply does not say no to the United States Navy—not out of hand, anyway.

An appointment was set up in my office for the producer-writer of the series, a tall, affable young man named Henry Salomon who, for reasons of his own, was nicknamed Pete, to fill me in. It was to be a series, called *Victory at Sea,* made up of twenty-six half-hour programs winnowed from over a million feet of film from the files of some ten different countries, Axis as well as Allied. Each segment would deal with a phase of our Navy's activities, the only addition being a voice-over commentary and musical score.

It was tempting. Apart from *Love Me Tonight,* I'd never before written any background music, nor had I ever written anything for television. In addition to the appeal of working in a new field in a new medium, I would meet a new array of heroes and heroines. Any composer would have been intrigued by the challenge of creating music to accompany the movements of ships, planes and submarines.

But I held back; to be frank, I was concerned about my ability to do the job. All my previous work had been in the theatre or films. In many ways, this would be a far more demanding job than anything I had ever done. It required an almost continuous stream of music, unaided by song titles or lyrics. I asked for two weeks to make up my mind.

During those two weeks, desire finally overcame doubt; of course I could do it. Despite my inexperience in the field, I couldn't let this opportunity slip through my fingers. No matter what was required, it would still be music, would still deal with emotions, would still be used to enhance dramatic situations. If I could reach people in a theatre audience, I was confident that I could also reach them in their homes, and if the U.S. Navy and NBC thought that I was the man for the job, who was I to disagree?

When I told Salomon that I'd undertake the assignment, I made one stipulation. Since the United States government was involved, I did not think *Victory at Sea* should be a moneymaking project, at least not until the initial series had appeared. After the twenty-six programs were shown for the first time, the network could make whatever syndication arrangements it wished, and I would be only too happy to share in the proceeds. NBC agreed, and I soon found myself back in the world of Guadalcanal, the Aleutians, Anzio and Leyte Gulf.

The months of working on *Victory at Sea* were one of the most satisfying periods of my life. Pete Salomon, who died only a few years after the documentary was shown, was a tremendous help, and together we evolved an agreeable *modus operandi*. I had neither the time, patience nor aptitude to sit in a cutting room hour after hour going over thousands of feet of film with a stopwatch in my hand in order to compose themes that fit an inflexible time limit. We agreed that Pete and the film editor, Isaac Kleinerman, would first do the rough cutting and editing, and then let me see sections of the episodes. They also supplied me with written breakdowns—or logs—of all the action. In this way, with the visual image in my mind and the logs in my hand, I was free to compose the music on my own time in whatever surroundings I chose.

I took those logs everywhere with me. Whenever I had some spare moments, I'd take them out and read, say, "Airplane carrier. Planes landing on deck," which would trigger the mental image I needed to write the music I thought appropriate to accompany the scene. During this period Dorothy and I took a vacation in Florida, and every afternoon I'd consult my logs and scribble away for an hour. It was fragmented work, not like sitting down and composing a symphony, or even a score for a show. Often there was little continuity from one sequence to another. Many of the segments were extremely short, some lasting no more than a minute and a half.

As a result, what I composed were actually musical themes. For the difficult technical task of timing, cutting and orchestrating, I turned to my old friend Russell Bennett, who has no equal in this kind of work. He fully deserves the credit, which I give him without undue modesty, for making my music sound better than it was.

Victory at Sea was successfully launched late in the fall of 1952. Since it attracted huge audiences right from the start, NBC was immediately inundated with offers of commercial sponsorship. True to our agreement, however, they waited until the twenty-six weeks were over before entering into any syndication arrangements. Apart from the public's continued approval, which kept the series running for years, I also had the gratification of being honored with the Navy's Distinguished Public Service Medal.

In addition, the *Victory at Sea* score has become a best seller in RCA's classical-records division.

Soon after this program began, I was invited to conduct the St. Louis Symphony, with Marguerite Piazza, Thomas Hayward, Claramae Turner and Robert Weede singing a program of my songs. The concert was scheduled for the afternoon of Washington's Birthday at the Keil Auditorium in St. Louis. Since the hall seats nearly fifteen thousand people, I told the sponsors that I couldn't imagine anything near that size crowd willing to sit still at a concert during a holiday afternoon. They told me to stick to conducting; they'd worry about filling the hall. It turned out to be a sellout, which was especially gratifying since it was the first time I'd ever conducted a full symphony orchestra.

The fact that *Victory at Sea* can sell in the millions as a classical-record album and that a program of theatre songs performed by a symphony orchestra is able to fill an enormous auditorium is a healthy indication of the universal appeal of music of all kinds. Unfortunately, too many people still believe that there are only two kinds of women and two kinds of music —one too popular to be good, the other too good to be popular. Why should we assume that goodness and popularity can't coexist?

In school I can even remember being taught that there were two kinds of "good" music, program and absolute—in other words, descriptive and abstract. There was always a snide connotation that descriptive music lacked the purity of the abstract composition and was thus of a lower order. This undoubtedly grew out of the fact that the great symphonies are allegedly abstract. I say "allegedly" because I believe that while it may be possible to create an unspecific work, the listener supplies his own description. He will hear surf pounding on rocks, relive the parting from a loved one, or even feel impending doom creep down his spine. Painters often see color combinations while listening to music, and I'll bet that the Schumann Piano Concerto makes a first-class cook water at the mouth. The horn solo in the second movement of Tchaikovsky's Fifth has always evoked my mother because it has a contralto voice, as she had, and because it even sounds the way she looked.

Musical labels have always bothered me, in part because the terms in common usage are imprecise and confusing. Is every "classical" work a classic? Aren't there any unpopular "popular" songs? Are we to assume that all forms of music other than "serious" must be "frivolous"? Is there no heavy "light" music—or light "heavy" music? All too often such words merely serve to build barriers around each form, attracting one group of people while putting off others. What we enjoy should have nothing to do with the descriptive labels currently in fashion. The most important function of any composition, whether song or symphony, is that it has the power to affect its listener's emotions. I cannot simply admire a piece of music; I must also feel it. In fact, when I feel it strongly enough the hairs on my arms actually stand straight out.

People have an emotional need for melody, just as they need food or personal contact. By this I don't mean to denigrate the contributions of atonal, so-called "modern" music. Nothing should be brushed off because it is not immediately understood. What may be far-out to one listener may very well be near-in to another. When I was a kid and first heard a Strauss tone poem I found it exciting but I didn't really understand it. Now it's too easy. I can't say that I fully appreciate rock music, but there's no denying that it fills an emotional need for a large part of the population.

Personally, I'd like to see musical labels disappear entirely. Whether it's Bach or Bacharach, the important thing is not the label or the name of the composer, but the music itself. Symphonies abound with dance tunes. The popular music of Italy is grand opera. Within the last ten years or so the theatre music of Gershwin, Bernstein, Kurt Weill, Fritz Loewe and others has become a fixture in the repertories of symphony orchestras. Whenever barriers crumble, the result can only be the broadening and strengthening of music's appeal.

In a small way, I did a little barrier-breaking myself. In my "symphonic" score for *Victory at Sea* was a theme for an episode called "Beneath the Southern Cross" that I wrote as a languid tango to accompany the activities of our Navy in South American waters. The motif attracted a considerable amount of interest as soon as it was heard, and I felt sure that I could find a place for it in a Broadway score. The opportunity presented itself in the very next Rodgers and Hammerstein show, *Me and Juliet,* and Oscar supplied the words and title, "No Other Love."

Me and Juliet grew out of our fascination with the theatre. It was our second production not adapted from a specific literary source, and while it fared a bit better on Broadway than *Allegro,* it was not a wholly satisfactory work. One of our aims was to avoid all the clichés usually found in backstage stories. Though the plot focused on various people associated with a stage musical, we established the fact at the beginning that the show within a show was a success. The backer didn't pull out, the star didn't quit and the chorus girl didn't take over. We simply used the production as a framework for a love story, though of course we did take advantage of the theme to reveal some aspects of the world of the theatre. For the actual setting, we decided to restrict the action to the theatre building itself, thereby giving the production a unity that we felt would contribute to its dramatic impact. For example, the number "Keep It Gay" began with an electrician on a light bridge singing along with the actor supposedly on the stage below during a performance of our play within a play. Then blackout, and the audience saw the same number being danced by the onstage chorus. Then another blackout, and the dancers were in practice clothes continuing the routine on a bare stage during a rehearsal.

This musical gave us the chance to put into song some of the things we felt about the theatre. One piece, "The Big Black Giant," dealt with that indispensable and unpredictable element, the audience. Another number, "Intermission Talk," opened the second act with the familiar sight of theatregoers having a smoke in the lobby between the acts. Here we first picked up the chatter—no one can remember how the songs go—which then leads into one group singing, "The theatre is dying,/ The theatre is dying,/ The theatre is practically dead . . ." Though another group cites currently successful shows, these "Happy Mourners" continue their gloomy predictions of the theatre's demise. Eventually the more satisfied patrons become dominant and end by proclaiming, "The theatre is living!"

It's nice to end on a positive note, but the truth is that the theatre has always been a Fabulous Invalid. Somehow, though, it always pulls through. I don't deny the multitude of problems that currently exist, but many of them have nothing to do with the theatre itself. It cannot accept responsibility for the disreputable elements invading the Times Square area or the fact that you can't get a taxi. Nor can it be held accountable for the high cost of living. It's easy to say that tickets cost too much. Of course they do, but so does everything else. In 1943 the top price for an orchestra seat for *Oklahoma!* was $4.80. Today the highest weekend price for a musical is $15. That's an increase of a little more than three times in over thirty years, which is about the same as that of a loaf of bread or a quart of milk. A New York subway ride costs seven times as much as in 1943. And these are necessities, not luxuries.

But if we can't be optimistic about the state of the Broadway theatre today, we can't deny that it not only survives but even thrives on occasion. When a worthwhile production comes along, nothing can keep the audience away. There is no force quite like that magnetic strength which the theatre has to draw people out of their homes to spend an evening with others watching real actors on a real stage.

Because Jo Mielziner's brilliant scenery for *Me and Juliet* was complicated, we opened the pre-Broadway break-in tour at the more commodious Hanna Theatre in Cleveland rather than the usual Shubert in New Haven. The next stop was Boston.

When a show is in good shape you don't have to wait for the newspapers to tell you; you can feel it in the air. In the same sensory way, you also know when a show is not in good shape. Whatever flickering optimism any one of us may have had about *Me and Juliet* was quickly doused when we heard people raving about the sets, without a word being said about the rest of the show. We opened on Broadway late in May 1953 and received the expected unenthusiastic notices, but thanks largely to a healthy advance sale still managed to run for ten months. As it turned out, early in the fall Oscar and I had four productions running in New York at the same time: *Me and Juliet* at the Majestic, *The King and I* at the St. James, *South Pacific* at the Broadway, and in a Jean Dalrymple revival, *Oklahoma!* at the City Center.

Shortly after the opening of *Me and Juliet,* Oscar and I became involved in our first venture as film producers. Just as soon as *Oklahoma!* had begun its record-breaking run, we were receiving offers from major studios for the screen rights. At one point Paramount, figuring to make their money solely out of the distribution rights, offered us 100 percent of the profits if we chose them. But this was early in the show's run and we thought it wiser to wait until the stage production ended before coming to terms with Hollywood. What sold us on the outfit that eventually did produce the picture was a film process called Todd-AO.

The "Todd" of Todd-AO stood for a pugnacious, imaginative showman named Michael Todd. Mike had been involved with Cinerama, the wide-screen three-camera screen process, and was anxious to perfect a wraparound projection that used a single camera and a single projector. He made a deal with the American Optical Company—the "AO" in the name —which agreed to undertake the research. Eventually the firm came up with an entirely new wide-angle camera, complete with new lenses, new 65-mm. film, and a magnetic sound track equipped for full stereophonic sound.

It was Arthur Hornblow, the Hollywood producer responsible for getting Larry Hart and me to write the score for *Mississippi,* who first told Oscar and me about Todd's new process. Arthur was associated with Mike's production company and he was anxious that the first Todd-AO movie be *Oklahoma!* He assured us that we would have complete artistic control over the picture, and that we would become part of the company then being organized to release films in Todd-AO.

Along with Sam Goldwyn, Arthur was one of the few men in Hollywood in whom I had total confidence, and in August, Dorothy and I traveled to Buffalo to see a demonstration of the new process at the Regent Theatre. We both came away tremendously impressed. The audience felt that it was part of the action, and the depth, clarity and sound were all remarkably lifelike. Best of all, Todd-AO didn't have those irritating jumpy seams that divided Cinerama into three panels. The filming of *Oklahoma!* would have been an important event in any case, but making it the debut of this exciting new process made the offer even more appealing.

To finance the process and the production, a company called Magna Theatre Corp. was set up, with George Skouras, head of United Artists Theatre Circuit, as president, and Arthur Hornblow as vice-president. At a preliminary meeting Todd and Skouras got into a furious name-calling brawl. Oscar and I were there with our lawyer, Howard Reinheimer, and after we left I said that I didn't want to have anything further to do with these people. Oscar's opposition was, if anything, even stronger.

To my amazement, without consulting me Oscar and Reinheimer went back to the Magna people a day or two later and told them we'd be delighted to become associated with them in the *Oklahoma!* production. Reinheimer must have thought the deal was so good that he was able to convince Oscar. Had I made an issue of this, I'm sure it would have caused a serious rift between Oscar and me, and this was one thing I wanted to avoid. Furthermore, I had to admit that my opposition was based solely on the behavior of Todd and Skouras at one meeting and had nothing to do with the business arrangement. So I said nothing and went along. Actually, though I approached the enterprise with a good deal of trepidation, the contract was highly satisfactory, both artistically and financially, and all things considered, the movie itself turned out to be creditable.

Except for location scenes (filmed near Nogales, Arizona, because the terrain was closer to turn-of-the-century Oklahoma than 1954 Oklahoma), most of the film was shot on the M-G-M lot in Culver City. Oscar and I flew to California in the summer and were met at the airport by assorted production and publicity wheels, who went to great lengths to describe the cottage on the M-G-M grounds that they had refurbished for our use. As we drove toward it my mind raced back twenty years. This was the very house that had been Irving Thalberg's office, where I had gone to say good-bye the day Larry Hart and I left Hollywood. Then Thalberg hadn't had the slightest idea who I was; now, with many a flourish, I was being royally welcomed to the very same place.

Though Oscar and I were the "executive producers," the actual producing chores were handled by Arthur Hornblow. The director we chose was Fred Zinnemann, who had recently won high praise for his work on

High Noon but who had never before directed a musical. As musical-theatre insurance, we signed Agnes de Mille to restage her dances. Oddly enough, she turned out to be the most temperamental person associated with the project. On one occasion she had the door locked on a sound stage during a dance rehearsal and made Arthur and me—both her employers—wait outside until she deigned to let us in.

Visually, parts of the film were impressive, with some stunning shots of elephant-eye-high corn, the surrey ride, and the cloud-filled Arizona sky. But the wide-screen process was not always ideal for the more intimate scenes, and I don't think the casting was totally satisfactory. At any rate, from then on—except for *South Pacific*—Oscar and I left moving pictures to moving-picture people and stayed clear of any involvement with subsequent film versions of our musicals.

We were both anxious to get back to New York to start work on a project we had been interested in for about two years. As I have mentioned earlier, Elaine and John Steinbeck had long been our good friends. John had once tried to adapt his *Cannery Row* stories into a musical, but it didn't work out and instead he wrote a novel called *Sweet Thursday,* using some of the characters in the stories. The producing team of Cy Feuer and Ernest Martin wanted to turn this into a musical, but it never got off the ground. It was then that John approached Oscar and me.

We read the book and were enchanted by the raffish characters and the colorful California locale. As soon as we returned East, we began plans for what eventually became known as *Pipe Dream*.

Sometime during the summer of 1955, I started feeling a pain in my left jaw which I assumed was caused by a tooth. My dentist examined me and told me not to worry, but asked me to return for periodic checkups. It didn't get any better, and one day in mid-September he took one look and told me that I was in trouble. Five minutes later I was in my doctor's office, and that evening my doctor and my brother made an appointment with Dr. Hayes Martin, a specialist in head and neck surgery, for the next morning. After the examination Dr. Martin asked me to sit with Dorothy in the reception room while he talked to Morty in his office. The wait was interminable, and I knew something serious was going on. Finally we were ushered into the office where Morty and Dr. Martin's colleague, Dr. Amoroso, were also waiting. Dr. Martin looked at me calmly and said, "It isn't too early but it still isn't too late." This was his way of telling me I had cancer. While the realization was disturbing, I somehow found the mournful expressions on the faces around me—particularly Dorothy's and Morty's—even more upsetting than the news itself.

It was a Friday. Dr. Martin made arrangements with Memorial Hospital to admit me the following Tuesday, with the operation scheduled for Wednesday. The rest of the morning was spent with an X-ray specialist whose office was a block away.

By coincidence, *Pipe Dream* was to begin its rehearsals on the Tuesday that I was to enter the hospital. Over the weekend I wrote a new song and finished three piano manuscripts. Because I was anxious to see the *Pipe Dream* cast in action and because I thought it was important that they see me, I managed to get permission to spend Tuesday morning at the rehearsal. At noon I took Dorothy to lunch at Dinty Moore's, and then she drove me to the hospital.

That afternoon there was a steady stream of medical and surgical technicians popping in and out of my room. It was all good-natured, without any gloom or tension, which helped overcome any feelings of fear. All I needed was one pill to give me a good night's sleep.

In the morning there were a couple of hypodermic injections, and shortly after noon I was wheeled upstairs. There was one more shot, this time Sodium Pentothal. What a miracle it is! I never felt the sensation of falling asleep or even blacking out. The next thing I knew I was conscious again in the recovery room, minus one malignant growth, a part of one jaw, and numerous lymph nodes. What actually woke me was the unexpected sound of applause, which came from the patient in the next bed being shown the headline in the *Daily News:* "MARCIANO KAYOS ARCHIE MOORE."

Sometime later they wheeled me back to my own room. I had no real pain, only enormous pressure from the bandages, and the first thing I did was walk unaided to the bathroom. Thereafter I received nothing stronger than an aspirin derivative, and at night only a mild sleeping pill. Oddly, I discovered that it was more comfortable to sleep in a chair than in a bed.

I can't say that the surgical and medical procedures of my hospital experience were enjoyable, but there was nothing horrible about them either. What sticks in my mind was the infinite patience of Dr. Martin and Dr. Amoroso, and the pervasive atmosphere of optimism in an institution where terror is thought to be the common emotion. I'm also aware that my recovery was greatly helped by Dorothy, who managed to remain cool and unhysterical at all times, no matter what she may have been going through inside. She also had the marvelous faculty of being exactly in the right place whenever I needed her.

On the eighth day after the operation, Dorothy took me for a ride in the park. I felt miserable. On the ninth day she took me to a movie. I was bored. On the tenth day, still making my home in the hospital, I went to a rehearsal of *Pipe Dream*. I loved every minute of it.

I left Memorial Hospital on the twelfth day after the operation, and went right back to work. I found it tremendously stimulating. Going to rehearsals, surrounded by healthy young people was the greatest possible boost for my morale.

For the first month or so I had handicaps but no visible scars. I couldn't eat properly or speak well, because my tongue hadn't yet learned how to behave. For a while, too, my left arm was quite stiff and I was afraid I'd never be able to play the piano again. But I insisted on going to New Haven and Boston for the *Pipe Dream* tryouts. My wife was my only nurse, and I can't imagine a professional one being more understanding or efficient. Since then, I have had no physical trouble that could be related in any way to the operation. My left jaw is slightly out of line, but it's far from being a major deformity.

If I learned anything from this particular episode, it was simply that the more honest we are about our ailments, the better off most of us will be. Though we recognize that our attitude is illogical, many of us are reluctant to admit that we've had cancer, even after a complete cure. People seem to feel that there is some sort of stigma attached to it, almost as if it were a social disease. The point is that if there are signs of trouble, a person should go for early help—not in fear but in hope.

Had this episode been made into a movie in the heyday of Hollywood musicals, the scenario would have ended with the composer recovering from his operation just in time to attend the opening-night performance of his latest work. With tears in his eyes he acknowledges the thunderous ovation signaling his crowning achievement. Well, if there were any tears in my eyes, it was because *Pipe Dream* was universally accepted as the weakest musical Oscar and I had ever done together.

Just before the Broadway opening we had written a piece for the *New York Times* in which we admitted: "It is not likely that *Pipe Dream* will prove to be exactly what is expected of us. We only know that the rule of thumb of 'expectability' is just about impossible for us to follow."

And that was the problem: we had simply gone too far away from what was expected. People were unwilling to accept the show on its own terms. It had to be compared with our other works and that indefinable thing called the Rodgers and Hammerstein image. Had we been a couple of unknowns, I'm convinced that *Pipe Dream* would have been better received. Which is not to say that it was an unflawed gem; far from it. We were well aware that it was something of a mood piece with little real conflict, and that we weren't as well acquainted as we might have been with bums, drifters and happy houses of prostitution. Also, we made mistakes in casting, and signing opera star Helen Traubel as a warm-hearted madam was certainly one of them. It wasn't Helen's fault; we chose her after Dorothy and I had heard her in a Las Vegas night club, and that was terribly misleading. We did, however, have two fine musical-theatre talents, Bill Johnson and Judy Tyler, in the romantic leads. By tragic coincidence, both died within a year after *Pipe Dream* closed.

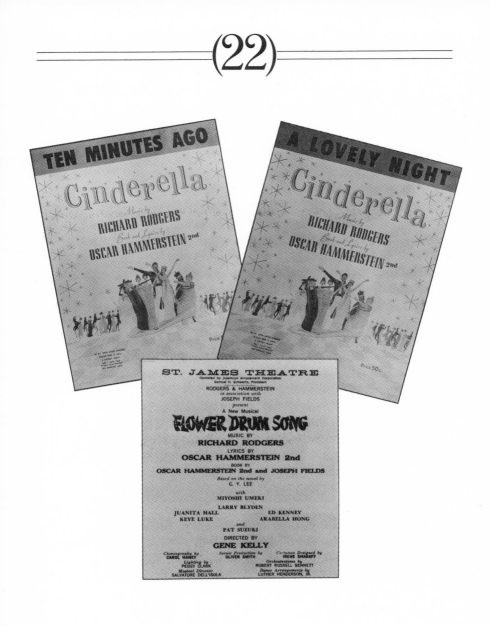

22

I n 1956, Lerner and Loewe's *My Fair Lady* glided, waltzed and skipped into town to win immediate acceptance as a classic of the musical theatre. Not only was it a rich and endearing work, it also served to establish Julie Andrews as Broadway's most radiant new star. There wasn't a composer or lyricist who didn't start dreaming of songs for her to sing or roles for her to play.

Luckily, Oscar and I didn't have to do any dreaming at all. One day in late summer I received a telephone call from Charles Tucker, Julie Andrews' agent. Hesitantly, he wanted to know if Oscar and I might be interested in writing a television adaptation of *Cinderella* for his client. At the time, thanks largely to Mary Martin's success in *Peter Pan*, children's stories were much in demand for television, but what sold us immediately was the chance to work with Julie. Casting her as Cinderella was like casting Ethel Merman as Annie Oakley. It was right right from the start.

The CBS production took shape quickly, with Dick Lewine, a distant cousin of mine and close friend, as producer, and Ralph Nelson as director. In writing the story and songs, Oscar and I felt that it was important to keep everything as traditional as possible, without any "modernizing" or reaching for psychological significance. One of the major changes, though, was making the two stepsisters less frightening and more comic. We also decided to make our Fairy Godmother an attractive young woman—played by Edie Adams—rather than the customary old crone.

Most good collaborations between a lyricist and a composer depend on give and take, a willingness to accept suggestions and make concessions in the interest of the project as a whole. This was one of the most rewarding aspects of working with Oscar. He was never afraid to voice his ideas if they differed from mine, nor did he ever make me afraid to voice mine if they differed from his. Since we respected each other's views, even in our own particular bailiwicks, we were always grateful for the other's help.

In November 1956, during the early stages of our work on *Cinderella*, Oscar and his Dorothy spent a few weeks in Australia—Dorothy was born in Tasmania—at the Olympic Games. Because we were separated during this period by over ten thousand miles, we had to thrash out whatever problems we had by mail. To document our method of collaborating, I have extracted sections from four letters dealing with the writing of the song "Do I Love You Because You're Beautiful?"

From Oscar:

I've been brooding about a line in "Do I Love You Because You're Beautiful?" I don't like "Am I *making believe,* etc.?" "Making believe" (outside of the fact that I cashed in on that phrase some years ago) seems an unimportant expression in this connection. How about this?

Am I telling my heart I see in you
A girl too lovely to be really true?

Let me know what you think.

The last time we went over this number, I suggested that you stay up on the higher notes, going into the phrase: "Are you the sweet invention, etc.?" First, you said you had wanted to finish in minor, then you said you could do what I was asking for and still finish in minor.

Now I have a new idea. Would it not be more exciting and psychologically sounder to finish the refrain in major, even though you have started in minor? It is my conception that although the last line is a question, the lover really believes she is "as beautiful as she seems." So after starting with doubt (minor key) the major finish would imply: "Oh, hell, I love you and I really think in my heart of hearts that you *are* as beautiful as you seem." This is based, of course, on the assumption that it is not musically ungrammatical to start with minor and finish with major.

From me:

I have no particular qualms about using the line "Am I making believe, etc.?" It occurs to me that this is simply a part of the language and it is not connected with you any more than it is with dozens of other authors. I am not devoted to the line "A girl too lovely to be really true," for the simple reason that it sounds like a split infinitive.

Apparently you don't remember that you gave me a pretty good briefing on the subject of going into a climax on the phrase, "Are you the sweet invention, etc.?" At the time I agreed that you were absolutely right and I changed the tune to subscribe to your suggestion. It still reaches higher for its climax and ends in major rather than minor. There is absolutely nothing ungrammatical about ending in major when you start in minor. It is quite conventional and extraordinarily effective. I think you will find that you have the lift at the finish that you expected.

From Oscar:

> My reason for wanting to change "make believe" was not chiefly because of my earlier use of the phrase. In my letter to you I mentioned that only parenthetically. I think it is a "little" phrase and I think "telling my heart" has more emotional importance. You, apparently, don't because you don't even mention it. Let us wait until we get together, which will be in two weeks. I don't share your split-infinitive phobia, but I tried very hard to dodge "really" and couldn't get out of it. I even considered asking you to eliminate the two notes and substitute a long one, thus: "a girl too lovely to be true," but feared it was less interesting musically.

From me:

> As I said in my last communication, once you and I sit down in a room and discuss these matters of syllables and notes there isn't the remotest possibility of disagreement. I know we can conform to what the other would like to do quite easily. In any event, it will be good to have you back and to sit down and talk things over.

When Oscar returned, we discussed this problem—and we compromised. Oscar agreed that "Am I telling my heart" was not appreciably stronger than "Am I making believe." And I agreed to accept "too lovely to be really true" because, no matter how it sounded, it wasn't really a split infinitive.

All this may strike some readers as more of a case of splitting hairs than infinitives, but the fact is that songwriting is made up of small things. It is concerned not only with emotional expression but with emotional compression. An inexact note or an imprecise word can ruin the desired effect simply because a song must convey a particular feeling within a relatively constricted form.

In mid-March, two weeks before the scheduled *Cinderella* telecast, we mounted a full-scale production—not just a dress rehearsal—which we recorded via kinescope. Though it lacked an audience, it was our equivalent to a New Haven tryout. We studied the production carefully and did whatever rewriting or restaging was necessary. A week later we ran a second kinescope—the Boston tryout—which helped us with last-minute polishing.

Other than mechanical differences, putting together a television musical is really not much different from working on a Broadway or Hollywood musical. We still had to create a show intended to produce an emotional reaction in the audience, to create musical sequences that conformed to the action and the mood of the piece. The main difference about writing for television is that the very size of the screen dictates a more intimate approach, while the rigid time limitations prescribe stories that can be told as succinctly as possible.

Though a few of its songs have become popular, our score for *Cinderella* is another example of what theatre music is really all about. No matter what the medium, a score is more than a collection of individual songs. It is, or should be, a cohesive entity whose words and music are believable expressions of the characters singing them. When the lonely, bullied heroine sings "In My Own Little Corner," it's not merely a song, it's a revelation of the girl herself. When she finishes, we know something more about her than we had before—her sense of humor, her naïve optimism, her imagination and her relationship to the rest of her family. It's fair to say that this song is familiar to a vast number of people, but it has never made anyone's hit parade and never will; it is simply part of a score, and it is the score *in toto* that either succeeds or fails. Like a symphony, concerto or opera, some portions have greater appeal than others, but it is the work as a whole that makes the overall impression.

Because there was no video tape in 1957, *Cinderella* was given one performance only, on March 31. By coincidence, this was also the fourteenth anniversary of the Broadway opening of *Oklahoma!*, a fact that invites a startling comparison of the number of people who saw both productions. *Oklahoma!*, our longest-running Broadway show, took over five years in New York to play to more than four million people, and ten years on the road to play to almost eight million. According to CBS, the single performance of *Cinderella* was seen by 107 million viewers.

Seven years after the live show was broadcast, CBS decided to film *Cinderella* with a new script and a new cast. The Rodgers and Hammerstein score remained the same, except that I added the song "Loneliness of Evening," which had been cut from *South Pacific*. Because it is on video tape, this production has been shown annually since 1964.

Early in the spring of 1957, soon after my work for *Cinderella* was completed, I first became aware of a new and mystifying illness: depression. I began sleeping late, ducking appointments and withdrawing into long periods of silence. I lost all interest in my work and barely spoke either to Dorothy or to my children. I simply didn't give a damn about doing anything or seeing anyone. One of the most disturbing manifestations was that I began to drink. This never grew to the point of my becoming an alcoholic, but it was a symptom of my emotional condition.

As these periods of depression became longer and more intense, those around me became increasingly worried, and so did I. What was especially upsetting was that I had no idea of its cause. It had nothing to do with my work. I'd had flops before *Pipe Dream,* and successes before *Cinderella,* and I didn't suffer from a loss of confidence. I am not a doctor, so I cannot speak from scientific knowledge, but I've always felt that the one thing that might have triggered the situation was my returning to work so soon after the cancer operation. It was great for my morale at the time, but one's nervous system is unpredictable and unfathomable, and there's no telling when or how it will react to an experience such as having part of one's jaw removed. Whatever, it is the only reason I can come up with for an extremely baffling and frightening period of my life.

During this time I was never so far gone that I was unaware of what was happening to me. I knew something drastic had to be done. One weekend Dorothy and I asked both my doctor and a psychiatrist to come up to visit us at our house in Connecticut. After discussing my condition we all agreed, calmly and rationally, that the best thing for me would be to spend some time at the Payne Whitney Clinic. So in the summer of 1957 I voluntarily separated myself from my family, from my work, from life itself.

Once I was in the clinic, untroubled by problems and pressures, I felt fine. My spirits soon picked up, and before long I was so well adjusted that I became something of a doctor's helper. Dorothy visited me, as did Oscar and a few close friends, but most of the time I read, played cards or chatted with the other patients, some of whom were confined for the same reason. The time passed quickly.

After a self-imposed exile of twelve weeks, I returned to my family and my work as if nothing had happened. Fortunately, it has never happened again. Fortunately, too, I soon plunged into a rewarding new project.

As the reader knows, I had always been close to Lew Fields and his family, both socially and professionally. Lew had given me my start in the theatre, Herb was the librettist for most of the Rodgers and Hart shows in the twenties, and Herb and Dorothy had written *Annie Get Your Gun.* But there was still one writing member of the family, Lew's eldest son, Joseph, with whom I had never worked. Our chance came in 1958.

Joe had read a book called *The Flower Drum Song,* by a Chinese-American novelist named C. Y. Lee, which dealt with the conflicts between the older and younger generations of Chinese Americans living in San Francisco. Joe saw the dramatic possibilities, secured the rights and approached Oscar and me about collaborating on a musical version. We were charmed by the story and before long we were under way.

While all of the characters in the play were of Chinese ancestry, it was impossible to find Chinese actors to fill every part; in fact, most of our leads were played by non-Chinese. Josh Logan had told me about a Japanese girl named Miyoshi Umeki who had a slight but adequate voice, and she turned out to be just right for the shy heroine. In the brassier role of a night-club stripper was a Japanese-American song belter named Pat Suzuki. For other main roles we cast Juanita Hall, who was black; Ed Kenney, who was Hawaiian; and Larry Blyden, who was Houston, Texas. Keye Luke, formerly Charlie Chan's number-one son, was the only actor of Chinese background who had a major part.

This ethnically mixed cast certainly didn't lessen the total effect; what was important was that the actors gave the illusion of being Chinese. This demonstrates one of the wonderful things about theatre audiences. People want to believe what they see on a stage, and they will gladly go along with whatever is done to achieve the desired effect. Ask them to accept Ezio Pinza as a Frenchman, Yul Brynner as Siamese or a heterogeneous group of actors as Chinese, and they are prepared to meet you nine tenths of the way even before the curtain goes up.

In selecting a director, we did the unexpected and went to Gene Kelly. I had known Gene ever since he was our Pal Joey, and had helped him get the job of choreographer for *Best Foot Forward*. Though his directing experience was limited to the screen—including Joe Fields' last picture— we were confident he could do a beautiful job. He did.

Rather than book *Flower Drum Song* into the Shubert in New Haven, we decided to go straight to Boston, where the show remained a full month. Part of the time was needed to rehearse Larry Blyden, who took over one of the leading parts. Musically, our major problem was with a song, "My Best Love." At first it was sung by Keye Luke, but that didn't work. Then we gave it to Juanita Hall, and that didn't work either. Then Oscar and I decided to scrap the number completely and write something new for another character in the same scene. That was the role played by Larry Blyden, who initially had an exchange with Miyoshi Umeki, his intended "picture bride" from China, in which he tried to talk her out of marrying him. Oscar simply put the dialogue into a lyric, "Don't Marry Me," and I set it to music on a piano I'd discovered in the Shubert Theatre's ladies' lounge.

One other song is particularly interesting because of the poetic form Oscar used. This was "I Am Going to Like It Here," which Miyoshi sang soon after her arrival in San Francisco. To achieve an appropriately naïve, singsong flavor, Oscar went back to an ancient Malaysian form called the "pantoum," in which the second and fourth lines of each four-line stanza become the first and third lines in the following stanza. It was meticulously worked out, though it's unlikely that many people were conscious of the technique—which is just as it should be.

Oscar was a perfectionist not only about his own work but about every aspect of a production. He was also the most self-controlled person I've ever known. During the Boston tryout of *Flower Drum Song* one of the actors, despite repeated warnings, continued to sing a line incorrectly for seven straight performances. Oscar may have been seething inwardly, but the strongest reproach he could muster was, "I'm not very good-natured about this any more."

The musical opened in New York on December 1, 1958, and ran for a year and a half on Broadway. Later it toured for another year and a half and also had a successful London run. The entire experience of working on *Flower Drum Song* was rewarding in many ways, not the least of which was that it convinced me that I had overcome all traces of my depression. My only thought was to keep on doing what I was doing, and I saw nothing in the future that could stop me.

23

Most people have a strong desire for continuity. One way we continue ourselves is through our work; what we create or accomplish is our method of reaching out and becoming part of others. But the most basic way we manifest our desire for continuity is by having children. This is biological continuation, but it can also be a form of creative continuation when one's children become involved in the same field that we are.

Both our daughters, Mary and Linda, have many traits and characteristics that are to be found in Dorothy and me, but from a purely selfish point of view, it is especially gratifying to me that not only do they have a strong love of music, they also have been gifted with the ability to perform and compose. (Geneticists may note, however, that all but one of Mary's five children have shown little interest in the musical arts but, like their grandmother, have demonstrated notable aptitude for the visual arts.)

Naturally, Mary and Linda grew up surrounded by music, and I did what I could to encourage their interest. I remember that we used to make a game of ear-training. For example, I'd strike a minor sixth and the girls would try to compete in identifying it first. In the early forties, when I began taking piano lessons again, the fact that I was always rushing to the piano to practice made it all the more desirable for Mary and Linda. If the old man could bang away at the keyboard for hours, maybe it wasn't so boring after all.

Though I have tried to help my daughters' ambitions, my attitude has always been that encouragement should remain within the confines of our home. While it is vital that young people interested in the theatre get as much practical experience as possible, I think it would have been wrong to have employed either of my daughters to work on any of my shows. Whatever talents they possessed had to be recognized on their own, without any close identification with me. I don't deny that the name Rodgers may have opened some doors, but both Mary and Linda were smart enough to realize that to keep those doors open, their work would have to possess both quality and individuality. Nobody hires a composer on the basis of having a relative in the business.

Linda was the first to exhibit musical talent. Since she is four years younger, this turned Mary away from music for a while. Dorothy and I then became convinced that Mary's talents lay more in words, but she surprised us all by majoring in music at college.

Though for a time Mary diligently pursued a career as a composer, she has recently emerged as a successful writer of fiction with two well-received books, *Freaky Friday* and *A Billion for Boris*. In addition, she and her mother write a column, "Of Two Minds," for *McCall's* magazine, which answers written-in questions about problems facing wives and mothers today. The column is an offshoot of the book they wrote together, *A Word to the Wives*. On her own, Dorothy has brought further literary distinction to the family by writing *My Favorite Things* (her feelings about various people, places and objects) and *The House in My Head* (her experiences in the building and decorating of our country house).

For their first stage score our daughters collaborated, with Linda as composer and Mary as lyricist. It was a charming mini-musical for kids called *Three to Make Music*, which Mary Martin performed in concert and on television.

Mary first won recognition as a composer with her score for *Once Upon a Mattress*. Mixed with my pride in her accomplishment was my concern that she should receive all the credit that was her due. Because it is always a temptation for outsiders to assume that I must have had a hand in the writing, I studiously avoided giving suggestions about the music or the show. I was, in fact, so sensitive about it that once when a photographer asked me to pose at the piano with Mary listening, I insisted that the positions be reversed: Mary was photographed at the piano while I was doing the listening.

Six months after the opening of Mary's first musical, Rodgers and Hammerstein's last musical, *The Sound of Music*, opened on Broadway.

The production's genesis, so far as Oscar and I were concerned, went back to the beginning of the previous year. Mary Martin, her husband Richard Halliday and producer Leland Hayward had just seen a German-language film, *The Trapp Family Singers*, and were all agog over its stage potential. But initially they envisioned it as essentially a dramatic play, featuring authentic Trapp family songs with one new number by Rodgers and Hammerstein.

Oscar and I saw the picture and agreed that it had the makings of an impressive stage production, but we disagreed with their concept. If they wanted to do a play using the actual music the Trapps sang, fine, but why invite a clash of styles by simply adding one new song? Why not a fresh score? When I suggested this to Leland and Mary they said they'd love to have a new score—but only if Oscar and I wrote it. We had to explain that we would be tied up with *Flower Drum Song* for a year, but they came back with the two most flattering words possible: "We'll wait."

Rodgers and Hammerstein joined Hayward and Halliday as co-sponsors, though the actual staff was recruited from the Hayward office. Because Howard Lindsay and Russel Crouse had already been signed to supply the libretto before Oscar and I became involved, *The Sound of Music* was one of the few productions for which Oscar's writing was confined to lyrics.

In creating their story, Howard and Russel tried to steer clear of making it one more old-fashioned dirndl-and-lederhosen Austrian operetta, and to keep the plot believable and convincing. Admittedly, it was a sentimental musical, but the truth is that almost everything in it was based on fact. No incidents were dragged in to tug at heart strings. This, more or less, is what had happened:

A young postulant named Maria Rainer went to work as governess for the children of an autocratic army captain named Baron Georg von Trapp. Postulant and baron fell in love, the girl left her order, the two were married, organized a family singing group and eventually were forced by the Nazis to flee Austria.

Had such a story come out in any way other than sentimental it would have been false. To be sure, too much of anything is harmful. No one is comfortable with an excess of hearts and flowers, but there is no valid reason for hiding honest emotion. This has always been a major element in the theatre, and it's my conviction that anyone who can't, on occasion, be sentimental about children, home or nature is sadly maladjusted.

My concentration on *The Sound of Music* during its preparation was tempered by my concern for Oscar. He was not a well man. During the writing he began to complain of discomfort, and in September, just before rehearsals began, he was operated on for an ulcer. Though they hid the truth from Oscar, the doctors told his family—and Dorothy and me—that he had cancer, and that there was only a slim chance of his pulling through.

It was devastating news. Still, we always clung to the chance that somehow he would be able to lick the disease just as I had. The seriousness of his condition was simply too awful to grasp. This couldn't be allowed to happen. Oscar would get over it; there was still time; somewhere, we were confident, there had to be a cure. Unfortunately, we were all afflicted with what Larry Hart had once called "the self-deception that believes the lie."

Oscar was too sick to go to New Haven for the first tryout stop, but he did get to Boston to write the lyric for a melody that Von Trapp sang as an expression of his love for his homeland. "Edelweiss" was the last song Oscar and I ever wrote together.

For this one, as well as for all the other songs in the score, it was essential that we maintain not only the genuineness of the characters but also of their background. "The Sound of Music," the first real song in the play, was an arm-flinging tribute to nature and music. "Do-Re-Mi" offered an elementary music lession that Maria employed to ingratiate herself with the Von Trapp children. "My Favorite Things," a catalogue of simple pleasures, had a folkish quality, while "The Lonely Goatherd" and the instrumental "Laendler" evoked the atmosphere of the Austrian Alps. "Climb Ev'ry Mountain" was needed to give strength to Maria when she left the abbey, and at the end to the whole family when they were about to cross the Alps.

One musical problem confronting me was the opening piece. Rather than begin with the customary overture, we decided to open immediately on a scene in Nonnberg Abbey, in which the nuns are heard chanting a Catholic prayer, "Dixit Dominus." Since I had been so strongly against a score that combined old music with new, I could hardly fall back on using a traditional melody for the mass. Writing "Western" songs for *Oklahoma!* or "Oriental" songs for *The King and I* had never fazed me, but the idea of composing a Catholic prayer made me apprehensive. Given my lack of familiarity with liturgical music, as well as the fact that I was of a different faith, I had to make sure that what I wrote would sound as authentic as possible.

So for the first time in my life I did a little research—and it turned out to be one of the most rewarding music lessons I've ever had. Through friends I got in touch with Mother Morgan, the head of the music department at Manhattanville College in Purchase, New York. She was not only willing to help; she even invited Dorothy and me to a specially arranged concert at which the nuns and seminarians sang and performed many different kinds of religious music, from Gregorian chants to a modern work by Gabriel Fauré. An unexpectedly amusing moment came when Mother Morgan, waving her arms like a cheerleader at a football game, was vigorously conducting a particularly dramatic passage. As the music built to its peak, above the singing could be clearly heard Mother Morgan's booming command: "Pray it!"

Working with Mary Martin again made me appreciate even more what an extraordinary trouper she is. During rehearsals and during the run of the show on Broadway she was constantly in training, both vocally and physically. Nothing we ever suggested was considered too demanding. Even after it seemed impossible to do anything more with the part, Mary was still working to improve her interpretation. In all the years I've known her, I have never seen her give a performance that was anything less than the best that was in her.

Nor have I ever known Mary to be anything less than kind to everyone. She does, however, have one unusual trait. Possibly because of her family background, she cannot utter even the mildest form of profanity. Strangely, though, her strait-laced innocence has led her to use euphemisms that sound even more scatological than the words she carefully avoids. Instead of saying "Oh, damn!"—or worse—Mary always substitutes "Oh, plop!" The strongest expression I have ever heard her use about anyone—and he has to be a true monster to earn it—is "He's a son-of-a-bear!"

The Sound of Music opened in New York almost exactly a year after *Flower Drum Song*. The line-up of talent ensured a healthy advance sale at the box office, but the notices were decidedly mixed, with most carping aimed at the book, which, predictably, was labeled too sentimental. Still, the production remained on Broadway for over three and a half years and had a London run of almost twice as long. Its longevity in the West End was all the more remarkable because of blistering first-night reviews—again chiefly because of the play's alleged sentimentality. Fortunately, the English have a habit of making up their own minds.

As we'd all feared, Oscar was getting progressively worse. During the following winter I continued to make believe—at least in front of him—that everything was fine. We held auditions for cast replacements, discussed possible future properties and even flew over to London at the end of March for the West End premiere of *Flower Drum Song*. Early in the summer I also tried to keep from thinking about the inevitable by becoming involved in the writing of the background score for a television series, *Winston Churchill—The Valiant Years*.

But Oscar could not be kept from the truth indefinitely. One morning he went to his doctor and insisted on knowing exactly how serious his condition was. That afternoon we met for lunch, and Oscar told me what his doctor had said. He had three alternatives: he could have another operation, which would leave him in great discomfort but would still not cure him completely; he could go down to Washington, where they had a highly sophisticated X-ray machine, but this treatment would also prove both painful and temporary; or he could do nothing. He revealed this quietly, in a calm, matter-of-fact voice, as if he were discussing a series of rhyming alternatives. He also told me that he had already chosen the third alternative: he would do nothing. "I'm just going down to Doylestown," he said, "and stay on the farm until I die."

Then he talked of the future. He had no financial problems, so his family would be well taken care of. As for me, he said he thought I should try to find a younger man to work with; it would prove stimulating for me, and he was sure that my experience would be of great help to someone just beginning. We discussed many things that day, two somber, middle-aged men sitting in a crowded restaurant talking unemotionally of the imminent death of one and the need for the other to keep going. Toward the end of lunch, a man seated a few tables away came over to us with his menu in his hand. He introduced himself, told us he was from the Midwest, and asked for our autographs. After we had scribbled our names, the man said, "I hope you won't mind my saying this, but one thing bothers me. You're both extremely successful men, at the top of your profession, and I'm sure you don't have a worry in the world. I was just wondering what could possibly make you both look so sad."

Oscar did as he said he would. He went back to his farm to spend his last remaining days with his family in the countryside that he loved. He died on August 23, 1960.

Larry Hart's death had affected me deeply, but Larry was a man whose death could have been predicted at any time during the twenty-five years we knew each other. When he did succumb he was only forty-eight with a career that was all but over. Oscar's death was the greater blow simply because almost to the day he died everything about him was an affirmation of life. He was then in his sixty-sixth year, but he was infused with a faith and an optimism that only grew stronger as he grew older.

In many ways Oscar was a study in contrasts. He was a passionately loving man, yet he never gave any overt indication of that love except through his lyrics. He was a meticulously hard worker, yet he'd roam around his farm for hours, even days, before putting words to paper. In business dealings he was practical and hard-headed, yet he was always willing to lend his support to idealistic causes. He was quiet-spoken and gentle, yet I saw him rise to heights of fury at the injustices around him, especially those dealing with the rights of minorities. He was a genuinely sophisticated, worldly man, yet he will probably be best remembered for his unequaled ability to express the simplest, most frequently overlooked pleasures of life.

For all his days Oscar sang with a clear voice about everything that was good and decent and enjoyable. It's still a clear voice, but now we must do his singing for him.

24

Of all the theatrical art forms, none is more of a collaborative effort than the musical play. While most of the essential components—the libretto, direction, dancing, set designs, lighting, and the others—can be and usually are handled by a single person in each area, the one department that generally requires the services of two people is the score. A composer can provide only half the finished product; without a lyricist he simply cannot function.

Composer-lyricist partnerships seldom last long. A writer must be able to work with someone new whenever the occasion arises. At the time of Oscar's death I had spent over forty years in the theatre, and in all that time I'd had only two partners. I don't think such fidelity has ever been equaled. When I turned to Oscar because of Larry's problems, there were never any adjustment difficulties, chiefly because our outlook on life and work was so similar. With Oscar gone it was simply too much to expect that I could adjust to anyone else without a lengthy interval between.

Still, there was never any question of my determination to continue. Primarily this was a matter of creative drive. After the shock and grief of the loss of a dear friend and partner it's easy to consider chucking everything and spending the rest of your life puttering around a garden or traveling around the world. Had I succumbed to that feeling I'd be dead —not physically, perhaps, but mentally and emotionally dead. For me, work is simply a matter of survival. I was only fifty-eight at the time of Oscars' death, and while my career had been long and fulfilling, I could not imagine spending the rest of my days reliving past glories and withdrawing from the vital, exciting world that I loved.

Under the circumstances, there was only one logical path: I had to try to write my own lyrics. The roster of men who are adept at writing both words and music is not long, but it does include some of the elite members of my profession. Frank Loesser, Cole Porter, Irving Berlin, Noël Coward and Harold Rome all have excelled in both fields. While I had no illusions about matching their lyric-writing skills, I knew that something must have rubbed off on me after all those years with Larry and Oscar. In fact, I had already had some limited experience; because of Larry's numerous disappearances, I'd frequently been forced to supply additional lyrics of my own during out-of-town tryouts. After Larry's death, I was also called on to update some of his lines for revivals of our shows.

Luckily, I had the chance to test my ability as a lyricist even before I was faced with writing a new score. At this time 20th Century-Fox was planning a remake of *State Fair*. Perhaps suffering from the misapprehension that anything bigger is necessarily better, they planned to change the locale from Iowa to Texas, and they also wanted some additional songs. I told them that I intended to write my own lyrics, but that if I didn't like them, they'd never see them. I also assured the studio that if they didn't like what I'd written, they didn't have to use it. Within a few weeks I sent them three songs which apparently won their approval because they then asked me for two more. While they weren't exactly world-beaters—and neither was the picture—they did give me enough confidence to plan on writing the lyrics for my next show, whatever it would be.

One evening in April 1961 I switched on the television set to watch Jack Paar's program, which I often used as something of a talent audition. That night his guest was the stunning Diahann Carroll, a singer whom I'd greatly admired ever since seeing her in Harold Arlen's musical, *House of Flowers*. I had even tested her for the lead in *Flower Drum Song*, but we never were able to make her appear Oriental. On Paar's program she sang an old Johnny Mercer number, "Goody-Goody," with such distinctiveness that it sounded like a brand-new song written expressly for her. But there was more to Diahann than vocal ability. Wearing a black chiffon cocktail dress with her hair in a stylish bouffant, she looked as if she had just stepped off the cover of a fashion magazine. Her singing and her appearance immediately gave me the idea of starring her in a musical in which she would play a chic, sophisticated woman of the world. She would not represent a cause or be a symbol of her race, but a believable human being, very much a part of a stratum of society that the theatre thus far had never considered for a black actress. Such casting, I felt, would be more effective than anything strident or preachy in breaking down racial stereotypes that had persisted far too long on Broadway.

This concept became so fixed in my mind that the very next day I called Diahann on the phone, and that afternoon we met for a drink. I told her my general idea—and at the time it was nothing if not general—and she responded to it immediately. Simply having a black actress in the starring role would, we both felt, give the play an extra dimension that made it unnecessary for anything in the dialogue or action to call attention to the fact. Rather than shrinking from the issue of race, such an approach would demonstrate our respect for the audience's ability to accept our theme free from rhetoric or sermons.

Now that I had a star and a general concept, as well as a fledgling lyricist, my job was to find a librettist to devise a suitable story. In thinking of various writers, I kept coming back to Sam Taylor. He had never before written a musical-comedy book, but I had known him for many years and admired his work. After Oscar and I had produced his first play, *The Happy Time,* Sam went on to write such equally charming comedies as *Sabrina Fair* and *The Pleasure of His Company.* Another factor was simply that I felt comfortable with Sam. He was a thoughtful, accommodating, highly skilled craftsman, with just the right outlook the project needed. We talked the matter over, he liked the idea, and I had a book-writer.

Early in the summer Dorothy and I went up to Sam's place in East Blue Hill, Maine, where we discussed various aspects of the story which by now we had decided to call *No Strings.* It was then that the basic form emerged: Diahann would play an American model living in Paris who meets and falls in love with another American, a former Pulitzer Prize-winning novelist who is now just another expatriate bum sponging off wealthy tourists. The girl helps restore his self-confidence and his desire to resume writing, but the distractions of the affluent life around him are too much. He can only work if he returns home to Maine—Sam's only autobiographical touch—but when he asks the girl to go with him they both realize that it could never work out, and they part. Even at the end, when the reason for the breakup is clearly because of anticipated racial prejudice, we were careful to avoid mentioning the issue directly.

With the outline and the basic characters decided on, I began work on the score. I soon discovered the major benefit of writing one's own lyrics: I was always there when I wanted me. Of course I missed Oscar's help, but I also was stimulated by being able to do the entire job myself. I loved the independence it gave me. If I wanted to, I could work until four in the morning—or I could get up at four and start working. I've always had a compulsion to finish something once I've started it, and at last I had the opportunity of polishing off a complete song at one sitting.

As any songwriter will tell you, writing lyrics is more demanding than writing music. Music is created with broad strokes on a large canvas, whereas lyrics are tiny mosaics that must be painstakingly cut and fitted into a frame. I found that I never really had any method of self-collaboration. Sometimes the title of a song and the first few bars would occur to me simultaneously and I'd finish them together. At other times I'd jot down a few lines of a lyric which would suggest a melody. Occasionally this would be reversed and I'd think of the musical phrase first. Never, however, did I write a complete lyric and then set it to music.

As I became more deeply involved in the production, I discovered that the theme lent itself to a technical innovation that had never before been attempted in the theatre. In any musical production, there is a built-in chasm, the orchestra pit, that separates the audience from the performers, and it has long been accepted as a convention that singers sing on the stage and musicians play in the pit. Since our story was of such an intimate nature, I began to think about putting the musicians on the stage, both in the wings and in full view of the audience. Instrumental soloists and small groups of musicians could then be involved visually with the play and players, thereby providing physical as well as musical cohesion.

Most of this aspect of the show was worked out with our director, Joe Layton, a tall, lean, intense fellow who heretofore had been known primarily as a choreographer. I had first become familiar with his work in my daughter Mary's show, *Once Upon a Mattress,* and later the same year Oscar and I hired him to stage the musical numbers in *The Sound of Music.* Since then he had done other impressive choreography and musical staging on Broadway. As *No Strings* began to evolve, it seemed to require the kind of fluidity of movement that could only come when the choreographer and the director were the same man, and I was convinced that Joe had the ability to handle the overall production.

Because it was important that audiences accept our concept right from the start, we did away with the overture and had the curtain rise on a darkened stage with Diahann Carroll, strikingly gowned in white, picked out by a spotlight. But she isn't alone. As she sings "The Sweetest Sounds," a musician plays a flute obbligato. The song is then sung by the male lead (played by Richard Kiley) with a clarinetist near him playing the accompaniment. Even though as an augury of their future romance they sing together, the girl and boy are unaware of each other's existence, and the instrumentalists, though in full view, are meant to be musical abstractions rather than characters in the story.

This was further developed in other scenes. During the song "Love Makes the World Go," we used a trombonist in an even more direct manner for comic effect. For the last scene in the first act, which takes place in the heroine's apartment, an invisible drummer first beats out a tense rhythm while the lovers express their feelings in "Nobody Told Me." Then, as they disappear into the bedroom offstage, a panel rises and the spotlighted drummer brings the act to a close with a blazing interpretation of their passion.

It should be stressed that while these innovations worked within the context of this play, they were not introduced to impress people with our cleverness. It was simply that given the kind of story we had, it seemed imperative that the entire musical and dramatic effect come from a single source—the stage—without the distractions of the structural chasm yawning in front of it.

Since we were trying so many innovations, we decided on a few more. To help maintain the flow of the narrative, which covers a number of French locales, we decided to have mobile sets moved by the dancers in full view of the audience. In one scene, at Honfleur, the beach was represented by a sand-colored slab. Because there were only two characters on the stage, at the end the girl changed the setting simply by tilting up one end of the slab—and the couple was now on a terrace overlooking the water.

Two major songs were sung during the beach scene. One was "Look No Further," a plaintive love song written in traditional "AABA" form. Here the only rhymes used in each "A" section fell on the two successive words in the fourth and fifth bars. Then, to start the next line, I repeated the second rhymed word, though with a slightly different meaning:

I.
Don't move an inch away, stay.
Stay with one who loves you.

2.
This is the journey's end, friend.
Friend has turned to lover.

3.
Making it all complete, sweet.
Sweet it is to hold you.

While there was no direct reference to race in either lyrics or libretto, the song "Maine," also sung in the Honfleur scene, was intended to make audiences aware of the disparity in background of the two leading characters. Even here, though, the mood was light and the attitude nostalgic. At first the boy sings:

Let the snow come down
Before the sun comes up.
Maine is the main thing.
Let the lake and hills
Become a frozen cup.
Twenty below in Maine . . .

Then, to the same melody, the girl sings:

When the sun goes down
The kids are up and out,
East of the Hudson.
There's a sidewalk symphony
Of song and shout
Up north of Central Park . . .

While the play's title fitted the situation of the story, during the preparation of the show we also decided to make it refer to the fact that aside from a harp, our orchestra would consist entirely of brass, percussion and woodwinds.

No Strings had an unusually lengthy break-in period—two months—during which we played Detroit, Toronto, Cleveland, and New Haven. We took our time primarily because so much of what we were doing technically had never been tried before. Musicians had to feel comfortable onstage, and dancers had to become familiar with stage markings in order to move the scenery with grace and precision.

We opened at the 54th Street Theatre (later the George Abbott) in New York in March 1962. In general, the reviewers applauded the physical production, raved about Diahann, were complimentary about the music and lyrics, and had reservations about the book. Though no smash, *No Strings* had a successful run of seventeen months.

But most important to me was the assurance it gave me that I could pick up the pieces of my career and start all over again with new people and new techniques. Well-meaning friends complimented me for my daring in attempting so many innovations, but this was only because they didn't know what I knew. Playing it safe is really playing it dangerous. Taking a chance is always far less risky, and it's a lot more fun.

25

Although I scarcely considered myself Broadway's latest lyric-writing genius, I felt generally satisfied with the job I had turned in on *No Strings*. There was no question in my mind that if necessary, I could always do it again. But once I'd proved this to myself, I was anxious to team up with a new partner.

Why? Simply because having worked with the two men who were the best in the field, I wanted the benefit of working again with a lyricist of comparable stature. There is nothing more stimulating to the creative process than the interchange of ideas with someone who is both a gifted writer and one with whom you can also establish a close personal rapport.

Almost inevitably, this led me to Alan Jay Lerner. He had written brilliant lyrics and librettos for a notable succession of musicals—*Brigadoon, My Fair Lady, Camelot*—to music by Frederick Loewe. Because of failing health, Fritz had decided to retire, and I was told that Alan was looking for a new collaborator. Anyone's list of Broadway's outstanding lyricists at that time would have to place Alan's name at the top, but even more important to me was the kind of theatre he had come to represent. It had taste and style, and it "said something." From what I knew about Alan, his general philosophy and attitude toward the musical theatre seemed closest to mine of any lyricist then active on Broadway. Further, since I was more than fifteen years older, working with him would even follow Oscar's advice to collaborate with a younger writer.

Early in 1961, at about the same time I began thinking of *No Strings,* Alan and I had a few preliminary meetings. One of his ideas, which I didn't like, was a musical about Coco Chanel; another, which I did, was to be an original story about extrasensory perception. Soon after *No Strings* opened, we agreed to work together on the ESP musical, which we called *I Picked a Daisy.*

It didn't take too long, however, for me to realize that Alan's working habits were far different from mine. I knew that he was then occupied with the screen version of *My Fair Lady,* but I couldn't understand why, once having made an appointment, he would often fail to show up or even offer an explanation—or if he did arrive, why the material that was supposed to be completed was only half finished. On one occasion, the Friday before the Labor Day weekend in 1962, Alan told me that he was planning to remain in New York and work during the three days because no one would be around to disturb him. The next morning, just before driving to the country, I telephoned him. The maid answered the phone: "Mr. Lerner 'e is not 'ere. 'E is in Capri."

It wasn't all Alan's fault. Perhaps he felt uncomfortable working with someone he found too rigid, and so had to show his independence. In any case, by the summer of 1963, when it was clear that nothing would come of it, we agreed to terminate our partnership. Soon afterward Alan found another composer, Burton Lane, with whom he apparently felt more compatible, and eventually the ESP musical—now called *On a Clear Day You Can See Forever*—was presented on Broadway. Though it caused no box-office crush, it did benefit from a score that I have always felt was one of the finest either man has ever turned out.

Devoting so many unproductive months to this enterprise was extremely frustrating, particularly at this stage of my career. Fortunately, at about this time I was given something else to think about: a new theatre.

William Schuman, the president of Juilliard, had recently resigned to accept the highly prestigious presidency of the newly completed Lincoln Center. I had known Bill for some time, primarily because of our mutual interest in Juilliard, and one day he asked me to lunch. He was satisfied, he told me, with the progress of all the component elements at the Center except for one, the New York State Theater. The New York Opera Company and the New York Ballet Company filled the theatre during most of the year, but he was worried about the summer months. What he had in mind was the creation of an autonomous producing organization, to be called the Music Theater of Lincoln Center, which would offer a series of musical revivals, and he wanted me to be in charge.

Bill touched a highly sensitive nerve. Ever since my abortive effort to get Columbia University to establish a center for the arts, I have tried to encourage such projects. Everyone knew that Lincoln Center was going to be the country's major performing arts center, and now I was being offered the opportunity to become part of it. There would be no salary—nor did I want any—but I was assured complete artistic control of a separate division which would be on an equal footing with those of concert music, opera, ballet and drama. How could I possibly refuse?

The initial plan was to offer two productions during the summer, each running a little over a month, which would then go out on tour. These would not be hand-me-down revivals, but would be mounted as carefully as if they were being shown on Broadway for the first time. There was one problem: the theatre was so huge that we had to limit our choices to musicals that required sizable casts.

Our first two productions, shown in 1964, were *The King and I* and *The Merry Widow.* Aided by the attraction of the glittering new playhouse, both shows did extremely well. We maintained the policy of two shows per season for three years, until rising costs forced us to cut down to one. Despite the size of the theatre and the expenses involved, we somehow managed to turn a profit during the first five years. Perhaps because it had been revived too often, the only production to lose money was *Oklahoma!,* the attraction for our sixth and final season.

One of the most exciting revivals was that of *Annie Get Your Gun* in 1966. After twenty years Ethel Merman was back in her original role, with possibly even more energy than before. Irving Berlin helped make the production truly memorable by writing two new songs, though one had to be dropped during the Toronto tryout. The song that remained, "An Old-Fashioned Wedding," was the kind of contrapuntal number that Irving writes with such skill that it always stops the show.

The second production that summer was *Show Boat,* which turned out to be an unusually expensive undertaking. The greatest acclaim was won by Constance Towers, a tall willowy blonde who auditioned for Magnolia but ended up playing Julie, the mulatto, in a black wig. Connie has a magnificent voice and more nerve than almost any actress I know. After singing "Bill" seated on top of an upright piano, she never failed to receive enthusiastic and prolonged applause. She also never failed to milk it by walking into the wings and then strolling back to the piano, picking up the pocketbook that she had presumably forgotten, and then strolling off again.

By 1969 the operation of the State Theater had been taken over by the New York City Center people, and they seemed agreeable that I continue the Music Theater seasons. For some reason, however, they began pressing me in the fall for my plans for the following summer. Obviously it was impossible for me to come up with anything definite so far in advance.

Sometime in January a representative of the City Center came to my office.

"When do you have to have my decision?" I asked him.

"Well, we'd like to have it pretty soon."

"You've got it now. I'm not going to do anything."

Despite his surprise, my impression was that this was really what the man wanted to hear. It was becoming obvious that the City Center management wanted to run things alone, which was perfectly all right with me. Quitting certainly caused no financial hardship; simply on a time basis, a minimum of a third of my year—as well as that of my office staff—was involved with the Lincoln Center operation. Unfortunately, the result of the City Center takeover was that for the first time the State Theater had what Bill Schuman had feared—a dark house during the summer.

Besides launching the Music Theater of Lincoln Center in 1964, I also helped launch a more modest theatrical undertaking, one which in a way meant even more to me: the Amphitheater in Mt. Morris Park. The park had changed, of course, since the days when I played there as a kid, and so had the neighborhood, but I still felt close to it and I wanted to do something both for the city and this particular area. Somehow the idea of contributing money for the construction of an outdoor theatre seemed appropriate; happily, the city thought so too.

The two architects, John Stonehill and Oliver Lundquist, came up with an interesting concept. The backstage, which ordinarily would be for dressing rooms, was also designed to include rooms for different functions, such as art classes and places where the elderly might go to play chess or cards. The productions themselves would be given without charge, with the community itself deciding on the different kinds of entertainment to be presented. Dorothy and I were there the day the Amphitheater was dedicated, and were joined by Mayor John Lindsay and Jerome Weidman, an old friend, and his wife.

Following the brief ceremony, the Weidmans and the Rodgerses walked over to the house at 3 West 120th Street, where I had lived as a boy.

As we approached the brownstone building I could see a sign where once "WILLIAM RODGERS, M.D." had been. Now it read "COME INTO MY HOUSE, MY CHILD." We climbed the steps and walked in to discover that the house was a drug rehabilitation center for kids up to fourteen years old. Not a thing seemed familiar. I remembered the spacious reception room for my father's patients and Pop's imposing office, with its huge Mussolini desk; now it all looked cramped and tiny. As happens so often, everything had shrunk in scale.

Though my association with Alan Jay Lerner had proved fruitless, it did nothing to lessen my resolve to keep on looking for the right partner and the right property. I had spent an unusually long unproductive period and I was eager to get going again. Given a good idea and some talented people who were willing to work, I was sure we would come up with something.

The next something was *Do I Hear a Waltz?*, based on Arthur Laurents' play *The Time of the Cuckoo,* in which Shirley Booth had appeared on Broadway. Later a movie was made of it called *Summertime,* with Katharine Hepburn. I'd always liked the story, and when Arthur and Stephen Sondheim came to me with the idea of making it into a musical, I told them I was their man.

Steve, who was almost half my age, had already demonstrated his considerable gifts as Leonard Bernstein's lyricist for *West Side Story* and as Jule Styne's for *Gypsy.* He displayed further ability by creating the music as well as the words for *A Funny Thing Happened on the Way to the Forum.* Three hits in three times at bat is a pretty good average in any league.

What also gave our partnership a certain blessing was that Steve happened to be something of a protégé of Oscar Hammerstein, who had taken him under his wing and taught him a good deal. Steve was opinioned but terribly self-critical and totally dedicated to his craft, and I thought it would be especially challenging to work with someone so thoroughly trained in music as he was.

At first we worked closely and well. There was no particular *modus operandi*. Sometimes a quatrain would start me thinking of a melody; sometimes it would be a completed lyric. Occasionally I thought of a melodic theme first and Steve would then write the words. If I changed his lyric pattern, we'd discuss it, and Steve would either rewrite or we'd agree to discard the number entirely. I was working again and I was happy again.

From the start Arthur, Steve and I decided that we would purposely avoid the clichés that we could easily fall into with a story about an American tourist in Venice. We weren't going to resort to tarantellas or a comic ballet featuring gondoliers; in fact, there would be no formal choreography at all, or any booming choral numbers. Instead, under our director, John Dexter, the aim was for stylized movement which would convey the quality we wanted. The story was touching and intimate, and this was exactly the way we planned to keep it. Every element was going to have so much integrity that we were all practically shining each other's halos.

Unfortunately, when we put our touching, intimate story on the stage, we found that instead of a musical we had a sad little comedy with songs. It simply didn't work. During the tryout in New Haven, we held a conference and decided to call in a choreographer, Herb Ross, to put some life into the show. This was especially needed in the first-act scene on the Piazza San Marco, where the heroine sits alone surrounded by tourists and Venetians. Originally she had a song called "Two by Two," which was accompanied by strollers acting out the lyric by walking around two by two. There was no real development or commentary. Then Steve and I wrote a new song, the self-mocking "Here We Are Again," and Ross devised dance steps for the amorous couples that emphasized and contrasted with the girl's loneliness.

This helped, but not enough. Changes of this sort are always tricky. When you start rebuilding a show you must always be careful that the number you may feel is delaying the action does not actually support the dramatic structure of the entire play. If you replace a song, you may find yourself with a problem in another scene fifteen minutes later. It's like pulling out one seemingly inconsequential brick from a wall, only to find the entire wall collapsing. And no one ever really knows why.

There was one fundamental problem with the story that I never realized until too late. It wasn't only that Elizabeth Allen, the actress playing the heroine, was younger and less spinsterish than either Miss Booth or Miss Hepburn; it was simply that in a crucial scene in the second act the girl gets drunk and tells a young wife that her husband has had a dalliance with the owner of their *pensione*. I felt that this made the heroine unsympathetic and that audiences would not accept it, no matter what the provocation might have been, but despite my objection, Sondheim and Laurents were adamant about retaining the scene.

The more we worked on the show, the more estranged I became from both writers. Any suggestions I made were promptly rejected, as if by prearrangement. I can't say that all this tension was to blame for the production being less than the acclaimed triumph we had hoped for, but it certainly didn't help. *Do I Hear a Waltz?* was not a satisfying experience.

Given the impermanence of life, it is only natural that people cling to the security of certain objects and places that seem impervious to time. Perhaps this is especially strong in me because of the intangibility of my work and the entertainment world of which I am a part. Ever since 1949, our place in Southport, Connecticut, had been more of a home to Dorothy and me than our city apartment. Rockmeadow was our refuge and retreat, where we enjoyed entertaining friends and where, just in walking through the grounds, I often thought of melodic themes or ideas for musical development. By mid-1965, however, it was no longer a haven of durability and dependability; it had simply become too difficult for Dorothy to maintain. The house itself, with three floors and numerous guest rooms, required constant cleaning, polishing and waxing. Outside, there were seemingly endless lawns to mow, hedges to trim and earth to reseed. It was a place that required year-round, sleep-in help, and we were unable to get it.

To Dorothy, the solution was to move not merely to a new house, but to a newly built house. Only in this way, she felt, could we live in a country place that would accommodate our particular needs. This meant a place that would require a minimal amount of care, with everything as functional as possible, while still possessing the features that enhanced the style of life we enjoyed.

When Dorothy first revealed her need for a change, I strongly resisted it. I could understand and sympathize with her many problems, but I didn't see why a less drastic solution wouldn't work as well. Couldn't we cut down on entertaining? Couldn't we live in just one wing? Couldn't we try to import help from Europe? And, most important, how could we possibly build a new house that would be ready for us to move in the following summer?

As patiently as she could, Dorothy shot down all of my arguments. Her strongest point was that it was wrong for us to make our lives conform to a house, no matter how much we loved it. Eventually—and grudgingly—I consented. Because we had definite ideas of what we wanted, Dorothy felt that the wisest course was to engage an architect without too many fixed ideas of his own. This led us to John Stonehill, who had been one of the designers of the Mt. Morris Park Amphitheater. A cousin of Dorothy's and a frequent guest at Rockmeadow, he had never designed a private home before. With his approval, Dorothy and I selected an area in Fairfield County of about ten acres of farmland, which we bought from our friends Margot and Roy Larsen.

We spent our last days at Rockmeadow on Labor Day weekend in 1965. Leaving the place was a painful experience for me. I felt comfortable there and hated the idea of change. With her miraculous ability to picture things to come, Dorothy had the joy of looking forward to a new house, new surroundings and a new life. I found the prospect intimidating, and it took months before I was able to appreciate what she had done.

The foundation for the new house was laid in the fall. With Dorothy and John supervising every step of the way, the contractor, true to his word, had the place ready for us to move in the following July. What they had accomplished was truly remarkable. Though functional and far from palatial, the house had a feeling of spaciousness and warmth that made it seem a part of the surrounding landscape. Everything fit comfortably on one level, without stairs to climb or wasted areas. There was one large central room, with plenty of space for both the piano and the dining area. I also appreciated the fact that I could go from my bedroom directly to the swimming pool without having to walk through the rest of the house. As Dorothy has said, our only regret is that we didn't build the place ten years earlier.

After the experiences with my most recent collaborators, it had become increasingly clear that I would probably never again have the kind of long-term working relationships I had enjoyed with Larry and Oscar. Each partnership would have to be for a specific project. If a lyricist came to me with an idea I liked, I'd work with him; if I thought someone the right person for a project I was interested in, I'd get in touch with him—and if I thought I could do the lyrics myself, that would be all right too. Most important, despite my recent setbacks I was determined to keep working.

In 1967 I was approached to write the score for a television adaptation of Bernard Shaw's *Androcles and the Lion,* with a book by Peter Stone. Since I could choose my own lyricist, I simply went back to my *No Strings* collaborator—me—and we got along just fine. The show itself didn't come off well, I'm afraid, but it did give me the chance to be professionally associated with Noël Coward, who played Julius Caesar as a wickedly charming Noël Coward.

Though I find satisfaction working in any medium, nothing can match the exhilaration of the Broadway theatre, and I was anxious to return to it. During this period I heard many ideas and read many scripts, some actually scheduled for production, but for some reason—perhaps because I had become overcautious—none of them ever got off the ground.

Eventually, early in 1969, one finally looked promising.

Martin Charnin, a young lyricist who had written songs with my daughter Mary, came to me with the idea for *Two by Two*. (Neither the title nor the title song had anything to do with the discarded number from *Do I Hear a Waltz?*) I liked Marty and admired his work, but what really excited me was the concept—a musical version of Clifford Odets' *The Flowering Peach*. The story dealt with Noah and the flood, and though written in 1954, covered such contemporary themes as the generation gap and ecology. There was even a parallel between the flood and the atom bomb. We got in touch with Peter Stone, who had just had a tremendous hit with *1776*, and he agreed to join us as librettist. In June we announced our plans to the press. Since Dorothy and Mary were off on a trip to the Soviet Union that summer, I looked forward to an extended period of concentrated work.

One Friday morning in July I was getting ready for a weekend in Fairfield, where my production manager, Jerry Whyte, and his wife, Jean-nette, would be my guests. I bent over to tie my shoelaces, and when I straightened up I had trouble catching my breath. A bit concerned, I telephoned my doctor, Frode Jensen, and his nurse told me to come right over.

After doing a cardiograph and giving me a thorough examination, Frode said, "You're not going to Fairfield, you're going to Lenox Hill Hospital. I want you where I can keep an eye on you. Your blood pressure is going crazy and I can't find your pulse."

I did as I was told. At the hospital I spent a reasonably comfortable day on Saturday, but on Sunday morning, as I was leaving the bathroom, I collapsed. The next thing I was aware of was a soothing voice saying, "Breathe normally," and I opened my eyes to see a roomful of doctors and nurses and an oxygen tank near the bed. Only then did I know I'd had a heart attack.

Later that day I was transferred to the coronary-care unit. When my daughter Linda was allowed to see me, the first thing she said was, "You're going to be sore as hell, but we're sending for your wife." I confess that it didn't make me sore at all.

But what nobody realized was how difficult it would be to make contact with Dorothy and Mary, who were then in Leningrad. In fact, it was only with the help of Mayor Lindsay that Linda and her husband, Danny Melnick, were able to put the call through. Dorothy and Mary immediately canceled their trip to Finland, scheduled for the following day, and through Danny's efforts, managed to get a reservation on the once-a-week flight to Paris, which fortunately left Leningrad on Monday. They spent that night in Paris, and on Tuesday were on the Air France flight to New York.

Later Dorothy told me that she had expected to see a desperately ill patient; instead, she found me reasonably strong and in excellent spirits—unquestionably due to the fact that she was there. If I learned anything from my experience, it was that the best place to be at the time of a cardiac arrest is in a hospital. Had I been in my apartment, on the street or in Fairfield, it is doubtful that I'd be writing about it today.

Possibly, too, this is the reason I never felt fear at any time. I had total confidence in my doctors and the hospital staff. I knew that they would do everything necessary and that all I had to do was put myself in their hands. My attitude was not merely one of hope or expectation; just as in the case of my cancerous jaw, I was sure I'd pull through.

This illness served to bring me in contact again with a remarkably dedicated young woman. Several years before, during the building of our new house, Dorothy had broken her knee and was operated on at the Hospital for Special Surgery. One of her nurses was a bright-eyed little Irish girl named Eileen Gurhy. After Dorothy was well enough to leave the hospital, we took Eileen with us to Fairfield, where she saw Dorothy through the transition from wheelchair to crutches to cane. Because of a problem in getting nurses following my heart attack, one of the first things Dorothy did after her return to New York was to telephone Eileen. Eileen's roommate said that she was home in Ireland but that she would call her and tell her what had happened. Soon afterward, Eileen telephoned Dorothy from Cork, and on Thursday morning at 8 A.M. she was in my hospital room ready for duty.

With the kind of care I received from Dorothy and Eileen, my recovery was rapid enough for me to return to *Two by Two* without much delay. One of our first steps was to sign Danny Kaye for the role of Noah. The notion of Danny in the part was especially intriguing. Though he hadn't been in a Broadway show since the early 1940s and was primarily identified as a zany comic, Danny was anxious to try something meatier than the parts he'd been given in the movies. Our script called for a bravura performance, requiring the actor to appear both as a doddering old man of six hundred and a bounding youth of ninety, and we were confident that it would benefit from his special brand of showmanship.

Two by Two has left a sour taste in my mouth not because of the mixed reception (it ran almost a year and showed a small profit), but because of Danny's behavior after the show had opened in New York. Early in February 1971 he tore a ligament in his left leg during a performance and had to be hospitalized. Apparently unable to submit to the discipline of the theatre, when he returned to the show he decided to adapt the entire production to his infirmity. He appeared with his leg in a cast and either rode around the stage in a wheelchair—in which he sometimes would try to run down the other actors—or hobbled around the stage on a crutch—which he used to goose the girls. In addition, he began improvising his own lines and singing in the wrong tempos. He even made a curtain speech after the performances in which he said, "I'm glad you're here, but I'm glad the authors aren't." Apparently there was a certain curiosity value to all this, because people actually went to see *Two by Two* because of Danny's one-by-one vaudeville act. Others, of course, were appalled and expressed their irritation in letters to the *Times.*

What was especially disturbing was that there was nothing I or anyone else could do about all of this; Danny simply could not take criticism. The minute someone faulted him, he'd just sulk and slow down, and figuring that slowing down was worse than cutting up, we reluctantly said nothing.

Coda

At the time I am writing these words—April 1975—I find that I am probably more active than at any other period during the past ten years. Even though I shall soon be seventy-three, this would hardly be worth mentioning except for the fact that nine months ago I underwent a laryngectomy. The operation was successful, I feel perfectly well and, thanks to therapy, I have mastered what is known as esophageal speech. So my days are happily devoted to assisting with the production of a Rodgers and Hart revue slated for Broadway, attending auditions for a revival of *Oklahoma!* at the Jones Beach Theatre—and working on the score for a new musical. Of course it is impossible to foresee what will happen to the musical by opening night, but what's important to me is that I have a new show, and there's no feeling like it in the world. Nothing else matches the exhilaration of helping to conceive, plan and create something that has no purpose other than to give people pleasure.

Yet there is more to it than that. Naturally, I'd like the show to be a hit, but it has to be creatively new, not just chronologically new. I don't want more of the same; I want everything I do to make some contribution, no matter how small, to push out the theatre's walls a bit further. The past is helpful; it can guide us in giving shape and direction to our work. But no production ever succeeds by looking over its shoulder. I know the form can be expanded because every day people are doing it, whether through a new approach in stagecraft, a new theme or a new sound in music.

I am often asked where I think the musical theatre is heading. It's one question I always try to dodge because I don't think it's heading anywhere until it's already been there. One night a show opens and suddenly there's a whole new concept. But it isn't the result of a trend; it's because one, two, three or more people sat down and sweated over an idea that somehow clicked and broke loose. It can be about anything and take off in any direction, and when it works, there's your present and your future.

There is a traditional trick that theatre people have played as long as I can remember. A veteran member of a company will order a gullible newcomer to find the key to the curtain. Naturally, the joke is that there is no such thing. I have been in the theatre over fifty years, and I don't think anyone would consider me naïve, but all my life I've been searching for that key. And I'm still looking . . .

Index